THE EDITORS: Vladimir G. Treml, Associate Professor of Economics at Duke University, has written many articles on Soviet economic affairs and is the author of a two-volume study, *The 1959 Soviet Intersectoral Flow Table,* published in 1964.

Robert Farrell, an editor for the Institute for the Study of the USSR and a former staff member of the U.N. Bureau of Economic and Social Research, is co-editor (with Robert A. Rupen) of *Vietnam and the Sino-Soviet Dispute.*

The Development of the Soviet Economy

Other books published for the
Institute for the Study of the USSR
General Editor: Edward L. Crowley

SOVIET LITERATURE IN THE SIXTIES
An International Symposium
Edited by Max Hayward and Edward L. Crowley

SOVIET AGRICULTURE
The Permanent Crisis
Edited by Roy D. Laird and Edward L. Crowley

THE MILITARY-TECHNICAL REVOLUTION
Its Impact on Strategy and Foreign Policy
Edited by John Erickson
Associate Editors: Edward L. Crowley and Nikolai Galay

RELIGION AND THE SEARCH FOR NEW IDEALS
IN THE USSR
Edited by William C. Fletcher and Anthony J. Strover

VIETNAM AND THE SINO-SOVIET DISPUTE
Edited by Robert A. Rupen and Robert Farrell

The Development of the Soviet Economy
Plan and Performance

Edited by

VLADIMIR G. TREML

Associate Editor: ROBERT FARRELL

Published for the
Institute for the Study of the USSR

FREDERICK A. PRAEGER, *Publishers*
New York • Washington • London

FREDERICK A. PRAEGER, PUBLISHERS
111 Fourth Avenue, New York, N.Y. 10003, U.S.A.
5 Cromwell Place, London S.W. 7, England

Published in the United States of America in 1968
by Frederick A. Praeger, Inc., Publishers

Printed in the United States of America

Preface

The studies offered here grow out of a series of papers on the Soviet economy presented to a conference on the theme "The October Revolution: Promise and Realization" held in Munich in October of 1966 under the auspices of the Institute for the Study of the USSR. The international flavour of the conference is reflected in this volume, which contains a fairly representative sampling of Western scholarship on Soviet economic affairs. There are contributions by specialists from France, Germany, the United Kingdom, and the United States. Each of the contributors is a recognized authority on a particular aspect of the Soviet economy. The studies differ in scope and format, ranging from broad inquiries into policy alternatives and the dynamics of economic growth to specific sector analyses, and it would seem that the initial purpose of the conference, a comprehensive survey of the development of the Soviet economy over the past fifty years, has been met.

At the conference, the principal papers were discussed by other specialists invited for this purpose. Unfortunately, space limitations make it impossible to include a record of the discussions, but since the contributors to this volume have had the opportunity to review and revise their original papers in the light of these discussions, on their behalf the editors wish to thank Mssrs. Keith Bush, N. K. Novak-Decker, Simon Kabysh, Constantine Olgin, A. Popliuko, Dimitri Pospielovsky, Phillip Raup, Hans Raupach, and Karl-Eugen Wädekin for their valuable, constructive criticism. Thanks are also due to Mr. Edward L. Crowley and other members of the Institute staff for working to make the conference a success, and to Dr. John Hardt and others who contributed to the organizational effort in individual countries. Mr. Robert Farrell of the Institute deserves the major credit for his invaluable assistance with the technical and stylistic editing of the volume.

V. G. T.

Contents

Introduction

Doubtless, readers of this volume will not be overly surprised to find its assessment of Soviet economic development essentially critical. After all, as Western scholars have expanded the scope and depth of their studies, the performance of the Soviet economy has appeared less and less impressive. To a large extent, moreover, this critical evaluation is reinforced by the increasingly somber tone of Soviet economic writings themselves. Their ever-widening reexamination of most of the basic postulates of Soviet-type socialism relating to economics and planning, and their frank preoccupation with deficiencies and shortcomings in the Soviet economic system do little to contradict this deprecatory view.

This is not to say, of course, that the popular press in the Soviet Union has lost its predilection for describing the progress of the economy largely by emphasizing output levels for basic industrial products. Output figures for steel, oil, electric power, and machinery, especially in comparisons with relevant data for 1913, a customary practice, do indicate that the USSR has substantially increased its productive capacity and is undeniably a major world power in terms of its share of the world's industrial output. Once one goes beyond the crude magnitudes of total output, however, and investigates such measures as capital and labour productivity, yields per acre, rates of adoption of new technology, rates of introduction of new productive capacity, average length of time for construction, consumption per capita, quality of output, capacity utilization, effectiveness of distribution mechanisms, and the like, the picture that emerges is far less favourable.

Most, if not all, of these measures are more meaningful, more reliable indices of the efficiency and viability of an economic system than figures for total output of selected industrial products. In the case of the Soviet Union, they suggest that economic progress over the past fifty years has been rather modest, and that economic development lags behind that of other industrial nations in terms of overall efficiency. Even the much-vaunted distinctions of rapid industrialization and fast economic growth—prime claims to fame for the Soviet economy in the past—have worn somewhat thin in recent years, because other developing countries have achieved higher rates of growth than those of the USSR with lower human costs, and because a marked retardation of the Soviet Union's own rates of growth has occurred since the late 1950's.

It is too early yet to assess fully the impact of the economic reforms announced by Premier Aleksey Kosygin in September of 1965, in part because introduction of the new methods of planning and administration is lagging behind schedule, and in part because some of the measures—the price reform, for example—have turned out to be more conservative than anticipated. One thing nevertheless is unmistakably clear: the new system represents a major break with the past. This factor alone is indicative of the frustrations being experienced by the political leadership. Surely, the official insistence that the new system is justified by changed conditions sounds rather hollow when it is remembered that the reforms constitute a rejection of what for years was held to be the Soviet model.

It is also true that the mechanism of central economic planning and control, which for years has commanded the attention of Western statesmen and economists, has proved to be crude and ineffective. Though Soviet planners and economists have pioneered in central economic planning, possessing a twenty-to-thirty-year head start in developing and perfecting central economic controls and planning tools, none of these innovations has turned out to be exportable from or adaptable outside the Soviet bloc. In elaborating economic planning systems, France, Great Britain, and other West European countries have found little or nothing useful in the Soviet experience. Similarly, in working out programmes for industrialization, the underdeveloped economies of the world have, by and large, come to reject the techniques for growth and development employed by the Soviet Union, even if, one must add, not for lack of trying them out. Gross shortcomings in the Soviet model have also been dramatically underscored by developments in East Europe, where practically all the socialist countries have by now embarked on various reforms leading away from the principle of a command economy.

All this, of course, adds up to the conclusion, shared not only by most Western observers but also by a growing number of economists in socialist countries and an increasingly vocal minority of them in the USSR itself, that the Soviet economy is now and has been in the past singularly inefficient in the use of its productive resources and in meeting the needs of its population. The growth record, impressive as it might have been through the mid-1950's, also suggests that rapid industrialization and quick gains have been achieved in a manner detrimental to the long-term prospects for development of the economy.

Rigorous analysis probably calls for an evaluation of the rationality behind the time schedule for rapid industrialization and the concomitant policy of forced collectivization and for an appraisal of the alternatives open to Stalin when he selected the most urgent variant of programmes for post-war reconstruction at great costs to a war-weary population. Even in this context, however, it can still be said that the country could most likely have achieved the present level of economic development and power at substantially lower human costs, and that the sacrifices extracted from the population have, in effect, been unnecessarily excessive.

The dismal record of the Soviet economy, so graphically defined by mounting evidence of inefficiencies in the economic system as a whole and of crudeness and lack of effectiveness in the planning apparatus in particular, must be especially painful to the Soviet political leadership as it looks back over the past fifty years to the hopes and expectations of the October Revolution. Economic growth and autarkic economic power have always occupied a uniquely important position in the Communist Party's set of goals. From the beginning, as the initial momentum of revolutionary fervour spent itself, the political leadership was able to reconstrue the priorities relevant for post-revolutionary conditions. Gradually, the loudly proclaimed aims of changing all aspects of life—of elaborating new art forms and establishing human corrective penal institutions, of evolving new patterns of family life and creating more rational labour-management relations—were either abandoned or given lower priorities, and more and more attention was given to economics. Economic growth, industrialization, economic self-sufficiency, and centralized control of productive resources were transposed into the overriding objectives of the system. The "brave new world" launched in Russia in October of 1917 came to emphasize things economic almost to the exclusion of the cultural, social, and legal aspects of life in the new society.

In the eyes of the Party, economics thus evolved into the singularly important, if not the only, testing ground for the validity of Soviet-type socialism and its presumed superiority over other systems. By now, of course, this narrow interpretation of the nature of conflict between different socio-political systems has been fully incorporated into the official ideology, a circumstance well illustrated by a recent commentary on economic reforms made by S. Pervushin, an old hand at interpreting the Party line: "...to allow for retardation of economic growth would mean putting off fulfilling the task of surpassing the capitalist world in the sphere of material production. In the end, this would mean not only an economic but also an *ideological* retreat in the face of the bourgeois world."[1] The growing realization of the failure of the Soviet economic system as a

---

[1] *Novy mir*, No. 6, 1966, p. 151, italics added.

showcase for socialism and as a proof of the alleged superiority of Soviet-type socialism over alternative systems must indeed disturb the political leadership of the USSR.

The professed and implied goals of any society represent some mix of the aspirations of the constituent groups in the society. Usually, these goals are somehow weighted by the respective political and economic influence wielded by the different member groups of the society. In the Soviet Union, the interests of consumers have, to say the least, been traditionally underrepresented in the formulation of economic policies and the goals of the system. The Party, or more accurately the leaders of the Party, have always assigned a low priority to consumer welfare. This factor, coupled with extremely ambitious and time-urgent aspirations in such areas as growth of heavy industry and the build-up of the administrative apparatus and military machine, has resulted in very low levels of consumption throughout the fifty years of Soviet economic history.

It is, of course, possible to dwell on the unfulfilled promises and pledges made by the Bolsheviks in the early months and years after the revolution, turning the rather long list into a well-documented condemnation of the system. Do we have to go any further than to recall Lenin's ringing challenge made in December of 1920, just a few months before the start of one of the most devastating famines Russia experienced: "We place great importance on eliminating hunger everywhere. You capitalists are incapable of eliminating hunger, but we know how to do it."[2] As if this were not enough, the Soviet population had to live through two more famines of tragic proportions, one accompanying the forced collectivization of agriculture and the other following the end of the war. And, it must be added, there is sufficient evidence to place the major share of the responsibility for the last two famines on the economic policies of the political leaders.

Standards of living in the Soviet Union have always been low, and state plans for expanding food and related industries and for increasing production of consumer goods have been consistently understated compared with other sectors of the economy. Sacrifices extracted from the population have not merely been restricted to low standards of consumption. Indeed, for practically the entire period of the Soviet experiment, the people of the USSR have been under continuous and relentless pressure to produce and overproduce, to excel and give their utmost to the constantly changing, always urgent economic tasks of the Party. Campaign has followed campaign. Frequently, a new crisis has come along before the last one has

---

[2] V. I. Lenin, *Sochineniya* (Works), 4th ed., Vol. 31, Moscow, 1963, p. 424.

been resolved. The people have always been in a frenzy, being spurred to even greater costs and sacrifices. Looking back, many so-called emergencies seem to have been unjustified and excessively costly, and some campaigns designed to undo and correct the results of previous ones.

In a recently published poem, Evgeny Evtushenko attacks these aspects of the economic and political system in his country. In a thinly veiled allegory, he describes a little ship fighting its way to a lighthouse only to discover that the beacon it has been following has been a mirage. The poet laments all the false leads that the ship has been given, including "the compasses that have always lied, and the weather forecasts that have always lied," while the exhausted crew has been long overdue for a rest in a quiet harbour. He goes on to tell how the cheerful captain of the ship is again goading the helmsman towards a new beacon, but how this time the helmsman refuses to share the enthusiasm of the leader and contemptuously dismisses the captain's exhortations by flatly stating: "It's a mirage."[3]

If the consistently low standards of consumption in the Soviet Union are viewed in the context of the built-in pressures of the system, one tends to agree with Professor Alexander Gerschenkron, one of the most prominent American economic historians, who concludes that "a policy of rapid increase in the level of consumption may, in the short run, bridge political difficulties, but in the long run it is likely to create bothersome problems. Plentiful supplies of consumer goods produce a climate of relaxation among the populace which is not congenial to dictatorships. Once the stress and strain have been reduced, the problem of political liberty is almost bound to arise."[4] At the same time, in assessing the viability and the record of the Soviet economic system, one must go beyond assertions of the Party's failure to honour promises made to the people. An analytically important question that must be broached is whether the Soviet system has met and is meeting the expectations of those in control, that is, of the leaders of the Communist Party. Clearly, the social costs of forced industrialization and total regimentation of the economy have been immense. Were Stalin's brutal and arbitrary methods of pursuing his grand design really necessary in the light of the results achieved? Or, to pose the question differently, given the Party's own goals, were there any alternative routes to be taken? It appears that many of the difficulties that the Soviet economy faces today can be traced to the past, to the unbalanced growth

---

[3] Evgeny Evtushenko, "Ballada o lozhnykh mayakakh," *Yunost*, No. 1, 1968, p. 4.

[4] Alexander Gerschenkron, *Economic Backwardness in Historical Perspective*, Cambridge, Massachusetts, Harvard University Press, paperback ed., 1962; New York, Frederick A. Praeger, 1966, pp. 267–8.

patterns of the 1930's and 1940's, to the neglect of social overhead capital, and to the rigidities of the planning mechanism that have tended to perpetuate imbalances and distort the optimal path of technological progress.

Marx maintained that those capitalist institutions conducive to progress at earlier stages in the development of industrial societies were later to become fetters on the further development of productive resources. It is now quite evident to Western observers and to a growing number of Soviet economists that the problem Marx posed of the compatibility of existing institutions with the continuing development of economic potential is very relevant to the Soviet situation itself. The Party, having realized this, has had to agree to the economic reforms sponsored by Kosygin and has had to close its eyes to the fact that these reforms amount to a rejection of what for several decades has been held to be the successful Soviet socialist model. Thus, at the fiftieth anniversary juncture, one may legitimately ask whether the Soviet system has not only betrayed the expectations of the population but also the aspirations of those in control of the system, whether, that is, the system has, in a way, betrayed itself.

Durham, North Carolina   *Vladimir G. Treml*

Soviet Economic Development and Policy Alternatives

John P. Hardt

Background

Soviet Economic Development in Perspective. The aim of this survey of fifty years of Soviet economic development is to appraise performance in the light of developmental and doctrinal alternatives. For this purpose, the fifty years is divided into three periods: the pre-industrialization period of 1917–1928 and two development periods from 1928–1967. Soviet economic development after the New Economic Policy (NEP) thus falls into two periods or *Wirtschaftsstufen :* the Stalinist period, from 1928 to about 1955; and the current period, from 1955 to date.[1] These two periods are distinguished by rather marked differences in political objectives, economic institutions, and overall performance. At the same time, they bear similarities with economic doctrines of earlier times: the Stalinist period, with some aspects of mercantilism in England and certain characteristics of the physiocratic school in France; the current, later period of Soviet economic development, with the beginning of libertarianism in English politics and the epoch of the classical economics of Adam Smith.

This qualitative evaluation of economic development and doctrine is intended to complement Stanley Cohn's study of fifty years of Soviet growth and efficiency in economic performance. Common to both studies is the theme that the path of Stalinist economic development diverged from the classical Western model by forcing the pace of industrialization at the expense of consumer welfare. An appraisal of the quantitative record requires some perspective of the choices for economic development open to the Soviet Union in 1928 and again in the post-Stalin period. The economic prescriptions of Nikolay Bukharin, Leon Trotsky, Joseph Stalin, and others participating in the industrialization debates of the twenties are therefore considered. These views are compared with alternative economic doctrines and theory, and the Stalinist view is likened to that of the eighteenth century English mercantilists and French physiocrats. The same unity of effective groups with analogous goals of national

---

[1] Walt Whitman Rostow, *The Stages of Economic Growth, a Non-Communist Manifesto*, Cambridge, England, Cambridge University Press, 1960; W. Hoffman, "Stadien und Typen der Industrialisierung," *Probleme der Weltwirtschaft*, No. 54, Jena, Kiel University Press, 1931, p. 166.

aggrandizement that led to the type of economic theory supported by the mercantilists and physiocrats in the eighteenth century in England and France may have obtained for the Soviet Union in 1928. Just as the diversity of groups that arose in libertarian England gave rise to the emergence of classical economics, the growing diversity of social groups in the post-Stalin era may have led to a regeneration of economics in Russia.

In evaluating Stalin's objective of overcoming economic backwardness, economic rationality is thought of primarily in the sense of internal consistency.[2] Thus, the focus of concern is not primarily on the excesses of the system in collectivizing agriculture and limiting foreign trade, but on evaluating the fulfillment of the economic development goals chosen by Stalin. How, then, after the first half-century of Soviet power does the performance of the Soviet planned economy measure up to its promise, or to the expectations of its architects? Have the ideological precepts of Marx, Engels, and Lenin, which influenced both the political revolution of 1917 and the economic revolution of 1928, given way to a new pragmatism arising from the need for efficient administration of a modern Soviet state? Has Soviet success in overcoming economic backwardness been offset by failure to develop the efficient allocation and administration necessary to cope with the increasing demands of a modern society?

Summary Trends. The dictatorial-democratic centralism of Leninist precepts and the egalitarian, humane aspects of the teachings of Marx and Engels were combined as compatible guides to economic development in the period of revolution and war communism from 1917 to 1920. It was only with the beginning of economic recovery and the initiation of economic planning, in the period from 1921 to 1927, that contradictions began to surface, especially in the controversy over wage policy. This debate was resolved in 1928 with the establishment by Stalin of political dominance and the initiation of an economic plan designed to augment the power of the state he controlled.

Though tsarist and reconstruction period (1921–1928) policies provided a basis from which a developmental "take-off" could be launched, this legacy did not limit the route to be taken to the specific pattern preferred by Stalin, especially in respect of agriculture and foreign trade. Soviet economic development under Stalin may not have had an alternative to concentration on high-priority industrial sectors, given the monolithic institutional preference for overcoming the problem of economic back-

---

[2] A. Gershenkron, "Rates of Growth in Russia," *Journal of Economic History,* Supplement, New York, 1947, pp. 144–73; *Industrialization in Two Systems: Essays in Honor of Alexander Gerschenkron by a Group of His Students,* edited by Henry Rosovsky, New York, John Wiley & Sons, Inc., 1966.

wardness in a very short time. To say that the human or moral cost of Stalinist-type development was too great or was not rational is largely to question Stalin's neo-mercantilist and Leninist views on the relationship of economic development to national power. Considering his priorities and time pressures, Stalin's pattern appears, in the main, internally consistent. Some deviations from consistency are characteristic of the volatile process of economic development in any country. Nonetheless, excesses in the application of the Stalinist pattern are apparent in Soviet agriculture and foreign trade.

After Stalin's death, the Soviet Union still had the same choice to make between the alternatives for economic development prescribed by Stalin and those posed by Bukharin. However, the alternatives suggested by Bukharin and Trotsky in the period 1924–1928 may have been more apparent than real, given the political priorities for developing national power. In the current period, the arguments of Adam Smith and other economists against the physiocrats and mercantilists seem relevant. Moreover, the current political setting, which requires attention to alternative economic ends, suggests, some three decades after he presented his case, that Bukharin may have been right. Indeed, in the changed political and economic environment of the post-Stalin period, the countervailing forces of elite groups within the Party, which is no longer monolithic, have given rise to a form of pluralism that has made Bukharin's argument for more balanced economic growth the relevant and perhaps even requisite alternative. Concomitantly, the Leninist view of the role of the Party in Soviet society has been called in question.

Though today balanced growth would be facilitated by a larger resource base, its pursuit in a partially modern, partially primitive economy would be more difficult than it would have been in 1928. Economic backwardness in the industrial-defence base has given way to backwardness in the economic analysis and management capabilities necessary for effective choice among the resource claimants of a more advanced economy and essential for more effective use of the resources that are to be allocated to meet popular needs. The evidence suggests that this latter type of backwardness became deeply rooted in the Soviet system during the era of Stalinist development and that a satisfactory way of overcoming it would require a major reorientation of the politico-economic framework of the system.

True, the Stalinist solution yielded very rapid growth and ultimately proved itself by successfully providing economic support in wartime, but it did so at the cost of inefficient use of resources and by means of postponing essential consumer and infrastructure investments. As long as growth could be sustained by massive infusion of man power and capital and as long as resources could be used in ways that did not contribute directly to national power objectives, this atypical path of development could be followed, and the economic institutions supporting it could remain basically unaltered. However, towards the mid-fifties, as the pool of resources no longer appeared to be inexhaustible, the effect of their inefficient utilization on the growth process became more evident. Supply constraint was made more acute by proliferation of priority demands. The leadership was gaining an increasing awareness of the importance of consumer welfare objectives for the enhancement of national power.

The resulting need of belatedly directing resources towards consumer-oriented objectives has meant that the pattern of Soviet development has had to veer towards more traditional market economy paths and suggests that it is likely to do so to a greater degree in future years. Meanwhile, the leadership has been obliged to reconsider the suitability of the Stalinist institutional structure. Thus, at the half-century point, there is a paradox in the economic basis of Soviet power. Stalin's major aim has been attained: the Soviet economy has raised the USSR to the level of the second great power in the world. At the same time, the performance of the economy appears, year by year, to be falling ever more short of felt needs for investment in transportation, housing, and balanced economic development on the whole.

Between the Political and Economic Revolution

Conflict of Leninist and Marx-Engels Ideological Precepts. The Soviet revolution of 1917 preceded the economic revolution of the First Five-Year Plan by a full decade. During the pre-industrialization period, the contradictions surrounding the promises of the revolution did not have to be opened to question. The Leninist prescription for revolution called for the destruction of the tsarist administrative apparatus and its replacement by a new administration directed by the Communist Party.[3] At the time, no contradiction was perceived between this approach and the Marx-Engels precepts of an egalitarian relationship between the state and the individual, with primary emphasis on the proletariat—the workers and the peasants—and on the withering away of the authoritarian state once the purposes of the dictatorship were established. As later became clear

---

[3] V. I. Lenin, "Chto delat?" (What Is to Be Done?), *Sochineniya* (Works), 4th ed., Moscow, 1950, V, 321–23; V. I. Lenin, "Imperializm, kak vysshaya stadiya kapitalizma" (Imperialism, As the Highest Stage of Capitalism), *ibid.*, XXII, 173–290; V. I. Lenin, "Gosudarstvo i revolyutsiya" (The State and Revolution), *ibid.*, XXV, 353–462; and Bertram D. Wolfe, *Marxism: One Hundred Years in the Life of a Doctrine,* New York, Dial Press, 1965.

in the Stalinist era, democratic centralism and dictatorial control of the state by the Party are not compatible with these concepts. During the revolution and the period of war communism, however, this incompatibility was not yet manifest, a circumstance duly reflected in the spirit of the 1919 Party Programme.[4]

According to the Leninist concept of democratic centralism, a small core of professional revolutionaries should decide for the masses when changes should take place and how they should be consummated. The conscious will of this elite—that is, the Party—was thus to express the will of the masses. The spontaneous expression of the majority was regarded as antithetical to the Leninist view. During the period of war communism, the contrasting views of Lenin and of Marx and Engels could be stated together in official policy, as they were in the 1919 Party Programme, without the contradictions being apparent.

Marx provided very little specific guidance for the development of the Soviet economy. As aptly put by E. H. Carr:

> What Marx bequeathed to posterity was, therefore, not an economic prospectus of socialism but an economic analysis of capitalism; his economic tools were those appropriate to the capitalist system. "Political economy," with its familiar categories of value, price, and profit, was something that belonged essentially to capitalism and would be superseded with it . . .
>
> But the economic policies of the transition period through which the revolution must pass in the struggle to create the socialist order had to be worked out empirically by the workers who had made the revolution.[5]

Certain notions of Marx and Engels nevertheless were incorporated into the revolutionary lexicon: egalitarianism, mass support and participation, particularly by the proletariat, and a dialectic process of change oriented towards reducing the coercive instruments of state power. The apparent contradictions raised by the adoption of these ideas were not clarified in the statements of Soviet leaders. Again, in E. H. Carr's view, Lenin himself was not entirely clear, or perhaps candid, about the rationale for war communism:

> But Lenin was not wholly consistent in his diagnosis of the driving forces behind war communism. In one of the two speeches which introduced NEP to the Tenth Party Congress he ascribed war communism to "dreamers" who supposed that it would be possible in three years to transform the "economic base" of the Soviet order; in the other he described war communism

---

[4] Philippe J. Bernard, *Planning in the Soviet Union*, London, Pergamon Press, Ltd., 1966.

[5] E. H. Carr, *The History of Soviet Russia : The Bolshevik Revolution*, London, Macmillan & Co., Ltd., 1952, pp. 5, 9.

as "dictated not by economic, but by military needs, considerations and conditions."[6]

Economic Recovery and the Surfacing of Contradictions. With the advent of NEP in 1921, the need to begin to establish a new state apparatus brought the two ideological faces of the Bolshevik revolution into conflict.[7] By 1920, the problems of administering the economy were coming to take precedence over the task of seizing and holding power.[8] The lines of a Soviet planned economy were already being drawn at the Tenth Party Congress in December 1920, when Lenin personally initiated the comprehensive plan put forward by Goelro (State Commission for the Electrification of Russia).[9] The Party, led by Lenin, was beginning to turn to the development of the state and its economy. Lenin chose to emphasize the heavy industrial sectors characterized by electric power—the so-called commanding heights of the economy. Still, he was not, at that point, able or required by the economic conditions in a war-ravaged country to choose a course of total economic development. He decided to concentrate efforts on development of key, controlled sectors. For the rest, the uncontrolled economy, he opted for recovery, thus postponing the more basic choice of a plan for the entire economy. The period of NEP was, in Lenin's view, an explicit ideological and political retreat from the promises of the revolution and war communism. However, in the view of a leading Party ideologist, Bukharin, it was a transition or step forward.[10]

Forced to turn to administration, in the period 1920–1922, Lenin appeared to uphold contradictory views. Some Marxian humanism was evident in his adoption of the so-called rule of poverty, and some egalitarianism in the principle of wage payments and work assignments. Each cook, in his words, was to be capable of governing the state.[11] The growing contradiction between these egalitarian notions and Lenin's own idea of Party dominance in economic planning was not yet resolved when Lenin became incapacitated in 1922. After Lenin's death in 1924, Stalin gave unequivocal support to the view of the dominant Party, aban-

---

[6] *Ibid.*, p. 275.

[7] Lenin, *op. cit.*, XXXII. See, especially, his speeches at the Tenth Party Congress (pp. 141–247) and the Tenth All-Russian Conference of the Party (pp. 377–413).

[8] P. I. Lyashchenko, *History of the National Economy of Russia*, New York, Macmillan & Co., Ltd., 1948.

[9] Lenin, *op. cit.*, XXXI, 456–500.

[10] Nikolay Bukharin, *Ekonomika perekhodnogo perioda* (The Economics of Transition), Moscow, 1920.

[11] Barrington Moore, *Soviet Politics—The Dilemma of Power*, Cambridge, Massachusetts, Harvard University Press, 1950, p. 175.

doning the more humane prescriptions of Marx and Engels. It can only be inferred that Lenin, had he lived after 1924, would have followed the same path.

The confrontation between these conflicting views came later, in the wage policy debate of 1926 and in the abandonment of equalitarian wage policy in 1931. These events formed the theoretical underpinning for the eventual adoption of the highly progressive, highly differentiated, piece-rate wage plan and the Stakhanovite system. An atypical quotation from Karl Marx's "Critique of Gotha Programme" established the Stalinist rationalization for this abandonment of Marxian egalitarianism.[12] The slogan "Each according to his contribution!" rather than "Each according to his need!" was the basis for abrogating egalitarian policy.[13] Similarly, the proletarian nature of the Soviet state came to be changed. The promise of a Soviet labour policy based on Marxian views was progressively minimized.[14]

Though there was a retreat from control by workers in industry with the introduction of "the bourgeois specialists," the influence of the latter was countered by the participation of trade unions and Party members in management—the so-called triangle.[15] This modified proletarian influence, tempered by the needs of economic recovery, gave way to state control with the establishment of one-man rule and to control by the Red Directors with the initiation of the Five-Year Plan.[16]

Subsequently, Stalin began to disinherit the concept of "the withering away of the state."[17] Many Bolsheviks had held the view that control institutions would gradually disappear as the state moved towards socialism and eventually towards communism. This interpretation of things was discredited by Stalin, and the subsequent progressive development of coercive institutions of state economic planning clearly reflects the departure from Engels' view of the appropriate historical process.

By 1926–1928, a recovery had taken place in Soviet factories and on Soviet farms; basically, 1913 levels of production had been regained. The

---

[12] A. Bergson, *Soviet Wage Policy*, Cambridge, Massachusetts, Harvard University Press, 1946.

[13] Carr, *op. cit.*, p. 4.

[14] For detailed discussion, see the study by Norton Dodge in this volume.

[15] J. R. Azrael, *Managerial Power and Soviet Politics*, Cambridge, Massachusetts, Harvard University Press, 1966.

[16] *Ibid.*

[17] Joseph Stalin, *Marxism and Linguistics*, New York, International Publishers, 1951, p. 43.

Soviet economy had got back to its take-off point.[18] Then, an economic decision could be made—indeed, in the view of the post-Lenin leadership, apparently had to be made—on the overall course of economic development. From the time of Lenin's death in 1924 until 1928 there was a debate among Soviet leaders on economic development. This was the so-called industrialization debate.[19] Its resolution in 1928 in favour of the group sed by Stalin signalled the commitment of the Soviet Union to rapid industrial development. This decision in 1928—not in 1917—constituted the economic revolution in the Soviet Union.

Economic Development under Stalin

The Resolution of the Debate. The Stalinist pattern of economic development grew out of the resolution of the industrialization debate. With the initiation of the First Five-Year Plan, the debate was formally resolved. Ostensibly, Stalin's view had prevailed over that of the Left, personified by Leon Trotsky, and that of the Right, personified by Nikolay Bukharin, though, in fact, Stalin accepted most of the premises and policy proposals advanced earlier by elements of the Left.[20]

In the period 1924–1928, the post-Lenin leaders theoretically faced problems similar to those perceived by their tsarist predecessors in 1913: establishment of an industrial-defence base consonant with other ingredients of national power, including population, natural resources, and physical size; creation and expansion of the urban-rural infrastructure of a modern society; and improvement of levels of consumption consonant with the economic capabilities of a great power in the modern world. Stalin and his opposition approached these problems with very different views on priorities, timing, and means of attainment.[21]

The Left, led by Leon Trotsky, took the view, still evident as late as 1931, in the German policy of Karl Radek, that economic development in Russia could be linked to an industrially advanced economy in a communist

---

[18] Jürgen Nötzold, "Agrarfrage und Industrialisierung in Russland am Vorabend des Ersten Weltkrieges," *Saeculum*, Freiburg-Munich, Vol. 12, 1966.

[19] Alexander Ehrlich, *The Soviet Industrialization Debate, 1924–1926*, Cambridge, Massachusetts, Harvard University Press, 1960.

[20] Ehrlich, *op. cit.*

[21] V. I. Lenin, *The Development of Capitalism in Russia : The Process of the Formation of a Home Market for Large-Scale Industry*, Moscow, 1956; Mikhail Tugan-Baranovsky, *Modern Socialism in Its Historical Development*, London, S. Sonnenschein, 1910; Nicholas Spulber, *The Soviet Economy : Structure, Principles, Problems*, New York, W. W. Norton, 1962; Mikhail Tugan-Baranovsky, *K luchshemu budushchemu* (Towards a Better Future), St. Petersburg, 1912.

Germany.[22] This led to continuation of revolution outside the Soviet Union, a policy that easily accommodated the Marxist idea of industrial development failing to occur in rural Russia. In his debates with the Trotskyite Left, Stalin took the view that socialism in one country, the dominance of domestic considerations over foreign affairs, was preferable to permanent revolution. His view was presumably influenced by the succession of failures to bring about revolution not only in Germany but also in Hungary and China.[23]

The Right, led by Bukharin, offered another view. Bukharin recommended the economic option of balanced growth: gradual development of a heavy industrial base and defence industry concomitant with improvement of the infrastructure of an urban and rural society and with increased consumption. This conflicted with Stalin's support for concentrating investment on the industrial-defence establishment at the expense of non-priority sectors such as transportation, housing, and consumption. The Right, in effect, argued for a continuation of the New Economic Policy, which it viewed as transition rather than retreat. Bukharin's views seem appropriate for a pluralistic society attempting to meet simultaneously the multiple needs of the expanding power base in a developing great state, the infrastructure of a modern society, and consumption improvements for the average citizen. Nevertheless, post-Lenin Russia was not a pluralistic society. There was, at best, factionalism within the small Party elite in the post-Lenin succession period, 1924–1928, with competition for control of the dictatorial Party. In contrast, the Party's view of the imperative needs of the state was for rapid transformation from an agriculturally based, weak national power to an industrially based, strong great power.[24]

At the time, the imperative, in the Party's view, was to enhance Soviet national power rapidly; judging by this criterion, both Trotsky's and Bukharin's solutions were inadequate. The continuing failures of the revolution abroad, which, if they had been successes, might have complemented Soviet power, weakened Trotsky's case for permanent revolution; pragmatically, there was little promise of early revolutionary success elsewhere. Bukharin's solution, because it envisioned a gradual approach, failed by definition to meet urgent time requirements. Stalin's counter-solution, which based economic power on developing a domestic base at the expense of

[22] Max Beloff, *The Foreign Policy of Soviet Russia, 1929–1941*, London, Oxford University Press, 1949.

[23] E. H. Carr, *A History of Soviet Russia : Socialism in One Country*, Cambridge, Massachusetts, Harvard University Press, 1960.

[24] Joseph Stalin, *Voprosy Leninizma* (Questions of Leninism), 11th ed., Moscow, 1953, pp. 355–363.

other objectives and doing it rapidly, appeared to be the proper solution because of the political imperatives facing the leadership at the time.[25]

The Stalinist Pattern. The Stalinist decision to direct maximum resources to heavy industry in the shortest possible time was embodied in the First Five-Year Plan. It required deemphasis of other economic ends and deferral of many longer-range programmes. Levels of consumption were depressed, since resources for light industry and agriculture were concentrated on increasing current production of energy and metals and on expanding machine-building.[26] Heavy industrial increments were then used primarily to meet military needs and additional investment requirements in the same preferred industries.

This approach was effective in providing substantial industrial growth, but it posed some basic questions:

(1) How could sufficient food be obtained from the countryside to feed an expanding urban-industrial population without producing consumer goods incentives for the peasants? The answer was to replace the market mechanism, which limited the cities' food supplies in the 1920's, by state control over the distribution of the harvest and over prices. State control of grain procured at low prices was the essential feature of the collectivized system of agriculture.[27] Soviet agricultural policy was influenced by the procurement difficulties during NEP referred to as the "Scissors Crises."[28] In 1923, largely because prices of goods purchased by the peasant increased as their supply decreased, coincident with a fall in grain prices, deliveries by the peasants to the cities fell and bread shortage crises developed in the cities.

(2) How could incentives be provided—even for urban-industrial workers in heavy industry—with a deemphasis on the production of consumer goods? The response to this problem was the progressive, piece-rate system, which, by unequal distribution of limited real income, compensated for a stable or declining income per capita.[29] Moreover, the wage policy was supplemented by punitive economic laws and extensive inspection

---

[25] Alec Nove, *Economic Rationality and Soviet Politics*, New York, Frederick A. Praeger, Inc., 1964.

[26] Alexander Baykov, *The Development of the Soviet Economic System*, Cambridge, England, Cambridge University Press, 1950; Maurice Herbert Dobb, *Soviet Economic Development Since 1917*, London, International Publishers, 1948.

[27] See Jerzy Karcz, this volume.

[28] Dobb, *op. cit.*

[29] Janet G. Chapman, *Real Wages in Soviet Russia Since 1928*, Santa Monica, California, The RAND Corporation, 1963.

and control systems for both workers and managers.[30] This policy was supplemented by a labour draft that led to an unprecedented shift of man power from agriculture to industry.[31]

(3) How could scarce resources for export be controlled to provide a maximum contribution from imports towards the fulfillment of economic plans? The state trading monopoly was the instrument put to work here, and the policy was primarily that of importing selectively to meet bottleneck needs in industrialization.[32]

(4) How could the transition from controlling the key sectors to planning the entire economy be effected with limited data and economic intelligence? The method of balanced estimates offered a crude but effective method of planning, in physical terms, for meeting the requirements of a limited number of critical sectors. The aim, quite simply, was to increase the physical output of key industrial products—for example, steel, electrical energy, and coal—as rapidly as possible. This short-run goal was met remarkably well.[33]

Excesses of the Stalinist Approach. Though it may be argued that the Stalinist pattern was necessary, given the political priorities of the Soviet Party leadership for rapid improvement of the economic basis of state power, some programmes cannot be defended in the form in which they were adopted. The Stalinist policies of collectivization of agriculture, direct control of labour and differential wage policy, state control of foreign trade, and balanced estimates planning of physical output were, in the main, consistent and possibly necessary, but the degree of control and coercion was, in many cases, excessive. In general, the control of all aspects of Soviet life, including the arts, and the extreme coercion employed during the purge period after 1937, were surely counter-productive. More specifically, the pace of collectivization during the First Five-Year Plan and the degree of self-sufficiency developed in foreign trade are examples. To be sure, after 1928, the Soviet leadership had considerable basis for concern over the problem of adequately feeding the cities, since there could only be limited production of consumer goods available in the agricultural market to pay through a market mechanism for deliveries of grain from the farms. Therefore, some system of collectivized forced deliveries at fixed prices was necessary to facilitate both rapid industrialization and maintenance of minimum diet requirements for industrial-urban dwellers. The Scissors

---

[30] *Ibid.*
[31] See Stanley H. Cohn, this volume.
[32] For detailed discussion, see Leon M. Herman, this volume.
[33] Hans Hirsch, *Quantity Planning and Price Planning in the Soviet Union*, Philadelphia, University of Pennsylvania Press, 1961.

Crisis of 1923 had brought home to all Soviet leaders the implications of agricultural procurement prices and deliveries based on plans of the state. However, as suggested by Jerzy Karcz, the analysis of the grain procurement problem that was carried out by Stalin and Professor Nemchinov on the eve of the First Five-Year Plan and that led to the aggressive collectivization programme probably anticipated more severe procurement problems than were likely to occur.[34] Moreover, Stalin may not have wished the collectivization process that developed to have happened. As noted by O. Narkiewicz:

> Every piece of evidence suggests strongly that while Stalin (in line with most other Bolshevik leaders) believed that a certain degree of collectivization would be necessary under the five-year plan, in order to ensure a constant supply of food to the industrial centres, he had no intention, as late as the beginning of October 1929, of carrying out anything so drastic as even a 25% collectivization . . . It was the incompetence of the local administration in carrying out the grain procurements, together with the lack of technical means and transport and storage facilities, which set off the peasant revolts. Once these revolts had occurred, some way had to be found of cloaking them under the overall term of "counter-revolution." Very little ingenuity was needed to show that the peasants were rebelling against collectivization and not against grain procurements; and this was in fact done, thus confusing not only the peasants themselves, but also serious students of the situation. Stalin needed this excuse desperately, not so much to protect himself from the population, as to protect himself from both the Central Committee and the expelled opposition leaders, who had for two years been predicting just such an event.[35]

In any event, the extreme collectivization drive and the resistance in the countryside to the policies of the state may have been of the essence. The artel form of collective farm, adopted in the Second Five-Year Plan, allowed for a private plot, some ownership of livestock, possession of some agricultural implements and tools, and a collective farm market to augment the income of the peasant from the sale of produce grown on his private plot. Had the artel been gradually and effectively introduced in 1928, then the extreme programme that preceded Stalin's speech "Dizzy with Success," given in 1930, and that aimed at eliminating the kulaks might have been avoided.[36] More specifically, short-term losses—almost one-third of all Soviet livestock and much of the harvest in the Ukraine during the First Five-Year Plan—might have been avoided.[37] The mistake

[34] Jerzy Karcz, *Soviet Studies*, Glasgow, Scotland, Vol. XVIII, No. 4, 1967, pp. 399–434.
[35] *Soviet Studies*, Vol. XVII, No. 7, 1966, pp. 36 f.
[36] Stalin, *op. cit.*, pp. 331–36.
[37] Naum Jasny, *The Socialized Agriculture of the USSR : Plans and Performance*, Stanford, California, Stanford University Press, 1949.

was acknowledged, as evidenced by Stalin's speech at the time. It is also true that post-Stalin leaders criticized the similar approach taken by the Chinese in the Great Leap Forward of the late 1950's.[38]

Nevertheless, this approach may have had broader long-term effects and costs than indicated by the short-run losses in livestock and harvest. As argued by Boris Pasternak in the epilogue of *Doctor Zhivago*, once the regime had committed itself to a policy as important as commune collectivization and the policy had been a noteworthy failure, further political consequences were inevitable. Those who argued publicly that it was a failure and continued to resist its development had to be silenced. This, in Pasternak's view, established a war or combat relationship between the state and the countryside that later broadened into a basic opposition between the state and Soviet society and provided a milieu conducive to the terror and purges of the late 1930's. It is clear that economic production declined during the period of the terror, from 1937 to 1940, just when all steps were being taken to mobilize resources for maximum production.[39] Assuming, then, some relationship between commune collectivization and the terror, the full costs of the commune might even be thought to include the poor overall performance immediately preceding the German invasion.[40]

Autarkical foreign trade policy was a less clear excess in the Stalinist model. Self-sufficiency was an uneconomic and unnecessary application of the general logic of the Stalinist process of priority development. Indeed, the evidence suggests that before the initiation of the First Five-Year Plan, Soviet planners anticipated, planned for, and were willing to accommodate far more extensive economic relations with the West than resulted. Soviet importation plans, however, fell victim to a foreign trade scissors. Major products for export—raw materials, including grain—met with drastically declining world market prices; whereas products for importation, including skilled personnel and engineering products, maintained a rather stable position in the world market.[41] Other discriminatory foreign trade practices, growing out of non-payment of tsarist debts or based on political considerations, tended to preclude the consummation of a more logical or rational foreign economic policy at the time.[42] This disastrous

---

[38] *Pravda*, April 29, 1964.

[39] See the study by Stanley H. Cohn in this volume.

[40] *Diversity in International Communism*, edited by Alexander Dallin, with Jonathan Harris and Grey Hodnett, New York and London, Columbia University Press, 1963.

[41] Dobb, *op. cit.*

[42] Harold Moulton, *Russian Debts and Russian Reconstruction*, New York, McGraw-Hill, 1924.

experience during the First-Five Year Plan may have led to a hypercautious trade policy subsequently. Likewise, lingering concern over so-called capitalist encirclement may have fortified an isolationist economic policy.

Historical Parallels: The English Mercantilists and the French Physiocrats. That Soviet leaders under Stalin chose routes of unbalanced, high-priority economic development is consistent not only with the policies of some of their tsarist predecessors, such as Peter the Great, but also with certain ideas of the English mercantilists and French physiocrats of the eighteenth century. Like the aims of these Western predecessors, Stalinist economic goals were designed primarily to enhance the power of the state. As in mercantilist England and physiocratic France, in Stalinist Russia the various institutional forces of the society—e.g., the military and Party apparatus, the economic and management apparatus, science groups, etc.— were all bent towards one view: attainment of the economic basis of a great power. This institutional unity assured the success of a single-minded planner's preference. The economic objectives of Stalinism, in the short run at least, were to postpone consideration of other major economic objectives—that is, development of the infrastructure of the society and improvement of consumption levels, in ways consonant with the expansion of the economic power of the state.

The elaboration of economic doctrine to maximize the economic basis of the state is clearly reflected in mercantilist policy in England. The capacity of such economic policy to enhance the power of the state was noted by one of the leading French physiocrats in a plea for unity of institutional and planner's preference:

> The sovereign authority should be one, and supreme above all individual or private enterprise. The object of sovereignty is to secure obedience, to defend every just right, on the one hand, and to secure personal security on the other. A government that is based upon the idea of balance of power is useless.[43]

Similarly, Sir James Stewart, the most articulate of the English mercantilists, declared that

> ... a statesman should develop a grand scheme of economic mobilization and frame the necessary laws and regulations to compel the citizens of the

---

[43] Francois Quesnay, *Maximes*, Paris, 1758. The physiocrats were in favour of a national assembly, but would give it no legislative power. It was to be just a council of state concerned chiefly with public works and with the apportionment of the burden of taxation. See M. Esmein's *memoire* on the proposed National Assembly of the Physiocrats in *Comptes rendus de l'Academie des Sciences Morales et Politiques*, Paris, 1904.

country to do those things which he as a statesman sees are conducive to national economic prosperity.[44]

The central authority held control over industry and foreign commerce. Moreover, in mercantilist England, distribution and pricing of grain was controlled by public authority. A representative of the crown, known as the clerk of the market, set prices and licensed dealers in grain.[45]

The French physiocrats differed, of course, from their own mercantilists and from the English mercantilists.[46] They did, for example, lay down the beginnings of a liberal economic doctrine and of a more or less systematic view of the entire economy, but these were fully developed only when Adam Smith came along, and translated into public policy only much later. Moreover, parallel with differences in Marxian and Leninist views, noted above, the concept of private intent and *laissez-faire* discussed by François Quesney and developed by Adam Smith might be related to concepts of consciousness or voluntarism, which were relevant in the post-Stalinist discussion and antithetical to Lenin's views of the Party and state.

As Stalin did in Russia, the physiocrats in France had an obsession with maximum development of one key sector of the economy—in their case, agriculture. This was perhaps consistent with the identity of interests between landed aristocracy and public authority. The single-sector focus probably limited concern to developing concepts of value and scarcity. As in Soviet development, value became important when choices were required. This was true in the more pluralist post-Stalinist period as well as in libertarian England.

While not condoning the inhumanity of the Stalinist system, it ought to be pointed out that it may well have been the only appropriate economic vehicle for meeting the priorities and goals defined by the Soviet leadership at the time. In this context, the efficacy of the Stalinist pattern as a form of neo-mercantilism, an idea set forth in 1934 by Wesley Claire Mitchell, may be reconsidered:

> There is abundant skilled testimony in favor of the opinion that provided we can have a market for all the goods that we can make, with our present knowledge, our present labor force, and present industrial equipment, it would be possible for us to increase the national income by a very substantial amount above the best records that we have ever attained . . .

---

[44] Wesley C. Mitchell, *Lecture Notes on Types of Economic Theory*, as delivered at Columbia University in 1934–35, New York, Augustus M. Kelley, 1949, p. 51.

[45] *Ibid.*

[46] Charles Gide and Charles Rist, *A History of Economic Doctrines*, 2nd ed., Boston, D. C. Heath, 1948.

Well, are these engineers right? We are a bit concerned as we watch the Russian experiment, as in these last few months we have watched the efforts of our own government, we have been concerned with the question whether a planned economy really is effective. *Have we drawn too hasty a conclusion from the downfall of mercantilism?* Was Adam Smith really right when he argued that if everyone were left to choose the occupation which is most advantageous in his own eyes the wealth of the community as a whole will improve at the most rapid rate? If Adam Smith was right in that opinion with respect to the conditions in his time, have conditions perhaps not changed in such a fashion as to justify very substantial modifications in the conclusions to which economists for three or four generations assented with very little difficulty? We want to know whether business cycles with their concomitants of recurring depressions in which a very considerable fraction of the working classes are unemployed for long periods and in which a very considerable proportion of our investors lose part of their savings cannot be obviated by more skillful economic organization.[47]

Post-Stalin Economic Development

Institutional Stagnation and Economic Retardation.[48] Even before Stalin's death in 1953, changes were taking place in the Soviet body politic and its economic institutions. Since his death, changes have accelerated, especially from 1955 to date. It should be acknowledged that Stalin succeeded in his major aim—overcoming economic backwardness and establishing the Soviet Union as a strong national power. By the middle 1950's, only the United States and a potentially economically unified Europe could claim an industrial-defence basis for power rivalry with the Soviet Union. Moreover, toward the end of the decade, Nikita Khrushchev could credibly claim that overtaking and surpassing the United States in some reasonably short period of time—for example, by 1970—was a realistic possibility.

At the same time, faltering economic performance was becoming increasingly evident. The coming of the nuclear space age to the Soviet Union led to spiraling resource costs.[49] Likewise, the inflexibility of the Stalinist system hampered the accommodation of the traditional coal and steel industrial base to the technology of modern industry. Without Stalin's close political control, the various economic institutions could no longer be forced to pursue unquestioningly the old Stalinist goals.

---

[47] Mitchell, *op. cit.*, pp. 6–7 (italics added).

[48] John P. Hardt, Dimitri M. Gallik, and Vladimir G. Treml, in *New Directions in the Soviet Economy*, Joint Economic Committee, U. S. Congress, Washington, D. C., Government Printing Office, 1966, pp. 19–62.

[49] See the study by Stanley H. Cohn in this volume.

In respect of the first period of Stalinist Soviet economic development (1928–1955), it has been argued that even though there were unnecessary excesses in the Stalinist system, especially in the damaging collectivization programme, the Stalinist pattern was consistent and perhaps even necessary in the political context of the times. In the current, post-Stalin period, the rigidities of the system, limiting changes as they do, again raise the question of the *raison d'etre* of the Stalinist pattern. Is lack of flexibility an organic element of a Stalinist-type system? Or does it merely reflect the impact of Stalin's own peculiar personality? This is extending Alec Nove's question: "Was Stalin really necessary?"[50] to include the issue: "Did Stalin live too long?" As a matter of fact, it may be argued that Stalinist-type objectives do require a Stalinist-type system and a Stalinist-type personality. In this scheme, the role of Stalin as a person may be overstated.[51] Perhaps this is the answer to Wesley C. Mitchell's question as to the appropriateness of Adam Smith's theory for the Soviet Union of the First Five-Year Plan. Perhaps the single-minded pursuit of *any* overriding objective, including national power, necessarily imposes rigidities that are difficult to overcome. Or is the answer to the first question of consistency or necessity to be found even deeper, as suggested in the earlier discussion of the conflict between Leninist and Marxian views? Is flexibility rooted in the Leninist principle of democratic centralism? Institutions die hard even in the more loosely ordered pluralistic society. Would they not be much harder to eliminate or modify in a system in which practically all initiative flows only from the pinnacle of power, as it did in the system ruled by Stalin?[52]

What appears to be needed in order to bring about more efficiency is the following: (1) A macroeconomic view of the economy, relating all aspects of it in a reliable, consistent fashion, with better reporting of data to provide a basis for consistent valuation of economic activities throughout the economy. (2) Improved valuation of economic activities so a price system could be employed as a basis for efficient decision-making among alternative needs. (3) More resource allocation for investment in longer-term payoff, e.g., in the infrastructure of the economy and changing technology. (4) More resource allocation for consumption throughout the economy to provide incentives for increased productivity by workers and peasants.

---

[50] Nove, *op. cit.*

[51] George Plekhanov, *The Role of the Individual in History*, New York, International Publishers, 1940.

[52] *Toward a New Soviet Economics, Underlying Macroeconomic Trends*, edited by John P. Hardt, Washington, D. C., Johns Hopkins Press, forthcoming.

The macroeconomic approach and the adoption of a more rational price mechanism strike at the core of the Stalinist method of planning. Essentially, under Stalin, only the priority heavy industrial sectors were planned, with critical links or potential bottlenecks in the other sectors, e.g., grain procurement for the cities, importation of critical industrial goods, labour supply to industry, etc. This was a microeconomic or partial equilibrium type of approach to planning. Because choices between heavy industry and other economic activities were not central to economic policy, the concept of value, as discussed in Western economics, did not directly intrude. However, as more sectors rose to importance in Soviet economic policy, in conjunction with falling performance and reevaluation or expansion of priority sectors, the need for good data on the entire economy became evident. Linear economics—that is, input-output analysis and linear programming —have been given increasing attention along with the problem of data collection and manipulation.[53] Improved data and macroeconomic analytical tools can improve the economic decisions made among newly relevant economic alternatives. The value basis of choice expressed in monetary terms, i.e., the use of a price mechanism, can substitute for the Stalinist reliance on physical measurements and direct methods of formulating plans and measuring performance.

Improved economic performance may result from improvement in labour productivity throughout the economy or from a reduction in the capital output ratio, i.e., from improved capital efficiency.[54] With limits on the supply of labour and capital, their efficient use has become the major concern. Labour efficiency was stimulated by administrative means in the simplified Stalinist approach. Highly differentiated income, especially in industry, with stable or falling average real income of the Stalinist period, no longer could be relied on for desired results. During the 1950's, per capita income rose and the inequalities of income distribution narrowed.[55] However, the satisfaction from increasing income has not been proportionate. The shift from a seller's to a buyer's market has given rise to consumer choice and rejection of low quality. Rising inventories have led to economic reforms centering on a shift from direct measures of performance such as physical production to indirect measures such as sales, profitability, etc.[56]

---

[53] See R. Judy and V. Treml in *Mathematics and Computers in Soviet Planning*, edited by J. Hardt, M. Hoffenberg, N. Kaplan, and H. Levine, New Haven, Connecticut, Yale University Press, 1967.

[54] See the study by Stanley H. Cohn, this volume.

[55] See the study by Norton T. Dodge, this volume.

[56] Eugène Zaleski, *Planification de la Croissance et Fluctuations économiques en U.R.S.S.*, Paris, Societe d'edition d'enseignement superieur, 1962.

The increasing capital required for increased output reflects the long-term effects of deemphasizing and postponing investment in all but the key sectors of the economy. Modernization of the industrial base and broadening of investment allocations to include transportation, housing, and agriculture are all designed to improve overall economic performance.

The Emergence of Pluralism in the Elite. Economic retardation is not alone the basis for the new trends toward macroeconomic analysis in Soviet planning. As in Adam Smith's time, the development of countervailing public forces in the society has given rise to concern over choices and an improved measure of value. The Stalinist unity of the Party has been shattered.

In the post-Stalin era, the military professionals, the economist-planner group, the physical scientists associated with the Academy of Sciences, the Party bureaucrats centering around the obkoms (regional committees of the Communist Party), and the intellectuals represented by *Novy Mir* and other liberal Soviet journals have all gained more influence over policies by virtue of their own professional expertise.[57] They have had a common interest in securing greater delegation of power from the Party and in encouraging it to maintain a *laissez-faire* attitude towards the elite groups, even as each competed within its own group and with other institutional groups for the allocation of resources to strengthen its own objectives, e.g., to strengthen the defence establishment or a particular institution. The emergence of pluralism in the Soviet elite may underlie the broadening of the economic objectives of the leadership. The overall economic objective of the Soviet Union is no longer limited to mere augmentation of the industrial-defence establishment. The Soviet Union is now also concerned with improving the infrastructure of the economy, with allocating scarce resources to transportation and housing, and with paying more attention to consumer needs.

Success in overcoming the economic backwardness limiting the power of the state means that the elite groups are no longer tied together in single-minded purpose. With more power and resources, the broader needs for continued progress require different solutions. Each group has differing views and priorities. As no group has overwhelming power, decisions result from an interplay of countervailing forces or a form of consensus.

Resistance to Change and Improved Performance. The emergence of pluralism and economic retardation may mean that it is now appropriate to consider the proposals made by Bukharin in 1928. Bukharin's views may have been expressed thirty years too early, but realization of his alternative of more

---

[57] *Toward a New Soviet Economics, op. cit.*

balanced economic growth in the economy is perhaps even more difficult now than it would have been earlier. The usual problems of balanced growth are compounded by the imbalances allowed to grow to the critical point under Stalin.

Developments in transportation offer a case in point. An austerity programme of three decades has limited construction of new rail lines and concentrated the movement of cargo on an outmoded rail system.[58] To be sure, a revolution in transportation was initiated with the Seven-Year Plan in 1959, which called for a shift from steam, coal-fired locomotion to diesel and electrified locomotion. This shift has been carried out at considerable expense and has probably led to substantial improvements in efficiency. Similarly, a shift from rail transport to pipelines and other means of transportation, previously exploited very intensively elsewhere, has now been heavily invested in, if at a late date, and has improved the efficiency of Soviet economic performance.[59] Yet the question can still be raised: Does this short-term, though expensive, programme of transport investment, compensate for the costs of long-term deemphasis on Soviet transportation? At the same time, will not the inappropriate locations of industries and the lack of specialization of Soviet industrial plants be a relatively permanent or at least highly resistant legacy from transport planning, possibly resulting in many generations of inefficiencies? Likewise, investments in neglected urban developments, including housing, may be rather late to make planning in this sphere effective. In order to meet the consumption needs of the populace, both the current and the deferred costs of neglect have become evident.

The costs of expanding production in sectors that have become important since Stalin is not just a problem of resource allocation. Such problems as inventory accumulation in consumer textiles suggest that there is a broad range of efficiency problems requiring a refurbishing of the underdeveloped segments of the economy—a bequest of the Stalinist pattern of uneven economic development. As in the case of an underdeveloped nation, the Soviet Union's investment process requires more than capital goods input. It requires, for example, a broadening of its education base and the development of an improved information-gathering and processing system. The substantial additional resources needed to achieve higher production levels in previously neglected sectors of the economy promise somewhat

---

[58] H. Hunter, *Soviet Transportation Policy*, Cambridge, Massachusetts, Harvard University, 1957; Ernest W. Williams, Jr., *Freight Transportation in the Soviet Union*, Princeton, New Jersey, Princeton University Press, 1962.

[59] H. Hunter, *The Soviet Transport Sector*, Washington, D. C., The Brookings Institution, 1966.

uncertain returns. Moreover, the ratio of new capital to incremental output is likely to be high just in the process of learning to plan and just in the course of rectifying the mistakes of neglect in sectors of deferred investments.

The mechanical solution for some of the production and investment problems in neglected sectors outside of the industrial-defence establishments often appears simple in theory: if some collective farms would just correctly apply more fertilizer, then grain yields would substantially increase; or, if certain textile plants would just use available resources more efficiently to meet the needs of Soviet citizens, then increased production would substantially ease the clothing shortage. But these sectors outside the high-priority pale became atrophied during the course of Stalinist development.More than increments of men and material are necessary to move towards a high production level and greater consumer satisfaction in these long-neglected, deemphasized sectors. The cumulative list of required investments is a major deferred cost of the Stalinist pattern of economic development that must now be borne. Moreover, a tight supply plan for capital, labour, and raw materials becomes even tighter with the expansion of priority sectors and the complexities of choice. No buffer sectors can easily be tapped to yield additional labour or ensure greater production when input efficiency or other factors fall below expectation. Agriculture in particular ceases to be a reservoir of labour supply and has become a problem area for planning increased yield and factor productivity.

Perhaps an even greater cost to the Soviet state from the Stalinist type of economic development is the heritage of control involved in decision-making. Stalinist-type control can no longer be imposed to direct institutions towards a single purpose as was true in the case of the early Five-Year Plans. The new power of institutions is largely that of constraint on change. Each of the various institutional groups in the now pluralistic power elite— the professional military, the economist-planners, the physical scientists, and the Party bureaucracy—appears to have enough strength to maintain the elements of *status quo* but not enough to improve the performance by their criteria. Thus, the professional military may be effective in withholding resources from agriculture that are necessary for improving agricultural productivity; traditional elements in the Party may be able to frustrate economic price reforms that might, by improving overall efficiency in planning, reduce their power in economic matters; the physical scientists may be able to defend the continued enormous costs of the Soviet non-military space programme, which is carried on at the expense of other investment programmes, such as the military programme on missile defence.[60] Even within each of these groups, the elements working for change and improvement of efficiency in overall performance have difficulty in carrying through their programmes. In an era requiring rapid changes to improve economic deficiency, this institutional rigidity imposes a cost that mounts with each successive year. The unsettled leadership post-Khrushchev may be a result of this process or may be a constraining factor on the resolution of it.[61]

The form of this debate is suggested by the following apparent reference by Party leader Dmitri Polyansky to other Party and perhaps military critics of the current expensive agricultural investment and incentives programme:

> What is needed to successfully implement all these measures? Above all, to insure strict fulfillment of the plans envisaged, there must be full allocation and the best possible utilization of planned capital investments and material-technical means. This has to be said because the good results of the last agricultural year have gone to the heads of some comrades. Some people are beginning to argue that collective and state farms are now able to develop with less substantial aid, that melioration plans can be cut and supplies of technical equipment and mineral fertilizers reduced. Such arguments are extremely dangerous, for they could delay implementation of the planned programme, and any attempts in that direction must be resolutely nipped in the bud.[62]

Spurred by the growth of new requirements, as perceived by the leadership, the pressure of attaining high performance mounts year by year. The steep rise in desired performance—indeed required performance—and the very modest increase in actual performance lead to an ever-expanding gap creating an increasingly unstable situation. Herein Adam Smith's critique of the French physiocrats appears to have a current application to the latter's modern emulators in the Soviet Union.

> It is thus that every system which endeavors, either, by extraordinary encouragements, to draw towards a particular species of industry a greater share of the capital of the society than what would naturally go to it; or, by extraordinary restraints, to force from a particular species of industry some share of the capital which would otherwise be employed in it; is in reality subversive of the great purpose which it means to promote. It retards, instead

---

[60] "Soviet Space Programs, 1962–65; Goals and Purposes, Achievements, Plans, and International Implications," Staff Report for the Committee on Aeronautical and Space Sciences, United States Senate, Eighty-ninth Congress, Washington, D. C., United States Government Printing Office, 1966.

[61] *Soviet Affairs, Number Four*, edited by Michael Kaser, Oxford, England, Oxford University Press, 1966.

[62] A Radio Moscow speech of March 3, 1967. See Polyansky speech, USSR Regional Affairs, Moscow Domestic Service in Russian, Foreign Broadcasting Information Service.

of accelerating, the progress of the society towards real wealth and greatness; and diminishes, instead of increasing, the real value of the annual produce of its land and labour.[63]

At the same time, the same type of institutional rigidities exhibited in the Soviet economy appears in other economies, as indicated by the *New Statesman* critique of British and United States government institutions:

> In the US, Congress functions much as it did in the days of George Washington; the methods of the House of Commons have changed little, in essentials, since Disraeli first entered it; Whitehall still administers the country on principles laid down in the mid-19th century . . .
>
> The truth is that the government, with the best intentions in the world, is working in the dark. It lacks the detailed, industry-by-industry, factory-by-factory information on which to base selective decisions; and even if it had that information, it lacks the legislative and administrative machinery to enforce them. It is trying to operate socialist policies with a free-market civil service structure, and with a statistical machine which Gladstone himself might have found inadequate. Hence it falls back on the blunt instruments of fiscal measures, which are both socially unjust and economically inefficient.[64]

However, in the case of the Soviet Union, the stakes are higher. Whether the economic performance is improved or continues to stagnate has profound political implications. What is now being called in question is the basic Leninist concept of a non-equalitarian, dictatorial political process of economic development. With the proliferation of countervailing forces in the leadership, this concept is being increasingly challenged. It was this concept that in the short run appeared to make the Stalinist approach appropriate and consistent with Leninism. In the long run, the post-Stalin period's new requirements may call forth not only a reexamination of Bukharin but a return to Marx. As well put by E. H. Carr:

> Marx's method was historical: all changes in the destinies and organization of mankind were part of an ever-flowing historical process. He made the assumption—the only postulate which he did not attempt to demonstrate—that modern society would *in the long run* always seek to organize itself in such a way as to make the most effective use of its productive resources.[65]

---

[63] Adam Smith, *Wealth of Nations*, Cannan Edition, Vol. I, Bk. IV, Ch. 2, p. 421; Everyman Edition, Vol. I, pp. 400–401; Modern Library Edition, p. 423.

[64] *New Statesman*, London, September 23, 1966, p. 1.

[65] E. H. Carr, *The Bolshevik Revolution, 1917–1923*, London, Macmillan & Co., Ltd., 1952, II, p. 3.

The Soviet Economy: Performance and Growth
Stanley H. Cohn

The aim of this study is to evaluate quantitatively the performance of the Soviet economy during its first half century. Soviet economic development and the particular growth formula selected for it will be compared with the approaches and performances of the other major industrial powers, both concurrently and during stages of their development analogous to those of the USSR from 1928 to the present. The technical medium is national accounts analysis, both in terms of GNP (gross national product) and its main elements. In addition, the behaviour of the production function of GNP will be comparatively analyzed as an indicator of economic efficiency. In order to provide historical perspective on Soviet performance, the legacies of the tsarist and reconstruction periods will be evaluated. Within the years of centralized planning, growth analysis will be differentiated by appropriate intervals that reflect significant changes in developmental policies. Though it is worthy of extensive separate treatment, the economic experience of World War II will not be evaluated as a distinct phenomenon, but will be looked at only as a phase in the long-term trend of the economy.

This examination of fifty years of Soviet growth and efficiency in economic performance is intended to complement John Hardt's evaluation of economic policy and organization. The theme common to both studies is that the path of Stalinist economic development diverged from the classical Western model by forcing the pace of industrialization at the expense of consumer welfare. As pointed out in Hardt's study, tsarist and reconstruction period (1921–1928) policies provided a basis from which a developmental "take-off" could be launched, but did not limit the path of development to the one preferred by Stalin. Though the Stalinist solution yielded very rapid growth and ultimately proved itself by successfully providing economic support in time of war, it did so at the cost of inefficient use of resources and by means of postponing essential consumer and infrastructure investments. As long as growth could be sustained by massive infusion of man power and capital and as long as resources could be used in ways that did not contribute directly to national power objectives, this atypical path of development could be followed, and the economic institutions directing the effort could remain unaltered. However, towards the mid-fifties, as the pool of resources no longer appeared to be inexhaustible, the effect of their inefficient utilization on the growth process became more acute. This supply constraint was compounded by a proliferation of priority demands as the leadership became more aware of the identification of national power with consumer welfare objectives. The resulting need of belatedly directing resources towards consumer-oriented objectives has meant that the pattern of Soviet development has had to veer towards more traditional market economy paths and suggests that it is likely to do so to a greater degree in future years. At the same time, the leadership has been obliged to reconsider the suitability of the Stalinist organizational structure.

In terms of the general theme of promise and fulfillment underlying the studies in this volume, the record of the Soviet economy during its first half century has been one of empty promises in respect of the welfare of the Soviet citizen, but one of fulfillment, at high cost, in respect of the aims of expansion of national power. Through the stresses and strains of war, reconstruction, and intensive industrialization, it was possible, for a time, to absorb consumer dissatisfaction with pie-in-the-sky promises of rewards tomorrow for sacrifices today. Within the past decade, however, the regime has come to realize that considerably larger regard for consumer welfare is essential if traditional national power aims are to be realized. Much of the present ferment in the Soviet system is to be explained by the realization of the regime that a thoroughgoing reassessment of resource priorities and economic institutions is vital to the effectiveness of the Soviet economy.

The Tsarist Legacy

An appraisal of economic performance over the half century of Soviet hegemony would be incomplete without reference to the state of the economy in the tsarist period. In his book, *Economic Backwardness in Historical Perspective*, Professor A. Gerschenkron systematically demonstrates numerous parallels in the techniques and conditions of industrialization under both the tsars and the Soviets: stress on heavy industrial development to support military capabilities, extraction of surplus from agriculture through rigid controls, high rates of forced saving through consumption taxes, and alterations of periods of intensive development with periods of economic recuperation. Though Soviet leaders, by their ruthless command over resources, were able to generate growth much more rapidly and steadily than the tsars, this was a difference of degree rather than of basic orientation.

What were the accomplishments of the tsarist regime and what was the level of economic development in 1913? Gross national product increased at an average annual rate of about 2.5 per cent between 1860 and 1913. Though respectable compared with the growth rates of the major industrial economies, this was, nonetheless, somewhat lower than the rate for Germany and considerably lower than that of Japan and the United States (see Table 1). In per capita terms, Russian growth averaged only 1.0 per cent, a rate lower than that of any major power except Italy. As was true later in the Soviet era, growth was very uneven among economic sectors. Industrial output increased by about 5.0 per cent annually,[1] or about double the GNP growth rate, whereas agricultural output advanced by only 2.0 per cent, suggesting a per capita increase of no more than 0.5 per cent.[2] Since exports rose rapidly, per capita domestic availabilities probably declined, Thus, large imports of foreign capital for industrialization, were, in part, financed by channelling food crops from domestic consumers for export.

Table 1

Comparative GNP Growth Rates Prior to 1913

(Average Annual Rates)

	Aggregate	Per Capita
Russia	2.5	1.0
United Kingdom	2.2	1.3
France	1.6	1.4
Germany	2.9	1.8
Italy	1.4	0.7
Japan	4.8	3.8
United States	4.3	2.2

NOTE: Data relate to 1860–1913 for Russia, 1878 for Japan, and 1870–1913 for other countries.

SOURCES: Raymond Goldsmith, "The Economic Growth of Tsarist Russia, 1860–1913," *Economic Development and Cultural Change*, Chicago, April, 1961, pp. 472–473; Angus Maddison, *Economic Growth in the West*, Twentieth Century Fund, New York, 1964, pp. 28 and 30; and *Historic Statistics of the Japanese Economy*, Bank of Japan, Tokyo, 1962.

As a result of this uneven development, the industrial position of Russia at the outbreak of World War I was higher than its general economic status warranted by historical analogy with other major economies. About 75 per cent of the labour force was still in agriculture, and per capita income was perhaps no more than a fifth or sixth of that in the United States and a third of that in Western Europe.[3] Yet, according to official Soviet estimates, which, it seems, would be prone to minimize

---

[1] Raymond Goldsmith, "The Economic Growth of Tsarist Russia, 1860–1913," *Economic Development and Cultural Change*, Chicago, April, 1961, p. 471.

[2] *Ibid.*, pp. 453–454.

[3] See Appendix I, Table I-1, this study.

tsarist accomplishments, Russia ranked as the world's fifth industrial producer in 1913,[4] behind the United States, Germany, the United Kingdom, and France. On a per capita basis, its position would have been less auspicious, placing it behind such small industrial powers as Belgium, Sweden, and Canada. Much of Russian industrial plant was foreign-owned and foreign-staffed, but the economy did possess the human and physical nucleus for an industrial civilization. Progress in agriculture had been slow, but there was the luxury of an agricultural surplus from which to extract savings required for development. Though considerably behind Western Europe in most respects, the Russian educational system did have almost three-quarters of the ratio of university students per capita as in the major West European countries (see Table 14). The illiteracy rate was, nevertheless, much higher than in the leading countries of the West. In the European part of the country, there existed an extensive rail network. Though the Russia of 1913 was backward by advanced market economy standards, it still possessed many of the essentials for a developmental "take-off," and, in this respect, was far ahead of most of the underdeveloped Asian, African, and Latin American countries of today.

Period of Consolidation of the Revolution

In terms of the economy, the years between the Bolshevik seizure of power in 1917 and the inauguration of intensive planning in 1928 were characterized by disruptions of the civil war period and efforts to restore the levels of output that prevailed before the onset of war and revolution. Inclusion of these years within the spectrum of the performance of the Soviet economic system is based on the thesis that seizure and consolidation of power are as much elements of the system's performance as of its ability to generate growth.

As a result of long years of economic chaos and recovery, the world position of the Soviet Union slipped behind the fifth place it had held in 1913.[5] It held sixth rank in production of iron ore and steel, seventh in production of coal, and eighth in production of electric power, cement, paper, and sulphuric acid. Had the growth rates that prevailed between 1900 and 1914 continued through 1928, the level of GNP would have been higher by 35 per cent, of industrial output by 200 per cent, and of agricultural output by 15 per cent. Therefore, the cost of World War I,

---

[4] *Narodnoe khozyaystvo SSSR v 1964 godu* (The Economy of the USSR in 1964), Moscow, 1965, p. 92.

[5] There is no overall ranking for industrial output, but the USSR slipped one rank in coal, steel, and electric power, and two ranks in iron ore, between 1913 and 1928. See *Narodnoe khozyaystvo SSSR v 1964, op. cit.*, p. 93.

the revolution, and the ensuing civil war, by 1928, may be estimated at roughly fifteen years of growth.

However, on the eve of its explosive growth phase, the Soviet economy had progressed in two important respects. Industrial output had advanced little since 1913, but output per man hour had risen by 37 per cent, or over 2 per cent as an annual average.[6] That this increase in productivity was largely compressed within the four or five years immediately preceding 1928 suggests that the system was capable of rapid assimilation of Western technology. A beginning had been made in the mass educational effort that distinguished Soviet policy in later years. During the 1920's, there was a widespread programme of adult education to reduce illiteracy and to train a pre-industrial population in modern technological skills. By 1928, enrollment in elementary and secondary schools had increased by more than 70 per cent over the pre-war level (pre-1939 boundaries).[7] The ratio of university students per 1,000 of population was higher by half than in 1914 and equalled or exceeded comparable ratios in Western Europe (see Table 14).

On the eve of the Stalinist era, the Soviet economy had changed little in terms of development from 1913. Per capita income levels (based on 1964 prices) ranged between $200 and $350, or between a seventh and a fifth of the level of the United States (see Appendix Table I-1), or a fifth and a third of that of the major West European economies. Almost 71 per cent of the labour force was in agriculture (see Table 13), a proportion similar to that in present-day India, Korea, and Mainland China,[8] and to that of the United States and the principal countries of Continental Europe in the early years of the nineteenth century.[9]

Thus, in terms of factor availabilities and motivation on the part of the regime, the thesis that the Russian economy was ready for a take-off is even more applicable to the Soviet economy of 1928 than of 1913. For, whereas the tsarist economic ministers had broken the path of pioneer industrialization and infrastructure investment, their Soviet successors possessed, in addition, advantages of growth motivation, intensive educational efforts, and an updated backlog of advanced Western technology.

---

[6] G. Warren Nutter, *Growth of Industrial Production in the Soviet Union*, Princeton, Princeton University Press, 1962, p. 164.

[7] Nicholas DeWitt, *Education and Professional Employment in the USSR*, Washington, D. C., National Science Foundation, 1961, p. 577.

[8] Frederick Harbison and Charles Myers, *Education, Manpower, and Economic Growth*, New York, McGraw-Hill Book Co., 1964, p. 46.

[9] Simon Kuznets, "Industrial Distribution of National Product and the Labor Force," *Economic Development and Cultural Change*, July, 1957.

Stalinist and Post-Stalinist Periods

General Growth Performance. When the Stalinist programme of intensive industrialization was introduced in 1928, the USSR had a national product approximately equal to that of the principal West European economies and about a fifth the size of that of the United States (see Appendix Table I–2). Since its product was heavily agricultural in origin, its economic power position was relatively lower, as its industrial ranking illustrates.[10] In terms of GNP per capita, the USSR stood seventh among the major powers, at perhaps a seventh of the United States and a fourth of the West European level (see Appendix Table I–1). In the fiftieth year of Soviet power, the USSR has become the world's second economy, some half the size of the United States and equal to the combined GNP of West Germany, France, and Italy. In per capita terms, the USSR has moved up to fifth position, reaching two-fifths the level of the United States and two-thirds that of Western Europe. Industrially, the Soviet economy is in second position, with about half the output of the United States and double that of the major West European powers.[11]

This achievement in growth has varied markedly from one period to another since 1928 (see Table 2). The rate between 1928 and 1937, during the most intensive, frenetic years of industrialization, averaged from 4.8 to 11.9 per cent annually, depending on the weights selected (see Note to Table 2). Though these rates are high by international standards, and though they are certainly much above those of Western powers caught in the throes of depression (see Table 3), they are not historically unique. At similar or lower per capita levels, the United States approached the lower limit from 1870–1890,[12] and Japan equalled the lower limit from 1890–1900, surpassing it between 1920 and 1930.[13] After 1937, the rising spectre of Hitler forced the Soviet leadership to shift resources into armaments on a massive scale. As a result, the growth rate fell drastically, to 3.6 per cent per year between 1937 and 1940. The destructive effects of World War II on the economy meant, in effect, that there was no net increase in GNP between 1941 and

---

[10] Abram Bergson, Hans Heymann, and Oleg Hoeffding, *Soviet National Income and Product, 1928–1948, Revised Data*, Santa Monica, California, The RAND Corporation, 1966, p. 13.

[11] Stanley H. Cohn, in U.S. Congress, Joint Economic Committee, *Annual Economic Indicators for the USSR*, Washington, D. C., Government Printing Office, 1964, Table VIII-6, p. 97.

[12] Angus Maddison, *Economic Growth in the West*, New York, Twentieth Century Fund, 1964, pp. 201–202.

[13] Michael C. Kaser, "Education and Economic Progress," *The Economics of Education*, edited by E. A. G. Robinson and J. E. Vaizey, New York, St. Martin's Press, 1966, p. 169.

1948.[14] In the post-war years, national product increased at an average annual rate of 7.1 per cent between 1950 and 1958, but declined to a rate of 5.3 per cent between 1958 and 1964. Growth during these years was not uniquely high among large, developed economies: most market economies have experienced growth surges since 1950. In the earlier post-war period, Soviet growth was less than that of West Germany, a country with a considerably higher per capita income; in the latter period, less than both West Germany and France, economies with higher per capita incomes. In the latter period, it also fell behind Italy, a country with a slightly lower per capita income, and far behind Japan, a country with 80 per cent of the Soviet per capita income level. This slowdown in growth has been a major concern of the leadership as the golden anniversary of the revolution has approached.

Table 2

Growth Rates of Soviet Gross National Product

(Selected Periods. Average Annual Rates)

	GNP		GNP per Employed Person		GNP per
	Aggregate	Per Capita	Man-Year	Man-Hour	Capital Unit
1860—1883	2.25	0.75	—	—	—
1883—1900	2.75	1.25	—	—	—
1900—1913	2.20	1.10	—	—	—
1913—1928	0.50	—0.10	—	—	—
1928—1937[1]	4.8—11.9	3.8—10.8	1.7—7.9	1.8—8.0	—0.1—6.1
1937—1940	3.60	0.70	0.8	—0.4	—4.5
1940—1950[2]	1.8—2.2	2.6—3.2	1.0—1.3	1.3—2.4	1.3—2.4
1950—1958	7.10	5.20	5.3	5.8	—1.2
1958—1964	5.30	3.50	3.3	4.7	—3.7

[1] Lower limit based on valuation of ruble factor cost in 1937 prices; upper limit on valuation in 1928 prices.

[2] Lower limit based on valuation of ruble factor cost in 1950 prices; upper limit on valuation in 1937 prices.

NOTE: The dilemma of selecting an appropriate base period in which to measure economic trends constantly bedevils the analyst in the use of time series. This is the familiar index-number problem in which there must be a choice between equally appropriate sets of relative prices or outputs over the period being measured, the former variable in the case of GNP indexes. The more rapidly the structure of an economy is evolving, or the longer the period under consideration, the greater will be the divergence between the results obtained from early and late period weights. Since there is a tendency in a progressive economy for relative price trends to vary inversely with output trends, early year price weights will yield a faster growth rate than later year weights, as the products which show the most rapid growth trends carry higher prices in earlier years. The Soviet economy was industrializing very rapidly from 1928 to 1937, so the

---

[14] The ability of the Soviet system to survive tremendous war-time losses, sustain a victorious military effort, and support rapid recovery is a theme worthy of detailed, separate analysis. In this study, it will only be noted in summary fashion.

choice of price weights markedly influences the GNP indexes. Since neither set of weights is conceptually superior to the other, the rate of growth of output has been expressed as a range, with the limits representing later and early (1937 and 1928) weights, respectively. The same observations apply to the period 1940–1950, in which both 1937 and 1950 price weights have been used. In the post-war period, structural changes have been more gradual, so only a single set of price weights (1959) have been used.

The problems of intertemporal comparisons are further complicated by those of an inter-spatial nature in the expression of of aggregate and per capita GNP time series in common dollar terms (see Appendix Tables I-1 and I-2). If the GNP of any economy is revalued in terms of the relative prices prevailing in any other economy, its relative national product will be overstated, i.e., if the GNP of country A is valued in prices of country B, the magnitude of country A's GNP relative to that of country B will be inflated. This phenomenon is produced by the inverse relations which exist between prices and output. In the hypothetical example, sectors with high output in country A would be valued at high country B prices rather than lower A prices, and sectors of relatively low output would be valued at low B prices rather than higher A prices.

The degree of divergence in relative price patterns and output structures is the greater, the wider the difference in stages of development of the two economies. The choice of an appropriate conversion ratio between the prices of a relatively advanced and a relatively backward economy is analogous to that in a GNP index between prices of an early and a late period. For purposes of simplification, the conversion ratios selected between foreign and dollar prices are single values—the geometric means of foreign and dollar prices. While not inherently preferable to some other conversion ratios, the geometric means do have the advantage of consistency. They reflect more accurately the relative purchasing power of a country's currency than do official rates of exchange.

SOURCES: Raymond Goldsmith, "The Economic Growth of Tsarist Russia, 1860–1913", *Economic Development and Cultural Change*, Chicago, April, 1961, pp. 470–473; Simon S. Kuznets, *Economic Development and Cultural Change*, October, 1956, p. 81; Frank Lorimer, *The Population of the Soviet Union*, New York, League of Nations, 1946, p. 135; Abram Bergson, *The Real National Income of Soviet Russia Since 1928*, Cambridge, Massachusetts, Harvard University Press, 1961, pp. 210, 217, 226, and 232; Stanley H. Cohn, "Soviet Growth Retardation: Trends in Resource Availability and Efficiency", *New Directions in the Soviet Economy*, U. S. Congress, Joint Economic Committee, Government Printing Office, Washington, D.C., 1966, pp. 105 and 115; Abram Bergson, "National Income," *Economic Trends in the Soviet Union*, edited by Abram Bergson and Simon Kuznets, Cambridge, Massachusetts, Harvard University Press, 1963, p. 4; and *Narodnoe khozyaystvo SSSR v 1964 godu* (The Economy of the USSR in 1964), Moscow, 1965, p. 68.

Efficiency of Growth Performance. If the criterion of performance is taken to be some measure of efficiency in the use of resources, such as productivity of labour or capital, the record of the Soviet economy since 1928 is considerably less noteworthy. Output per man-hour in the period 1928–1937 rose at an average annual rate of 1.8 to 8.0 per cent and declined in the period 1937–1940 by 0.4 per cent. Within the perspective of international experience, all the major Continental European economies as well as that of the United States considerably exceeded the lower limit of man-hour productivity advancement during the decades of the nineteenth century in which their per capita income equalled that of the Soviet Union between 1928 and 1937 (see Table 4). This relatively poor productivity record is explained by the prodigous infusion of man power into urban occupations

Table 3

Comparative Trends in Gross National Product
(Average Annual Rates)

AGGREGATE

	1913—1964	1928—1964	1950—1958	1958—1964
USSR	2.1	4.4—6.3	7.1	5.3
France	1.9	2.1	4.4	5.4
West Germany	2.8	3.7	7.6	5.8
Italy	2.6	2.8	5.6	6.1
United Kingdom	2.1	2.3	2.4	3.9
Japan	3.6	4.3	6.1	12.0
United States	3.2	3.4	2.9	4.4

PER CAPITA

	1913—1964	1928—1964	1950—1958	1958—1964
USSR	1.1	3.3—5.4	5.2	3.5
France	1.6	1.8	3.5	4.0
West Germany	1.8	2.6	6.4	4.6
Italy	1.9	2.2	5.0	5.4
United Kingdom	1.6	1.8	1.9	3.1
Japan	3.1[1]	2.6[2]	4.8	11.0
United States	1.4	1.4	1.2	2.7

PER MAN-HOUR

	1913—1964	1928—1964	1950—1958	1958—1964
USSR	—	2.8—4.4	5.8	4.7
France	1.6	1.9—2.1	3.9	4.4
West Germany	0.9	2.8—2.9	5.9	5.4
Italy	1.9	2.8—3.2	3.9	5.5
United Kingdom	1.7	1.9—2.0	2.0	3.5
Japan	—	2.5[2]	3.2	11.0
United States	2.4	2.2—2.4	2.4	2.2

[1] Initial year: 1910.

[2] Initial year: 1930.

SOURCES: Raymond Goldsmith, "The Economic Growth of Tsarist Russia, 1860—1913," *Economic Development and Cultural Change*, Chicago, April, 1961, pp. 470—473; Simon S. Kuznets, *Economic Development and Cultural Change*, October, 1956, p. 81; Frank Lorimer, *The Population of the Soviet Union*, New York, League of Nations, 1946, p. 135; Abram Bergson, *The Real National Income of Soviet Russia Since 1928*, Cambridge, Massachusetts, Harvard University Press, 1961, pp. 210, 217, 226, and 232; Stanley H. Cohn, "Soviet Growth Retardation: Trends in Resource Availability and Efficiency," *New Directions in the Soviet Economy*, U. S. Congress, Joint Economic Committee, Government Printing Office, Washington, D.C., 1966, pp. 105 and 115; Abram Bergson, "National Income," *Economic Trends in the Soviet Union*, edited by Abram Bergson and Simon Kuznets, Cambridge, Massachusetts, Harvard University Press, 1963, p. 4; Central Statistical Administration, *Narodnoe khozyaystvo SSSR v 1964 godu*, Moscow, 1965, p. 68; Angus Maddison, *Economic Growth in the West*, New York, Twentieth Century Fund, 1964, pp. 28, 232—233; Michael Kaser, "Education and Economic Progress," *The Economics of Education*, edited by E. A. G. Robinson and J. E. Vaizey, New York, St. Martin's Press, 1966, p. 169; and *Historical Statistics of the Japanese Economy*, Bank of Japan, Tokyo, 1962.

during the Stalinist years. Employment rose by 3.7 per cent annually from 1928 to 1937 and by 3.0 per cent annually from 1937 to 1940 (see Table 5). No other economy has even remotely matched the Soviet rate of labour influx at comparable periods of development.

Such a rapid increase in employment without a proportional increase in population was achieved through a rapid jump in the participation ratio— that is, the labour force as a per cent of the work-age population (15 to 64). This went from 56.8 per cent in 1928 to 70.1 per cent in 1937 (see Table 6). Within the periods for which statistics have been compiled, no other economy has experienced so rapid a rise in the participation ratio. In fact, since 1913, the ratio has fallen in most West European countries.[15] The increase in the ratio between 1928 and 1940 is mainly a function of the shift from underemployed agriculture to fully employed urban occupations, whereas in the post-war years it is a function of the rising proportion of females in the labour force.[16] In other words, the rapid rise in employment, in full-time labour equivalents, was a function of the unusually rapid transfer of man power out of agriculture, a phenomenon to be analyzed at a later point in the discussion.

After the powerful upsurge of the thirties, until 1958, the participation ratio, excluding the war years, remained on a plateau. The delayed impact of low war-time and early post-war birth rates on the rate of entry of youth into employment became evident in the late fifties. As an offset to this constraint, the regime accelerated the flow of youth into employment by cessation of the trend toward universal secondary education and by inducing an even greater ratio of remunerative employment for women. By 1964, the Soviet participation ratio was the highest among the major industrial powers, and probably it cannot be increased further.[17]

During the post-war years, the Soviet economy exhibited considerably greater efficiency in use of man-power resources. Its rise in man-hour productivity compared favourably with the performances of other major economies, though slipping in both rate and rank after 1958 (see Table 3). This great improvement in labour productivity is to be explained, at least in part, by a much slower rate of increase in employment, 1.7 per cent annually from 1950 to 1958, and 2.0 per cent annually between 1958 and

---

[15] Maddison, *op. cit.*, p. 31.

[16] Warren W. Eason, "Labor Force," in *Economic Trends in the Soviet Union*, edited by Abram Bergson and Simon Kuznets, Cambridge, Massachusetts, Harvard University Press, 1963, p. 87.

[17] Stanley H. Cohn, "Soviet Growth Retardation : Trends in Resource Availability and Efficiency," in U.S. Congress, Joint Economic Committee, *New Directions in the Soviet Economy*, Washington, D. C., Government Printing Office, 1966, p. 114.

Table 4

Comparative Historical Trends in Growth of GNP per Man-Hour
(Average Annual Rates)

	Period	Rate
USSR	1928—1937	1.8—8.0
	1937—1940	—0.4
France	1880—1890	2.5
	1890—1900	2.2
Germany	1871—1880	2.5
	1880—1890	2.4
	1890—1900	1.9
United Kingdom	1880—1890	3.8
	1890—1900	1.2
United States	1871—1890	2.7
	1890—1900	2.2
Italy	1900—1913	2.6

NOTE: For derivation of historical analogues see Appendix I.

SOURCES: Raymond Goldsmith, "The Economic Growth of Tsarist Russia, 1860–1913," *Economic Development and Cultural Change*, Chicago, April, 1961, pp. 470–473; Simon S. Kuznets, *Economic Development and Cultural Change*, October, 1956, p. 81; Frank Lorimer, *The Population of the Soviet Union*, New York, League of Nations, 1946, p. 135; Abram Bergson, *The Real National Income of Soviet Russia Since 1928*, Cambridge, Massachusetts, Harvard University Press, 1961, pp. 210, 217, 226, and 232; Stanley H. Cohn, "Soviet Growth Retardation: Trends in Resource Availability and Efficiency," *New Directions in the Soviet Economy*, U.S. Congress, Joint Economic Committee, Government Printing Office, Washington, D.C., 1966, pp. 105 and 115; Abram Bergson, "National Income," *Economic Trends in the Soviet Union*, edited by Abram Bergson and Simon Kuznets, Cambridge, Massachusetts, Harvard University Press, 1963, p. 4; Central Statistical Administration, *Narodnoe khozyaystvo SSSR v 1964 godu*, Moscow, 1965, p. 68; and Angus Maddison, *Economic Growth in the West*, New York, Twentieth Century Fund, 1964, p. 232.

1964 (see Table 7). If the sharp reduction in the length of the work week after 1958 is taken into account, the man-power input increased at a rate of only 0.6 per cent. The impact of demographic losses in the war-time period on the rate at which school graduates entered the labour force was felt during these years. In order to sustain growth, it was necessary to substitute other productive factors for the depleted labour reservoir. Necessity, of course, does not guarantee success, but through a combination of maintaining a high rate of capital input (see Table 7) and reaping the return on a more highly educated labour force as well as on the intangible improvements to efficiency that must have accrued from the more relaxed atmosphere following Stalin's death, the economy managed to improve its labour productivity performance greatly (see Table 2), with some deceleration after 1958.

Table 5

Comparative Historical Rates of Increase in Labour Force

(Average Annual Rates)

	Period	Rate
USSR	1928—1937	3.7
	1937—1940	3.0
United Kingdom	1821—1831 to 1851—1861	0.9
	1851—1861 to 1871—1881	0.7
Germany	1851—1855 to 1871—1875	0.7
	1871 to 1886—1895	1.4
	1886—1895 to 1907	1.7
United States	1874—1889	2.8
	1889—1914	2.4
Japan	1883—1887 to 1903—1907	1.0
	1893—1897 to 1913—1917	0.6
	1918—1922 to 1938—1942	0.9
Italy	1861—1881	0.2
	1881—1901	0.2
	1901—1921	0.3
	1921—1936	0.3

SOURCE: Simon S. Kuznets, *Economic Development and Cultural Change*, Chicago, July, 1961, Part II, pp. 34, 35.

Table 6

Trends in the Labour Participation Ratio in the USSR

	Work-Age Population	Employed Population	Paritcipation Ratio
1928	87,000,000	49,400,000	56.8%
1937	98,000,000	68,700,000	70.1%
1950	115,100,000	82,500,000	71.7%
1958	133,900,000	94,800,000	70.8%
1964	140,100,000	106,600,000	76.1%

SOURCES: Abram Bergson, *The Real National Income of Soviet Russia Since 1928*, Cambridge, Massachussetts, Harvard University Press, 1961, pp. 442, 443; James Brackett (working paper), "Estimated Population of the USSR by Single Years and Sex," Model 3, Foreign Manpower Division, Bureau of Census, Washington, D.C.; and Murray Feshbach, "Manpower in the USSR," U.S. Congress, Joint Economic Committee, *New Directions in the Soviet Economy*, Washington, D.C., Government Printing Office, 1966, p. 746.

Whereas the Soviet economy was wasteful of labour resources during the 1930's, it has been wasteful of physical capital throughout the entire period since 1928. With the exception of the atypical war and recovery decade of 1940–1950, the rate of change in inputs of fixed capital per unit of output has been negative—that is, the marginal capital output ratio has been rising (see Table 2). Historical estimates for the United States and post-war estimates for Western Europe indicate that such a persistent

Table 7

Growth Rates of Employment, Fixed Capital, and Educational Stock in the USSR

(Average Annual Rates)

	Employment		Fixed Capital	Educational Stock
	Man-Years	Man-Hours		
1928—1937	3.7	3.6	10.4—12.0	11.2—11.8*
1937—1940	3.0	3.8	8.1	
1940—1950	0.3	0.6	−0.2—0.5	4.8—5.0
1950—1958	1.7	1.2	8.3	7.1
1958—1964	2.0	0.6	9.4	4.7

* These figures are for 1926—1939.

SOURCES: See Appendix II, this study.

negative trend is probably unique.[18] The expectation of a decline, or at least a relatively constant marginal capital output ratio, would appear to be particularly applicable in an economy like the Soviet one, with extensive technological borrowing possibilities and the presence of a large corps of trained engineers, scientists, and managers to assimilate the technology. Post-war experience in Western Europe, where, unlike in the USSR, capital output ratios have tended to remain low, below historical trends, supports this generalization.[19]

This persistent inefficiency in utilization of fixed capital may be explained by the rapid rate of increase in capital stock (see Table 7). Except

---

[18] Simon S. Kuznets, *Capital in the American Economy*, National Bureau of Economic Research, Princeton, Princeton University Press, 1961, p. 80; John W. Kendrick, *Productivity Trends in the United States*, National Bureau of Economic Research, Princeton, Princeton University Press, 1961, p. 167. Kendrick's estimates, which exclude housing and government capital, show no negative trends for any decade between 1869 and 1953. Kuznets' estimates, which include both of these factors to the extent that data are available, show a rising ratio of gross capital to GNP through 1919, with a secular decline through 1955. Estimates of United States capital stock based on Bulletin F depreciation rates indicate that the post-1919 trend has persisted into the 1960's. The post-war estimates for Western Europe are preliminary calculations by Edward Denison, as reported in Michael Boretsky, "Comparative Progress in Technology, Productivity, and Economic Efficiency: USSR versus U.S.," *New Directions in the Soviet Economy, op. cit.*, p. 212.

[19] For a comparison of post-war, fixed, non-residential output ratios, see Cohn, "Soviet Growth Retardation," *New Directions in the Soviet Economy, op. cit.*, p. 120. If historical ratios of investment to output, as computed by Simon Kuznets, are compared with post-war ratios, as computed by this author using techniques and sources described in the article cited, ratios for Germany and Italy prove to have been at historic lows after World War II and those for Japan at the lowest level in this century.

during the disrupted decade of the 1940's, increments to capital stock, exclusive of retirements, have not been less than at an annual rate of 8 per cent. During the middle nineteenth century, the comparable rate for the United States ranged between 4.5 and 4.8 per cent.[20] According to conventional economic theory, any tendency towards diminishing returns ought to have been offset by the technological advance embodied in new capital invested. However, in the Soviet case, this expectation may have been undercut by the very high rate of increments to capital stock, as evidenced by high capital-labour ratios (see Table 8). Substitution of capital for labour was especially prominent after 1958. Incremental fixed capital-labour ratios in the United States in the nineteenth century were far lower than any experienced by the Soviets, except during the atypical war and recovery decade.[21]

Table 8

Incremental Capital-Labour Ratios: Average Annual Rates

(Increase in Fixed Capital, Net of Retirements, Divided by Increases in Man-Hours)

USSR		UNITED STATES	
1929—1937	2.9—3.3	1879—1889	1.5
1937—1940	2.1	1889—1899	2.2
1940—1950	0.3—0.7	1899—1909	1.7
1950—1958	6.9	1909—1919	2.1
1958—1964	15.7	1919—1929	2.9

SOURCES: See Table 7, this study, for respective rates of growth for the USSR. Simon S. Kuznets, *Capital in the American Economy*, National Bureau of Economic Research, Princeton, New Jersey, Princeton University Press, 1961, p. 64; and John W. Kendrick, *Productivity Trends, in the United States*, National Bureau of Economic Research, Princeton, New Jersey, Princeton University Press, 1961, pp. 308–310, 328–331.

Undoubtedly, the peculiar nature of the Soviet system of pricing played a role in the disproportionate infusions of capital through the absence of an interest charge. In a market economy, with the imposition of interest charges, diminishing returns to, or marginal productivity of, capital investment would become evident long before attaining the rate of investment reached by the Soviet economy. This condition would have been particularly relevant for the 1930's, a period in which scarcity of capital would have led to very high implicit rates. Bent as it was on fostering rapid industrialization, the regime may have ignored the rising cost of a high rate of investment, but at least it would have possessed an adequate criterion

---

[20] Reliable estimates of capital stock are not available for other major economies for years prior to World War II, thus limiting the comparison to the economy of the United States.

[21] *Kuznets, op. cit.*, p. 64.

for determining an appropriate investment ratio and for making choices among investment alternatives.

Total Factor Productivity. The efficiency of the economy is best measured by including the maximum number of productive factors in the estimating equation. In this way, unknown influences on growth are minimized. The multi-factor model used in this study combines man power (man-hours), fixed capital (net of retirements, gross of depreciation), agricultural land, and productive livestock. For the post-war period, educational stock has been added to the other four factors (see Table 9).

Table 9

Soviet Gross National Product per Unit of Combined Inputs
(Average Annual Rates)

	Four-Factor Model	Five-Factor Model
1928—1937	1.0—7.9	—
1937—1940	—0.2	—
1940—1950	1.2—1.6	—
1950—1958	3.9	3.4
1958—1964	2.3	2.0

SOURCES: See Appendix II, this study.

The performance of the economy between 1928 and 1937 is obscured by the widely varying results that alternative price weights yield. If 1937 weights are employed, there is little increase in productivity; with 1929 weights, the rate of increase is 7.9 per cent. In the armament years, from 1937 to 1940, output per unit of combined inputs was slightly negative. In the early fifties, combined factor productivity sharply increased for reasons previously noted in the discussion of labour productivity. Since 1958, the rate of growth in combined factor productivity has decelerated, with stagnation in agriculture and falling productivity in industry.

What has been the relative importance of the increases in factor inputs and of the productivity of these inputs for Soviet growth? Some perspective may be gained on this question by comparing the historical growth experience of the Soviet Union and the United States (see Table 10). With the exception of the period 1950–1958, which was influenced by the liberalizing effects of de-Stalinization, Soviet growth has depended more on inputs of factors than on the increased efficiency of their utilization. In the twentieth century, in the United States factor productivity has been considerably more important than increases in volume of factors, though the Soviet-type pattern was prevalent in the last three decades of the nineteenth century. The significance of parallel experience during years of comparable levels of per capita income must be left for further investigation.

Table 10

Growth Contributions of Factor Inputs and Combined Factor Productivity

(Average Annual Rates)

USSR

	Inputs	Productivity
1928—1937	3.7	1.0—7.9
1937—1940	3.8	−0.2
1940—1950	0.6	1.2—1.6
1950—1958	3.2	3.9
1958—1964	2.9	2.3

UNITED STATES

1869—1878 to 1899—1908..	3.0	1.5
1899—1908 to 1929	1.5	1.8
1929—1948	0.4	2.2
1950—1957	1.2	2.4
1957—1963	0.8	2.4

NOTE: Figures for inputs represent weighted values for man-hours, fixed capital, farm land, and productive livestock. Productivity equals index of GNP divided by index of inputs.

SOURCES: See Appendix II, this study.

It would appear that any margin of growth that the Soviet economy has achieved over the United States can be entirely explained in terms of factor inputs rather than factor productivity.[22] Such a comparison casts doubt on the efficiency of Soviet planning, as distinguished from its ability to command productive resources.

Resource Allocation Trends and Policies. Having reviewed trends in Soviet growth and the efficiency of the growth process, let us now turn to an analysis of the resource policies that facilitated this performance. In general terms, rapid growth occurred because the regime could channel a large share of national product into investment. This policy, of course, meant that a relatively small share of national product could be used to satisfy consumer needs, a share that was further reduced as defence claims burgeoned after 1937 (see Table 11).

Even in 1928, before the progressive squeezing of the consumer, aimed at directing resources into growth, and later, additionally, into defence, the share of GNP allocated for purposes of private consumption was low by

---

[22] Data suitable for constructing production functions for West European economies are available only for the post-war years and are limited to factors of man-years and business capital investment. In West Germany, France, and Italy, between 1950 and 1962, the preponderant influence on growth was exerted by factor productivity rather than factor inputs. See Boretsky, *op. cit.*

the historical standards set in other major economies at similar levels of per capita GNP. Abram Bergson's estimate of 64.7 per cent compares with 83.0 per cent for the United Kingdom in 1860–1869, 82.6 per cent for Germany in 1851–1860, 79.7 per cent for the United States in 1867–1878, 84.1 per cent for Italy in 1891–1900, and 82.0 per cent for Japan in 1931 — 1940.[23] Equally without historical precedent is the rapidity with which the

Table 11

Trends in Allocation of Soviet GNP at Factor Cost

(Per Cent of Total)

	1928	1937	1940	1950	1955	1964
Private Consumption	64.7	52.5	51.0	51.0	50.6	46.5
Communal Consumption[1] ..	5.1	10.5	9.9	8.0	8.2	9.4
Investment[2]	25.0	25.9	19.2	23.0	25.3	30.5
Defence[3]	2.5	7.9	16.1	13.3	13.0	11.3
Other[4]	2.7	3.2	3.8	4.7	2.9	2.3

[1] Outlays for public education, health, and science.

[2] Fixed investment and inventories.

[3] Budgetary category of defence, 1928–1940; budgetary plus estimates of defence expenditures under other portions of state budget, 1950–1964.

[4] Largely composed of governmental administrative expenditures.

NOTE: The pre-war and post-war proportions of GNP should not be directly compared with one another, except as general orders of magnitude, because of methodological differences. The first difference concerns adjustment of market prices to factor cost. The pre-war Bergson estimates, after deduction of turnover taxes from the prices of farm products and consumer goods, do not include an allowance for agricultural rent; whereas the post-war estimates, based on the 1955 national accounts constructed by Morris Bornstein, include an estimate of land rent. The Bergson estimates value farm income in kind at average realized farm prices, while the original Bornstein estimates use the higher valuation of weighted state retail and collective farm market prices. Lastly, the Bergson estimates compute investment as a residual between calculated total incomes and expenditures, while the Bornstein estimates compute investment directly from official estimates and assumptions as to unspecified state budgetary expenditures of an investment nature. The net effect of these methodological differences is to give private consumption a lower proportion and the other end uses, particularly investment, higher proportions in the Bergson than in the Bornstein calculations. For further analysis of differences in methodology, see Abram Bergson's source noted below; Morris Bornstein and Associates, *Soviet National Accounts for 1955*, Center for Russian Studies, Ann Arbor, Michigan, University of Michigan, 1961; and Stanley H. Cohn, "Comment on 2½ Percent and All That," *Soviet Studies*, Glasgow, Scotland, January, 1965.

SOURCES: Abram Bergson, *The Real National Income of Soviet Russia Since 1928*, Cambridge, Massachusetts, Harvard University Press, 1961, p. 237; Stanley H. Cohn, "Soviet Growth, Retardation: Trends in Resource Availability and Efficiency," *New Directions in the Soviet Economy*, U. S. Congress, Joint Economic Committee, Government Printing Office, Washington, D.C., pp. 129, 132.

[23] Simon Kuznets, "The Share and Structure of Consumption," *Economic Development and Cultural Change*, January, 1962, pp. 72–74. Also, see Appendix I, this study, for estimates on which the choice of analogues is based.

proportionate claim of private consumption on GNP declined, reaching a share of 52.5 per cent in 1937. No other major economy approached this low proportion in peacetime until Japan did in the late 1950's.

The initial diversion of GNP from private consumption went into investment. Beyond this initial surge of investment, there was little further increase in the GNP share allocated to investment through 1937, and a considerable drop thereafter, as defence requirements loomed ever larger. Instead, through 1937, there was considerable emphasis on communal, at the expense of private, consumption, with a subsequent levelling off in the communal share until the outbreak of war. This trend reflected in particular the massive educational effort, and can be quite properly evaluated as an ingredient of growth policy: large-scale physical investment could not yield returns without concomitant investment in human capital.

Consumption Trends. The process of economic development is normally accompanied by a decline in the share of private consumption. The rate at which this decline takes place and whether this decline is absolute or relative on a per capita basis reflects the changes in consumer welfare during the development period. The 12 per cent reduction in the share of private consumption in GNP required only 9 years in the USSR. In Germany, it took 40 years; in the United Kingdom and Italy, 50; in the United States, 30; and it was not attained in Japan until the 1950's.[24]

Another way of gaining perspective on Soviet consumption policy is to compare rates of change in per capita private consumption levels in other major economies during periods when they had similiar levels of per capita income (see Table 12). Depending on the base-year prices used, Soviet per capita private consumption either declined steadily from 1928 through 1941, and very drastically during the war, or showed a moderate increase between 1928 and 1937, and declined during the following three years. If there was an increase, it was more nominal than real, as much of it would reflect the cost of urbanization, i.e., the commercial purchase of services and commodities formerly supplied by the consumer himself in a rural environment. In no case, did consumption decline in other economies at a similar stage, nor were increases so largely reflective of urbanization costs, because shifts out of agriculture were more gradual.

In contrast, the rate of increase in communally supplied consumption was very large, averaging around 15 per cent annually in this period. Defence claims after 1937 halted further progress in this sphere until after the war.

---

[24] *Ibid.*

Table 12

Comparative Trends in Per Capita Private Consumption
(Average Annual Rates)

	Period	Rate
USSR	1928—1937	−1.0—2.6
	1937—1940	−1.0
	1940—1944	−8.1— −8.9
	1944—1950	9.5
	1950—1958	5.3
	1958—1964	2.2
United Kingdom..........	1880—1889 to 1890—1899	1.7
	1890—1899 to 1900—1909	0.6
	1950—1958	1.6
	1958—1964	2.8
Germany	1851—1860 to 1861—1870	1.9
	1861—1870 to 1871—1880	1.4
	1871—1880 to 1881—1890	0.8
	1881—1890 to 1891—1900	1.8
	1950—1958	6.2
	1958—1964	4.2
Italy	1861—1870 to 1871—1880	0.1
	1871—1880 to 1881—1890	—
	1881—1890 to 1891—1900	1.2
	1950—1958	3.5
	1958—1964	5.7
United States	1869—1879	4.2
	1879—1889	2.0
	1889—1898 to 1899—1908	2.9
	1950—1958	1.1
	1958—1964	2.6

SOURCES: Abram Bergson, *The Real National Income of Soviet Russia Since 1928*, Cambridge, Massachussetts, Harvard University Press, 1961, p. 236; Stanley H. Cohn, "Soviet Growth Retardation: Trends in Resource Availability and Efficiency," *New Directions in the Soviet Economy*, U.S. Congress, Joint Economic Committee, Government Printing Office, Washington, D.C., 1966, p. 107; and Simon S. Kuznets, "The Share and Structure of Consumption," *Economic Development and Cultural Change*, Chicago, July, 1961, pp. 80, 82, 86.

The post-war period, particularly the years following Stalin's death, was the only time in Soviet history in which the consumer enjoyed a continued, rapid advance in his living standards. Between 1950 and 1958 the Soviet economy distinguished itself among major economies in growth of per capita consumption. A primary factor was the upsurge in agricultural output. The year 1958 marked the end of this trend, with the onset of agricultural stagnation. Since 1958, per capita increases in private consumption have been less in the USSR than in any other major industrial nation.

Investment Policy. Ultimately, the rapid rate of industrialization in the USSR after 1928 was a function of the high rate of investment. As the ratio of private consumption to GNP was unusually low in terms of the historical experience of more advanced economies, so the ratio of investment was unusually high. Customarily, low income economies cannot invest a large portion of their national product, as consumption cannot be easily diverted from a population living close to the margin of subsistence. Through its close control over resources, especially in agriculture, the state was able to sequester the savings that enabled the economy to enjoy a high rate of investment.

No other major economy—in historical periods in which per capita income was similar to that of the Soviet Union in 1928–1937—has been able to invest anything like the quarter of GNP that the USSR did in these years. In the middle of the nineteenth century, the British economy was able to divert only about an eighth of GNP for this purpose; the German economy, only about a seventh. By the end of the nineteenth century, the German economy was able to contribute as much as a fifth of GNP for investment; the Italian economy, early in the twentieth century, a seventh; the Japanese economy, in the 1920's and 1930's, only as much as a sixth; and the United States, in the 1870's and 1880's, with a higher level of per capita income than the USSR in 1928, a fifth.[25] It was only in the 1950's that some large market economies began to approach the high Soviet investment ratios, and none of these has a relative defence burden comparable to that of the USSR.

The ability of the Soviet economy to devote so large a share of national product to investment at low per capita income levels appears all the more unique if it is realized that the entire burden of saving occurred within national boundaries. In contrast, other economies at the stage of development of the USSR in 1928–1940 were able to draw on capital inflows from more highly developed nations. The United States was partially dependent upon foreign sources of financing until the 1890's. Foreign sources provided about 11 per cent of its net capital formation in the 1870's and probably considerably more earlier.[26] Japan was heavily dependent on foreign investment until World War I and Italy for most of the period under review. Such dependence was particularly important for countries like Canada, Australia, and Argentina.[27]

---

[25] Simon Kuznets, "Long-Term Trends in Capital Formation Proportions," *Economic Development and Cultural Change*, July, 1961, pp. 10–11.

[26] Simon Kuznets, *Capital in the American Economy, op. cit.*, p. 133.

[27] *Ibid.*

Another distinguishing characteristic of Soviet investment has been its concentration in growth-supporting sectors. The most graphic illustration of this propensity has been the unusually small portion of fixed investment devoted to housing. Between 1928 and 1940 the proportion was only 15.5 per cent,[28] compared with around 25 per cent for the United States in the 1870's and 1880's, a third for Germany from 1851–1890, a quarter to a third for Italy from 1861 to 1915, and a quarter for Japan from 1887 to 1906.[29] The small Soviet proportion is even more significant, given the rapid rate of urbanization in these years. The combination of circumstances led to a drastic decline in housing standards, with per capita availabilities falling from 5.8 square metres in 1928 to 4.6 in 1937[30] and only increasing to 6.4 in 1964.[31]

During the period of relaxation following Stalin's death, the share of housing in fixed investment increased to around 21 per cent, just under the proportions for the United Kingdom, Germany, and Italy.[32] However, in the investment productivity constraint that developed after 1958, the regime chose to sacrifice housing in favour of an accelerated rate of productive investment. As a result, the housing share fell to less than 20 per cent, considerably below the proportions for all major economies other than the United Kingdom. In fact, there was an absolute decline in the annual volume of housing investment from 1959 to 1964.[33]

Lack of available data precludes historical comparison of distribution of fixed investment on a more disaggregated basis, other than bilaterally between the United States and the Soviet Union. Using the same historical time analogues, Norman Kaplan has demonstrated that Soviet investment in the period 1928–1940 was much more heavily oriented towards industry and agriculture and correspondingly less towards trade and services than in the United States in the middle of the nineteenth century.[34] He also in-

---

[28] *Kapitalnoe stroitelstvo v SSSR* (Capital Construction in the USSR), Central Statistical Administration, Moscow, 1961, pp. 39, 187.

[29] Simon Kuznets, *Economic Development and Cultural Change*, July, 1961, pp. 65, 73, 97, 116.

[30] Janet G. Chapman, "Consumption," in *Economic Trends in the Soviet Union*, edited by Abram Bergson and Simon Kuznets, *op. cit.*, p. 238.

[31] Timothy Sosnovy, "Housing Conditions and Urban Development in the USSR," *New Directions in the Soviet Economy*, *op. cit.*, 1966, p. 533.

[32] Cohn, "Soviet Growth Retardation," *New Directions in the Soviet Economy*, *op. cit.*, p. 118.

[33] *Ibid.*, p. 117.

[34] Norman M. Kaplan, "Capital Formation and Allocation," *Soviet Economic Growth*, edited by Abram Bergson, Evanston, Illinois, Row and Peterson, 1953, p. 59.

dicates that Soviet industrial investment was much more directed towards the metallurgical and machinery sectors.[35] In the post-war period, Soviet investment orientation towards industry and agriculture has been conspicuously high among the leading economies, with relative neglect for the service sectors and transportation.[36]

Structural Transformation. The rapid industrialization of the Soviet economy after 1928 was accomplished, as noted earlier, by heavy infusions of man power and capital into productive enterprises. This process was accompanied by a rapid transformation in the structure of the system. In terms of the proportion of the labour force employed in agriculture, the Soviet economy of 1928 was far less industrialized than other major market economies at comparable levels of per capita income (see Table 13). The forced transfer of labour from farm to urban occupations, through collectivization and organized recruitment, reduced the proportion of the labour force employed in agriculture by 20 percentage points.

The shift was far more rapid than in the large market economies, with shifts of comparable proportions requiring 60 years in France, 65 in Italy, 40 in the United States, and 30 to 35 in Japan (see Table 13). Yet, because of the huge size of the farm population in the Soviet Union initially and the rapid increase in population as a whole, agricultural employment actually increased by 2.4 million between 1928 and 1937 and by another 4.0 million between 1937 and 1940. The latter increase is largely explained by the territorial acquisitions of the Soviet Union in 1939–1940.

The unbalanced nature of Soviet growth between 1928 and 1940 is reflected in divergent sectoral productivity trends. In terms of man-hours, industrial labour productivity increased within an average annual rate range of 3.1–10.4 from 1928 to 1937 and at an average annual rate of 2.7 from 1937 to 1940.[37] In contrast, in agriculture, the rise in employment was coupled with a decline in production,[38] implying, of course, a fall in productivity. Historically, especially since World War I, in market economies the transfer of labour out of agriculture has been accompanied by rising labour productivity trends at rates not too different from those of industry.[39] In no instance has agricultural productivity declined. Though the rapid

---

[35] *Ibid.*, p. 63.

[36] Cohn, "Soviet Growth Retardation," *New Directions in the Soviet Economy, op. cit.*, p. 118.

[37] Estimates of Raymond Powell, in *Economic Trends in the Soviet Union*, edited by Bergson and Kuznets, *op. cit.*, pp. 88, 178.

[38] Estimates of Gale Johnson, in *ibid.*, p. 218.

[39] Deborah C. Paige, "Economic Growth: The Last Hundred Years," *National Institute Economic Review*, London, England, July, 1961, p. 39.

reduction in the share of employment in agriculture in the Soviet Union and the apparent decline in production were not functionally related, they both stemmed from the drastic collectivization campaign, with its emasculation of incentives and wholesale destruction of working and productive livestock.

Table 13

Agricultural Employment as Proportion of Total Employment

	Year	Proportion		Year	Proportion
USSR	1928	71	Japan	1897—1902	70
	1937	54		1907—1912	63
	1940	51		1920	54
	1950	46		1940	42
	1958	41	Germany	1882	42
	1964	34		1895	36
France	1788	75		1907	34
	1845	62		1925	30
	1866	52		1939	27
	1886	48	England and Wales..	1841	23
	1906	43		1861	19
	1926	39		1881	12
Italy	1861	62		1901	9
	1881	57	United States	1870	50
	1901	59		1890	42
	1921	56		1900	37
	1936	48		1920	27
Japan	1877—1882	83		1940	17
	1887—1892	76			

SOURCES: Abram Bergson, *The Real National Income of Soviet Russia Since 1928*, Cambridge, Massachussetts, Harvard University Press, 1961, p. 443; Murray Feshbach, "Manpower in the USSR," and Stanley H. Cohn, "Soviet Growth Retardation: Trends in Resource Availability and Efficiency," *New Directions in the Soviet Economy*, U.S. Congress, Joint Economic Committee, Government Printing Office, Washington, D.C., pp. 112 and 786; and Simon S. Kuznets, "Industrial Distribution of National Product and Labor Force," *Economic Development and Cultural Change*, Chicago, July, 1957, pp. 84, 85, 88, 89, 91, 93.

The lack of balance between industrial and agricultural development is a corollary of the policy of suppression of consumption in favour of investment. Within the aggregate of industrial production, output of industrial raw materials and producer durables rose much more rapidly than that of consumer goods, inclusive of home-processed food and clothing. Within the broad category of services, production- and investment-oriented services increased far more swiftly than did consumer services. This dichotomy makes generalizations about output and productivity trends in the services sector as a whole meaningless as a guide to developmental policy.

In the post-war years, following Stalin's death, the former pattern of unbalanced sectoral growth was considerably rectified, with rapid progress in agriculture through 1958. Since the rapid increase in output was extensive in nature, being partially based on an 18 per cent increase in cultivated acreage,[40] as well as on greater incentives for production on private plots, farm employment actually increased by a million from 1950 to 1958.[41] Though the proportion of man power on the farm continued to fall, the relative decline was far slower than the breakneck pace of the period from 1928 to 1940.

These were years of rapid growth and technological progress throughout the Western world in all spheres of economic activity. In most market economies productivity in agriculture since 1950 has risen more rapidly than overall productivity.[42] In contrast, in the USSR, the average annual increase in man-hour productivity in agriculture was 5.5 per cent from 1950 to 1958 and 3.0 per cent between 1958 and 1964.[43] For the economy as a whole, the rates were, respectively, 5.8 and 4.7 per cent.[44] As a result, the proportionate decline in the share of total employment in agriculture was less in the Soviet Union than in any other major economy.[45] It would appear, therefore, that unusually rapid structural transformation in the early years of planning, with its unfavourable impact on consumption, has led to an unusually slow transformation in the post-war years as higher priority has been accorded to consumer interests.

Prospective changes in the structure of the economy will reflect the belated necessity to pay the full costs of industrialization. By suppressing consumer interests, it has previously been possible to economize on investment in such areas as housing, agriculture, and consumer services. Solution of the critical agricultural problem through mechanization, greater use of fertilizers and insecticides, and some degree of decentralization of decision-making is capital intensive in all respects and should lead to reduced labour requirements, thus enabling the economy to reduce substantially the

---

[40] Douglas B. Diamond, "Trends in Output, Inputs, and Factor Productivity in Soviet Agriculture," *New Directions in the Soviet Economy, op. cit.*, p. 353.

[41] Murray Feshbach, "Manpower in the USSR," *New Directions in the Soviet Economy, op. cit.*, 1966, p. 786.

[42] Angus Maddison, "Soviet Economic Performance," *Banca Nazionale del Lavoro Quarterly Review*, Rome, Italy, March, 1965, p. 13.

[43] Diamond, *op. cit.*, pp. 348, 381.

[44] Cohn, "Soviet Growth Retardation," *New Directions in the Soviet Economy, op. cit.*, p. 115.

[45] *Ibid.*, p. 111.

present high proportion of the labour force in agriculture. Much of this reduction would take the form of a reduction in female participation rather than in a transfer of man power from the countryside to the city. The need to expand the labour-intensive consumer-services sectors, including retail trade, will result in a higher proportion of employment in the services. The historical, atypical structure of the Soviet economy thus reflects a resource allocation policy of forced industrialization, and as the economy is compelled to invest belatedly in infrastructure and consumer needs, its structure will begin to resemble the normal developmental pattern.

Educational Development and Policy. Just as the pattern of Soviet economic development has featured unusually high allocation of resources to investment in plant and equipment, so has it been distinguished by heavy emphasis on investment in human resources. Without a concomitant effort in educational development, the great commitment in physical investment would not have yielded the resulting high growth of accomplishments. In the pre-war years, the main objective of educational policy was mass literacy through universal elementary education and an extensive programme of adult education. Since the war, the emphasis has been on universal secondary education and rapid expansion of higher and technical education.

The most meaningful indicator of educational effort would be enrollment ratios giving the proportion of a particular age group enrolled in school; however, lack of data precludes use of this measure for international comparisons in all but the most recent years. As a substitute, the comparison made here is in terms of the ratio of university students per thousand of population. Such a ratio may be affected by the age distribution of the population, but not in a large enough magnitude to distort the comparison. The Soviet ratio of 1.2 per thousand in 1928 was far higher than that of other countries, except Japan, at comparable historical levels of per capita. This ratio was not attained by the United Kingdom until the 1930's, by Germany until just prior to World War I, by France and Italy until the 1920's, and by the United States until the 1880's (see Table 14).

Though the increase in the ratio for most other market economies was slow until after World War II, the Soviet ratio rose steadily during the years of comprehensive planning, reaching 3.3 by 1937, 4.7 by 1950, and 6.7 by 1964. Since 1932, the Soviet university enrollment ratio has been second only to that of the United States, with the exception, since 1958, of Japan, even though the relative per capita income level of the Soviet Union warrants a much lower ranking. The parallel between the USSR and Japan in this respect is striking, as it is in terms of other comparative developmental features.

Table 14

Comparative University Enrollments per Thousand of Population

	Year	Ratio		Year	Ratio
United Kingdom ..	1901	0.9	Japan	1950	2.9
	1911	1.1		1958	7.1
	1921	0.9	USSR	1914	0.8
	1931	1.1		1928	1.2
	1937	1.1		1932	3.2
	1951	1.9		1937	3.3
	1958	2.2		1940	3.0
Germany	1901	0.9		1950	4.7
	1911	1.1		1958	6.4
	1922	1.8		1964	6.7
	1932	1.9	United States	1870	1.3
	1937	1.1		1890	2.5
	1951	2.5		1910	3.8
	1959	3.7		1920	5.6
				1930	8.9
France	1921	1.1		1940	11.3
	1931	1.5		1950	17.6
	1954	3.3		1960	20.0
	1959	3.7	Italy	1881	0.4
Japan	1890	0.3		1901	0.8
	1910	0.9		1921	1.3
	1920	1.3		1941	3.2
	1930	2.5		1951	3.1
	1940	3.2		1958	3.4

SOURCES: Nicholas DeWitt, *Educational and Professional Employment in the USSR*, National Science Foundation, Washington, D.C., 1964; Central Statistical Administration, *Narodnoe khozyaystvo SSSR v 1964 godu* (The National Economy of the USSR in 1964), Moscow, 1965, pp. 667, 678; and Michael C. Kaser, "Education and Economic Progress," *The Economics of Education*, edited by E. A. G. Robinson and J. E. Vaizey, New York, St. Martins Press, 1966. pp. 99–105, 165–173.

The effect of educational policy on economic growth can be measured by estimates of rates of increase in educational stock. This magnitude is defined as the capitalized value of the varying levels of educational attainment among the employed population on the bench-mark dates of the historical trend.[46] Until 1958, the stock of human capital was rising at about as rapid a rate as the stock of physical capital and considerably more

---

[46] More explicitly, each level of attainment is valued as the total cost expended for education per person, including incomes forgone by the students. The procedure is based on the methodology developed by Nicholas DeWitt in "Costs and Returns in Education in the USSR," an unpublished doctoral dissertation of Harvard University, 1962.

rapidly than that of employment, whether measured either in man-years or man-hours (see Table 7). A similar realtionship has been measured in the United States in recent years. According to Theodore Schultz, educational stock in the United States increased at an average annual rate of 4.1 per cent from 1929 to 1957,[47] while fixed capital increased at less than half this rate (1.5 per cent from 1929 to 1955 and 1.9 per cent from 1939 to 1955).[48] Employment increased at a much lower rate, 1.2 per cent.[49] Earlier experience in the United States is less clear, but Edward Denison estimates the rate of increase in average educational attainment among the labour force from 1909 to 1929 at only a little more than half the rate from 1929 to 1957, while the growth rate for fixed capital was some two-thirds higher in the earlier period.[50] These rough approximations would imply that the growth rate for physical capital exceeded that for the human variety prior to 1929. If this observation for the United States is generalized for the other major market economies, with their much lower enrollment ratios, the Soviet stress on human capital investment appears unique.

The decision in 1958 to suspend progress toward universal secondary education and expanded higher education in order to satisfy short-term man-power needs reduced the annual rate of increase in human capital to half that of physical capital. Continuation of this growth discrepancy would eventually restrict rapid expansion through a deficiency of a sufficient inflow of technically qualified man power. The new Five-Year Plan reinstates the former policy of attainment of universal secondary education. Of course, the huge rates of growth in educational stock realized prior to 1958 cannot be expected to continue once universal secondary education is a fact, and further expansion must occur on the higher level. Moreover, this prospect does not imply lessened investment expenditure, since per student costs in higher education are two to three times above those on the secondary level. However, since the USSR has not hesitated to support an even relatively greater educational burden in the past, it can be expected not to hesitate to support this one in the future.

[47] Theodore W. Schultz, "Reflections on Investment in Men," *Journal of Political Economy*, Supplement, Chicago, October, 1962, p. 6.

[48] Simon Kuznets, *Capital in the American Economy, op. cit.*, p. 64.

[49] Maddison, *op. cit.*, p. 224.

[50] Edward F. Denison, *The Sources of Economic Growth in the United States*, Committee for Economic Development, 1962, p. 148.

Appendix I

Historical Trends in Per Capita and Aggregate Gross National Product

Per capita GNP has been selected as the most convenient index of stage of economic development (see Table I-1 of this appendix). Since most analogues in major market economies to Soviet per capita income levels before World War II are to be found in the early or mid-nineteenth century, historical time series have been derived. For the United States and the United Kingdom, estimates are not available for early enough periods to match 1928 Soviet levels, but the approximations for the earliest dates are close enough to the Soviet levels to be relevant.

Most of the time series for the market economies have been obtained from Michael C. Kaser, "Education and Economic Progress: Experience in Industrialized Market Economies," *The Economics of Education*, edited by E. A. G. Robinson and J. E. Vaizey, *op. cit.* They have been supplemented and checked by estimates of Angus Maddison, *Economic Growth in the West, op. cit.* Both Kaser and Maddison base their estimates on post-war official data adjusted to a common conceptual framework that takes historical estimates of private scholars and official statistical agencies into consideration.

Estimates are in terms of 1964 dollars. Methodology and source of derivation are described in Table 7 of my article in *New Directions in the Soviet Economy, op. cit.*, p. 108. The 1964 estimates are moved either to 1950 or to 1958 by the growth rates noted in Table 2 of the article. Pre-1950 Soviet levels are based on the growth rates noted in Table 1 of this study. Kaser's and Maddison's indexes have been used for pre-1950 or 1958 series for the market economies.

The estimates are subject to two limitations in interpretation. The validity of much of the early data is questionable by current standards. National income accounting is largely an art developed within the past 30 years. As a result, many earlier statistics are based on limited indicators. However, the directions, as distinguished from the degree, of the indicated trends are probably not seriously distorted.

The other important limitatation is that of the index-number problem (see Note to Table 2), which is greatly magnified over a time span as wide as a century. Though most of the scholarly estimates are noted in secondary sources as being in constant prices, they are actually in linked series, the validity of which cannot be tested without close perusal of the original sources. Time limitations have precluded this investigation. It is improbable, however, that any systematic bias would arise from the selection of base period weights or methods of linkage. The same methodological remarks and source citations govern the derivation of the aggregate GNP trends in Table I-2 of this appendix. In their derivation, the principal source for estimates prior to 1950 is Maddison with confirmation from Kaser.

Table I-1

Historical Levels of Per Capita Gross National Product
(1964 Dollars)

	Year	Level		Year	Level
USSR	1913	207—374	Japan	1940	554
	1928	204—368		1950	382
	1937	500—531		1958	556
	1940	510—542		1964	1,040
	1950	699	France	1851	293
	1958	1,049		1872	369
	1964	1,289		1881	445
United States	1870	452		1891	525
	1880	725		1901	667
	1890	868		1921	690
	1900	1,049		1931	1,017
	1920	1,417		1950	1,172
	1940	1,886		1958	1,544
	1950	2,536		1964	1,953
	1958	2,790	Germany	1860	338
	1964	3,273		1870	423
United Kingdom..	1861	557		1880	581
	1871	699		1900	780
	1881	742		1911	938
	1891	960		1925	827
	1901	1,073		1937	1,101
	1921	1,032		1950	1,001
	1937	1,234		1958	1,644
	1951	1,393		1964	2,154
	1958	1,592	Italy	1881	339
	1964	1,910		1901	399
Japan	1880	97		1921	488
	1890	128		1941	580
	1900	184		1951	626
	1920	252		1958	866
	1930	442		1964	1,187

Table I-2

Comparative Historical Aggregate Levels of GNP
(Billions of 1964 Dollars)

	1913	1928	1937	1950	1958	1964
USSR	30—58	32—62	90—93	124	215	293
United Kingdom....	36	45	56	68.	83	104
France	38	46	42	50	70	96
Germany	32	34	43	50	90	126
Italy	17	23	27	28	43	61
Japan	11	28	37	32	51	101
United States	132	203	228	387	487	629

Appendix II

Derivation of Combined Factor Inputs and Productivity

Indexes of factor productivity are based on the conventional Cobb-Douglas production function in which trends in GNP are explained by trends in explicit factors of production, weighted according to their marginal productivities, and by trends in unmeasured productive factors. This last term can be alternatively considered as the combined productivity of the explicit production factors. In its simplest version: $P = aL^{\alpha} K^{1-\alpha} Z$ where P = percentage change in GNP; a = autonomous variable; L = employment (man-hours); α = proportion of GNP accruing to labour; K = capital stock; $1-a$ = proportion of GNP accruing to capital; and Z = combined factor productivity or contribution of unmeasured productive factors.

The production function, as used in this study, has been expanded to include land and livestock in addition to employment and physical capital in the pre-war period for the USSR and a fifth factor of educational stock in the post-war period. The first four factors are used throughout the historical comparison for the United States. Man power is measured in terms of man-hours.

Soviet Factor Productivity Weights. The pre-war weights are those of Bergson. The "B" alternative comes from his article in *Economic Trends in the Soviet Union, op. cit.*, p. 19. The "B" alternative has been selected, because it assumes the same return of 8 per cent on fixed capital as assumed in the post-war weights. My estimate for the post-war weights begins with proportions for three factors: 69.7 for man power, 26.6 for capital, and 3.7 for land.[1] The weight for land is determined by the estimate for land rent. The weight for capital is the sum of interest return on fixed and working capital and depreciation charges. The weight for man power is the sum of wages and supplements and incomes in kind. The weight for livestock is taken from Douglas Diamond's estimate for capital in this form and for agricultural capital as a whole.[2] Diamond provides an estimate in 1955 rubles for the value of productive livestock in 1959. As in the case of other forms of capital, an 8 per cent annual rate of return is assumed to prevail for this productive factor. The land weight of 3.7 and the livestock weight of 0.8 are subtracted from the previously computed weight for capital. This breakdown comprises the four-factor model. For the five-factor model, the weight for educational capital stock is based on Nicholas DeWitt's estimate for 1959.[3] The return on educational stock is assumed to be 8 per cent—that is, the assumed return on physical capital.[4] The resulting weight of 9.6 is subtracted from the previously computed man-power weight. The weights are presented in Table II-1.

[1] Stanley H. Cohn, *Derivation of 1959 Value-Added Weights for Originating Sectors of Soviet Gross National Product*, McLean, Virginia, Research Analysis Corporation, TP-210, 1966, p. 21.

[2] Douglas Diamond, "Trends in Output, Inputs, and Factor Productivity in Soviet Agriculture," U.S. Congress, Joint Economic Committee, *New Directions in the Soviet Economy*, Washington, D. C., Government Printing Office, 1966, p. 373.

[3] Nicholas DeWitt, "Costs and Returns in Education in the USSR," unpublished doctoral dissertation, Harvard University, Cambridge, Massachussetts, 1962, p. 273.

[4] Stanley H. Cohn, "Derivation of 1959 Value-Added Weights," *op. cit.*, p. 17.

Table II-1

Soviet Factor Productivity Weights

(Percentages)

	Pre-War	Post-war Four-Factor Model	Post-war Five-Factor Model
Man Power	80.5	69.7	60.1
Capital	8.3	25.8	25.8
Land	10.0	3.7	3.7
Livestock	7.0	0.8	0.8
Education	—	—	9.6

Soviet Factor Input Indexes. Indexes for 1928 through 1950 are estimates of Bergson, *op. cit.*, p. 4. Post-1950 indexes are derived from several sources: those for man power and educational stock, from Stanley H. Cohn, "Soviet Growth Retardation," *New Directions in the Soviet Economy, op. cit.*, p. 131; those for capital stock, from *Narodnoe khozyaystvo SSSR v 1964 godu, op. cit.*, p. 68; and those for land and livestock, from Diamond, *op. cit.*, p. 373.

United States Weights and Indexes. Factor inputs and weights and indexes for the United States through 1948 are those of Bergson, *op. cit.*, p. 25. Man-power indexes are based on unpublished estimates of the Bureau of Labour Statistics. The capital stock index is based on estimates of George Jaszi, Robert Wasson, and Lawrence Grosse, "Expansion of Fixed Business Capital in the United States," *Survey of Current Business*, Washington, D. C., November, 1962, and unpublished estimates of the Office of Business Economics. The Bulletin F depreciation alternative is used. Land (cropped acreage) and livestock indexes are Department of Agriculture estimates obtained from the Council of Economic Advisors, *Economic Report of the President*, Washington, D. C., 1966, p. 296.

Planning for Industrial Growth

Eugène Zaleski

Though the Soviet Union can now claim to have the longest experience of any modern major industrial economy in centralized planning, the lessons to be drawn from this experience are difficult to evaluate. The very concept of planning is not always clear. Often, confusion arises between general goals laid down by central authorities for the country as a whole and specific plans elaborated by constituent authorities to fulfill these goals. Confusion also arises over the various means used to work out a plan in a way consistent with overall goals. If a plan drawn up by central authorities is in the nature of projected goals, without specification of means of implementation, it is termed indicative planning. If fiscal, monetary, price, or budgetary provisions are made for its implementation, it is called flexible planning. If its targets are disaggregated in an authoritarian way among enterprises, it is known as administrative planning.

This division into systems of planning is not always well defined, since in an actual economy different ways of carrying out a plan coexist. Part of the task may be left to market forces, another part may depend on fiscal or monetary measures, and still another part may be directed from the top. For this reason, a variety of models for planning systems exists. The experience of the Soviet Union has primarily been with administrative planning. Flexible planning was in effect only for about seven of the last fifty years, that is, during the period of the New Economic Policy (NEP). Still, since the nature of administrative planning has differed markedly over the years, it is impossible to speak of a single type of administrative planning system. In fact, at least three can be distinguished: the integral type of administrative planning, featuring replacement of market demand and money by authoritarian allocation of resources; the Stalinist type of administrative planning, featuring maintenance of market demand and money primarily for consumer goods, labour, and accounting needs, and using some monetary and fiscal tools; and the less rigid type of administrative planning, featuring reduction of the number of centrally planned indexes of output, enlargement of the market to include some production activities, and increased reliance on fiscal, monetary, and budgetary tools.

Because many different kinds of planning have been tried in the Soviet Union, separate and detailed comparisons are needed for different periods.

Unfortunately, available documentation is not particularly helpful in this regard. There are, for example, no detailed versions of long-range plans after 1934 or of annual plans after 1941. Moreover, no official, comprehensive quarterly plan has ever been published. Thus, for most of the Soviet period, one must reconstitute plans in the manner of an archeologist, and precise knowledge of plan implementation remains out of reach. It is extremely difficult to evaluate a single, definite variant of the general plan, for the very essence of planning lies in substituting different planned variants throughout the process of implementation. The main concern here is with Soviet flexible planning and the three types of Soviet administrative planning mentioned above. Obviously, imperfect means of investigation can yield only tentative answers.

Soviet Flexible Planning

It seems somewhat risky to describe the period of NEP as characterized by flexible planning, owing to the tendency to overstate the case, but the principal features of flexible planning, as now defined in the Soviet Union, did exist from 1922 to 1928. The period of NEP was launched by the resolutions of the Tenth Party Congress in March 1921. For 4,000 small industrial enterprises accounting for 75 per cent of all retail trade and 20 per cent of all wholesale trade, it meant the reintroduction of private property. NEP also brought the inauguration of free trade for peasant products and the establishment of market relations among state industrial enterprises and trusts. Centralized allocation of raw materials and equipment was gradually replaced by free contracts among enterprises. The monetary reform begun in the period 1922–1924 established the use of taxation and budgetary subsidies as tools for economic policy.

The plans of the early part of the NEP period, 1922–1925, differed from those of the later part, 1926–1928. In the early years, the idea of a general economic plan was never carried out. The Goelro Plan (Plan of the State Commission for the Electrification of Russia), adopted in December 1921 by the Eighth Congress of Soviets, was, in effect, indicative planning, since the government took no formal steps to implement it. The plan could be used only for study purposes and soon became outdated.[1] At this time, partial plans for a number of economic activities were drawn up by the State Planning Committee (Gosplan). The most generalized of these were plans formulated on a five-year basis for different economic

---

[1] A formal revision of the Goelro Plan was ordered on February 19, 1927. See *Direktivy KPSS i Sovetskogo Pravitelstva* (Directives of the CPSU and the Soviet Government), Moscow, 1927, Vol. I, pp. 648–652.

sectors—for industry, agriculture, and transport, for example. In this period, in other words, no general, annual economic planning was done.

In the later years of NEP, 1926–1928, Soviet officials were able to elaborate general plans for different periods. A fifteen-year plan for the period 1925–1926 to 1940–1941 was prepared by Gosplan. Variants of the First Five-Year Plan were made up by Gosplan and the Supreme Council of the National Economy (VSNKh) each year from 1925 to 1929. Annual plans, in the form of control figures, were also drawn up each year after 1925–1926. The plans of the NEP period, except perhaps for the 1927–1928 plan, were not operational. No orders were given for enterprises to pursue targets set by annual control figures, and no formal links existed between the targets of the Five-Year Plan and the annual control figures. The only importance of plans during this period was their influence on governmental fiscal and budgetary policy. How great this influence was is difficult to say, and a special study would be necessary to make such an evaluation. It is interesting to note, however, that the planned targets of annual control figures for the period 1925–1926 to 1927–1928 were in general fulfilled, that the goals for industrial production and transport were in general overfulfilled, and that agricultural production came very close to the planned target.[2]

Finally, it should be said that the NEP period as a whole does not constitute a pure example of a flexible planning system. During the early years of NEP, some vestiges of the practice of authoritarian allocation of resources survived. During the later years, administrative implementation of certain planned targets became more frequent, and authoritarian allocation of resources was in large part reintroduced through the creation of the USSR Council of Unions (*Sindikaty*) in 1926. It should also be said that even without centralized general planning, the Soviet state, by controlling about three-quarters of industrial production through the VSNKh, had the means of directing productive activities without using fiscal or budgetary instruments.

Soviet Integral Planning

Though an integral economic planning system in direct control of all natural and human resources has never existed in the Soviet Union, at times Soviet authorities have come very close to this "ideal." The following three periods can be distinguished: the period of war and civil war from 1918 to 1920, the period of the Stalinist leap forward from 1930 to 1932, and

---

[2] For more details, see Eugène Zaleski, *Planification de la Croissance et Fluctuations économiques en URSS*, Paris, 1962, Vol. I, p. 46.

the period of war planning for World War II from 1941 to 1945. The main characteristics of integral planning in the Soviet Union have been almost complete nationalization of productive activities in industry, transportation, trade, and agriculture; increased authoritarian allocation of raw materials and equipment; partial replacement of retail trade by distribution of food and manufactured goods through closed factory shops; and severe restrictions on labour mobility with recurrent extension of forced and prison labour.[3]

These characteristics, of course, varied from period to period. During the period of war and civil war planning, 1918–1920, a deliberate attempt was made to eliminate money and the market. Almost all handicraft and other small industries were nationalized, and the same action was taken in respect of transport, foreign and domestic trade, and banks. Almost all agricultural production was subject to Party requisitioning, even though agriculture as such remained in the private sector, with the government trying to extend its authority over allocation of resources and labour. That the market was not totally eliminated was not owing to liberalism on the part of the state but to the practical impossibility of eliminating the black market and introducing paramilitary organization of labour.

During the other two periods of Soviet integral planning, the Soviet government took the experience of the civil war period into account and did not try to eliminate the market completely. It legalized the black market by introducing the so-called collective farm market and by tolerating the so-called bazaar. It no longer tried to introduce military control over labour, but, instead, reinforced labour discipline and introduced legal obstacles to changing jobs. Nevertheless, the government did not succeed in stopping the increase in labour turnover and eventually had to resort to the expedient of substantially expanding the volume of forced labour. These two later periods, 1930–1932 and 1941–1945, represent a more organized, in some ways more coherent, planning system, but the earlier centralization of political power, with nationalization and collectivization of the means of production, created the necessary preconditions for the reintroduction of integral planning.

All Soviet experiments in integral planning have shared one thing in common: an inability to introduce long-range or current annual plans for

---

[3] Theoretically, in the 1930's, agriculture was not "nationalized" but only "collectivized" with the introduction of the collective farm. Nevertheless, government control over the management and production activities of collective farms was as strong as for industrial enterprises, the essential differences lying in the method of paying collective farmers and the nature of agricultural production. The maintenance of private plots was, however, a serious limitation on the extent of collectivization of agriculture.

the country as a whole. This circumstance suggests that power at the centre does not necessarily facilitate the elaboration and implementation of plans from the centre. Centralization of power coupled with authoritarian allocation of resources helps to preserve some priorities in an unstable situation. Planning, after all, involves setting goals and providing means of realizing them in a given period. Extreme centralization therefore offers an alternative solution to planning in a troubled period. In this context, it seems paradoxical that it has been well-nigh impossible for the Soviet Union to introduce central and general plans during periods of integral planning.

During the civil war period, efforts were made to draw up semi-annual plans for 1919 and an annual plan for 1920. These plans never got beyond the stage of being put on paper, however, and had no practical influence on the plans of enterprises. During World War II, no attempt was made to draw up annual or long-range plans, and the government instead limited itself to annual forecasting for purposes of the budget. Nevertheless, during the period of the Stalinist leap forward, from 1930 to 1932, annual, five-year, and longer-range plans had been prepared and had received considerable publicity. On the surface at least, these plans appear to have been an exception to the generally observed inability of the government to elaborate central plans during periods of integral planning. Despite much publicity by the state, however, the annual plans of 1931 and 1932 were never operational. They were not used as the basis for quarterly plans and as a result remained documents for internal use by planning agencies. At this time, the main role in implementing governmental priorities was played by planning agencies through the authoritarian allocation of resources. A similarly important role was played by rationing and the requisitioning of peasant production, measures which were introduced during this period. The three- and five-year plans drawn up at this time merely represented extrapolation of past trends and changed with the yearly economic situation. The second Goelro Plan (1932–1942 or 1945) remained only a preliminary document. It was never approved, and no attempt was made to change it to accord with the new variant of the five-year plan for 1933–1937, which was drawn up at the end of 1932.[4]

Stalinist Administrative Planning

The Stalinist type of administrative planning lasted the longest of all the Soviet planning experiments. In operation for about twenty-eight years,

---

[4] See Eugène Zaleski, *Planification de la Croissance et Fluctuations économiques en URSS*, Vol. II (in preparation).

from 1933 to 1941 and from 1946 to 1965, it represents an accommodation of the integral planning system to a longer stretch of peacetime or, at least, to a less troubled period. Stalinist administrative planning adhered to almost all the ideological premises of the integral planning system, especially nationalization and collectivization of the means of production and authoritarian distribution of producer goods. Now, however, the market for consumer goods and for labour was integrated into the system. The Soviet population could buy consumer goods freely and, to a lesser extent, supply its labour potential freely. The Stalinist type of market for consumer goods was not a free market: the state monopolized supply and introduced a rationing system on the wholesale trade level; it controlled the circulation of money, though it had to take into account effective demand for consumer goods in planning the non-market sector.

Under the Stalinist system of planning, central plans for the whole economy were elaborated in considerable detail. During this period, the Soviet press announced the preparation of several long-range plans (1938–1953, 1946–1960, 1957–1972, and 1961–1980), many five-year plans (1933–1937, 1938–1942, 1943–1947, 1946–1950, 1951–1955, 1956–1960, 1959–1965, and 1966–1970), and the customary annual plans.[5] Quarterly plans were drawn up regularly until 1946; after 1946, they were drawn up for a limited number of planned indicators.

The Stalinist plans were not merely schemes on paper or attempts to conceal present difficulties by *des lendemains qui chantent*. A real effort was made to distribute the planned targets among enterprises and to have the central authorities approve individual plans through a complicated administrative process. Though the final versions of plans, which were supposed to be coherent, were never approved in time, the earlier, preliminary, unbalanced versions had considerable influence on the plans of economic units. This was particularly true of annual and quarterly plans. Five-year and long-range plans were usually derived by extrapolating current trends, and they had constantly to be revised, a difficult task in view of the rigidity of the Stalinist administrative system.

The Stalinist annual and quarterly plans were generally considered to be operational. This was certainly true of plans at the enterprise level. At the national level, annual and quarterly plans were the sum of enterprise plans, with many corrections. The national plan as such required so many correc-

---

[5] The plan for 1943–1947, drawn up in 1941, was never made into a general plan for the whole economy. That for 1959–1965 was a seven-year plan. Preliminary versions of the plan for 1966–1970 were already drawn up in 1963 and 1964.

tions within the planned period that it was practically impossible to take account of all of them in the time given. Some parts of the national plan would be operational, while others had already been by-passed. In other words, the Stalinist plan was not implemented but was disintegrated as it was carried out. The Stalinist planned economy became a directed economy with imperfect competition between government agencies for materials, equipment, and labour. The system of centralized supplies, with its own priorities for emergencies not foreseen by the plan, and the continuous bargaining that went on, introduced special rules into the centralized, non-market sector. In this scheme, one can hardly speak of plan implementation.

The Stalinist method of fulfilling plans renders comparisons of planned and actual figures pointless. The plans are a means of carrying out a policy that changes during the planned period. Results can hardly be compared with projections that have long been out of date. Rather, they can be used as indicators of economic policy and of the tautness of plans.

To give some idea of economic policy as reflected in Soviet plans of the Stalinist administrative type and to give some notion of the real economic policy of the government during the planned period, in Table 1 the main goals of the Second Five-Year Plan (1933–1937) and of the Seven-Year Plan (1959–1965) are compared with the results of these plans. Comparison of the Second Five-Year Plan and the Seven-Year Plan is of interest since these plans fall at the very beginning and the very end of the experiments with the Stalinist type of administrative planning. The same features appear in the annual plans, but the disparity between planned targets and results is less important, especially for aggregate indexes.

The principal characteristics of Soviet economic policy as seen in the long-range plans are the following: (1) Absence of any real choice. No economic sectors and no economic activities were to be sacrificed in order to obtain higher rates of growth in priority sectors. (2) Semblance of balanced growth. All activities were to increase at specified rates, and all gains were to be achieved through a rise in productivity. (3) Elaboration of a plan for the national economy as if it were a plan for an enterprise. Final results in terms of consumption and investment rates—that is, higher outputs—were to be achieved with smaller inputs of labour and transportation and with relatively slow increases in use of raw materials and proliferation of intermediary products—that is, low input coefficients. (5) Pursuit of a deflationary policy. This was to be accomplished through a small increase in planned money wages, reduction or stability of retail prices, and high growth rates for retail trade and for planned real personal income.

Table 1

Comparison of the Main Goals
of the Second Five-Year Plan (1933–1937)
with Those of the Seven-Year Plan (1959–1965)

Second Five-Year Plan

NATIONAL INCOME

	Growth Planned for 1937	Actual Growth in 1937	Per Cent of Plan Fulfilled in 1937
	——— (1932=100)- ———		
Official Soviet Calculations .... (Constant Prices)	220.2[1]	211.6[1]	96.1
Western Estimates	—	146.0[3]	66.3[4]

INDUSTRIAL PRODUCTION

	Growth Planned for 1937	Actual Growth in 1937	Per Cent of Plan Fulfilled in 1937
Official Soviet Calculations	214.1[1]	220.8[1]	103.0
Western Estimates:			
Jasny	—	173.9	81.2[4]
Kaplan & Moorsteen	—	161.7	75.5[4]
Shimkin & Leedy	—	161.7	75.5[4]
Nutter........................	—	199.3	93.1[4]

PRODUCER GOODS (Group A)

	Growth Planned for 1937	Actual Growth in 1937	Per Cent of Plan Fulfilled in 1937
Official Soviet Calculations	197.2[1]	238.9[1]	121.1

CONSUMER GOODS

	Growth Planned for 1937	Actual Growth in 1937	Per Cent of Plan Fulfilled in 1937
Official Soviet Calculations	233.6	199.5[1]	85.4

AGRICULTURAL PRODUCTION

	Growth Planned for 1937	Actual Growth in 1937	Per Cent of Plan Fulfilled in 1937
Official Soviet Calculations	200.1[1]	148.1[1]	74.0
Official Soviet Calculations .... (Comparable Prices)	—	125.3[6]	62.6[4]
Western Calculations:			
Jasny	—	153.3	76.6[4]
Johnson and Kahan:			
Real 1926–1927 Prices	—	138.1	69.0[4]
Average 1925–1929 Prices...	—	137.6	68.8[1]
1953 Prices	—	132.1	66.0[4]

EMPLOYMENT

	Growth Planned for 1937	Actual Growth in 1937	Per Cent of Plan Fulfilled in 1937
Workers and Employees .... (National Economy, Total)	126.0	118.1	93.4

RAILROAD TRAFFIC

	Growth Planned for 1937	Actual Growth in 1937	Per Cent of Plan Fulfilled in 1937
Total Ton-Kilometres	177.0	209.6	118.3

WAGES

Money Wages:	Growth Planned for 1937	Actual Growth in 1937	Per Cent of Plan Fulfilled in 1937
	———(1932=100)———		
Workers and Employees .... (National Economy, Total)	123.0	212.9	173.1

Real Wages:

Official Soviet Calculations:

Workers and Employees .... (National Economy, Total)	196.0	201.0	102.5

Western Calculations:

Jasny.........................	—	122.4	62.4[4]
Zaleski	—	123.2	62.9[4]

REAL INCOME

Official Soviet Calculations:

Collective Farmers	—	—	—

Western Calculations:

Collective Farmers (Jasny)	—	162.7	67.2

RETAIL TRADE

Official Soviet Calculations:

State and Cooperative Trade	250.7[8]	148.5[9]	59.2

Seven-Year Plan

NATIONAL INCOME

	Growth Planned for 1965	Actual Growth in 1965	Per Cent of Plan Fulfilled in 1965
	———(1959=100)———		
Official Soviet Calculations .... (Constant Prices)	162—165	159[2]	96.3—98.1
Western Estimates	—	—	—

INDUSTRIAL PRODUCTION

Official Soviet Calculations	180	184[5]	102.2

Western Estimates:

Jasny.......................	—	—	—
Kaplan & Moorsteen	—	—	—
Shimkin & Leedy	—	—	—
Nutter	—	—	—

PRODUCER GOODS (Group A)

Official Soviet Calculations	185—188	197	104.8—106.4

CONSUMER GOODS

	Growth Planned for 1965	Actual Growth in 1965	Per Cent of Plan Fulfilled in 1965
	——(1959=100)——		
Official Soviet Calculations	162—165	160	97.0—98.7

AGRICULTURAL PRODUCTION

Official Soviet Calculations	170	115	67.6
Official Soviet Calculations .... (Comparable Prices)	—	—	—
Western Calculations:			
Jasny	—	—	—
Johnson and Kahan:			
Real 1926–1927 Prices	—	—	—
Average 1925–1929 Prices..	—	—	—
1953 Prices	—	—	—

EMPLOYMENT

Workers and Employees .... (National Economy, Total)	122	137	112.3

RAILROAD TRAFFIC

Total Ton-Kilometres	139—143	150	105.4—108.3

WAGES

Money Wages:			
Workers and Employees ...... (National Economy, Total)	126	122.9	97.5
Real Wages:			
Official Soviet Calculations:			
Workers and Employees	—[7]	—	—
Western Calculations:			
Jasny	—	—	—
Zaleski	—	—	—

REAL INCOME

Official Soviet Calculations:			
Collective Farmers	140	—	—
Western Calculations:			
Collective Farmers (Jasny)	140	130	92.9

RETAIL TRADE

Official Soviet Calculations:			
State and Cooperative Trade...	162	158.7	98.0

[1] Prices for 1926.
[2] Prices for 1958.
[3] Estimated on the basis of Jasny's calculations for 1928 and 1937.
[4] Calculated from planned growth according to official Soviet calculations.
[5] July 1, 1955 prices.

[6] Comparable prices replaced 1926–1927 prices for agricultural production in official Soviet statistics. This figure appeared for the first time in *Narodnoe khozyaystvo SSSR v 1958 godu* (National Economy of the USSR in 1958), Moscow, 1959, p. 350.

[7] The Seven-Year Plan gave an increase of 40 per cent for real income of workers and employees in the national economy and of 40 per cent for income of collective farmers. These two categories cover almost all the population employed in the USSR and hence this figure was assumed to apply to the income of the whole population.

[8] Prices for 1932.

[9] Prices for 1940. In view of the considerable inflation between 1932 and 1937, the price increase is too small and the percentage of fulfillment hence too low. See Zaleski, *Planification de la Croissance et Fluctuations économiques en URSS*, Vol. I, pp. 358–360.

SOURCES: Zaleski, *Planification de la Croissance et Fluctuations économiques en URSS*, Vol. II, 1933–1952 (in preparation); *Vneocherednoy XXI Sezd Kommunisticheskoy Partii Sovetskogo Soyuza* (Extraordinary Twenty-first Congress of the Communist Party of the Soviet Union), January 27–February 5, 1959, Moscow, 1959, Vol.I, pp. 25–54, and Vol. II, pp. 492–493, 499, 524–525; *Narodnoe khozyaystvo SSSR v 1965 godu* (National Economy of the USSR in 1965), Moscow, 1966, pp. 59–60, 259–262, 457, 558, 567, 593, 627–628, 653.

The Stalinist type of administrative planning was unable to implement plans drawn up on this basis. The real choice is always made at the moment of actual plan execution, and as can be seen from Table 1, agriculture and the consumer goods industry were usually the areas of the economy that were sacrificed. Lower outputs (national income) and lower consumption, also lower investment, were obtained with higher inputs.[6] In its deflationary policy, Stalinist administrative planning was at least partially successful. There was considerable inflation in the period 1933–1941, but the deflationary policy was generally successful in the period 1948–1965. This still did not mean that the goals for real wages or real income were fulfilled.

Though the overall characteristics of the Stalinist type of administrative planning are clearly reflected in Table 1, there are some important differences in the economic situation in each period. The Second Five-Year Plan started when the level of consumption was very low owing to the so-called leap forward. This explains the relatively higher growth rates for consumer goods. It also accounts for the huge planned increase in real wages and retail trade. More generally, the higher growth rates during the Second Five-Year Plan were the result of the lower level of Soviet economic development at this time, and the difference between that period and 1959–1965 does not imply any difference in economic policy.

---

[6] See Table 2. Higher inputs than planned can be seen in the overfulfillment of the goals for employment and transportation. For employment, the Second Five-Year Plan is an exception in Stalinist-type planning caused mainly by the fact that the flow of peasants to the cities during the First Five-Year Plan was reduced after the collectivization drive and that further rapid migration was impossible because of the housing problem.

Table 2

Distribution of Industrial Products According to Percentage of Plan Fulfillment, Second Five-Year Plan (1933–1937) and Seven-Year Plan (1959–1965)

(Number of Products)

Percentage of Plan Fulfillment	PRODUCER GOODS		CONSUMER GOODS	
	Second Five-Year Plan	Seven-Year Plan	Second Five-Year Plan	Seven-Year Plan
130.0 and Over	1	1	1	—
110.0—129.9	3	—	3	3
106.0—109.9	1	1	—	1
102.0—105.9	1	4	3	1
99.0—101.9	4	2	1	—
95.0— 98.9	2	5	2	1
90.0— 94.9	3	3	2	4
85.0— 89.9	3	2	4	1
80.0— 84.9	5	4	3	—
70.0— 79.9	4	3	2	2
60.0— 69.9	6	3	4	1
50.0— 59.9	5	2	3	—
49.0 and Lower	14	2	10	—
Total Number of Products	52	32	38	14
Median Percentage of Fulfillment..	72.2	88.9	77.8	93.7

SOURCES: Zaleski, *Planification de la Croissance et Fluctuations économiques en URSS*, Vol. II, 1933–1952 (in preparation); *Vneocherednoy XXI Sezd Kommunisticheskoy Partii Sovetskogo Soyuza*, Vol. I, pp. 25–54, and Vol. II, pp. 476–505; *Narodnoe khozyaystvo SSSR v 1965 godu*, Moscow, 1966, pp. 121–247.

As can be seen in Table 2, for the Second Five-Year Plan and the Seven-Year Plan, the Stalinist type of administrative planning did follow a certain pattern in the implementation of industrial plans. For producer goods and for consumer goods, the percentages of plan fulfillment varied widely, being concentrated mainly in the lower brackets. Some improvement in plan fulfillment appears to have taken place in recent years, but the figures must be examined more carefully.[7] In relative terms, the plan for consumer goods was better fulfilled than that for producer goods, despite the fact that in aggregate value terms the opposite was true (see Table 1).

The failure of the policy of trying to achieve higher outputs with lower inputs is also evident in more detailed comparisons of plan fulfillment

---

[7] For the Seven-Year Plan, the number of products included in Table 2 is much lower. The products included are mainly aggregated products, for which the percentage of fulfillment is usually higher.

for individual industrial products.[8] For producer goods, in both plans, percentages of fulfillment more than five points above the median were obtained for gas, bricks, steel, pig iron, electric power, rolled steel, iron ore, and coal. Performance was very poor in both plans for machinery and in the Seven-Year Plan for new products in the chemical industry (plastics and artificial and synthetic fibers). The constant difficulties in fulfilling plans in the Soviet lumber and wood industry can also be seen in these two plans. In the consumer goods industries, poor performances in both cases were the consequence of failure to fulfill the plan for agriculture, the results for meat being particularly poor (35.7 per cent in the Second Five-Year Plan and 72.7 per cent in the Seven-Year Plan) and those for cotton, woolen, linen, and rayon fabrics being equally deficient.

Defects of the Stalinist Planning System and Reform Proposals

The defects in the Stalinist type of administrative planning have often been alluded to in the Soviet Union, though no systematic criticism has ever been published. Two kinds of defects can be distinguished: those on the enterprise level and those on the national level.[9] The main defects on the enterprise level were the result of arbitrary pressures from higher authorities on management. These pressures took many forms. First, there were innumerable compulsory indexes imposed on enterprises. Almost all indexes for enterprise activity of any importance were fixed by higher authorities: in 1964–1965, a Soviet industrial enterprise had 500 indexes in its annual plan imposed from above.[10] Second, the Soviet enterprise could not freely carry out the plan fixed by higher authorities, because it was subject both to continuous plan adjustments during the year, and to arbitrary interference by many different administrative and Party bodies.

Another important defect on the enterprise level was lack of adequate success criteria. During most of the Stalinist planning period, the main criterion used was gross value of production. This only stimulated production of low-quality goods without sufficient demand (*vozdushnyy val*). Additional compulsory indexes, including output in physical terms, labour

---

[8] Calculated from the sources given in Table 2. For more details, see Eugène Zaleski, *Planning Reforms in the Soviet Union, 1962–1966*, University of North Carolina Press, Chapel Hill, 1967.

[9] See O. Nekrasov, "Otraslevoy printsip upravleniya promyshlennostyu i tekhnicheskiy progress" (The Sector Principle of Managing Industry and Technical Progress), *Voprosy ekonomiki*, No. 11, 1965, p. 3.

[10] The annual plan for the Tartar Autonomous Republic, for example, was adjusted almost 500 times in 1961. (See *Ekonomicheskaya gazeta*, November 17, 1962, p. 21.)

productivity, costs, and profits, and so-called accounting indexes that were not compulsory but were controlled from above, such as production per ruble of fixed capital, introduced a good deal of arbitrariness into judgements of an enterprise's performance. This was especially true when these indexes moved in opposite directions.

Administrative pressures and lack of valid criteria for judging performance were responsible for a lack of incentive among workers and management. Conflicts between the interests of the state, as represented by higher authorities, and of the workers, as represented by the enterprise, arose almost automatically. Enterprises tried to resist the imposition of too taut plans and of too high norms for input and labour by concealing their real productive capacities and performance. The agencies to which they were subordinated did not trust them and imposed higher production targets to be met with lower inputs of materials, labour, and investments.

The defects on the national level were the result both of the system itself and of Stalinist economic policy. In Stalinist administrative planning, a plan on the national scale was an aggregation of administrative dossiers. The main planned targets were distributed through hierarchical channels to enterprises. At each administrative stage, planned indexes became more precise, orders given more detailed, and decision-making powers of enterprises more limited. Informal bargaining on different administrative levels replaced a more careful examination of the plan's coherence, and the only valid criterion on the national level remained the approval of central Party authorities.

The Stalinist type of administrative planning was unable to produce coherent plans for purely technical reasons. Aggregation of the targets of enterprises into a national plan meant that any test of coherence would call for a huge input-output table, not only comprehending the 20 million commodities in the Soviet industrial classification, but covering the whole economy for past as well as future years. The latest Soviet input-output tables (124 by 124 in value terms) are very far from accomplishing this end.

These defects, which were in some ways inherent in Stalinist administrative planning, were amplified by the effects of Stalin's economic policy. High investment targets, stimulation of disproportionate growth, and heavy armament programs imposed sacrifices on the population. The planners were reluctant to admit this, preferring to assume high productivity increases and excellent internal and external conditions for plan fulfillment, and therefore preferring to write into the plans the highest possible output with the lowest possible input. Taut plans and the necessity for continual adjustments were the results of this policy.

Though rigid in its basic principles, Stalinist administrative planning was subjected to perpetual reforms. Until 1964–1965, however, all these reforms, in fact, aimed at consolidating the system. Changes in the number of ministries and other government agencies, changes in the areas of their jurisdiction, changes in the methods of elaborating plans, changes in the success criteria, and changes in the regulations for bonus payments were usually praised in the Soviet press as major reforms. The need for radical reform of the basic principles of the Stalinist system of administrative planning eventually became so strong that in the 1960's the Soviet government could no longer restrict discussion merely to measures of accommodation to the old system. This was the case with the so-called Liberman proposals in the fall of 1962, at which time the official debates on incentives for workers and employees spread into a more general discussion of the role of profit as a criterion of success for enterprises and verged upon a reexamination of the role of central authorities in economic planning. Though Khrushchev managed to put an end to the discussion after the Party Plenary Session in November 1962, the problem remained. Then, the poor economic performance of the Soviet Union in 1963 obliged the Soviet government to renew the discussion, broadening it to include considerations of fundamental changes in the planning system. Articles by V. Nemchinov, V. Trapeznikov, and Evsey Liberman set off the discussion, which, though not spectacular, was very frank and showed more signs of progress than the partisans of basic reform had given since 1962.[11]

It would take too long to go into all the details of the plans put forth by the proponents of reform. In fact, except for Nemchinov, no one had a clear idea of the function of a new planning system. Rather, the proposals made concentrated on a few distinct, basic improvements, which may be summarized in the following five points:

(1) Increase in the autonomy of enterprises. This was to be achieved by reducing the number of planned indexes and replacing them, in some cases, with noncompulsory accounting indexes. Liberman, Nemchinov, and many others supported this view. It was also to be achieved by abolishing the material supplies system and replacing it with state trade. Nemchinov and Birman called for this move. Finally, it was to be achieved by improving the legal statute of the enterprise, a measure recommended by Birman and Laptev.

(2) Modification of the success criteria for enterprises. The only fundamental reform proposed in this regard was the establishment of profit

---

[11] *Kommunist*, No. 5, 1964, pp. 75–76; *Pravda*, August 17, 1964; *Pravda*, September 20, 1964.

as the single or most essential criterion of success. This proposal was usually accompanied by the stipulation that profitability be calculated on the basis of fixed and working capital and that long-term profitability norms be introduced for groups of enterprises. Liberman, Vaag, and Zakharov were the proponents of this approach.

(3) Changes in the methods of calculating prices. A whole school of Soviet economists demanded the introduction of so-called production costs, including rent or interest payments, for capital. More basic reforms in the methods of calculating prices were proposed by Kantorovich and Novozhilov, who suggested calculating marginal prices and thereby introducing the concept of utility. Nemchinov advocated considerable decentralization of price formation.

(4) Improvements in accounting methods and greater use of computers. Two different tendencies can be distinguished among the adherents of this approach. Kobrynsky and others saw computers as possible allies of economic centralization and as a means of saving the authoritarian system. However, most mathematical economists—Glushkov, Dorodnitsyn, Kantorovich, Novozhilov, Belkin, and Nemchinov, for example—hoped that the introduction of mathematical methods would provide a basis for rational decisions and economic decentralization.

(5) Changes in the planning mechanism. This most important proposal called for the introduction of a flexible planning system. Compulsory planned indexes were no longer to be transmitted directly to enterprises. Operation of the system was henceforth to be controlled by financial and monetary decisions. Special funds were to be created to promote the most important activities of the government. The most prominent proponent of this reform was Nemchinov. Liberman also advocated some of these changes, favouring, for example, limitation of compulsory indexes to the level of the Sovnarkhoz (Regional Economic Council) in a *Pravda* article on September 9, 1962.

The Soviet government was no longer in a position simply to stop the discussion, but was obliged to act. The accumulation of stocks of unsold consumer goods, mainly textiles of low quality, led the Soviet leadership, on July 1, 1964, to introduce a liberal planning experiment in two clothing factories—Mayak in Gorky and Bolshevichka in Moscow. The two factories were allowed to plan their output independently on the basis of contracts with retail stores; to plan their costs, wages, and volume of sales; and to choose their own suppliers of materials. Nevertheless, their two success indicators—volume of marketed production and total profits—had to be confirmed by higher authorities, and several restrictions on invest-ment, pricing, and the right to make free delivery contracts were maintained.

The experimental system spread rapidly in the Soviet Union, and by the third quarter of 1965 the entire garment industry under the Moscow City Sovnarkhoz—including such cities as Leningrad, Kiev, Odessa, Khar-kov, and Lvov—had been transferred to it. In 1965, the direct-links system, to use the official name given to this experiment, was to cover 25 per cent of the garment factories, 28 per cent of the footwear factories, 18 per cent of the textile mills, and 30 per cent of the leather factories. The experiment was also partially introduced into the food industry, the retail trade net-work, and some heavy-industry enterprises.

The direct-links experiment was used by the Soviet government largely for propaganda purposes. The enterprises taking part in it increased their profits and improved their performance, and as a result, there was con-siderable pressure to extend the experiment. However, since the autonomy granted to a group of factories could not improve the basic administrative system, neither could the extension of this experiment to all industry. The consumer sector would be competing for scarce resources with the state, whose demands are effected through the budget, and this circumstance would have had important implications for the role of enterprise managers and higher economic administrative agencies. The government might lose its absolute control over the economy, thus leaving the door open for the much-feared flexible economic planning. All this must be kept in mind in order to understand the real meaning of Kosygin's reforms of October 1965.

Less Rigid Administrative Planning

The October 1965 reforms were outlined in Kosygin's speech of September 27, 1965, at the Party Plenary Session.[12] They were to be applied to all industry, in successive stages, during the period 1966–1968. On January 1, 1966, the first group of industrial enterprises, forty-three in all, was transferred to the new system. In April of the same year, 200 additional enterprises were transferred; in July, 400 more. On January 1, 1967, another 1,800 enterprises joined. Enterprises accounting for a total of one-third of industrial employment were scheduled to be transferred

---

[12] See A. Kosygin in *Pravda*, September 28, 1965, pp. 1–4. For more details, see Eugène Zaleski, *Planning Reforms in the Soviet Union, 1962–1966*, University of North Carolina Press, Chapel Hill, 1967, pp. 141–183. Also see *Ekonomiches-kaya gazeta*, No. 14, 1967, p. 9.

to the new system by January 1, 1967, and all industrial enterprises were to have been admitted to the system by the end of 1968. Kosygin's reforms represent a deliberate effort to effect changes in the Stalinist type of planning, and at the same time to maintain real governmental control over the economy. The extent to which these aims might be implemented can be seen from the changes that the new system introduced in the finances, profit-sharing, and planning autonomy of the enterprise.

The principal change in the enterprise's finances is the introduction of interest payments on capital. Only exceptionally will funds for investment be granted free from the state budget, and the present levies on profits will gradually be replaced by taxes on fixed and working capital.[13] Long-range profitability norms are to be established to enable enterprises to retain a share of the profits for meeting planned expenses and for financing an incentive fund. For 1966, the rental payments on an enterprise's capital have been fixed at the general level of 6 per cent. This provision is also intended to improve economic efficiency in the use of capital and to nationalize the internal autonomy of the enterprise. It is assumed that enterprises will use investment funds more cautiously, when, by 1968, about 80 per cent of investments in fixed industrial capital will be financed by their own resources and by long-term credit from the state. A special fund for the development of production—this formerly was included in the enterprise fund—is to guarantee increasing ability on the part of the enterprise to finance itself, for which purpose resources will also be provided by levies on profits and on part of amortization allowances and by proceeds from the sale of unused equipment.[14]

In the present system, the main source of incentive payments is the enterprise fund. Up to 40 per cent of the fund can be spent on bonuses, 40 per cent on housing and communal construction, and 20 per cent on the introduction of new technology and the modernization and extension of production. Six per cent of planned profits and 30 to 60 per cent of profits in excess of the plan can be paid into this fund on condition that the many planned, compulsory indexes of the enterprise's activity are fulfilled. This condition has rarely been met, however, and in September 1965 Kosygin pointed out that about half of all industrial enterprises did

---

[13] In 1965, credit was used to finance only 5.3 billion rubles of investment out of an aggregate of 48.3 billion rubles for the whole Soviet economy. More than half of the present investment is supposed to be financed in the near future by means of credit. (See *Ekonomicheskaya gazeta*, No. 32, 1966, p. 13.)

[14] These proceeds are at present paid into the state budget. The depreciation allowances in question are those for replacement of capital. Today these are distributed centrally for financing investment in general.

not have a fund based on profits. The other half, he added, only had funds of insignificant size.

The October 1965 reforms introduced three separate funds: the afore-mentioned fund for the development of production; a second fund for the insurance of material incentives; and a third fund for the expansion of social welfare and housing. The latter two funds are financed by levies on profits, the norms for which are set for a period of several years for groups of enterprises with similar rates of profitability and related kinds of working conditions. The amount of levies depends on the fulfillment of plans for marketed production, of plans for profit in the preceding quarter, and of plans for a specific assortment of major products. If the planned targets are not fulfilled, the levies on profits for the funds are reduced, but they must still be at least 40 per cent of the original share stipulated in the annual plan. This is an important concession to enterprise personnel and may improve their incentives. Another important provision for profit-sharing, aimed at discouraging enterprises from underestimating their potential, is reduction of the levies by 30 to 40 per cent for each percentage point by which the plan is exceeded.

The degree of autonomy that Soviet enterprises have in planning depends mainly on the precise definition given to their prerogatives and obligations in respect of "property" rights and relations with higher authorities and on the number of planned indexes imposed from above. The Kosygin reforms of October 1965 will doubtless increase the degree of autonomy of enterprises, but progress in this direction will be very slight. According to Kosygin, almost all the important planned indexes of enterprises will continue to be imposed from above, including volume of marketed production; classification of essential products defined in physical terms, with specification of export goods and details on quality; aggregate wage fund norms; aggregate profits and profitability rates; budgetary levies and subsidies; volume of centralized investment and of installation of new productive capacity financed by centralized investment; targets for introduction of new techniques; and supplies of materials and equipment from superior agencies.

The principal increase in the autonomy of the enterprise is to derive from reduction of the number of products centrally planned and of the number of products centrally supplied. The importance of this concession is difficult to assess. According to some statements, reduction of the number of centrally planned products will probably be insignificant in the case of producer goods but may be more substantial in the case of foodstuffs and light industry.[15] In theory, under the new system, the Soviet enterprise will be able to plan employment autonomously. In actual fact, this freedom seems quite limited since the ministries that have recently been reactivated will control employment and wage policies. Wage schedules and rates will continue to be fixed from above, and work norms will be fixed centrally. The number of people employed will, therefore, be predetermined largely by the volume of production imposed on the enterprise in physical terms. Another concession—autonomous planning of costs—is also a rather dubious feature of the new scheme, since, by controlling aggregate profits, higher authorities will necessarily supervise the plan for costs.

The number of concessions made to the autonomy of the enterprise is small, and an administrative planning system will still be in effect even if Kosygin's reforms should be completely successful. The immediate success of the reforms, however, depends on the solution of four problems: (1) Modification of prices. The new prices will certainly be brought closer to costs, but if price-fixing methods remain unchanged, the price system will remain almost as arbitrary as before.[16] (2) Grouping of enterprises according to profitability rates. In the first provisional arrangement, instead of long-run rates for groups of enterprises, short-term individual rates were used for the most part. A major difficulty appears to lie in the question of just how to group enterprises and how to know that a certain profitability rate will remain stable. In any case, the decision to remain in a particular group will not depend on the enterprise alone since the enterprise cannot determine its product mix. (3) Amelioration of material supplies. The present reforms do not guarantee abolition of authoritarian allocation of resources. In this situation, no enterprise can be sure that a plan maximizing profits or production can actually be realized. (4) Elimination of arbitrary interference in the operation of the enterprise. The new regulation on the rights of enterprises, dated October 4, 1965, is intended to forestall striking instances of arbitrary interference, but it gives all the necessary powers for accomplishing this to higher authorities, and the number of recent complaints against interference from the newly created ministries is very great.

---

[15] See A. Bachurin, "Sovershenstvovaniye planirovaniya" (Planning Improvement), *Ekonomicheskaya gazeta*, No. 47, 1965, p. 10.

[16] New gross prices for industrial production will be introduced on July 1, 1967. On April 1, 1967, 129 out of 139 new price lists for gross prices and tariffs were already approved by the government. (See *Ekonomicheskaya gazeta*, No. 14, 1967, p. 9).

Obviously, the present reforms, even if they succeed, are not sufficient to keep pace with the need for greater flexibility in the rapidly growing industrial economy of the Soviet Union. New reforms are, therefore, unavoidable. They may take the form of a greater diversification of the nature of Soviet enterprises through extension of existing economic reforms. New and more general concessions to the autonomy of the Soviet enterprise are also likely to be made in the future. Nevertheless, the present social and political opposition to real liberalization is so strong that unless there are some striking political changes, a new period of less rigid administrative planning is just starting.

Planning System and Economic Performance

The problem of economic performance is commonly related to the planning system. There is no doubt that such a relationship exists, but the extent of the influence of the planning system is not easy to judge. The most generally accepted success criteria for the system as a whole are growth rates. It is, therefore, interesting to compare Soviet industrial growth rates under different planning systems. This is done in Table 3. Growth rates in Soviet industry seem to have been highest in the period of flexible planning, during NEP, and lowest, declines mostly, during the period of integral planning. For the purpose of comparing planning systems, the conclusions drawn from Soviet and Western estimates seem to be the same. The only difference is in the evaluation of overall rates of growth; there is no difference in the comparison of growth for different periods.

It is clear from Table 3 that any conclusions to be made about the superiority of any one planning system, as measured by growth rates, would be false. The highest growth rates were, in fact, achieved during post-war recovery periods, 1922–1925 and 1947–1950, and during the period of continuous expansion that preceded collectivization, the Soviet leap forward, and world crisis. The lower levels from which growth started had more effect than change of the planning system; the same is true of times of large-scale perturbation, such as the Civil War and World War II. There was also a considerable slowing down of growth rates in

---

[17] The official Soviet average growth rate for 1930–1932 (19.1 per cent) is too high. It is strongly influenced by the introduction of new products, mainly machinery, for which the constant 1926–1927 prices are in fact replaced by current prices. For this reason, the Western estimates for this period, based on a more limited sample of goods, in physical terms, are more correct.

Table 3

Soviet Planning Systems and Average Annual Rates of Industrial Growth

Number of Years	Official Soviet Estimates	Jasny	Kaplan and Moorsteen	Nutter	Hodgman	Greenslade and Wallace	Noren
FLEXIBLE PLANNING (NEP)							
1922–25 (4)	28.4	—	—	32.6[1]	—	—	—
1926–29 (4)	21.2	—	—	12.6	—	—	—
INTEGRAL PLANNING							
1919–21 (3)	—17.0	—	—	—15.6	—	—	—
1930–32 (3)	19.1	—	—	8.0	—	—	—
1941–46 (6)	— 4.2	— 6.4	— 7.2	— 8.4	— 5.5	—	—
STALINIST ADMINISTRATIVE PLANNING							
1933–37 (5)	17.2	11.7	10.1	14.8	16.5	—	—
1938–40 (3)	13.2	4.8	2.0	3.9	5.1	—	—
1947–50 (4)	22.3	18.8	23.0	20.4	20.8	—	—
1951–55 (5)	13.1	—	9.6	9.6	—	10.1	—
1956–60 (5)	10.4	—	—	6.7	—	9.0	—
1961–65 (5)	8.6	—	—	—	—	—	7.4
LESS RIGID ADMINISTRATIVE PLANNING							
1966–67 (2)	7.8	—	—	—	—	—	—

[1] Industrial materials only.

SOURCES: *Pyatiletniy Plan narodno-khozyaystvennogo stroitelstva SSSR* (The Five-Year Plan for Economic Construction in the USSR), Moscow, 1929, Vol. I, p. 15; *Promyshlennost SSSR* (Industry of the USSR), Moscow, 1957, p. 31; *Narodnoe khozyaystvo SSSR v 1960 godu* (National Economy of the USSR in 1960), Moscow, 1961, p. 219; *Narodnoe khozyaystvo SSSR v 1965 godu*, Moscow, 1966, p. 122; *Pravda*, January 29, 1967, p. 1; N. K. Bajbakov, *Pravda*, December 16, 1966, p. 2; Naum Jasny, *Indices of Soviet Industrial Production 1928–1954*, Council for Economic and Industry Research, Washington, D. C., 1955, p. 40; Norman Kaplan and Richard Moorsteen, *Indexes of Soviet Industrial Output*, RAND Corporation, RM–2495, Santa Monica, California, 1960, pp. 234–235; G. Warren Nutter, *Growth of Industrial Production in the Soviet Union*, Princeton, New Jersey, National Bureau of Economic Research, 1962, Table D–1; Donald Hogman, *Soviet Industrial Production, 1928–1951*, Cambridge, Massachusetts, 1954, p. 89; Rush V. Greenslade and Phyllis Wallace, "Industrial Production in the USSR," *Dimensions of Soviet Economic Power*, Hearings, Joint Economic Committee, 87th Congress of the United States, 2nd Session, 1962, Washington, D. C., Government Printing Office, 1962, pp. 115–136; James H. Noren, "Soviet Industry Trends in Output, Inputs, and Productivity," in *New Directions in the Soviet Economy*, Joint Economic Committee, 89th Congress of the United States, 2nd Session, Washington, D. C., 1966, p. 280. Indexes are computed separately for sectors other than machinery and for machine-building and metal products. For the former, the indexes for different branches are aggregated with value-added weights, and the individual branch indexes are the sum of the value of sample commodities in July 1, 1955, prices. The machine-building and metal product index is taken from official Soviet statistics and reduced, respectively, by 10, 20, and 30 per cent. In the estimates cited here, the results for the total industrial production index are given for the 20 per cent reduction (*ibid.*, p. 281). For the 10 per cent deduction, the average annual growth rate for 1961–1965 is 7.8 per cent, and for the 30 per cent deduction, 7.0 per cent.

1930–1932, but dissaving and the shift from agricultural to industrial employment in 1930 had a strong influence on the growth rates for the whole period.

What seems to have been more important than the planning system was the economic policy—armaments, the fight against inflation, the agricultural policy, and the proportion of resources allocated to investment and consumption. There is no statistical evidence of the influence of the planning system on the rates of growth. More refined statistical criteria would have to be found to demonstrate such influence. In any case, the Soviet planning system could not help but be affected by the slowing down of industrial growth rates with the growing maturity of the Soviet economy, by the influence of the economic situation on the growth rates and the structure of the economy, and by economic, social, and political pressures calling for important changes. In the Stalinist period, the political pressures and so-called ideological deviations seem to have been of major importance. Now, the economic and social pressures, favouring greater flexibility in the system, can no longer be ignored.

Collectivization: New and Old Myths

Roy D. Laird

Inevitably, there has evolved among Soviet leaders a set of beliefs concerning collectivized agriculture. These are part of the total myth system, which, as defined by Professor Robert MacIver, comprises "the value-impregnated beliefs and notions that men hold, that they live by or live for." In MacIver's words, "all social relations, the very texture of human society, are myth-born and myth-sustained."[1] Soviet society would seem to be no exception. The assumption of this study is that in addition to the economic and political determinants of Soviet agricultural policies, there are also important beliefs that have influenced the decisions of the Soviet leadership in the realm of agricultural affairs. It should perhaps be made clear from the start that recognition of the importance of social or individual myths does not imply anything about "the grounds of belief, so far as belief claims to interpret reality." Beliefs may square with the most rigorous tests of modern science, or they may be the product of "the most grotesque imaginations of the most benighted savage."[2] To assume that myths, including both those that are scientifically valid and those that are rooted in dogmatic nonsense, have been a major determinant of Soviet agricultural policies is of little help in identifying either the particular beliefs that have influenced a given policy or the extent to which any enduring belief is rooted in Marxist-Leninist dogma rather than some more pragmatic influence. Of course, the tests of logic and consistency are helpful, but in the final analysis it is difficult to know if, for example, Brezhnev and Kosygin actually regard collective and state farms as the highest form of rural society and the best means of managing agricultural productivity because of doctrinal imperatives or because of personal conviction in the efficacy of collectivization as a highly satisfactory instrument of political and economic control.

Professor Alfred G. Meyer has written that "the leaders of the Communist Party really do believe in communism, as they understand it." He nevertheless goes on to ask if they are really communists, commenting:

---

[1] R. M. MacIver, *The Web of Government*, The Macmillan Company, New York, 1948, pp. 4 and 5.

[2] *Ibid.*

"I am not sure whether it should even be asked."[3] If Professor Meyer's test of being a communist is a measure of one's slavish adherence to religious doctrine, as might be the test for many communicants of more conventional religions, the evidence would tend to support the doubts his question raises. Indeed, as nearly as one can be sure of such judgements, Soviet agricultural policies have often been formulated in defiance of doctrine, representing instead a response to urgent political and economic needs—for example, Lenin's adoption of the New Economic Policy (NEP) in 1921. Much of the staying power of the Soviet system must be credited to the ability of the leadership to invent new non-communist myths in the face of pressing demands of the moment. Yet, surely, a major test of belief is the demonstrated need to argue, no matter how far-fetched the necessary rationalization might be, that a new policy accords with professed dogma. Regardless of how tortuous the task has been, the Soviet leadership has always managed to invent an argument with a Marxist-Leninist orientation to explain new policies that the Western observer views as obvious responses to pragmatic needs. This author therefore maintains that the myths catalogued below are best described as elements of an evolving Soviet belief system springing both from Marxist-Leninist doctrine and pragmatic responses to economic and political needs. The present view, it should be noted, moreover, goes further than that of Professor Meyer. Not only is it thought that Soviet leaders are communists; it is also held that since men are believing animals, any explanation of post-1917 policies in rural Russia based solely upon political (i.e., power) considerations and economic factors would be both sterile and misleading. Hobbes and Marx were right: aspirations for power and responses to economic imperatives are vital determinants of political behaviour; so, however, is man's need to quiet his conscience by making his actions conform with some view of the good and the true. Communism has been an oft-changed base for the emerging Soviet belief system. Marxist-Leninist descriptions of what ought to be, do more than just determine the leadership's description of what has been done. They also provide the word picture for much of what the leaders "live by and live for."

Marx and the Village Community

Though he claimed to approach human affairs from a universal standpoint, arguing that economic need determines all human activity and that the impact of the industrial revolution on the economic environment pro-

---

[3] Alfred G. Meyer, "The Functions of Ideology in the Soviet Political System," *Soviet Studies*, Glasgow, Vol. XVII, No. 3, 1966, pp. 273–285.

vides the key to all future change, Karl Marx's view was highly parochial and futuristic and thus blind to the immediate wants and needs of the bulk of mankind. His theories were built upon observations of the forces at work in the urbanization and industrialization of Western Europe and North America, but they largely ignored the great mass of the world's population living in rural areas of the globe in the middle of the nineteenth century, practically untouched by industrial change. One of the greatest ironies of modern history is that Marxist-Leninist revolutions have succeeded only in predominantly agricultural societies. With one curious exception, what little attention Marx and Engels devoted to rural problems rested upon the assumption that urban economic change would sweep the peasantry into the mainstream of the industrial revolution. The exception was that perhaps Hertzen had a point in stressing the special nature of the case for Russia. In line with Engel's view, in *Anti-Dühring*, that man had held land in common in the original state of nature, it was supposed that a communal seed of socialism had perhaps been preserved in the village community. Such a primitive socialist consciousness could provide an important spark for a communist revolution in Russia.[4] Marx's impact on agricultural thought was, nevertheless, based almost entirely upon his belief in the universal application of the industrial method of production. Therefore, his major contribution to the agricultural myth system was the conviction that as in the case of industry, agriculture was destined to be concentrated in fewer and fewer hands, becoming highly mechanized and adopting the managerial patterns evolved in industry. In short, large-scale industrialized farming operations would prove to be the most efficient form of food production and in time would dissolve the differences between urban and rural societies.

Lenin versus Stalin

The political key to correctly organizing society for abundant production was Marx's argument that only nationalization would allow the proper, equal relation of all members of society to the means of production. This meant that nationalization of the land was an explicit requirement for agriculture and that some sort of collective or state organization and management of large industrial farming units was an implicit requirement. Faced with the responsibility of leading a state created in the name of Marxism, Lenin was left with the task of working out the details necessary for putting theory into practice. The failure of the abortive revolution in 1905 had

---

[4] Frederick Engels, *Anti-Dühring*, Moscow, 1947, p. 133. See also the discussion on this point in David Mitrany, *Marx Against the Peasant*, The University of North Carolina Press, Chapel Hill, 1951, pp. 41–71.

provided him with lessons that would lead to success in 1917. These were embodied in two major revisions of doctrine: the Party had to be transformed into a highly disciplined vanguard representing a political elite capable of leading a successful revolution; success could be achieved only if the Party vanguard could effectively harness the forces for agrarian revolution.

In Lenin's eyes, though the class consciousness of the peasantry was less developed than that of the urban proletariat, its sympathies, especially those of the well-to-do (*kulak*) peasants, were largely bourgeoise. In addition, the great bulk of peasants who were landless or short of land were regarded as in a position, in relation to the rural means of production, that was analogous to the position of the exploited urban worker. Thus, in 1908, Lenin nominated that bulk of Russia's rural masses who were desperately poor to the role of a "semi-proletarian" class. His conviction was that the growing Russian crisis was taking place under conditions in which "the peasantry [was] being transformed into a rural bourgeoisie and a proletariat."[5]

Building upon such thinking, Lenin aggregated the promises of the 1917 revolution in the peasant-oriented phrase: "Peace, bread, land, and liberty!" Not only had he come to recognize that the success of the revolution depended upon the alliance of interests that he had helped to create with the peasants, he had also come to believe that the survival of Bolshevist power depended upon the concessions that might be fashioned to meet peasant demands. In the long run, however, agriculture was to be industrialized. "Communism," it was said, "is Soviet power plus the electrification of the whole country." What this was to mean in practice was some form of collectivization. Indeed, the need to adopt a system of large-scale collective and mechanized agriculture was seen as amounting to an indisputable theoretical truth.[6] Nonetheless, non-proletarian rural habits were so deeply ingrained in most of the peasants that if they were pushed too fast, the results could be disastrous. In short, Lenin perceived that communist construction in the countryside had to be gradual, built step by step upon voluntary peasant acceptance of the superiority of communist production forms. More than once he warned that it would be "absolutely absurd" to attempt to reshape the millions of individual small farms "in any rapid way." Again, the state was to effect the transition to collective

---

[5] V. I. Lenin, "The Agrarian Question in Russia Towards the Close of the Nineteenth Century," *Collected Works*, Vol. 15, Foreign Languages Publishing House, Moscow, 1963, pp. 129 and 131.

[6] V. I. Lenin, "Preliminary Draft Theses on the Agrarian Question," *Collected Works*, Vol. 31, Foreign Languages Publishing House, Moscow, 1966, p. 162.

farming "with extreme caution and only very gradually, by the force of example, without any coercion of the middle peasant."[7]

Stalin, of course, saw fit to abandon the strictures of Lenin against forced collectivization. Perhaps the heart of the matter lay in Lenin's undying belief that the revolution in Russia was primarily the staging ground for an imminent proletarian revolution in industrialized Europe. Surely, one can reasonably argue that had Lenin lived for a number of years after 1924, he, too, would have broken with the dream of European revolution and turned all his efforts to creating socialism in one country. In any case, once the Soviet leadership had given up the dream of there being, immediately, a communist Europe, collectivization represented far more than just a promise of bringing communism to the Russian countryside. Whatever Lenin might have done, Stalin concentrated all his thoughts and efforts on internal construction, concluding that heavy industry should be developed at the fastest possible pace and that by forcing the peasants onto collectives by means of "a revolution from above" he could create institutions permitting maximum control over peasant politics and maximum exploitation of peasant production to sustain the crash industrialization programme.

Though Stalin's concern with what he saw as the pragmatic demands of industrial construction determined his agricultural policies, he apparently believed that the overwhelming bulk of the peasantry simply joined the collective farms.[8] The Western critic may rightly disbelieve this judgement. Nevertheless, the resurrection of Lenin's trick of using "committees of the poor" to serve as the major wedge in defeating general peasant opposition was the key to achieving collectivization. At the least, Stalin believed there was a core of the rural proletariat capable of leading the struggle for higher production achievements once the proper organizational form for the struggle had been created. In sum, though Stalin's rural policy actions were dictated largely by his view of industry's needs, the conviction prevailed that collectivization had allowed the countryside to join the march to communism. This is evident from the literature of the time. In any case, Stalin could not have declared the arrival of socialism in 1936 if collectivization had not been achieved. Moreover, a new doctrine was proclaimed: the collective and state farms would prove to be so much more efficient than the old forms of production that soon the whole of the rural society would enthusiastically support them. Continued increases in the

---

[7] *Ibid.*, p. 157 and "Speech Delivered at the First Congress of Agricultural Communes and Agricultural Artels," *Collected Works*, Vol. 30, Foreign Languages Publishing House, Moscow, 1965, p. 196.

[8] *History of the Communist Party of the Soviet Union*, Foreign Languages Publishing House, Moscow, 1950, p. 374.

sizes of farms reflected the belief that the larger the farm, the greater the potential for efficient production. Stalinist literature also expressed the belief that the state farms (sovkhozes) were a higher form of organization of production than the collective farms (kolkhozes) and that a marriage of Marxist-Leninist ideology and natural science would create an alliance that ultimately would allow the transformation of nature to the point where agriculture would enjoy the same controlled conditions of production that had been achieved in much of industry. Meanwhile, of course, Lysenko had managed to incorporate the tenets of Marxism-Leninism into his teachings on genetics, promising increased production with minimum investment and thereby securing the favour of Stalin and the leadership of Soviet agricultural science.

Khrushchev and His Successors

At times, Stalin's successors may well wonder whether Lenin's voluntary path would not have been superior to the Stalinist road of force. Nevertheless, the collective and state farms that exist are part of the heritage, and there is no evidence that the post-1953 leadership has rejected the myth of the superiority of large-scale collectivized agriculture. Clearly, however, the new leadership believes that the system can be improved upon. Stalin saw little need for change. He stoutly rejected the suggestion that the *zveno* (link or team) might be superior to the huge brigade as the basic means of organizing work on the farms. The Machine and Tractor Stations (MTS) were declared to be sacrosanct, even long after extension of the Party's influence over the farm meant that the MTS monopoly over machinery, a key means of production, was no longer needed to assure continued control over the peasantry. Suggestions that the MTS machinery should be sold to the collectives were stubbornly rejected on the grounds that such an act would involve "a step in reversion to the old backwardness... trying to turn back the wheel of history."[9]

In contrast to Stalin's conservatism, the almost frantic actions of Khrushchev and his successors in carrying out various administrative reforms reveal an awareness on their part that when organizational relationships can be set right, the key will have been found to expanded production. The heretical idea of the *zveno* has been discussed and briefly tried again, if only to be rejected once more.[10] Most important is the new willingness to experiment with institutional forms and relationships. Though construction of heavy industry is still said to receive first priority

[9] J. Stalin, *Economic Problems of Socialism in the U.S.S.R.*, Foreign Languages Publishing House, Moscow, 1952, p. 100.
[10] See *Pravda*, January 20, 1966, pp. 1–2.

in terms of investment, the significant increases in investment in agriculture represent an important change from the old myth of all priority to industry. Stalin expressed concern in his valedictory work *Economic Problems of Socialism in the USSR* that the dragging feet of agriculture were holding back industrial progress, but now there is a new belief that many more rubles than before must be poured into agriculture if there is not to be a serious slowdown in the growth of the economy. A measure of this change in attitude is Brezhnev's observation that projected investment in agriculture for the new five-year period is "approximately as much as investment in agriculture during the nineteen years following the war."[11]

Khrushchev's belief that bigness is a concomitant of production efficiency was carried to the extreme with efforts to increase the average size of the collective farm by more than fourfold between 1950 and 1964. Brezhnev's early remarks imply a recognition that the mania for giganticness had got out of hand, and that the call for amalgamations had been somewhat overzealous. He commented: "Some kolkhozes became so huge that they proved to be unmanageable."[12] Similarly, the process of transforming many of the collective farms into state farms was said to have gone too far. Yet neither trend seems to have been reversed. Indeed, in comparison with 1964, the year 1965 showed a still further increase in the number of state over the number of collective farms, the number of the former increasing from 10,078 to 11,642 and the number of the latter decreasing from 38,300 to 36,900.[13]

The belief that Lysenko had a special insight into the relationship between Marxism-Leninism and natural science seems to have been laid to rest. Part of new investment in agriculture is to go towards new investigations of the application of science to increased production. Significant increases in the number of trained agricultural specialists were observable under Khrushchev, and this pattern has continued under Brezhnev and Kosygin. Whereas, under Stalin, very few trained specialists lived on the farms, by April 1, 1965, 40.7 per cent of engineers and technicians on collective farms, 67.3 per cent of collective farm chairmen, 10.1 per cent of production brigade leaders, and 10.8 per cent of heads of livestock sections had university or secondary specialized educations.[14] Obviously, the leadership hopes that the impact of this managerial revolution on the farms will be highly beneficial.

---

[11] *Pravda*, March 27, 1965, pp. 2—4.

[12] *Ibid.*

[13] *SSSR v tsifrakh v 1965 godu* (The USSR in Figures in 1965), Moscow, 1966, pp. 91—93. As the figures reveal, since there were some 164 more farms in 1965 than in 1964, the average farm was slightly smaller.

[14] *Kommunist*, No. 4, 1966, pp. 91—96.

The Commitment to Collectivization: 1966 and Beyond

To rephrase a saying of Will Rogers, the student of Soviet affairs knows only what he reads in Soviet newspapers. If he is wise, of course, he reads between the lines. (This is true whether he is reading *Pravda* or *The New York Times.*) The reason, simply if ominously enough, is that the private thoughts of leaders often differ significantly from their published utterances. Still, those who once thought that Soviet statistics were consistently falsified for Western consumption found no significant discrepancies between the secret state economic plan for 1941, which fell into German hands during the Second World War, and what had been published about it in the Stalinist press. The invention of the big lie is credited to Hitler, though he had published the truth in *Mein Kampf.* Doubtless, the Soviet leadership entertains private thoughts about collectivization and its future, and doubtless, pressing pragmatic demands will dictate the adoption of un-communist policies. Yet, reading both on and between the lines of the Soviet press leaves one with the impression of a substantial collectivization myth, not the least of which is the firm belief that, however reorganized in the future, the collectivized system is destined to continue, because it is the best possible means of organizing the countryside. Necessity has given a new lease on life to the private plot of the peasant, but there is little doubt that at some future date this malignancy will have to be removed from the system.

The Soviet leadership is constantly concerned about the proper education and indoctrination of its citizenry, and the collective farms are repeatedly credited with being valuable schools for communism. Under Stalin, only a small number of the farms could claim Party units, but by January 1, 1965, the average collective farm could boast a Party cell of some forty members.[15] The central leadership's faith in the increased presence of the Party on the farms, reinforced by the increased specialized training of cadres, seems to promise that the long-admitted need for greater decentralization of the decision-making process in production can now be realized. At the same time, a long history of unfulfilled promises, coupled with emphatic assignment of responsibility for "the operational direction" of farms to republic, rayon, and oblast and kray administration, to guarantee fulfillment of state procurement plans, seems to point in the old direction.[16] In short, the reluctance of an authoritarian system of leadership to relax central controls, along with new sociological evidence substantiating the long-held and little-disguised belief that the peasantry is

---

[15] *Ibid.*
[16] *Voprosy ekonomiki*, No. 6, 1965, pp. 1–13.

socially inferior, leads to the prediction that the Soviet leadership will
continue using the collective farms to exercise tight control over a backward peasantry. In a most revealing study, one that is quite unusual for
Soviet social science, statistics of the Russian Republic are cited to indicate
that the collective farmer's income from his private plot averaged 628 rubles
in 1961, whereas the state farmer's income from this source averaged
465 rubles. It is asserted that "the closer the private plot brings the collective
farmer to the urban worker materially, in level of income, the more strongly
they are separated in the social respect." Again, in a study of a representative farming area, it is indicated that only 7 per cent of homes in which
heads of families were engaged in skilled work had icons, whereas 57 per
cent of homes of unskilled labourers had icons.[17] If this is an accurate
reflection of the level of socialist development of the average peasant,
perhaps many district Party secretaries would tend to agree with the attitude
expressed by one their Mexican counterparts, an official responsible for
several collective *ejidos*. When asked by this writer, during the summer of
1966, what decisions the average members of the *ejido* make, he replied:
"They are incapable of making decisions."

Of course, there is also the belief that significant progress has been
made in expanding the social consciousness of the peasantry, and that the
differences between the cities and the farms are gradually disappearing.
Similarly, the major differences between the two forms of property, the
collective farms and the state farms, are said to have almost vanished.
Realization of the promise of a guaranteed collective farm wage, increased
investments in the collective farms, and the convergence of mental tasks and
physical labour are said to be "overcoming the socio-economic and cultural distinctions between the town and the country."[18] Though the press
in the post-Stalin period has repeatedly emphasized that collective and state
farms are to be regarded as virtually at the same place on the ladder of
socialist development, a hint of the slight superiority of the state farm per-
sists. Indeed, while arguing that the socialist development of collective and
state farms is virtually on a par, one collective farm chairman admits that
there is "a theoretical basis for turning weak collective farms into state
farms."[19]

The dream, fashioned perhaps from Russian feeling for the limitless
steppes, and certainly from Marxist-Leninist faith in the superiority of
large-scale industrialized agriculture, has not faded. Amalgamation of
already huge farms into even more enormous ones continues. Surely, this

[17] *Voprosy filosofii*, No. 6, 1966, pp. 51–61.
[18] *Pravda*, June 16, 1966, pp. 2–3.
[19] *Kommunist*, No. 8, 1966, pp. 20–26.

process must cease before the whole countryside is one massive state farm. It is possible that in the future some of the farms may be subdivided, but published studies on the optimum size of farms tend at present to support the concept of large units. As noted earlier, experiments in breaking the collectives into small production units (*zveno*) seem to have been discredited. The myth of the superiority of huge brigades endures. One manifestation of the pattern of gigantomania does, however, seem to have been modified: Khrushchev's vast new lands programme is no longer advertised as the answer to increased production needs. Rather, his successors seem to have concluded that the key to greater food output lies in increasing yields in established areas. Thus, there is considerable emphasis on a land melioration programme for "all areas of the country, every collective and state farm."[20]

The lie that the bulk of the peasants originally joined the collective farms voluntarily is still heard. Perhaps it eventually will be reputed. Yet, the belief that most collective farms are democratically managed, and that all of them can and should be so managed, is stoutly defended. For example, the collective farm chairman cited above stresses that "every member must actively participate in managing the affairs of the public farm."[21] In a reverse fashion, the continued dramatization in the press of the evils present on farms failing to live up to the democratic ideal is proof of the importance of this exercise in self-delusion. Those who might doubt the strength of this argument ought perhaps to be reminded of the millions of Americans who long expressed passionate belief in the near perfection of American democracy, in seeming ignorance of the second-class status of the Negro. Further evidence of the great importance of the myth of democracy on the collective farm is Podgorny's assertion at the Twenty-third Party Congress that the new Rules of the Agricultural Artels would provide "an improvement in the democratic methods of managing collective farm life."[22]

The myths of a society are not just fashioned from obvious environment. (This concept relates to Marx's famous dictum: "Social being is not determined by consciousness, but consciousness by social being.") They are much more subtly derived from the parts of environment that the leadership and the members of the society select as important. As suggested at the beginning of this study, the changing myths of Soviet collectivization are rooted both in Marxist-Leninist doctrine and the lessons of experience. However come by, after more than a quarter of a century, they seem to

---

[20] *Pravda*, May 28, 1966, pp. 1–3.
[21] *Ibid.*
[22] *Pravda*, April 1, 1966, p. 4.

describe a belief system, some of the more important elements of which are outlined below:

(1) The collective and state farms represent an enormous economic investment. Soviet maps, records, roads, and especially peasant settlements, agricultural machinery, and administrative headquarters, have all been designed to reinforce the vision of the superiority of huge farms and huge fields. The cost of changing to any fundamentally different system, inevitably involving much smaller production units, would be staggering and the disruption of production during the period of transition might be disastrous.

(2) The collective and state farms provide the Soviet leadership with a means of exercising tight control over the nations's food supply.

(3) The collective and state farms provide the Soviet leadership with a highly effective instrument for exerting political control over the peasantry.

(4) The collective and state farms constitute an emotional investment of more than a quarter century. If the system were abandoned, such an act would amount to an unprecedented admission of grave error on the part of the Party.

(5) Collectivization fits the demands of the ideology for bringing communism to the countryside.

(6) Ironically, in spite of wide advertisement of the inefficiency of the Soviet agricultural system, the collective and state farms constitute an existing model for organizing a revolutionary peasantry in developing countries. To abandon Soviet collectivization would be to undercut the most important argument for native revolutionaries in predominantly peasant-populated, developing nations to follow the Soviet lead.

For good or ill, then, it seems that nothing short of another revolution, or a series of production failures far more serious than those yet experienced, can be expected to result in a serious challenge to the basic myth associated with Soviet collectivization.[23]

---

[23] After preparing this paper, the author carefully reread an essay by Professor Alec Nove entitled "Ideology and Agriculture" (*Soviet Studies*, Vol. XVII, No. 4, 1966, pp. 397–407). The cast of his paper and the present essay are different. However, where the area of the two presentations does overlap, I find no substantive difference—with one major exception. Professor Nove writes: "My own personal prejudice inclines me to minimize its [ideology's] importance. Yet it is wrong totally to disregard it." Perhaps the difference of our prejudices in respect of ideology will explain why Professor Nove is a political *economist* and I am a political scientist, who is perhaps best described as an old-fashioned *political* economist. Whatever the cause of our differences, Professor Nove's interpretation of the impact of ideology on agriculture is largely negative, whereas the stress here has been that the Soviet myth system has often been a vital, positive determinant of Soviet agricultural policies.

From the Promise of Land and Bread to the Reality of the State Farm

Carl R. Zoerb

In the dynamic slogan "Land and Bread to the Peasantry!" Lenin found the spark to solidify the support of the peasants for the revolution. In the expropriation of the land and its distribution among the peasants, however, an established, large-scale agricultural system was broken up into an atomistic order of small-scale operations. Almost a third of the farming area in European Russian consisted of large holdings operated by landowners, the Church, and the state. This productive sector yielded most of the marketable farm products. It was the basis for improving breeds of livestock and superior plant varieties and for developing technology and progressive methods of farm management. In addition, a good number of estates operated ancillary industries, including distilleries, processing plants for farm products, and units for supplying building materials, thereby insuring stability of farm employment. Historically, the whole thrust of Russian agriculture had demonstrated the productive superiority of large-scale estate farming over the smaller farming efforts of the peasantry, and the Bolsheviks faced an ideological dilemma. With the nationalization of the land and the liquidation of large landholdings, the clamour of the peasantry for complete distribution of the land had to be met. This process was carried out impulsively by the seizure of land, cattle, and equipment by local peasant masses. At the same time, in order to salvage the productive assets of some of the estates and provide immediate sources of foodstuffs, the Bolsheviks organized socialist enterprises, which came to be known as state farms (sovkhozes).

The land nationalization decree of November 8, 1917, declared that "lands with highly developed forms of cultivation...should not be divided up, but should be transformed into model farms to be cultivated exclusively either by the state or by the communes, according to their size and importance."[1] The Party Programme, adopted by the Eighth Congress of the All-Russian Communist (Bolshevist) Party in March 1919, proclaimed:

---

[1] *Pravda*, November 10, 1917; *KPSS v rezolyutsiyakh i resheniyakh* (The CPSU in Resolutions and Decrees), Moscow, 1954, Vol. I, pp. 409–430.

The Soviet government, having carried out the complete abolition of private property in the land has already begun to carry out a series of measures directed to the organziation of socialist agriculture on a wide scale. The principal measures are the following: (1) the establishment of Soviet farms, i.e., large socialist economic enterprises; (2) assistance to societies as well as associations for the common cultivation of land; (3) organization by the state of the cultivation of all uncultivated acreage; (4) state mobilization of all agricultural forces for the purpose of taking the most energetic measures to increase agricultural productivity; (5) the support of agricultural communes as absolutely voluntary associations of agricultural workers for the purpose of conducting a communal system of economy on a large scale.[2]

The relative importance and weight the Bolsheviks originally attached to the state farms as compared with the agricultural communes or collective farms is clearly apparent from the Programme. Even so, only a small fraction of the land expropriated from large estates was socialized into state farms or agricultural communes. There were, for example, 5,923 state farms in the RSFSR in 1920, but they received only 6 to 7 per cent of the land expropriated.[3] Naum Jasny quotes a Soviet source to the effect that of 29 million hectares of land held in the form of large estates before the revolution, little more than 3 million hectares were turned into state farms.[4]

Phases of Sovkhoz Development

The development of Soviet state farms since the revolution falls into three distinct periods: (1) the period from 1918 to 1927, which extended from the Civil War through the time of the New Economic Policy (NEP); (2) the mighty sovkhoz revival, which occurred concurrently with the mass collectivization campaign, when the slogan "Factories in the field!" was heard, and which turned in 1935 into a time of disenchantment lasting until the end of the Stalin era; and (3) the great upsurge of the state farm system, which has lasted from 1954 to the present. The recent period will be the principal concern of this paper.

The Early Stage. The first state farms were organized in 1918, mainly as converted estates. By 1921, their number had reached 5,629, covering an area of some 3.5 million hectares. They ranged in size from 100 to 2,000

---

[2] *The Soviet System*, Meisel and Kozera, Ann Arbor, Michigan, 1953, pp. 115–161.

[3] Alexander Baykov, *Soviet Economic System*, Cambridge, Massachusetts, 1950, p. 22.

[4] Naum Jasny, *The Socialized Agriculture of the USSR*, Stanford, California, 1949, pp. 235–236.

hectares.[5] In the process of nationalizing the land, the peasants were allocated the major share of the confiscated estates. They showed a pronounced disinclination to join the state farms or the communes. The operation of the state farms further suffered from a lack of experienced managers. These were mostly industrial workers or revolutionary intellectuals. Other disadvantages were extreme fluctuations in the labour supply and pragmatic interpretations of communism that took the primary object of production to be satisfaction of the needs of workers and employees. Many industrial enterprises adopted a similar view of the food shortages that prevailed during the Civil War, organizing farms in surrounding areas to secure foodstuffs for workers. Such farms were simply considered auxiliary state farms.

During the period of NEP, with its emphasis on individualism in production and distribution, the position of the state farms was still further weakened. Apart from those farms with specialized crops, such as sugar beets, state farms operated at a loss and their number and area declined. After almost a decade of farming, state farms were cultivating only 1,550,000 hectares of land, or 1.4 per cent of the total crop area, and supplying less than 3 per cent of the grain marketed in 1927.[6] Even the official history of the Communist Party underscores the performance of the state farms as negligible, stating that the kulaks produced three times more grain for market in 1927 than the combined sales of the state and collective farms.[7] Clearly, apart from the failure to improve production and play a positive role in the countryside, the state farms had yet to demonstrate that large-scale farming was superior to individual peasant farming. Moreover, the system had not earned the good-will of the peasantry towards specialized

---

[5] The early history of the state farms is described in I. Ya. Solyarov, "Sovkhozy" in *Trudy gosudarstvennogo nauchno-issledovatelskogo instituta zemlyeustroystva i pereseleniya* (Works of the State Research Institute for Land Management and Resettlement), Moscow, 1928, Vol. V; A. Lavrentev, *Stroitelstvo sovkhoz i pervye gody sovetskoy vlasti 1917–20* (Construction of the State Farms and the First Years of Soviet Power 1917–20), Moscow, 1957. The apparent decline from the number of state farms said to have existed in 1920 (5,923) to the smaller number of state farms said to have existed in 1921 (5,629) is perhaps explained by the different sources from which the figures have been drawn. The fluidity of the situation in the Soviet Union at this time should also be kept in mind, however, which is to say that at least in part the decline may be attributable to the constant land rearrangements that took place during this period, including, of course, amalgamation of farms.

[6] W. Ladejinsky, "Soviet State Farms", *Political Science Quarterly*, New York, Vol. LIII, p. 65.

[7] *History of the Communist Party of the Soviet Union*, Moscow, 1960, pp. 418–419.

farming: the peasants opposed the creation of the state farms, because they felt that by right the land ought to be distributed to them.

Factories in the Field. With the developing grain shortage and the decision in 1928 to collectivize agriculture, the Party simultaneously launched a systematic campaign to strengthen and expand the network of state farms. Stalin maintained, in his speech "On the Grain Front," that one way out of the chronic grain problem was to replace the small-scale peasant farm by large, amalgamated, socialized farms, which were to be equipped with machinery, armed with scientific knowledge, and thus made capable of yielding a maximum of grain for the market; the other way out was through expansion and development of new, large state farms. Within three or four years, the state farms were to produce from 1.3 million to 1.6 million tons of marketable grain annually, and their size was to vary from 10,000 to 30,000 hectares.[8] In addition, Stalin assigned the state farms the task of spearheading the socialization of agriculture in the countryside. They were to be the vanguard of the reconstruction of the old order in rural areas.

This middle period in the history of sovkhoz development has been carefully documented by Western scholars and requires no elaboration.[9] However, as a participant in the forced "assault" that was part of the reconstruction of the rural economic order, this writer feels that it might be useful to comment on some developments that are probably not generally known. Encouraged by initial successes, especially in marginal dry areas in central and eastern Russia, where many of the new state grain farms were located, the Soviet Union expanded the system of establishing livestock farms. In early 1930, a cattle trust, a grain trust, a dairy trust, and a vegetable trust were organized under the Commissariat for State Farms. Soon after, specialized farms were created on either a national or republican basis. These included poultry, horse, and sheep farms.[10] That the Kremlin had considerable confidence in the pioneering role of the state farms is indicated by its decision to spend hard currency for essential imports. At a time when full-speed industrialization commanded all the resources in foreign exchange that the Soviet Union could muster, substantial sums of hard currency were

----

[8] J. Stalin, *Voprosy Leninizma* (Problems of Leninism), Moscow, 1954, pp. 253–255.

[9] The most complete account, particularly in respect of grain-producing state farms, is by Ladejinsky, *Soviet State Farms, op. cit.* See also Jasny, *The Socialized Agriculture of the USSR, op. cit.*, Chapter XI; L. Volin, *A Survey of Russian Agriculture*, 1951, USDA, Washington, D.C, pp. 69–80.

[10] By the end of 1930, there were 2,832 state farms, of which 370 were grain farms representing 41 per cent of state farm crop land. Livestock farms numbered, 1,046, many of which were in the process of organization. Forced collectivization actually aided the process of assembling livestock herds.

being expended for imports almost exclusively intended for the state farms: tractors and farm machinery, breed-improving livestock, and a variety of equipment and chemicals. In addition to the services of American engineers and tractor mechanics on grain farms, a group of thirty agricultural specialists from the United States was hired to work within the livestock trusts at central, republican, and farm levels. From time to time, experts from European countries were also called in for assistance and counsel. Thus, in the early part of the thirties, the climate for the development of the state farms was distinctly favourable.

In February 1931, the immediate objectives of the state farm network were outlined for the American specialists by a representative of the Commissariat for State Farms. The broad goals were twofold in nature: one aspect productive, the other educational. The state farms were to be models of successful, productive enterprises supplying the state with marketable produce. They were to introduce and demonstrate modern achievements in agricultural technology; to assist the collective farms in general and in particular to supply them with superior varieties of seeds and breeds of stock; to train peasants in the arts of agricultural production on a large scale; and finally, to pioneer the path for the socialist reconstruction of the countryside. In addition, for good measure, the farms were to be profitable enterprises.

The excessive size of the farms and their narrow specialization soon produced dislocations. This issue was widely debated at all levels, and the American advisors rather cautiously proposed to the Commissariat for State Farms that until a more intensive degree of mechanization could be assured and a more stable supply of skilled workers provided, the state farms ought to be reduced in size and their production diversified. The debate over the issue occurred in 1931, a circumstance that contrasts oddly with Stalin's accusation at the Seventeenth Party Congress that the Commissariat had not been involved in the problem and had not in fact done anything about it.[11] On the contrary, no operational issue was more discussed than the size and specialization of the farms.

Another issue, associated with the development of the state farm system but seldom given its weight as a determinant of the success or failure of the individual farm, has been the enormous construction effort that, apart from the war period, has continued to this day. Not even the confiscated estates had adequate buildings for the enlargement of farming operations, and when the programme of expansion was launched in 1928, it marked the beginning of a nearly endless cycle of construction. Because most of the

[11] See following quotation.

new farms were literally staked out on the steppe, extensive construction projects had to be undertaken. Grain farms had to build huge storage sheds and granaries, communal housing units and eating centres, and homes and offices for administrators, as well as provide schools, water supplies, and sanitary facilities. On the livestock farms, the need for mammoth barns and shelters and for storehouses for feed compounded the effort. Much of the original construction was faulty, necessitating frequent repairs. Wood was the principal building material; cement, paint, and nails were rarely available. A major share of investment in agriculture went towards building and repairs, a trend that holds true today. So great were the demands in this respect that some foreign agricultural advisors reported they spent a third of their time planning and supervising the construction of farm buildings.

A distinctive feature of the state farms as compared with the collective farms was the primacy of Party control. From the start, but particularly after 1928, each state farm had a primary Party organization with either a full-time or a part-time secretary. Though membership was small, it embraced all the administrative officials, a few of the specialists, and some of the skilled workers who exercised control over all farm activities. A striking feature of early state farm administrations was the youngness of the farm officials—directors in their late twenties or early thirties. At the sub-farm level, Party authority was considerably diluted; among the labour units in the fields, it was actually ineffective. The rank-and-file state farm worker of both sexes was young and single, and the paucity of families was another striking feature of state farm life. Reliance was had on the Komsomol (Young Communist League), but as state farm labour policy was one of "hire and fire," given the harsh living conditions and the seasonal work schedule of the specialized farms, the labour turnover was excessive and proved to be a serious impediment to agricultural development. In the main, the Komsomol was an ineffective Party instrument in shaping productivity. The impression of the foreign advisors was that many of the young people were only marking time, waiting to migrate to the cities. The small number of them who operated tractors and machinery often regarded their work merely as training for industrial employment. In introducing young peasants to machinery and technology, the state farms made a positive contribution to agricultural and industrial development. Yet, not entirely unlike their parents, who showed disinterest in and apathy towards the state farm system, younger peasants responded to the call of the Komsomol with less than zealous devotion. This attitude persisted until the late thirties, when urban labour shortages drew many young workers of both sexes from the farms and created more of a balance between younger and older workers on the farms.

A series of poor harvests, coupled with mounting operating deficits and breakdowns in labour discipline, set the stage for a number of investigations and trials of state farm workers in the early thirties. Scapegoats were found and the blame laid on class enemies. Credit must nevertheless be given to the state farms for being able to feed their workers during the 1932–33 famine in the affected areas of southern Russia. Starvation was confined to members of the collective farms and to the remaining peasants engaged in private farming. As the time for the Seventeenth Party Congress in 1934 approached, the great expectations of the Party for the state farms as productive factories in the field were redefined. In the words of Stalin:

> In regard to the state farms, it must be said that they still fail to cope with their tasks. I do not in the least underestimate the great revolutionizing role of our state farms, but if we compare the enormous sums the state has invested in the state farms with the actual results they have achieved to date, we will find an enormous balance against the state farms. The principal reason for this discrepancy is the fact that our state grain farms are too unwieldy; the directors cannot manage such huge farms. The farms are also too specialized; they have no rotation of crops and fallow land; they do not engage in live-stock-breeding. Evidently, it will be necessary to split up the state farms and make them less specialized. One might think that it was the People's Commissariat of State Farms that raised this question opportunely and succeeded in solving it. But that is not so.[12]

Disenchantment had set in. The state farms were subdivided into smaller units, and a degree of diversification was introduced. After 1935, over a million hectares of crop land were transferred to neighbouring collective farms. Other sources mention that one-fourth of agricultural land was turned over to the collective farms. Table 1 demonstrates the trend.

In terms of gross production, the state farms accounted for 10.6 per cent of total agricultural output in 1932. During the record harvest

Table 1

Development of the State Farm System: 1928—1938

	1928	1932	1938
Number of State Farms	1,400	4,337	3,961
Sown Area (Hectares)	1,700,000	13,400,000	12,400,000
Number of Tractors	6,700	64,000	85,000
State Procurements of Grain (Per Cent)	9	8	9

SOURCES: *Planovoye khozyaystvo*, No. 11, 1939, p. 100; A. Baykov, *Soviet Economic System*, Cambridge, Massachusetts, 1950, p. 333.

---

[12] J. Stalin, *Voprosy Leninizma, op. cit.*, pp. 614–615.

year of 1937, this proportion dropped to 9.3 per cent.[13] On the eve of the war, in 1940, when annexation of the western area of Poland and the Baltic republics led to an increase in the number of state farms, the share of state procurements from the state farms was 10 per cent for grain, 16 per cent for cattle, and 16 per cent for milk.[14] Thus, after a decade of state farm construction, collective farms and private plots still constituted the overwhelming source of food and fibre supplies in the Soviet Union. It cannot be denied that the state farms were a minor source of national income, but a 10 per cent increment to gross output is still a decisive factor in an economy, regardless of questions of the rationality of the resources allocated. Some specialized farms located near active markets did become productive and profitable, but the system as a bloc was unproductive, had to be subsidized by the state, and lent itself to relegation to a subordinate position in the economy. The state farm system was, nevertheless, essential for the stabilization of socialism in the countryside, and no functional or structural changes were made in its organization. In spite of its disappointing performance, in other words, the state farm system remained an indispensable political weapon.

The Great Upsurge. During the war, all agriculture suffered severe losses in occupied areas. N. Vosnesensky reports that 1,800 state farms were destroyed, most of their machinery lost or transferred, and the livestock herd of the whole system reduced by 60 per cent. In the postwar period of reconstruction, state farms, unlike the Machine and Tractor Stations (MTS), were not unduly favoured in respect of allocations of machinery. Important innovations in policy were, however, advanced. The 1947 Party Plenum called for greater diversification in production. To attract and keep workers on the farms, the allowable area of land for private plots was increased from 0.15 to 0.50 hectares. Bank credits were granted to farm workers and officials for construction of private homes. The big agrarian issues of the day largely passed the state farms by: amalgamation of the collective farms, measures to restrict violations of the kolkhoz charter. Even the brigade-*zveno* debate was more concerned with the less mechanized artels. Over the issue of the agrogorod, too, Khrushchev proposed the complete reconstruction of small, backward villages to transform them into modern, urban-like settlements. The aim of this was said to be elimination of the technical and cultural discrepancy between the city and the countryside. Khrushchev did not choose to

---

[13] *Sotsialisticheskoye selskoye khozyaystvo SSSR* (The Socialist Agriculture of the USSR), Moscow, 1939, p. 87, as quoted by Jasny.

[14] *Selskoye khozyaystvo SSSR* (Agriculture in the USSR), Moscow, 1960, p. 48.

uphold the state farm as an example, but in reality most of the state farms had been built from the ground up with the idea of creating large, well-appointed settlements with their own cultural and social services. As part of the agitation in rural areas during the thirties, the image of the state farm as a model to emulate in the drive to eradicate the technical and cultural gap between town and country was vigorously propagandized. Nevertheless, by 1951, disenchantment with the state farm as a model for abundant production was widespread among the peasantry, and Khrushchev wisely avoided insisting upon it.

The third and most powerful drive to increase the number of state farms began at the September 1953 Party Plenum when Khrushchev exposed the backwardness of Soviet agriculture. By the end of the Stalin era, industrial output had increased two and a half times, while gross agricultural production had risen only 10 per cent. Moreover, a disastrous situation existed in respect of livestock products, potatoes, and vegetables. Apart from hogs, numbers of livestock in 1953 were below the levels of 1928. This applied to crop yields as well. What really carried the economy, as during the war, was the astonishing performance of the private sector. In 1953, with little more than 3 per cent of the land, the private sector yielded nearly two-thirds of the total output of milk and potatoes, almost one-half of the total output of meat, vegetables, and fruit, and 90 per cent of the total output of eggs.[15] These are precisely the high-value, protective foods needed by a modern industrial society. In grain production, still the primary area, the share of state farm grain seedings in relation to sown area fell from 69 per cent in 1940 to 51 per cent in 1953. In the realm of procurement, in 1953 the state farms scarcely surpassed the share of deliveries they made to the state in 1940: of total procurements, they provided 12 per cent of the grain, 18 per cent of the livestock, and 17 per cent of the milk.[16]

The principal trend of Party decisions in agriculture in 1953–54 was towards immediate and massive expansion of the grain area by bringing under plow the virgin lands of Kazakhstan, Western Siberia, and the Urals. The thinking was that the shift of wheat-growing activities to the eastern lands would release crop land in the older farm areas for feed grain and fodder production as well as for technical crops. The stagnant livestock sector would benefit from enhanced feed stocks as well as from reduced procurement quotas of grain. Given the speed of the undertaking and the routine nature of grain-growing activities, the state farm system was the

[15] *Ibid.*, pp. 225, 240–243.
[16] *Ibid.*, pp. 47, 48.

logical and most effective organization to activate the crash programme. During the first half of 1954 alone, 124 new state farms with nearly 3 million hectares of crop land were established in the new lands; by the end of 1955, they totalled 425, averaging 25,000 to 30,000 hectares of arable land in Siberia and Kazakhstan. At the Twenty-first Party Congress in February 1956, Khrushchev reported that 581 new state farms had been established over the preceding two years.[17] The programme of expansion was followed by a sharp rise in the output of state farms, particularly in 1956, when there was a bumper harvest. The development of the state farm system in these years is traced in Table 2.

Table 2

Development of the State Farm System: 1953—1956

	1953	1955	1956
State Farms (Absolute Number)	4,857	5,134	5,098
Sown Area (Hectares)	15,500,000	25,800,000	31,500,000
Grain Area (Hectares)	7,800,000	17,800,000	22,300,000
Grain Deliveries (Tons)	3,700,000	5,100,000	15,300,000
Share of Total Deliveries (Percentage):			
Grain	12	18	28
Livestock	18	—	15
Milk	17	—	16

SOURCES: *Selskoye Khozyaystvo SSSR* (Agriculture in the USSR), Moscow. 1960, p. 47, 48; *Narodnoe khozyaystvo SSSR v 1956 godu* (The Economy of the USSR in 1956), Moscow, 1957, p. 135.

By 1956, the area of sown land had doubled; by the same date, the area of land sown to grain had almost trebled. The amount of grain delivered to the state was four times as large as that in 1953. The state farms now accounted for 28 per cent of grain procurements. The new land programme was obviously responsible for this growth.

About this time the sovkhoz-kolkhoz controversy arose. The amalgamation drive had reduced the number of cooperative farms from 254,000 in 1950 to 97,000 in 1952 and 76,535 in 1957. The problem of weak and backward artels nevertheless remained, and their conversion or transformation into state farms was advocated. The Minister of State Farms, Ivan Benediktov, was the spokesman for a persuasive group of Party hardliners who argued that the collective farms customarily delivered less grain per hectare to the state than the state farms and at a higher price: in Kazakhstan, the state farms sold an average of 52 poods of grain per hectare to the state; the artels, 36 poods, including payment in kind. The

---

[17] *Pravda*, February 15, 1956.

costs of the collective farms were said to be double those of the state farms. Though the artels furnished almost 50 per cent of the grain procurements in Kazakhstan in 1956, Benediktov argued that land "only formally" attached to them should be transferred to the state farms.[18] The number of state farms in Kazakhstan had increased from 628 in 1956 to 1,119 in 1961, while the number of collective farms had fallen from 2,611 to 655 in the same period. In the RSFSR, up to 1957, 693 state farms had benefited from acquisitions of collective farm land and equipment. There is considerable variation in available figures, because they do not always take into account instances in which two or more state farms had merged into one large farm or in which auxiliary farms had been similarly absorbed. Benediktov illustrated the pattern of incomplete reckoning, listing 656 new farms for the period 1951–1955, a time in which 515 small state farms were combined into larger units.[19]

The rate of transformation into state farms was stepped up during 1958–1960 with the plan to establish clusters of specialized farms in suburban areas to supply industrial centres with vegetables, potatoes, and milk. Over 600 specialized farms for growing potatoes and vegetables were set up at this time: 330 in the RSFSR, 182 in the Ukraine, 14 in Belorussia, and 22 in Kazakhstan.[20] This figure probably includes some existing state farms as well as some auxiliary units of state farms, but a good share of the total number of state farms must have been new or transformed enterprises, since the growth of state farms showed an increment of 494 farms for the period.

The decline in the number of collective farms and the increase in the number of state farms were thus brought about in two ways: (1) by internal amalgamation of the artels, and (2) by external absorption into state farms. In the process, the political climate, of course, changed. In 1957, Benediktov remarked: "Some time ago hostile attempts were made to dislodge the state farm system, allegedly because the state farms did not bring in any profits."[21] In 1963, Khrushchev was to disclose that the losses of the newly created farms reached more than 600 million rubles a year, and that some farms produced even less than when they were collective enterprises.[22]

[18] *Kommunist*, No. 18, 1956, p. 80.
[19] *Planovoye khozyaystvo*, No. 1, 1957, p. 32.
[20] *Ekonomika selskogo khozyaystva*, No. 1, 1960, p. 2.
[21] *Radio Moscow Home Service*, January 26, 1957.
[22] *Stroitelstvo kommunizma v SSSR i razvitiye selskogo khozyaystva* (The Construction of Communism in the USSR and the Development of Agriculture), Moscow, Vol. 8, pp. 62–87.

A tranquilizing gesture was made in respect of the sovkhoz-kholkhoz issue, however. Following the sale of the MTS machinery to the collective farms, and in reply to the arguments of some economists and literary personages who supported the collectives as "more democratic institutions," it was said that now in possession of the basic tools of production—that is, machinery—the collective farms were approaching a kind of coexistence with the state farms in the transition to communism and the liquidation of differences between town and country. The Party Programme

Table 3

The Rise of the State Farms

1959	1960	1961	1962	1963	1964	1965
NUMBER OF STATE FARMS						
6,000	7,400	8,300	8,600	9,200	10,100	11,600
NUMBER OF COLLECTIVE FARMS						
53,400	44,000	40,600	39,700	38,800	37,600	36,300
COLLECTIVE FARM CROP LAND (Millions of Hectares)						
130	123	111	111	114	111	—
STATE FARM CROP LAND (Millions of Hectares)						
54	67	80	87	90	87	—
SHARE OF CROP LAND HELD BY STATE FARMS (Percentages)						
30	35	42	44	44	44	—
SHARE OF GRAIN DELIVERIES FROM STATE FARMS (Percentages)						
39	38	43[1]	45	41	53	38
VEGETABLE DELIVERIES						
29	47	—	49	56	57	57
MEAT DELIVERIES						
27	32	—	39	39	42	45
MILK DELIVERIES						
23	32	—	36	38	40	41

[1] Since 1961, deliveries of auxiliary farms are included in the total for state farms. For grain, they are minute; for livestock and vegetables, they represent 5 to 7 per cent of total deliveries from state farms.

SOURCES: *Narodnoe khozyaystvo SSSR v 1960* (The Economy of the USSR in 1960), Moscow, 1961; *Narodnoe khozyaystvo SSSR v 1961*, Moscow, 1962; *Narodnoe khozyaystvo SSSR v 1962*, Moscow, 1963; *Narodnoe khozyaystvo SSSR v 1963*, Moscow, 1964; *Narodnoe khozyaystvo SSSR v 1964*, Moscow, 1965; *Selskoye khozyaystvo SSSR* (Agriculture in the USSR), Moscow, 1965; *Radio Moscow Home Service*, January 30, 1966.

adopted by the Twenty-second Party Congress in 1961 was specific in this regard: "The further advance of the countryside to communism will proceed through the development and improvement of the two forms of socialist farming—the collective and state farms." Nonetheless, in quantitative terms, a persistent trend in favour of the state farms is evident (see Table 3).

There has been an uninterrupted increase in the number of state farms and a corresponding decline in the number of collective farms since the drive to expand the state farm system began. At present, the ratio between the number of state and collective farms is one to three. The share of socialized crop land farmed by state farms has stabilized at the level of 44 per cent. This may appear to be an excessive share, but the state farms concentrate heavily on grain-growing, and the spatial dimensions of the grain farms are more apparent. Nonetheless, the total area of crop land farmed by the collectives has declined by 15 per cent since 1958. Moreover, in marketability of grain, the state farms have continued to make solid progress. Sales of grain to the state reached 53 per cent of the total marketed in 1964 but dropped to 38 per cent in the poor harvest year of 1965. In deliveries of vegetables, a sector in which suburban specialized state farms have concentrated since 1958, the share of marketable output reached 57 per cent of the total in 1964, surpassing the collective farms. However, vegetable production is the domain of the private sector, and state farm marketings represent little more than one-fifth of total vegetables harvested. The influence of suburban specialty farms is likewise felt in meat and milk deliveries, which reached, respectively, 45 and 41 per cent of deliveries to the state in 1964. Growth in the number of suburban state farms probably accounts for the progress in marketability of their products. This growth is shown in Table 4.

Table 4

Number of State Farms by Types of Production

	1958	1962	1965
Milk and Meat Farms	1,739	3,170	3,735
Vegetable, Fruit, and Potato Farms	816	1,222	1,548
Grain Farms	1,036	1,135	1,229
Sheep Farms	610	722	987
Swine Farms	622	573	581
Poultry Farms	202	443	613

SOURCE: *Narodnoe khozyaystvo SSSR v 1964 godu* (The Economy of the USSR in 1964), Moscow, 1965, p. 408.

It is significant that historically the state farms have dealt with the low-price products: grain and livestock. This circumstance has in part contributed to their chronic losses. The more profitable commodities, including cotton, sugar beets, sunflowers, and related technical crops, have customarily been grown on a smaller scale on the state farms, perhaps because the high labour demands that production of such crops entails make them better suited to the collective farms, which have a more abundant labour supply. In the new price lists, however, the prices for the specialty crops of state farms have been made considerably more firm, and the gap between prices paid by the state to the collective farms and the state farms for the same commodity has been narrowed.

In the dreary log of failures of the Khrushchev Seven-Year Plan, one planned goal was realized: targets of the state farms for deliveries to the state (see Table 5).

Table 5

Deliveries of the State Farms under the Seven-Year Plan

(Percentage of Total Deliveries)

	Plan	Actual
Grain	40	38
Meat	32	45
Milk.............	26	41
Wool	33	42

As the highest form of socialist organization of agriculture, the state farm system has been heavily favoured with capital investments, allocations of machinery and fertilizer, and technical innovations. This treatment contrasts with that accorded to the collective farm system. Despite preferential treatment, however, there has been a prevalent trend on the state farms towards excessive production costs resulting in recurrent deficits. Balancing chronic deficits requires sustained financial subsidies from the state year after year. The Party has been acutely conscious of this fiscal problem, but while openly admitting the running deficits, has released only incomplete supporting data on the subject. Stalin complained of the losses in general terms. Benediktov revealed that until the record harvest in 1956, the natural balance sheet for the farms had always been in the red.[23] Even in that year, he maintained, many farms stood to run deficits. At the 1958 and 1959 Party Plenums several speakers pointed to the losses as obstacles to farm progress. The most inclusive figures reported were for the year 1960, when, it was said, two-thirds of the 7,375 state farms oper-

[23] *Planovoye khozyaystvo*, No. 1, 1959, p. 35.

ated with "huge losses."[24] In the Ukraine, during the good harvest year of 1961, 41 per cent of the farms were unprofitable. It was thought, moreover, that operating losses would be at the same level in 1962.[25] *Izvestia* reported that nearly 70 per cent of the farms in the USSR incurred losses during 1963, a crisis harvest year to be true.[26] Low prices and incompetent leadership were blamed for the situation.

Two innovations of the Brezhnev-Kosygin leadership are directed at raising the profitability of the state farms: price increases for farm products, with stabilization of deliveries, and introduction of a new system of management for the state farm system. Following the September 1965 Plenum on industrial management, an experiment among a number of state farms was carried out to test a new system of management.[27] The main feature of this experiment is increased autonomy for farm management in the operation and planning of production under a scheme of full cost accounting. This implies maximizing profits, raising labour productivity, and offering a choice of commodities for production where supply and demand forces are favourable. The economic organization of each farm is to be the prerogative of the management. A state farm council chosen from specialists and workers will have the authority to make all decisions for the farm. The director will be the main organizer of production. The price schedule for commodities sold to the state will be comparable to that of collective farms in the same region. Transport of products from the farm will be the responsibility of the trade organization. The concept of a state farm council engaged in resolving major issues of farm management with the aid of cost accounting is a bold departure from the forty-year-old Stalinist pattern of one-man rule. In the 1958–1959 kolkhoz-sovkhoz controversy, the Minister of Agriculture described collective farm management as "more democratic" than state farm management.[28] The ode to the more democratic aspect of collective farm management became a recurrent theme in the last years of Khrushchev's rule.

One final trend in the development of the state farm system has been that while the number of farms has increased, the composition of the farms has moved in the opposite direction (see Table 6). What is striking is that sown area has declined on the average farm by 2,100 hectares, a 23 per cent decrease from 1963. In other words, the average size of the state farm is back to the 1956 level. This trend was no doubt

---

[24] *Ibid.*
[25] *Finantsy SSSR*, No. 3, 1961, p. 29.
[26] *Pravda Ukrainy*, December 7, 1962.
[27] *Izvestia*, November 25, 1964.
[28] *Pravda Ukrainy*, November 17, 1965.

Table 6

Composition of the State Farms

	1958	1963	1964	1965
Number of State Farms	6,002	9,176	10,078	11,642
Average Number of Workers per State Farm..	639	775	721	657
Average Sown Area per State Farm (Hectares)	8,700	9,800	8,600	7,700
Average Number of Cattle per State Farm....	1,370	2,356	2,201	2,098
Average Number of Hogs per State Farm	1,355	827	1,144	1,073

SOURCE: *SSSR v tsifrakh v 1965 godu* (The USSR in Figures in 1965), Moscow, 1966, p. 93.

prompted by the need to subdivide some "gigantic" farms in grain-growing and livestock-grazing areas. This process of splitting up the larger farms was accomplished without fanfare in the press, although the issue had been discussed publicly as part of the problem of rationalization of management. With the decline in the number of collective farms about equal to the increase in the number of state farms during the last two years, the impression that decollectivization is occurring seems misplaced. Nevertheless, the problem of organizing both the state and collective farms as operational units more manageable in size remains a decisive issue.

An Appraisal

The development of the Soviet state farm system is now midstream in the currents of an ebb-and-flow agricultural economy, and general conclusions are in order. The state farms now supply from 40 to 50 per cent of state purchases of some important commodities, whereas a quarter of a century ago the share was 10 to 15 per cent. The primary function of the farms has been to assure high marketability of foodstuffs for the urban population, and to that extent they have been successful. A high level of marketability on a low output base was, however, no assurance of an abundance of urban food supplies. Thus, for a long time, the heavy burden of supplying the urban centres was carried by the collective farms and in some commodities by the private sector.

As sources for high yields of agricultural produce, the state farms have failed to live up to their expectations. Apart from the more stable grain areas in southern Russia, where winter wheat has reached fairly consistent, high yields, the performance has been far below what was anticipated. In eastern Russia, the heartland of Soviet cereal output, where spring wheat is grown, yields are one-half those obtained in comparable parts of Canada and the United States. Average corn yields (for grain) are vastly below those of the United States; even yields of grain for fodder lag behind. The one crop with superior yields is cotton, but this is only a minor crop for the state farms. The same is true of sugar beets and sunflowers, which are primarily collective farm crops. In line with low cropping achievements, the record for the livestock industry has been even more discouraging. Despite excessive labour inputs and year-round feeding, milk yields have been only half or two-thirds those of countries in the West; likewise, meat production has required considerably greater feed inputs per unit of output than in the West.

Though yields have been low, the nemesis of development of the state farm system has been exorbitant production costs. The situation has not improved since Stalin charged the farms with unprofitability and heavy indebtedness to the state. Profitability and cost accounting were to be the twin criteria distinguishing the state farms, directives of the Commissariat of State Farms read. Jasny, in his definitive study on costs, concluded that the state farms had higher production costs than collective farms, and that the state farms were the most expensive producers of farm products in the world. Soviet data published in 1964 in *Narodnoe khozyaystvo SSSR* substantiate the first statement.[29]

The state farms did provide a spearhead for penetration into the countryside and socialization of agriculture, but they were more of an administrative fortress than an effective model for demonstrating the benefits of large-scale farming to the peasantry. It is doutful that the role of the state farms had any effect on collectivization; if so, collectivization would have proceeded at a slower pace. In any case, from 1929-1933, when collectivization engulfed the peasantry, the state farms were in no shape to exemplify the superiority of the system. Collectivization was forced on the peasantry by the state mobilizing every power and persuasive resource at its command. In fact, had the state farm been the model in the early period, it is entirely likely that the nature and form of the collective farm system, as well as the results of it, would have been quite different.

Any institutional organization of agriculture, particularly one forty years in construction, ought to have contributed some innovations to world agriculture. With a single exception, one searches in vain for a solid achievement in the history of the state farms. There has been no revolutionary development such as hybrid corn. There have been no advanced seed or livestock varieties. There have been no contributions to soil improvement. And there have been no surprises in the way of new machinery or equipment. The only major contribution of the state farms to agrobiological technology in the half decade of their existence has been adapta-

---

[29] A. Matskevich, *Pravda*, December 26, 1959.

tion of artificial insemination on a wide scale among certain types of live-stock. This adaptation of an old technique occurred on the state farms in the early thirties, and was soon taken up in the West and greatly improved upon. The Soviet Union was, however, the pioneer in mass adaptation of the technique on the farms.

Some observers look towards a gradual equalization of the collective and state farms. Since their inception, the collective farms have been a more effective supplier of foodstuffs to the state than the state farms: the artel assumed all risks in the enterprise, the cooperative peasants were residual claimants to the farm income after all delivery quotas to the state were met, the multiple price system was advantageous to the state, and no state subsidies were required. As the Germans discovered during the war, the collective farms were efficient organs for gathering produce from the peasantry. In production functions the collective farms were also superior: per unit of output they used less inputs from state resources than the state farms. Even the costs of commodity production, it is now officially ad-mitted, were less than on the state farms. Moreover, in the national ac-counts, the collective farms were net exporters of capital. If returns of the turnover tax on farm products are also considered, the collective farms have been decidedly superior to the state farms as sources of capital accumulation.

The advantages of the collective farms for the state will now be altered, since guaranteed wages have been introduced for collective farmers on the same level as state farmers doing similar work in the same region. In addition, the recently granted pension rights for collective farmers will contribute to costs. The immediate trend will likely show the collective farms becoming as high cost producers as the state farms unless a significant increase in labour productivity can be brought about. Both systems have been moving towards a common type of payment, guaranteed wages, which are a modified residual. This development is perhaps the most novel innovation in the recent reforms and will have an equalizing effect on both forms of agricultural institutions.

The pressing doubt that a form of equilibrium has been reached by the conversion of collective into state farms has already been indicated despite the protestations of the new Kremlin leadership. The apparent, continued transformation is counter to agro-economic science, which suggests that a subdivision of the unwieldy collective and state farms is the most rational process in management. Momentous decisions must be made: Will collective farm unions and their higher structure, the Kolkhoz Centre, ultimately give the farms the right to bargain with the central authorities over price and delivery schedules? Will the state farms participate in the bargaining? Or will the state farms form a union of their own, as a counterweight, or as a step towards ultimate amalgamation?

The impact of the mechanized team system, as the basic form of labour organization on the farms, with its stewardship over specific areas of land for a long time, portends a revolutionary approach to farm management and promises to be a positive lever in increasing labour productivity. The state farms will surely be given the same option if the charter grants the collective farms the right to organize the mechanized team system. The experiment of the sovkhoz councils, as part of the management reforms, offers possibilities for approaching the collective farms through "a more democratic form of farm management."

On balance, the state farm system, while showing positive development in the past decade, is not a model of a productive form of agricultural institution, either in terms of high yields or profitability, and ought not to be emulated by the underdeveloped nations. The promise—after nearly five decades—still looms larger than the performance. Unless far-reaching changes in the structure of the state farms are instituted, unless a sharp rise in labour productivity is achieved, unless large labour movements out of agriculture are effected, all backed by a sustained rate of investment, the Soviet Union will doubtless find it necessary to follow the path of many Western nations in subsidizing agriculture. There will be one distinguishing feature, however. The scale of the Soviet subsidies will of course relate to the larger size of Soviet farms.

Soviet Agriculture: A Balance Sheet

Jerzy F. Karcz

This is a most opportune time to review the performance of Soviet agriculture for reasons other than the proclaimed occasion of the fiftieth anniversary of the revolution. The research efforts of many Western and Soviet scholars have by now supplied values for many of the unknowns that have stubbornly resisted discovery and obscured the way for earlier analysis. It will be understood that a summary such as this necessarily reflects the work of others and that an attempt to assess the achievements of Soviet agriculture over a period of fifty years necessarily relies on historical as well as statistical analysis.[1] For obvious reasons, comparisons with pre-revolutionary performance ought to relate to the period 1909–1913 or to the year 1913 if the necessary data for the preceding five-year average are lacking. Indeed, many comparisons with performance in 1913 are made in Soviet specialized and general literature. Unfortunately, their meaning is beclouded by certain remaining deficiencies in underlying Soviet data.

The first problem to arise is that of volume of output in 1913, not only of Soviet agriculture as a whole but also of principal individual products, not only in terms of the current territory of the Soviet Union but also in terms of that of 1939. The history of Soviet attempts to estimate the volume of relevant output (hence, also of yields) is both instructive and revealing.[2] At least four such efforts have been made. Results were published in 1924–1925, 1926, 1937–1938, and 1959. For meat and milk, estimates of production in 1913 currently used by the Central Statistical Administration are higher than those made in 1924–1925, and 1926. The estimates for milk are, however, lower than those given in 1939. In fact, for most crops, successive estimates have been lower than their predecessors.[3] In the case of meat, the difference

---

[1] In particular, the work of Nancy Nimitz, Abraham Becker, Abram Bergson, Naum Jasny, and Alec Nove should be mentioned. On the Soviet side, the work of Arutyunyan, Vyltsan, and Malafeyev has resulted in publication of data that are invaluable for an understanding of agricultural developments.

[2] Arcadius Kahan in *Soviet Agricultural and Peasant Affairs*, edited by Roy D. Laird, Lawrence, Kansas, University of Kansas Press, 1963, pp. 137–138.

[3] For grain, the latest official revision has been explained by Yu. A. Moshkov in *Zernovaya problema v gody sploshnoy kollektivizatsii selskogo khozyaystva SSSR: 1929–1932 gg.* (The Grain Problem in the Years of the Complete Collectivization of Agriculture in the USSR: 1929–1932), Moscow, 1966, p. 20. Peasant, rather than estate, yields are now applied to areas rented by peasants from landlords.

may be due to exclusion of some components of output—as presently calculated—from earlier, pre-1928 estimates. Also, it is uncertain whether present estimates for 1913 include a reasonable valuation of output of edible sub-products, which, today, are included in production figures.

Manipulation of statistical data is, of course, objectionable on principle, even if the wisdom of such proceedings were not otherwise open to question. In the present instance, the issue has become so confused that any adjustment of current official data on the volume of output in 1913 is necessarily arbitrary. Since exactness is simply not to be achieved, adjustments made here are quite crude. For yields, this study adopts the expedient of using the data of Imperial Russia for 1913. Adjustment of the index of gross output is then made by increasing the value of the base year (1913) or of the base period (1909–1913) by 15 per cent.[4] This increase represents the relative difference between the area sown in 1913 on pre-war territory and that sown in the same year on the territory the Soviet Union now occupies. Neither adjustment is likely to have an appreciable effect on calculations, and the second correction may well err on the conservative side.

Use of official data on output or yield of grains and sunflower seed in the period 1958–1965 (hence, also, use of the official index of gross output for these years) raises another problem. Western analysts generally agree that Soviet data on production of grains and sunflower seed overstate the size of so-called barn yields or outputs and that this exaggeration is in part the result of a change in statistical reporting procedures introduced at the time of the 1958 harvest. An implicit admission of this has recently been made by the Central Statistical Administration.[5] For overall production of grains, a reduction of 10 to 15 per cent would appear to be in order, depending upon harvest conditions in given a year. Nevertheless, it is not clear to what extent yields or outputs of individual grains ought to be adjusted, even though it is known that a larger correction is in order for wheat than for any other grain. As a consequence of these considerations, no explicit adjustments of official data on yields or outputs of grains or sunflower seed are made in this study, and the reader is asked to bear in mind

---

[4] Actually, the value of output in most areas annexed in 1939–1940 is considerably higher than in the USSR on the average, excluding the Kazakh SSR. Cf. *Narodnoe khozyaystvo SSSR v 1964 g.* (The Economy of the USSR in 1964), Moscow, 1965, p. 248, for value of output, and pp. 270–271, for sown areas. This source is subsequently referred to as *Narkhoz*, with mention of the year of the expanded title.

[5] Cf. *Narkhoz-1964*, p. 298, 316.

the general caveat that details are to be found in the sizeable literature on the subject.[6]

Finally, there is the awkward problem, only partly related to the one just discussed, of reasonable trends in the official Soviet index of gross agricultural output for the years 1958–1965. A number of factors, including admitted deficiencies in reporting practices in 1959–1960 and again in the years 1962–1964, cast considerable doubt on the reliability of the index for the period of the Seven-Year Plan. This writer has already expressed some reservations on this score in another context, and nothing has happened to dispel them.[7] Still, the official Soviet index is the only one that covers the entire period under consideration in this study. Random calculations demonstrate that productivity indices would not be significantly affected by substituting the United States Department of Agriculture (USDA) index of net output for the official Soviet index of gross output. Though this would not be the case for trends in total or per capita output under the Seven-Year Plan, consistency and simplicity suggest using the official index. At the same time, alternative calculations are shown. So much for the statistical skeletons in the closet.

During the summer and fall of 1966, an outside observer of developments in Soviet agriculture might have pointed to a variety of topics calling for special attention. If he were at all familiar with the subject earlier, one of his first reactions would doubtless have been to the pervasive atmosphere of change. There were changes in cropping patterns, in farming and planning practices, and in the general attitude of Party officials. Some long-standing policies had already been reversed; others, including many deep-rooted practices, were evidently undergoing reexamination. The very foundations of the Soviet procurement system—a keystone of the official Soviet approach to agriculture since 1932—were being eroded by discussions in learned journals and specialized newspapers. Indeed, a mythical observer would have been wholly justified in referring to a general atmosphere of ferment and potential renewal.[8]

----

[6] For example, see the paper by Harry E. Walters and Richard N. Judy in *Soviet and East European Agriculture*, edited by J. F. Karcz, Berkeley, California, University of California Press, 1967.

[7] J. F. Karcz, "Seven Years on the Farm: Retrospect and Prospects," in U.S. Congress, Joint Economic Committee, *New Directions in the Soviet Economy*, Washington, D. C., Government Printing Office, 1966, p. 387.

[8] The discussion of structural changes in Soviet agriculture has by now subsided from the peak levels reached in the aftermath of the March 1965 Plenum and under the impact of the bumper crop of 1966: less is now heard of organizational innovation. Still, I believe the underlying issues will again come to the fore in the near future.

Rudolf Bicanic reminds us that "general phenomena must have a common cause."[9] The common cause of the ferment in Soviet agriculture in the fall of 1966 was the persistent failure of the system to live up to the expectations of Soviet policy-makers. A bird's-eye view of the performance of Soviet agriculture since 1913 may be gained from the data on crop yields and productivity of livestock herds in Table 1. Bearing in mind the special limitations of these data, the synthetic picture created by the table reveals to a large extent the unsatisfactory nature of the performance and explains much of the present concern.

Table 1 fails to support the claim that the methods used until now in Soviet agriculture are inherently superior. The data indicate a certain deterioration over the years in yields of wheat, oats, rye, barley, and sugar beets, and in productivity of hog herds. The improvement in yields of potatoes is small; it would be somewhat greater if comparisons were made with the period 1909–1913. Somewhat more of an improvement is indicated in yields of sunflowers and productivity of cattle herds. For purposes of comparison, Table 1 includes data on average yields and productivity in Eastern Europe and Europe as a whole for the period 1960–1964.[10] These figures clearly define the size of the gap between the Soviet Union and Eastern Europe in respect of productivity of land and of animal herds. Except for sunflowers and rye (a crop of the past), Soviet yields officially cited range from 49 to 66 per cent of average East European yields. Productivity of cattle herds in the period 1960–1964 was lower than that of any other country in Eastern Europe with the single exception of Yugoslavia.[11] In the same period, productivity of hog herds was lower than that of Bulgaria, Czechoslovakia, and Poland, and productivity of Soviet dairy herds lower than the average for Eastern Europe.[12] In general, production figures for many of the East European countries, including Bulgaria, demonstrate a steady improvement in agricultural performance over the past few years, but statistical trends for the USSR since 1958 demonstrate a significant decline.

Though in part revealing, the indicators in Table 1 in the main reflect the interrelationships of many complex factors and tell nothing of the causes of a rather unspectacular performance. An attempt to employ standard economic analysis in tracing trends in outputs, inputs, and various related

---

[9] *Foreign Affairs*, New York, Council on Foreign Affairs, July, 1966 (quoted from the author's manuscript).

[10] Eastern Europe, as defined here, includes Bulgaria, Czechoslovakia, East Germany, Hungary, Poland, Rumania, and Yugoslavia.

[11] Yugoslavia, though, exported sizeable numbers of live animals.

[12] Hungary also exported sizeable numbers of live pigs.

Table 1

Crop Yields and Productivity of Livestock Herds in Russia, the Soviet Union, Europe, 1913, 1960–1964

YIELDS

(Quintals per Hectare, Calculated from Data on Areas and Outputs)

	1913 Official Data	1913 Imperial Russia	1960—1964[1] USSR	1960—1964[2] Eastern Europe	1960—1964 Europe
Wheat[3]	9.0	9.8	10.1	17.5	19.4
Rye	8.0	10.2	10.4	11.2	17.5
Barley[4]	9.0	10.2	11.6	20.6	25.4
Oats	8.9	10.9	8.3	16.8	19.5
Potatoes	76.0[5]	88.0	92.0	140.0	160.0
Sugar Beets	168.0[6]	—	164.0	246.0	306.0
Sunflowers	7.6	—	10.8	11.8	10.7

MEAT PER 100 ANIMALS

(Tons per 100 Animals in Herds at Census Dates Not Identical for Different Countries)

	1913 Official Data	1913 Imperial Russia	1960—1964 USSR	1960—1964 Eastern Europe	1960—1964 Europe
Beef[7]	3.0	—	4.1	3.4—7.1[8]	4.6— 8.1[9]
Pork[10]	7.1	—	6.2	4.8—9.3[11]	6.8—13.5[12]

MILK

(Kilogrammes per Cow)

	1913 Official Data	1913 Imperial Russia	1960—1964 USSR	1960—1964 Eastern Europe	1960—1964 Europe
Milk............	—	—	1,672[13]	1,871	1,015—4,182[14]

[1] As noted in the text, Soviet yields of grains and sunflowers are now officially defined as "weight originally determined by farms" or so-called "bunker weight."

[2] Eastern Europe, as defined here, includes Bulgaria, Czechoslovakia, East Germany, Hungary, Poland, Rumania, and Yugoslavia. Data for Europe include, in addition, Austria, Albania, Denmark, Finland, France, Germany (Federal Republic,) Greece, Ireland, Italy, Luxemburg, Malta, Netherlands, Norway, Portugal, Spain, Sweden, Switzerland, and the United Kingdom.

[3] The underlying data for Bulgaria, Czechoslovakia, and Yugoslavia include spelt.

[4] All barley in 1913 for Imperial Russia.

[5] The official yield in 1909—1913 was 78 quintals per hectare.

[6] The official yield in 1909—1913 was 150 quintals per hectare.

[7] Calculated from data on herds as of January 1, 1914. Beef output is assumed to have been 1,900,000 tons.

[8] Yugoslavia—Hungary.

[9] Spain—France.

[10] Herd data as of January 1, 1914. Pork output is assumed to have been 1,800,000 tons.

[11] Hungary—Poland.

[12] Italy—France.

[13] Figure for 1961—1964.

[14] Italy—Holland.

SOURCES: Data for Imperial Russia are from I. V. Chernyshev, *Selskoe khozyaystvo dovoennoy Rossii i SSSR* (Agriculture in Pre-War Russia and the USSR), Moscow, 1926, pp. 82—84. Official data on 1913 yields are from *Selskoe khozyaystvo SSSR* (Agriculture in the USSR), Moscow, 1960, pp. 208—209. Other data are from the Food and Agricultural Organization of the United Nations, *Production Yearbook 1963*, Rome, FAO, 1964, pp. 37, 39, 41, 43, 72, 76, 128, 222, and *Production Yearbook 1965*, Rome, FAO, 1966, pp. 39, 41, 45, 74, 78, 135, 234.

factors on pre-war territory is made in Table 2, using the period 1909–1913 as a base. A few comments on the selection of bench-mark years for Table 2 are in order. Since no population data are available for the period 1909–1913, the selection of 1913 as a base year for calculating per capita data is self-explanatory. Special interest attaches to trends in 1928 and 1939, as they represent, respectively, performance in the last complete year of non-collectivized peasant agriculture and performance in the last complete year of uninterrupted agricultural activity on pre-war territory. As it happens, trends in output for 1928 and 1939 correspond very closely to

Table 2

Selected Performance Indicators, Soviet Agriculture, Pre-War Territory

	1909—1913 Average	1913	1928	1939	1936—1939 Average
Gross Output (Official)	93	100	124	121	121
Gross Output (Adjusted)	93	100	108	105	105
Per Capita Gross Output (Official) ...	—	100	115	99	102
Per Capita Gross Output (Adjusted) ..	—	100	100	86	88
Farm Marketings (Per Urban Head) ..	—	100	96	78[1]	78[2]
Food Marketings (Per Urban Head) ..	—	100	93	74[1]	74[2]
Sown Area	—	93	100	118	119
Capital Stock (Total)	—	—	100	100[3]	96[3]
Capital Stock (Excluding Livestock) ..	—	—	100	200[3]	—
Labour Input (Man-Days)	—	—	100	100	104
Output Index (Official)	—	—	100	98	98
Input Index (Weights I)	—	—	100	96	93
Input Index (Weights II)	—	—	100	93	92
Joint Productivity Index (Weights I) ..	—	—	100	96	93
Joint Productivity Index (Weights II)..	—	—	100	93	92

[1] The figure shown here is the 1938–1940 average, which is higher than the figure for 1939.
[2] The figure shown here is the 1936–1940 average, which is higher than the figure for 1936–1939.
[3] Estimates.

SOURCE: (Notes on the procedures used to derive the indices shown in Table 2 are to be found in Appendix II of this study.) *Selskoe khozyaystvo SSSR* (Agriculture in the USSR), Moscow, 1960; Arcadius Kahan, in *Soviet Agricultural and Peasant Affairs*, edited by Roy D. Laird, Lawrence, Kansas, University of Kansas Press, 1963; *Narodnoe khozyaystvo SSSR v 1958* (The Economy of the USSR in 1958), Moscow, 1959; *Narodnoe khozyaystvo SSSR v 1962* (The Economy of the USSR in 1962), Moscow, 1963; *Narodnoe khozyaystvo SSSR v 1964* (The Economy of the USSR in 1964), Moscow, 1965; *Kontrolnye tsifry narodnogo khozyaystvo SSSR na 1929—1930* (Planned Figures of the Economy of the USSR for 1929—1930), Moscow, 1930; Yu. A. Moshkov, *Zernovaya problema v godu sploshnoy killektivizatsii SSSR* (The Grain problem in the Year of the Complete Collectivization of Agriculture in the USSR), Moscow, 1966; Central Statistical Administration, *Kapitalnoe stroitelstvo v SSSR* (Capital Construction in the USSR), Moscow, 1961; Abraham S. Becker, *Soviet National Income and Product, 1958—1962*, Part II: National Income at Factor Cost and Constant Prices, RM-4881-PR, Santa Monica, California, The RAND Corporation, 1966; and Nancy Nimitz, *Farm Employment in the Soviet Union, 1928—1963*, RM-4623-PR, Santa Monica, California, The RAND Corporation, 1965.

trends in average output for the years 1926–1929 and 1936–1939. Since no data on the size of labour input or capital stock are available for 1913, trends for these factors are derived by comparison with 1928. By 1928, gross output had fully recovered from the ravages of World War I and the Civil War. A slightly lower level of output is indicated by both official and adjusted indices for the end of the thirties. This follows a decline of 17 per cent (judging by the official index) from 1930 to 1933. In per capita terms, the adjusted index shows complete recovery by 1928. In the period 1936–1939, per capita production was 12 per cent below the level reached on the eve of the Third Five-Year Plan.

Recovery of absolute level of output between 1913 and 1928 was achieved on a larger sown area, but the increase in output was proportional to the increase in land under crops. Trends in the volume of remaining inputs are unknown. In 1928, the productivity of livestock herds was probably somewhat higher than at the end of 1913,[13] and it may reasonably be assumed that total labour inputs remained roughly the same. If these guesses are correct, joint factor productivity in 1928 was not substantially different from that in 1913.

The next period to be considered is that from 1928 to 1939. In spite of excellent harvest conditions in 1940, average yields of potatoes and grains in the years 1938–1940 were still below the level of the late twenties. The index of labour productivity for 1936–1939 is 94 (1928=100).[14] Trends in the productivity of capital are more difficult to gauge. By 1939, total capital stock (including livestock) had almost regained the level of 1928.[15] However, a catastrophic decline in the size of livestock herds took place between 1928 and 1933–1934, as the data in Table 3 show.

Virtual recovery of the size of capital stock in 1928 must be interpreted in the light of these and other data. Capital stock (excluding livestock) approximately doubled. Yet in spite of an impressive increase in tractor park from 18,000 to 486,000 units of 15 horsepower, draft power in agriculture by the end of 1939 was no higher than in 1928.[16] In terms of adjusted

---

[13] Cf. Kahan, *op. cit.*, p. 138, and *Narkhoz-1962*, p. 302.

[14] Nancy Nimitz, *Farm Employment in the Soviet Union, 1928–1963*, RM-4623-PR, Santa Monica, California, The RAND Corporation, 1965, p. 33.

[15] According to *Narkhoz-1962*, p. 52, capital stock in 1940 was 23 per cent larger than in 1928. The comparison, however, is between the 1928 figure on pre-war territory and the 1940 figure on 1940 territory. The latter figure is first reduced by 15 per cent to take into account the territorial change. A deduction of investments in 1940 yields the approximate figure of about 100 per cent of 1928.

[16] *Selskoe khozyaystvo SSSR* (Agriculture in the USSR), Moscow, 1960, pp. 263, 409. A horse is taken as equal to 0.75 h. p. (This source is subsequently referred to as *Selkhoz-1960*.)

Table 3

Livestock Herds in the Soviet Union, 1918—1934

(Heads as of January 1)

	1928	1933	1934
Cattle...............	60,100,000	33,500,000	33,500,000
Cows...............	29,300,000	19,400,000	19,000,000
Hogs	22,000,000	9,900,000	11,500,000
Sheep	97,300,000	34,000,000	32,900,000
Goats	9,700,000	3,300,000	3,600,000
Horses..............	32,100,000	17,300,000	15,400,000

SOURCE: *Selskoe khozyaystvo SSSR* (Agriculture in the USSR), Moscow, 1960, p. 263.

1955 prices (used as constants in calculating investment data), the joint state and collective farm effort in the period 1929—1939 amounted to 4.6 billion new rubles. Reference is to productive investment alone. Expenditures for formation of livestock herds are excluded. In terms of prices used in the 1960 census of capital stock (or the 1962 census of collective farm capital stock), the value of capital stock in 1928, including livestock, was 16.3 billion new rubles. Still, average output for the period 1936—1939 was about the same as for that of 1926—1929 or slightly less than that of 1928.

Quite likely, changes in the structure of capital stock between 1928 and the eve of the Second World War tended to reduce the productivity of capital and especially of new, more modern implements. In respect of joint productivity of factors employed in agriculture, the indices derived by this author reveal that by 1939 (or 1936—1939), the level of productivity was from four to eight per cent lower than that reached in 1928.[17] The period under discussion, of course, brought with it fundamental structural changes in the system of Soviet agriculture. This was achieved through massive, abrupt, compulsory collectivization. Though tempted to let the figures speak for themselves, certain aspects of the overall impact of collectivization are not easily quantifiable. Before expressing any views on the matter, the performance of Soviet agriculture must be considered in the context of the rapid development of the economy as a whole.

With some alteration of the classification of B. F. Johnston and J. W. Mellor, the theoretical contribution of the agricultural sector to the develop-

---

[17] The weights used are those of Abraham Becker. They reflect factor shares for 1958 and alternative assumptions about the magnitude of rent (cf. sources for Table 2). Alternative calculations using very unlikely factor shares for control purposes yield almost identical results.

ment of the Soviet-type economy may be outlined as follows: (1) increase in per capita food production and expansion of marketings, thereby ensuring the required level of supplies for a rapidly growing urban population; (2) increase in production of raw materials, thereby ensuring adequate supplies from agriculture for growing domestic capacity in industries processing fibre crops, wool, tobacco, and the like; (3) maintenance (or, where possible, expansion) of agricultural exports, thereby providing supplies urgently needed at home by means of foreign exchange; (4) release of labour for new industrial or other non-agricultural undertakings; and (5) promotion of domestic capital formation, preferably without reducing consumption (that is, by means of increased agricultural productivity).[18] If the record of Soviet agriculture is looked at from this standpoint, the performance is much more impressive. Indeed, it might be said that Soviet agriculture made it possible for the Soviet economy to grow at the very high rates set in the period 1928–1940.[19] This is true, however, only in a very special sense. Though by 1933 the Soviet economy had virtually ground to halt,[20] its balance, as defined by Gregory Grossman,[21] had been maintained. This circumstance is doubtless an index of success, but it may also be convincingly argued that the nature of this success was rather precarious.

The question of food supplies will be considered first. (For statistical reasons, other issues of course become involved at the same time). Ideally, a measure of the contribution of food production to the development of the economy as a whole would be provided by an index of volume of sales per head of urban population. A somewhat less precise measure might be obtained from an index of net food marketings per head of urban

---

[18] B. F. Johnston and J. W. Mellor, "The Role of Agriculture in Economic Development," *American Economic Review*, LI: 4, Evanston, Illinois, University of Illinois Press, September, 1961, pp. 571–581. I add the supply of raw material for local industry to the five Johnston-Mellor criteria and omit the one suggesting that rising farm incomes might increase the size of the market. Since there is little room for induced investment in the usual sense and since—at least until 1952—the main Soviet problem was that of restricting rather than raising farm incomes, this last point is not relevant for purposes of this study.

[19] Depending on the nature of measurement, net national product grew at a rate of 4.2 or 9.3 per cent annually from 1928 to 1940. Cf. *Economic Trends in the Soviet Union*, edited by Abram Bergson and Simon Kuznets, Cambridge, Massachusetts, Harvard University Press, 1963, p. 6.

[20] Naum Jasny, *Soviet Industrialization, 1928–1952*, Chicago, Illinois, University of Chicago Press, 1961, p. 114.

[21] Cf. Gregory Grossman, "Notes for a Theory of a Command Economy," *Soviet Studies*, XV: 2, Glasgow, Scotland, University of Glasgow, October, 1963, pp. 101–102.

population or by an index of *sal'do sela*, the net balance of the village, as formerly calculated by Soviet statisticians in the twenties. Neither index can be computed for the period 1928–1939, and therefore trends in the index of gross food marketings per head of urban population, as presented in Table 2, must be relied on. The underlying data relate to all off-farm sales other than those within the farm sector. They include exports, supply of the armed forces and the urban population, changes in stocks, and quantities resold to the agricultural population for use as inputs or for personal consumption.

In the course of economic development, repurchase of farm products by the agricultural population tends to become an increasingly important factor as a result of the diminishing self-sufficiency of the individual farm or the individual farm household. The Soviet Union is no exception to this rule, even though in its case this process has been taking place in a rather special environment. In any event, an attempt to measure the contribution of agriculture by the index of gross food marketings in Table 2 is likely, as a consequence, to overstate the degree of improvement and understate the degree of deterioration. In spite of this, the indices of gross farm or food marketings may be interpreted as adequately reflecting total demand for farm products or foods at existing prices—that is, the demand by the state, institutions, and the population, through the retail trade network or the collective farm market. Urban population is used as the only available, if less than perfect, common denominator to reflect changes in the demographic structure of the country.

Two important observations may be made on the basis of data in Table 2. The first relates to the period 1913–1928. During this time deterioration of the index of per capita farm marketings was relatively moderate (4 per cent).[22] A somewhat larger, though still moderate, deterioration occurred in the index of per capita food marketings (7 per cent). In both instances reference is to indices computed on the basis of value weights for the two-year period 1925–1926 through 1927–1928. The second interesting feature of Table 2 is that it shows deterioration in per capita indices of both food and farm marketings between 1928 and the late thirties. Even the average index of food marketings for 1938–1940, a period that included the excellent harvest year of 1940, reflects a decline of 20 per cent in comparison with 1928. It should also be noted that the nutritional value of marketings in the years 1938–1942 was lower than that prevailing in 1928. Trends in the intervening years are likely to show that in 1932–1933 the entire operation

---

[22] The underlying data have been adjusted for differences in coverage, but the adjustments are not complete.

was hanging by a thread, and that the balance of the economy was mantained by terror alone.

In contrast, corresponding indices for all farm products (including fibre crops, wool, and tobacco) show slightly more favourable trends, especially in relation to 1913. This indicates that the function of supplying raw materials to domestic light industry was performed more effectively than the function of supplying food products to the urban population. Even so, production of domestic raw materials probably still failed to keep pace with increases in related processing capacity. It should be borne in mind, moreover, that production of technical crops took place in a special environment. Such crops enjoyed a privileged position both in terms of prices and supply of off-farm inputs. Indeed, if total farm income for the agricultural sector and total supply of off-farm inputs are seen as constraints, the policy of favourable treatment for technical crops may be seen either as a cause of poorer performance in food-producing or as an effect of the deliberate neglect of the latter.[23]

The next function to be considered is supply of exportable "surpluses" and increase of foreign exchange earnings. Judging by official data, in the critical period of the First Five-Year Plan, from 1929 to 1932, the value of agricultural exports was 4,548,000,000 rubles (converted to 1950 exchange rates). This was some 270,000,000 less than in 1925–1926. Meanwhile, in the same period, the share of agriculture in the total value of exports declined from 59.8 to 39.2 per cent.[24] In appraising these trends, some consideration must be given to the crisis in domestic food supplies calling for the introduction of rationing in 1929 and to the depressed level of world prices on farm products during the Great Depression. Notwithstanding these obstacles, the agricultural sector remained a crucial source of foreign exchange earnings. Its net contribution—net, that is, in terms of foreign exchange earnings used for imports of farm machinery—amounted to 3,577,000,000 rubles. This was almost enough to cover the value of all imports in the peak import year 1930.

---

[23] This means the government is assumed to have defined certain minimum and maximum limits within which total agricultural income was to fall and was prepared to offer a certain quantity of off-farm inputs to agriculture as a whole. Needless to say, the limits in question would have been rather vague.

[24] USSR Academy of Sciences, Institute of Economics, *Postroeniye fundamenta sotsialisticheskoy ekonomiki v SSSR, 1926–1932 gg.* (Building the Foundation of a Socialist Economy in the USSR, 1926–1932), Moscow, 1960, pp. 519–524. For trends in the period 1933–1940, see also USSR Academy of Sciences, Institute of Economics, *Sotsialisticheskoe narodnoe khozyaystvo SSSR v 1933–1940 gg.* (The Socialist Economy of the USSR in 1933–1940), Moscow, 1963, pp. 614 ff.

Alternatively, if the level of imports in 1926–1927 is taken as an index of "normal" imports in the period before industrialization, maintenance of agricultural exports at their actual level in the years 1929–1932 may be regarded as having enabled the Soviet Union to meet its increased import demand during the same period. These successes were, of course, achieved at the cost of tremendous human suffering. They pointedly recall Vyshne-gradsky's slogan, uttered some forty years before the advent of Stalin, "Let us starve but export!" Even granting the difficult situation for farm products on the world market, the foregone improvements in productivity would have enabled the Soviet Union to achieve the same results at a lower cost in lives and illness.

The task of tracing trends in the agricultural and, by implication, the non-agricultural labour force is simplified by the recent careful and diligent research of Nancy Nimitz. As she has shown, input of man-days on the farm rose by only 4 per cent from the average for 1928 to that for the period 1936–1939.[25] At the same time, the non-agricultural labour force more than doubled. Thus, virtually all natural increase in the employable population in the agricultural sector (reduced, as it was, by deficient food supplies at the beginning of the thirties) was chanelled into non-agricultural employment. Given the prevailing organizational structure, this was probably all the economy could bear without a further increase in its high rate of investment. Moreover, the frequent complaints about excessive mobility of cadres suggest that it was the young, the trained, and the more enter-prising element that was then, as now, leaving the villages.

The contribution of agriculture to domestic capital formation is not easily measured. That it did involve a reduction in personal consumption seems clear, since productivity trends evince a pattern of deterioration and farm marketings a much faster rate of growth than output as a whole. Some indication of this contribution, extracted through the system of compulsory deliveries and MTS (Machine and Tractor Station) payments in kind, may be gauged from data on the relative levels of various farm prices in the period 1932–1939.

Forty per cent of total grain deliveries by collective farms in the years 1937–1939 was paid for at low compulsory delivery prices. Another 45 to 51 per cent was covered by MTS payments in kind.[26] The compulsory delivery price of potatoes, unchanged through 1955, elicited the following

---

[25] Nimitz, *Farm Employment, op. cit.*, Table 1, and Warren Eason in Bergson and Kuznets, *op. cit.*, p. 77.

[26] *Postroeniye fundamenta sotsialisticheskoy ekonomiki v SSSR, 1926–1932 gg, op. cit.*, p. 474.

Table 4

Prices for Various Farm Products, 1932—1939

(New Rubles per Ton)

	Compulsory Deliveries	State Purchases	Collective Farm Market
Grains	7.5	16.4	119—691
Potatoes	3.6	11.0	37—200
Milk	16.5	46.5	118—254
Meat (Live Weight) ..	35.0	175.0	316—604

NOTE: The grain prices in the state sector are those of 1937, or about 10 to 12 per cent higher than in 1932. Collective farm market prices for 1932—1939 show the lowest and the highest annual prices as the limits of the ranges. Meat prices are converted to live weight using the coefficient of 2.1.

SOURCES: USSR Academy of Sciences, Institute of Economics, *Sotsialisticheskoe narodnoe khozyaystvo SSSR v 1933—1940 gg.* (The Socialist Economy of the USSR in 1933—1940), Moscow, 1963, p. 475; J. F. Karcz, *Soviet Agricultural Marketings and Prices*, RM-1930, Santa Monica, California: The RAND Corporation, 1957, Appendix E, with some adjustments based on more recent Soviet data; and M. A. Vyltsan, *Istoriya SSSR*, Moscow, No. 2, 1966, pp. 60—61.

conclusion from a high Soviet Communist Party functionary in 1958: "[For this money,] no self-respecting man would bother to load a centner of potatoes on the truck."[27] The government must have assumed that all farm administrators were self-respecting men, since it deprived them of the ability to plan their own outputs. This function, as well as those of planning sown areas and projecting the size of herds, was centralized in local government offices. The powerful apparatus of the Committee (later Commissariat) of Procurements ensured that products were ultimately delivered.

This leads to the issue of trends in farmer income and its various components. The problem has recently been given emphasis by the publication of archival data on the level of market prices in 1932—1939. Adjusting the calculations of Nancy Nimitz in the light of these more recent data, the values in Table 5 emerge for incomes in cash and kind (actually grain only), with the component of income in kind valued at current market prices.

In 1928—1929, the value of sales of farm products by the rural population came to 3,506,000,000 rubles in terms of prevailing prices—that is, to

---

[27] The All-Union Lenin Academy of Agricultural Sciences, *Materialy sessii Akademii posvyashchennoy dalneyshemu razvitiyu kolkhoznogo stroya i reorganizatsii MTS* (Materials of the Session of the Academy Devoted to the Further Development of the Collective Farm System and to the Reorganization of the MTS), Moscow, 1958, p. 192.

Table 5

Income Values in Cash and Kind

(Old Rubles)

	Per Man-Day		Per Man-Year	
	Cash	Cash and Kind	Cash	Cash and Kind
1932......	0.44	10.87	55	1,348
1933......	0.32	21.42	50	3,340
1934......	0.26	9.85	43	1,614
1935......	0.61	5.11	104	878
1937......	0.68	5.43	105	842
1938......	0.83	2.81	121	409
1939......	0.73	2.84	105	409
1940......	0.64	3.47	95	522

SOURCES: Nancy Nimitz, *Farm Employment in the Soviet Union*, 1928–1963, RM-4623-PR, Santa Monica, California, The RAND Corporation, 1965, p. 93; and M. A. Vyltsan, *Istoriya SSSR*, Moscow, No. 2, 1966, p. 61.

NOTE: The grain component has been revalued in collective farm market prices for a given year.

0.36 rubles per man-day.[28] It seems legitimate to assume a grain equivalent of 5 kilogrammes per day. In terms of free market prices in 1928–1929, this would amount to 0.72 rubles, making the value of total income in cash and kind 1.08 rubles per man-day.[29]

To compare the effectiveness of the collective farm with that of the private farm, these earnings may be deflated by approximating an index of prices paid by the farmers. (For such a restricted purpose, income derived from the household plot after collectivization may be ignored.) The assumption is made that one half of purchases occurred in retail trade and the other half at market prices. The assumption is legitimate for the late thirties but is less relevant for 1932.[30] It will be understood that results cannot be precise and are merely intended to illustrate the general order of magnitude and the direction of the trends. The resulting indices of income per man-day are enumerated in Table 6.

Obviously, the socialist sector of the collective farm system was an inadequate substitute for the private farm of 1928. Clearly, the household

[28] Gosplan USSR, *Kontrolnye tsifri narodnogo khozyaystva SSSR na 1929–1930 god* (Planned Figures for the Economy of the USSR for 1929–1930), Moscow, 1930, p. 478. Man-day input data are from Nimitz, *op. cit.*, Table 1.

[29] Price data are from *Ekonomicheskoe obozreniye*, Moscow, No. 1, 1929, p. 145, where the market price is given as 143 rubles per ton.

[30] *Planovoe khozyaystvo*, No. 9, 1938, p. 102. It is likely that in 1932 the share was considerably higher for collective farm market than in the late thirties to which these data refer.

Table 6

Indices of Income Per Man-Day
(1928 = 100)

	1932	1937	1938	1939	1940
Total Distributions	1,006	503	260	263	321
Cash Distributions	122	189	231	203	178
Deflator......................	928	766	696	882	1,346
Real Total Distributions	108	66	37	30	24
Real Value of Cash Payments	13	25	33	23	13

SOURCES: For sources and derivation of the deflator, see Appendix I.

plot was needed, not only to increase supplies of food for the urban population but also to sustain the individual farm household. The decision to allow the operation of the private sector, which had been a function of the adopted method of collectivizing agriculture, nevertheless had some far-reaching consequences; for, as has been said elsewhere: "Nowhere in Western Europe is peasant farming so inefficient in the employment of labor as it is on the plot farms in the Soviet Union."[31] The reasons for the diversion of labour to the private plot are all too evident. The share of cash distributions to collective farms, in the combined total of these distributions plus household income deriving from sales on the collective farm market, declined from 22 per cent in 1932 to 15 per cent in 1933. It then rose to 24 per cent in 1935. However, the following percentages illustrate the trend of uninterrupted decline after 1936: in 1937, the share was 22 per cent; in 1938, 20 per cent; in 1939, 15 per cent; and in 1940, 14 per cent.[32] The underlying ruble values may be deflated by the index of prices paid by peasants. (The distortion introduced by the omission of income from state procurements is not likely to be significant, since the value of such income is relatively small in comparison with the totals included in the calculation). The object is to focus attention on the larger question of the contribution of agriculture to domestic capital formation. Resulting indices of household incomes, from market sales and cash distributions in constant prices, with 1928 as the base year, are as follows: 1932 = 25; 1937 = 72; 1938 = 106; 1939 = 98; and 1940 = 61.

[31] Theodore W. Schultz, *Transforming Traditional Agriculture*, New Haven, Connecticut, Yale University Press, 1964, p. 123.

[32] Data for distributions are from the revalued calculations of Nancy Nimitz (cf. note to Table 5). Collective farm market data are taken from M. A. Vyltsan, *Istoriya SSSR*, Moscow, No. 2, 1966, p. 59 (cf. note to Table 4). For data on share of farms and households on the market, see J. F. Karcz, *Soviet Agricultural Marketings and Prices*, RM-1930, Santa Monica, California, The RAND Corporation, 1957, pp. 117–118.

The drastic decline from 1928 to 1932 dramatically illustrates the forcible effect of great inflationary pressures under the First Five-Year Plan. Since income in kind was obviously much more important in this period, little useful information can be derived from these figures for the purposes of this study. However, by 1937, the retail market was again functioning with reasonable effectiveness; rationing had been abolished in 1935. After the abolition of rationing, trends in the real value of peasant money income were quite favourable until 1939–1940. This may at first seem puzzling. When peasant terms of trade are measured by indices of retail prices, a steady deterioration is indicated, but such calculations ignore the fact that one half of peasant monetary income during the late thirties was spent on the collective farm market or in purchases of products (including inputs) from the collective farm.[33]

It may be concluded that in overall terms the gross share of agriculture in domestic capital formation was actually smaller than had been commonly supposed before the publication of Bergson's opus magnum.[34] It will be recalled that large expenditures of resources were required to regain the 1928 level of agricultural capital stock by the end of the thirties. When this is taken into account, the net contribution of agriculture to domestic capital formation in the years 1928–1940 turns out to have been much smaller than Bergson suggested in 1962. Some other factors must also be taken into account. As yet, it is not possible to compute dispersion of average peasant income for this period, and knowledge of the reliability of this average is incomplete. Nevertheless, one thing is clear. In 1937, more than one quarter of the entire income from state procurements by the collective farms and the private sector accrued to producers of cotton, and cotton prices rose more rapidly than other prices.[35] The system of triple farm prices resulted in very high, at times extraordinarily high, quasi-rents for low-cost producers and those located near large industrial centres. However, such producers, as well as producers of relatively privileged technical crops, comprised only a small minority of peasant producers. Hence, the wide dispersion of income distribution in the Soviet village at this time as well as later must also be taken into account if data on trends in mean income are not to be misleading.

Clearly, then, in Soviet agriculture the burden of contributing to capital formation was very unevenly distributed among the different strata

---

[33] This necessarily assumes that prices in the intra-rural trade moved in about the same fashion as those on the urban collective farm market.

[34] Abram Bergson, *The Real National Income and Product of Soviet Russia*, Cambridge, Massachusetts, Harvard University Press, 1962, p. 257.

[35] Karcz, *Soviet Agricultural Marketings and Prices, op. cit.*, pp. 313–314.

of the Soviet farm population. The inequitable distribution of forced savings was perhaps one of the more serious shortcomings of the Stalinist model of development, profoundly affecting the future course of events in the Soviet countryside by molding the attitudes of peasants and officials alike. Probably, it influenced many important policy decsions in the post-war period. The contribution of agriculture to Soviet economic growth in the period 1928–1940, though vital, still fell far short of reasonable standards. In view of this, it seems pertinent to ask whether alternative methods of extracting marketable surpluses and increasing the propensity of peasants to save would not have been more effective. Judging by the circumstance that no other socialist country in Eastern Europe chose to adopt the Soviet model unaltered for purposes of collectivizing agriculture, the answer, obviously, is yes.

The experience of Soviet collectivization was indeed so chaotic in the extreme changes it wrought on the Soviet countryside that it would be possible to explain virtually every shortcoming of Soviet agriculture today in terms of its consequences. This interesting intellectual exercise will not be engaged in here, but the reader should be reminded that such conclusions ignore a very essential factor: Soviet collectivization did not occur in a vacuum but was a function of the decision to adopt a high rate of growth and of subsequent decisions to increase this rate still further. Recently, M. Lewin's brilliant research has disclosed how Stalin drifted into adopting this expedient.[36] Though Lewin does not say it in so many words, he implies that the great collectivization drive and all its consequences are to be seen as the result of an attempt to solve long-run structural problems by means of short-run policy tools. Such an attempt is, of course, doomed to eventual failure unless proper steps are taken at a reasonably early stage to modify the combination of applied policy instruments. Nothing of the sort occurred in the Soviet Union, though it is now known that appropriate suggestions towards this end were made by some individuals.[37] Instead, a glorified version of *razverstka* (appropriation) was built into the edifice of the Soviet economy as a veritable cornerstone of so-called socialist agriculture, thus destining the collective farm to become an instrument of collection rather than of collective work.

Was this inevitable? A tentative answer to this question is called for, if only because many Soviet writers tend to explain too much by too little.

---

[36] M. Lewin, "The Immediate Background of Soviet Collectivization," *Soviet Studies*, XVII, No. 2, October, 1965, pp. 162–197.

[37] For example, in the thirties V. G. Venzher suggested the abolition of the MTS.

In particular, they tend to exaggerate the importance of the preparations for and the consequences of World War II.[38] An explanation in these terms is by far too simple and too appealing to be allowed to stand without further justification. On the basis of data from the annual plan for 1941, Naum Jasny has shown that Soviet preparations for this war were much less extensive than anyone, including the Soviet man in the street, had the reason or the right to expect.[39] True, an atmosphere of international tension is not conducive to liberating initiative or introducing innovations in organizational structures, but then neither was the phenomenon of the Great Purge of 1937–1938. It, too, narrowed the scope of possibilities for structural change in agriculture and elsewhere, though its causes were only remotely related to developments on the international scene. Far better ways exist for strengthening defensive potential than the virtual decapitation of the armed forces and the statistical apparatus.

If the war exerted any direct influence on agricultural policy, it was through the attempt to accumulate stocks of grain.[40] Even so, the basic reason for the failure to introduce meaningful corrections in the collective farm sector during the thirties ought, I believe, to be sought elsewhere. As said, by 1933, the entire operation might have been hanging by a thread except that the balance of the economy had been kept intact. When this is borne in mind, the issue of more efficient alternative methods of achieving the same or better results is no longer decisive. The great virtue of the Stalinist model—doubtless one that must have been thoroughly appreciated by its architect—is that it worked, no matter how precariously. Furthermore, there is no question that from the short-run standpoint of achieving marketable surpluses and additional savings from the village, the model seemed to be working better and better as the initial consequences of collectivization were overcome. Finally, there is the well-known fact that most bureaucracies—not to mention most dictators—are reluctant to tamper with a going concern.

----

[38] Even such an outstanding writer as V. G. Venzher declares it was the war that was mainly responsible for the relatively insufficient supply of tractors to agriculture in the post-war period. This, of course, assumes that no other policy for the allocation of capital could have been followed in that period, and Venzher's own writings point to the opposite conclusion. Cf. V. G. Venzher, *Kolhoznyy stroi na sovremennom etape* (The Collective Farm System at Its Present Stage), Moscow, 1966, p. 16.

[39] Jasny, *op. cit.*, pp. 177–194.

[40] Nancy Nimitz, *Soviet Government Grain Procurements, Dispositions and Stocks*, RM-4127-PR, Santa Monica, California, The RAND Corporation, 1964, pp. 14–15.

Some other consequences of the adopted method of collectivizing agriculture call for mention. The economist of the twenty-first century may well appreciate the fact that the USSR has unwittingly provided the world with a test case for the development of unbalanced sectoral growth. The model, after all, vividly illustrates the pitfalls of this type of growth in market-type economies. It is, of course, a matter of considerable interest for those who must make major development decisions. The impact of the Soviet drive for collectivization on the attitudes and mental processes of the peasant masses in Eastern Europe (and, for that matter, elsewhere) is also important. Truth has a way of leaking out in spite of the most formidable barriers to communications: perhaps no better tool for the making of anti-kolkhoz propaganda could have been devised by a rabid anti-Communist than an honest description of the true state of affairs in the Soviet countryside.

Ironically, the successes of Soviet armies in World War II helped to break down the barrier to communications, because Soviet troops came into contact with local peasantry on an extensive scale. Since the architect of the system persisted in calling it socialist, his claim was faithfully echoed by almost all obedient elements of the professional and daily press. As a result, irreparable damage was inflicted upon the cause of socialism and cooperative agriculture, regardless of their actual merits and demerits. Henceforth, in agriculture and elsewhere, what was understood as socialist was more often than not simply equated with what was known of Soviet reality. Worse yet, the emergence of what is now referred to as the cult of personality, coupled with these other factors, contributed to the elaboration of a single so-called socialist model of agricultural development. Another contributing factor may also have been the inability of the Soviet bureaucracy to cope with more than one organizational structure at that time. In any event, when communist governments acceded to power in Eastern Europe after the Second World War, they were unable to choose between several alternative models for creating a socialist agriculture. Though none of them chose to collectivize in a short period of weeks or months, serious and lasting damage grew out of efforts to adhere to other parts of the Soviet prescription. The existence of alternatives has been alluded to here. Hopefully, the reader is convinced by now that there ought to have been at least one other way of getting more value per ruble. This issue will be raised again after a review of trends since 1940 on current territory.

According to the adjusted index in Table 7, total output in 1940 was 23 per cent above that in 1913. Again, however, this increase was sufficient only to maintain per capita output at the level it had reached prior to World War I. It required, incidentally, an increase of 27 per cent in the area of land under crops. Hence, again, it seems fair to conclude that the record of Soviet agriculture is far from spectacular.

Shifting the basis of comparison to 1940, the pre-war level of output was approached in 1949–1950 and barely surpassed in the good harvest year of 1952. A more permanent move in this direction began only after the introduction of new policy measures following Stalin's death. It ought also to be noted that in spite of large population losses in World War II, per capita output in the period 1951–1955 was only 9 per cent greater than that on the eve of the war. The damage inflicted by occupying forces and military operations was very large indeed and the task of reconstruction correspondingly difficult. Reconstruction was, in fact, made even more difficult by the continuation and intensification of pre-war policies.

Once again, recovery of output was achieved on a larger sown area. The rise in productivity in the period 1951–1955 primarily reflects the impact of the new lands campaign. In the initial stages of this campaign, it was perhaps inevitable that the increase in land under crops would be greater than the increase in output. Trends in the productivity of capital

Table 7

Selected Performance Indicators, Soviet Agriculture, Post-War Territory

FIVE-YEAR AVERAGES

	1913	1940	1951–1955 Average	1956–1960 Average	1961–1965 Average
Gross Output (Official)	100	141	148	210	235
Gross Output (Adjusted)	100	123	129	183	204
Net Output (USDA Index)	—	—	—	—	108[1]
Per Capita Gross Output (Official)	100	116	125	163	168
Per Capita Gross Output (Adjusted)	100	101	109	142	146
Per Capita Net Output (USDA Index)	—	—	—	—	100[1]
Farm Marketings (Per Urban Head)	100	77	73[3]	88	89
Food Marketings (Per Urban Head)	100	71	65[3]	79	81
Sown Area	78	100	109	131	141
Capital Stock (Total)	—	100	122	192	285
Capital Stock (Excluding Livestock)	—	100	145	244	414
Labour Input (Man-Days)	—	100	104	102	107[4]
Output Index (Official)	—	100	106	150	168
Input Index (Weights I)	—	100	108	122	143
Input Index (Weights II)	—	100	108	124	145
Joint Productivity Index (Weights I)	—	100	98	123	117
Joint Productivity Index (Weights II)	—	100	98	121	116
Net Output (USDA Index)	—	—	—	—	108[1]
Joint Productivity Index (Weights I)	—	—	—	—	95[1]
Joint Productivity Index (Weights II)	—	—	—	—	95[1]

AVERAGE PERFORMANCE BEFORE AND DURING THE
SEVEN-YEAR PLAN

	1913	1940	1956—1958 Average	1959—1965 Average
Gross Output (Official)	100	141	203	231
Gross Output (Adjusted)	100	123	177	201
Net Output (USDA Index)	—	—	100[1]	107[2]
Per Capita Gross Output (Official)	100	116	160	168
Per Capita Gross Output (Adjusted) ...	100	101	140	146
Per Capita Net Output (USDA Index) ..	—	—	100[1]	99[2]
Farm Marketings (Per Urban Head)	100	77	86	89
Food Marketings (Per Urban Head)	100	71	77	81
Sown Area........................	78	100	129	139
Capital Stock (Total)	—	100	177	265
Capital Stock (Excluding Livestock) ...	—	100	219	376
Labour Input (Man-Days)	—	100	102	105[5]
Output Index (Official)	—	100	145	166
Input Index (Weights I)	—	100	119	138
Input Index (Weights II)	—	100	121	140
Joint Productivity Index (Weights I)....	—	100	122	120
Joint Productivity Index (Weights II)...	—	100	120	119
Net Output (USDA Index)	—	—	100[1]	107[2]
Joint Productivity Index (Weights I)....	—	—	100[1]	95[2]
Joint Productivity Index (Weights II)...	—	—	100[1]	96[2]

[1] 1957—1959 = 100.
[2] 1957—1959 = 100; 1960—1965 average.
[3] 1952—1955 average.
[4] 1961—1964 average.

SOURCE: (Notes on the procedures used to derive the indices shown in Table 7 are to be found in Appendix III of this study.) *Selskoe khozyaystvo SSSR* (Agriculture in the USSR), Moscow, 1960; *Narodnoe khozyaystvo SSSR v 1961* (The Economy of the USSR in 1961), Moscow, 1962; *Narodnoe khozyaystvo SSSR v 1962* (The Economy of the USSR in 1962), Moscow, 1963; *Narodnoe khozyaystvo SSSR v 1964* (The Economy of the USSR in 1964), Moscow, 1965; *Narodnoe khozyaystvo SSSR v 1965* (The Economy of the USSR in 1965), Moscow, 1966; Central Statistical Administration, *SSSR v tsifrakh v 1965 godu* (The USSR in Figures in 1965), Moscow, 1966; U.S. Department of Agriculture, Economic Research Service, *The USSR and Eastern Europe Agricultural Situation*, ERS-Foreign-151, Washington, D.C., U.S. Department of Agriculture, 1966; Nancy Nimitz, *Farm Employment in the Soviet Union, 1928—1963*, RM-4881-PR, Santa Monica, California, The RAND Corporation, 1965; *Kontrolnye tsifry narodnogo khozyaystva SSSR na 1929—1930* (Planned Figures of the Economy of the USSR for 1929—1930), Moscow, 1930; and Abraham S. Becker, *Soviet National Income and Product, 1958—1962*, Part II: National Income at Factor Cost and Constant Prices, RM-4881-PR, Santa Monica, California, The RAND Corporation, 1966.

were even less favourable. Between 1940 and 1951–1955 (average), the incremental capital output ratio rose to 3.7. A slight improvement of 2 per cent was registered in productivity of labour. The joint productivity index, regardless of weights employed, shows a decline of 2 per cent. Thus, the pre-war level of factor productivity in agriculture—such as it was—remained unsurpassed again until the bountiful harvest of 1956.

Table 7 also shows trends in the five-year averages for the periods 1956–1960 and 1961–1965, but it is more convenient to focus discussion on average performance in periods of different length—that is, 1956–1958 and 1959–1965, since this not only permits a comparison of performance under the Seven-Year Plan with that during the three preceding years, but also makes possible more meaningful comparisons of performance with trends in the USDA index of net output. In the years 1956–1958, the level of output was 37 per cent above that of the period 1951–1955. In per capita terms, the increase amounts to 28 per cent. For the first time, in terms of the periodization employed here, the increase in sown area was smaller than that in output. Productivity of capital is shown to have improved, since the incremental capital output ratio for 1956–1958, in comparison with 1951–1955, is 1.22. (If a comparison is made with 1940, the corresponding value is 1.71.) A drastic improvement occurred in productivity of labour, which rose by 39 per cent in comparison with the 1951–1955 average. (The improvement over labour productivity in 1940 comes to 41 per cent.) Finally, the indices of joint factor productivity show improvements of 22 to 24 per cent in relation to 1951–1955 and of 20 to 22 per cent in relation to 1940. Residual factors here, of course, include the weather; this period covers two out of the four best harvest years from 1940 to 1965. On the other hand, the increase in input indices is also smaller than in any of the other subdivisions.

In contrast, trends in 1959–1965 are much less favourable. Even the official index of output indicates painfully slow progress, amounting to 14 per cent in direct terms and 6 per cent in per capita terms. As already noted, trends in the official index over this period are not entirely credible, and doubtless the USDA index of net output offers a much more reliable measure of growth of gross output. It suggests a considerably smaller increase in output—7 per cent—and expresses a slight retrogression in per capita output.[41] Productivity trends depend, of course, on the choice of output index for a numerator, but even the use of Soviet indices yields a retrogression in comparison with the average results of 1956–1958. The degree of decline is correspondingly greater if the USDA index is employed. The productivity of land improves slightly if the Soviet index is applied and remains about the same in calculations incorporating the USDA

---

[41] Judging by Douglas B. Diamond's index of net output, the increase amounted to 9 per cent. Cf. U.S. Congress, Joint Economic Committee, *op. cit.*, p. 352.

index. Capital output ratios soar in both kinds of comparison. Calculations using the official index yield an incremental capital output ratio of 3.4; those using the USDA index, a comparable value of 7.1. (Both figures relate to a comparison with 1956–1958; in a comparison with 1940, calculations based on the official index yield a value of 2.2.) Depending on whether the official or the USDA output index is employed, labour productivity indices exhibit an increase of 11 or 4 per cent respectively in a comparison with 1956–1958. Finally, indices of joint factor productivity manifest a decline of 1 to 2 per cent in calculations with the Soviet index as a constant factor. For a somewhat different time period, 1960–1965, related calculations using the USDA index indicate a decline of 4 to 5 per cent (1957–1959 = 100). In view of the interest attaching to annual development under the Seven-Year Plan, all the variables entering into the calculations are shown in Table 8, which makes comparisons with values for 1958. The two joint productivity indices based on official output trends show monotonic declines until 1963. Recovery in 1964 fails to exceed the 1958 level. The USDA index (based on 1957–1959 = 100) yields slightly different results in calculations of joint factor productivity.

In sum, then, the pre-war level of output was exceeded only in 1953, after the introduction of new policies in the farming sector. This was also true in the case of joint productivity, primarily owing to improvements in the role played by labour. In all instances, the decisive years fall in the period 1956–1958. Thereafter, a further advance proved impossible in per capita terms, and a moderate decline in overall productivity took place. Instead of a projected improvement of 56 per cent in per capita terms, the Seven-Year Plan merely proved to be a holding operation.

The literature on agricultural policy under the Seven-Year Plan is by now quite voluminous,[42] and little purpose would be served by repeating its well-known arguments. Instead, as in the preceding section of this study, attention will be focussed on the contribution of agriculture to economic development. Trends in food supplies, measured by the index of food marketings per head of urban population, will again be considered first. That the level of 1913 has never been surpassed in this respect is in itself significant, though the explanation for this lies largely in terms of differing export balances and changing demographic trends. In any case,

---

[42] Cf. *ibid.*; J. F. Karcz and V. P. Timoshenko, "Soviet Agricultural Policy, 1953–1962," *Food Research Institute Studies*, Vol. IV, No. 2, Stanford, California, Stanford University, May, 1964; and Nancy Nimitz, "The Lean Years," *Problems of Communism*, Vol. XIV, No. 3, Washington, D.C., U.S. Information Agency, May-June, 1965.

Table 8

Selected Performance Indicators, Soviet Agriculture, Seven-Year Plan
(1958 = 100)

	1959	1960	1961	1962	1963	1964	1965
Gross Output Official	100	103	106	107	99	113	114
Gross Output Per Capita (Official)	98	99	100	100	91	102	102
Farm Marketings (Per Urban Head) ...	100	100	97	100	97	100	—
Food Marketings (Per Urban Head) ...	101	101	99	104	100	101	—
Sown Area	100	104	105	110	112	109	107
Capital Stock (Total)	108	115	123	136	146	160	173
Labour Input (Man-Days)	100	103	107	106	104	104	104
Input Index (Weights I)	101	105	109	112	112	114	117
Input Index (Weights II)	101	105	109	112	113	114	116
Joint Productivity Index (Weights I) ..	99	98	97	96	88	99	97
Joint Productivity Index (Weights II) ..	99	98	97	96	88	99	98
Net Output (USDA Index)	—	101	107	107	101	117	109
Joint Productivity Index (Weights I) ..	—	96	98	95	89	102	93
Joint Productivity Index (Weights II) ..	—	96	98	95	89	102	93

SOURCE: (Notes on the procedures used to derive the indices shown in Table 8 are to be found in Appendix III of this study.) *Selskoe khozyaystvo SSSR* (Agriculture in the USSR), Moscow, 1960; *Narodnoe khozyaystvo SSSR v 1961* (The Economy of the USSR in 1961), Moscow, 1962; *Narodnoe khozyaystvo SSSR v 1962* (The Economy of the USSR in 1962), Moscow, 1963; *Narodnoe khozyaystvo SSSR v 1964* (The Economy of the USSR in 1964), Moscow, 1965; *Narodnoe khozyaystvo SSSR v 1965* (The Economy of the USSR in 1965), Moscow, 1966; Central Statistical Administration, *SSSR v tsifrakh v 1965 godu* (The USSR in Figures in 1965), Moscow, 1966; U.S. Department of Agriculture, Economic Research Service, *The USSR and Eastern Europe Agricultural Situation*, ERS-Foreign-151, Washington, D.C.: U.S. Department of Agriculture, 1966; Nancy Nimitz, *Farm Employment in the Soviet Union, 1928—1963*, RM-4881-PR, Santa Monica, California: The RAND Corporation, 1965; *Kontrolnye tsifry narodnogo khozyaystvo SSSR na 1929—1930* (Planned Figures of the Economy of the USSR for 1929—1930), Moscow, 1930; and Abraham S. Becker, *Soviet National Income and Product, 1958—1962*, Part II: National Income at Factor Cost and Constant Prices, RM-4881-PR, Santa Monica, California: The RAND Corporation, 1966.

for 1940 the index of food marketings is 71 (1913 = 100). Then, in the war years, it undergoes a dramatic decline. (The index of food marketings for 1945, unadjusted for population changes, is 58.) Thereafter, a fairly rapid recovery takes place, but by 1952–1955 the per capita index has risen to only 91 (1940 = 100). Once more, a breakthrough comes in 1956–1958, when volume of food marketings per capita substantially exceeds the pre-war level. After 1958, the index fluctuates within a narrow range of 6 per cent. These trends help to explain the policy changes that were made in 1953 and 1964, but they fail to provide a clue to the reasons for the policy shift that was implemented in 1958. Trends in the index of all farm marketings, including technical crops and wool, are likewise revealing. Until 1958, the index of all farm marketings rises faster than that of food marketings. Its subsequent failure to maintain this trend reflects a policy that was in force after 1958 and until 1963 and that was less favourable in terms of prices and incentives.

As in the earlier period, grain is the chief crop involved in the fate of agricultural exports under the Seven-Year Plan. In 1940, in spite of a decline in farmer income and a policy of rapid accumulation of stocks, the Soviet Union exported 1,100,000 tons of grain. By 1952, the volume of exports had risen to 4,000,000 tons. In the period 1953–1955, it fluctuated between 2,100,000 and 2,600,000 tons. In 1956, and again in the years 1958–1962, net annual exports rose to somewhere between 6,100,000 and 7,400,000 tons, less than one-third of which went to non-socialist countries.[43] Any interpretation of these trends must take into account changes that took place in the economic environment of the country between the twenties and the post-war period. The need to acquire foreign exchange credit to pay for industrial imports was no longer so pressing, though post-war grain exports did help to pay for substantial quantities of East German and Czech machinery. In terms of hard currency, however, the contribution of agricultural exports was relatively small. Once more in Soviet history and for that matter in Russian history, grain exports were maintained— and even increased—in the face of rising domestic demand. An explanation for this is to be sought chiefly in the import requirements of other socialist countries during this period and to a much lesser extent in the desire to supply grain to underdeveloped countries. These requirements are, in turn, a function of changes in the economies of these countries and of the unwillingness or inability of their leaders to adopt the autarkic Soviet model of the thirties intact at the expense of domestic consumers.

Were it not for exports in the period 1960–1964, the Soviet government could have disposed of an additional 24,000,000 tons of grain to satisfy internal requirements.[44] No matter what alternative use might have been made of this grain, other than the maintenance of large stocks, the face of the Soviet countryside today would be very different, and Khrushchev might well yet endure at the helm of Soviet power. Thus, though the contribution of agricultural exports to the development of the Soviet economy was less significant than in the pre-war period, it was crucial in terms of developments in other countries of the socialist bloc. As the Romans and the British did in the past, the Russians discovered in the

---

[43] Nimitz, *Soviet Government Grain Procurements, op. cit.*, pp. 98–99.
[44] *Loc. cit.*

present that the cost of becoming the centre of an empire can be very high indeed.[45]

In turning to the issue of supply of labour, reliance is had once again on the calculations of Nancy Nimitz. As before the war, virtually the entire increase in able-bodied population has been chanelled into non-agricultural occupations. In fact, there are several indications that release of labour from agriculture has proceeded at too fast a pace. An unpublished calculation of Dr. Karl E. Waedekin shows that from 1959 to 1963, the number of able-bodied collective farmers declined by 37.5 per cent or by about 12,000,000 people.[46] Local labour shortages have occurred in agriculture in several areas, while surpluses of unskilled labour outside of agriculture have added to the difficulties of creating jobs and providing decent urban housing. The task of keeping the farmer on the farm is not yet as pressing as in Czechoslovakia, but the average age of the agricultural population in the USSR is now approaching 50 years,[47] and mobility of cadres remains a serious problem.

The question of the contribution of agriculture to domestic capital formation is to be viewed in terms of the changed economic environment of the post-war period. Agriculture is no longer the largest sector of the economy, having, in default of competition, to contribute heavily to domestic capital formation. In a sense, the problem is now reversed: the next stage of agricultural development is "capital intensive, labour extensive." Precisely because of the policies followed earlier, the agricultural sector alone is unable to meet its own capital requirements.

Reconstruction was the most urgent problem of the immediate post-war period. One might suppose that the very extent of war-time damage would have called for changes in agricultural policies and that special attention would have been given to trends in peasant income. In fact, the opposite happened as the policy line hardened. Cash distributions to collective farmers rose from 4.1 billion to 14.1 billion old rubles between 1940 and 1952. By 1952, collective farm market sales by households amounted to 45.5 billion old rubles as compared with 24.7 billion in 1940.[48] Thus, there is an apparent increase of 86 per cent in the money income of the farm population. It is not easy to deflate this figure. State retail prices for "peasant goods of mass consumption" appear to have risen by a factor of

[45] These countries were unable to follow a policy of autarky, but they also followed a more reasonable policy towards their peasants.
[46] Karl E. Waedekin, "Aktuelle Grundprobleme der agrarsozialen Struktur in der Sowjetunion," p. 11 of the mimeographed version.
[47] Nimitz, *Farm Employment, op. cit.*, Table 1, and *Kommunist*, No. 2, 1966, p. 88.
[48] Nimitz, *Farm Employment, op. cit.*, p. 96. It is again assumed that the share of households in total market sales came to 85 per cent.

about 2; collective farm market prices underwent an increase of only 4 per cent.[49] The difficulty lies in lack of knowledge of how expenditures were distributed between the two markets and of what the price trends were in the rural markets. It is clear that the tax burden rose somewhere from 300 to 350 per cent and that it became severe enough to lead to considerable disinvestment in the private sector. Such developments are hardly consistent with a rise in the real value of peasant money income.[50]

Trends between 1953 and 1958 were entirely different. The money income of households, from market sales and collective farm distributions, doubled, and retail prices for "peasant foods of mass consumption" fell about 20 per cent.[51] Collective farm market prices also fell by about six per cent. In this period, then, there is an apparent increase of some 130 to 150 per cent in the real value of peasant money income. Unfortunately, 1958 immediately became a "good old year." Trends in total income from sales of farm products, including procurements, and trends in collective farm market distributions are enumerated in Table 9 below.

Table 9

Income from Sales
of Farm Products and Collective Farm Market Distributions
(In New Rubles)

	Total Money Income from Agriculture	Collective Farm Cash and Kind Disbursements per Man-Day
1958.........	11,780,000,000	1.50
1959.........	11,750,000,000	1.40
1960.........	11,430,000,000	1.32
1961.........	12,480,000,000	1.61
1962.........	14,350,000,000	1.65
1963.........	16,380,000,000	1.72
1964.........	16,410,000,000	1.89
1965.........	18,160,000,000	—

SOURCE: "Seven Years on the Farm: Retrospect and Prospects," Joint Economic Committee, *New Directions in the Soviet Economy*, Washington, D.C., Government Printing Office, 1966, Appendix, Table 7.

---

[49] Indices of state retail prices for 1952 (1940=100) are as follows (cf. Central Statistical Administration of the USSR, *Sovetskaya torgovlya* [Soviet Trade], Moscow, 1964, p. 165):

Sugar	209	Leather Shoes	198
Salt	183	Tobacco Products	117
Vodka and Liquor	298	Matches	250
Cotton Textiles	243	Kerosene	213
Knitwear	193		

[50] Nimitz, *Farm Employment, op. cit.*, pp. 103–105.
[51] *Narkhoz-1962*, p. 533.

Thus, the economic record of the first two years of the Seven-Year Plan manifests retrogression. Moreover, until 1964, income in kind from agriculture failed to regain the level it had reached in 1958.[52] Once again, the attempt to extract forced savings from the agricultural sector is evident. Mention has already been made of the inability of the agricultural sector to satisfy its own capital needs. In view of this shortcoming, effective use of scarce capital resources acquires special importance not only for the agricultural sector of the economy but for the other sectors as well. Given the scarcity of capital, particularly in the context of the ambitious goals of the Soviet leadership, an incremental capital output ratio of 5.2, which prevailed from 1958 to 1965, is extremely difficult to tolerate.

Finally, to come to grips with essential causal relationships, it has been suggested in the preceding section of this study that most of the present Soviet difficulties in agriculture can be traced to the adoption of a model of unbalanced growth—unbalanced, that is, between agriculture and the other sectors of the economy. To a very large extent this statement is correct, but the issue is much more complex than is suggested. It is possible, I believe, to speak of the inexorable logic of a command economy without subscribing to one or another version of determinism. The point is that in the institutional environment of the USSR, where the machinery for the resolution of conflict is largely conspicuous by its absence, enactment and implementation of major institutional reforms necessarily entails formidable difficulties. These are further aggravated by problems of information flows (how else could Stalin have wished to extract another forty billion rubles from agriculture shortly before his death?) and by the predilection of the Soviet leadership to use short-run policy instruments for the solution of structural problems.

The harsh policy of the immediate post-war period, clearly oriented as it was to the disadvantage of the peasant, has already been alluded to here. Stalin's policies in the last eight years of his life are still not sufficiently elucidated to justify drawing conclusions about what motivated them, but it seems reasonable to suspect that he decided in favour of this harsh line while carefully watching the trends in the indices of farm and food marketings. In 1945, these stood at a level somewhere between 50 and 58 per cent of what they had been in 1940. At the same time, the population demand that these marketings had to satisfy must have been at least as large as, or larger than, that in 1940. Under these circumstances, a great deal of imagination and skill would have been required to introduce a major

[52] Abraham S. Becker, *Soviet National Income and Product, 1958–1962*, RM-4394-PR, Part I, Santa Monica, California, The RAND Corporation, 1965, p. 7.

policy shift. (Perhaps a suggestion to this effect constituted the real "crime" of Voznesensky). In any event, it must have appeared safer to rely on the well-tested methods that saw the Party safely through the difficult years of the Civil War and the First Five-Year Plan.

To summarize, the contribution of the agricultural sector of the Soviet economy to domestic capital formation in the post-war period was very great indeed. Failure to recognize that the economic environment had changed and that as a result a different agricultural policy was necessary is more understandable if other factors, such as requirements of reconstruction in industry, pressures to sustain other socialist countries in Europe, and continued, if unfounded, fears of foreign aggression, are borne in mind. The fact remains, however, that failure to recognize the need for a change in policy had consequences so far-reaching that they perhaps outweigh even the effects of war damage on the performance of agriculture. In spite of Draconian measures, it proved impossible to regain pre-war levels of food marketings per urban head. Even a complete recovery would have left the government in a difficult situation, since the size of the armed forces and the size of its own export demand were considerably greater than they had been in 1940. Trends in gross output in the period 1948–1952 suggest stagnation, defining, as they do, a steady deterioration in per capita production. Thus, notwithstanding annual investments of two billion new rubles in 1950–1952, the agricultural sector had ground virtually to a halt in the last years of Stalin's life. That no changes in policy were forthcoming is in itself an indication of the importance of the information problem in the command economy as well as of the stubborn refusal to recognize the seriousness of the situation. Indeed, it is interesting to speculate on the consequences of persistent use of the same policies had Stalin lived until, say, 1955 or so.

That other policies were introduced in 1953 confirms the existence of alternatives, and the satisfactory performance of agriculture in the period from 1953 to 1958 testifies to their effectiveness. The merits and shortcomings of Soviet agricultural policies since 1953 will not be discussed here. A substantial literature on the subject already exists.[53] What is remarkable about this time is that a successful policy was consciously abandoned in mid-stream. I have attempted to show elsewhere that the events of 1958 should be seen not only as monumental mismanagement of a much-needed structural reform of the MTS, but also as a reflection of a conscious shift

---

[53] See J. F. Karcz, "The New Soviet Agricultural Program," *Soviet Studies*, Vol. XVII, No. 2, October, 1965, and Keith S. Bush, "Agricultural Reforms Since Khrushchev," Joint Economic Committee, *New Directions in the Soviet Economy*, Washington, D.C., Government Printing Office, 1966.

in agricultural policy.[54] This shift may have been based in part on the belief that farm incomes had by then reached a desirable level and that the state should share to a greater extent in future gains in productivity. However, the events of 1958 were also a function of the famous so-called planner preferences, and there is no doubt that the priority of agriculture was considerably reduced while the Seven-Year Plan was being prepared. Upon further reflection, it seems fair to say again that the planners were unable to reconcile their own time preference, as it affected future trends in agricultural output, with the competing claims of other goals affecting the production of off-farm inputs, particularly machinery and fertilizers. In essence, the policy pursued from 1958 to 1960 represented a return to implementation of the exploitative practices of the thirties in a different, if nonetheless painfully meaningful, way.

The reasons why efforts to speed up the extraction of "surplus produce from the countryside" so rapidly misfired are simple enough. Unfortunately, for Khrushchev, the endeavour to launch his own version of the Great Leap Forward coincided with very unfavourable trends in the income elasticity of expenditures. These trends were in part the result of certain built-in characteristics of the Soviet command economy, in part the effect of unsound fiscal policies, and in part the outcome of failure to practice demand analysis.[55] In spite of repeated pleas, the demand for grain by other socialist countries could not be significantly reduced.[56] Khrushchev's predilection for applying campaign methods (corn, grasses, and fallow) violated the principles of sound agronomy and was not at all helpful. In addition, the weather failed to oblige. The rise in capital output ratios was not confined to the agricultural sector alone, and little help could be expected from other sectors of the economy.[57] Khrushchev's policy in this period might be described as overdetermined in that it employed too many policy tools indiscriminately. Measures suitable to the command economy were applied at the same time that market-type incentives were introduced, with the result that nothing seemed to work in the expected manner or at the expected time.

There is a certain Alice-in-Wonderland flavour about Soviet agricultural developments in this period that is quite instructive. The government

---

[54] See Karcz, "Seven Years on the Farm," *op. cit.*, pp. 402–410.

[55] *Ibid.*, pp. 388–391.

[56] See Khrushchev's poignant appeal in his *Stroitelstvo kommunizma i razvitiye selskogo khozyaystva v SSSR* (The Building of Communism and the Development of a Socialist Economy in the USSR), Moscow, 1962–1964, p. 109.

[57] On this matter see the paper by Ya. B. Kvasha in V. G. Venzher, *et al.*, *Proizvodstvo, nakopleniye, potrebleniye* (Production, Accumulation, and Consumption), Moscow, 1965, and Stanley Cohn's paper in this volume.

was investing in agriculture at the rate of nine billion rubles a year, but it was also attempting to keep farm specialists from leaving the village virtually by means of making them serfs. A good deal of time and effort was being spent in developing new varieties of wheat that yield more, while a drastic decline in the protein content of Soviet wheats was taking place as a result of various mistakes in procurement planning and farm organization. When farms attempted to scrap much of the obsolete equipment acquired from the MTS, the government responded with an edict that forbade disposing of such equipment prior to a bureaucratic determination of periods of useful life not only for machines as a whole but for crucial sub-assemblies as well. Prices were raised grudgingly, but they still failed to cover costs in the livestock sector. This as well as other defects in procurement planning interfered with specialization and prevented development of weaker farms. Ridiculously high plans were issued for production of animal products, but farms were forced to cut down rations and maintain so-called ghost herds since administrators refused to permit a reduction in numbers of livestock in the face of serious feed shortages.

Ultimately, the reason why Khrushchev failed where Stalin succeeded is that the latter was fully prepared to "drown the risings in blood."[58] To his lasting credit, Khrushchev himself foreclosed this avenue of approach, even though he, too, had to deal with civil disorders and riots such as those following the increase in prices of meat and butter in 1962.[59] One wonders whether Khrushchev felt the shadow of Bukharin at his shoulder on that fateful evening of October 14, 1964. For, in the end, it was the old problem of peasant incentives and responses to market forces and of yet another unsuccessful attempt to proceed with primitive socialist accumulation (this time in a developed socialist economy) that forced the introduction of the New Agricultural Programme in 1965. The details of this programme have been described elsewhere,[60] and it may be sufficient only to pinpoint what I regard as a major shift in emphasis represented by it. Soviet agriculture, for the first time, appears to have been put on a par with industry, at least insofar as there are signs of recognition that output cannot rise without a concomitant increase in input.

In closing, one last question calls for consideration: Have Soviet leaders chosen a method of improving agricultural performance regardless of costs? Judging by the best thinking on the subject in the West, the answer

---

[58] *Sotsialisticheskiy vestnik*, No. 9, 1929, p. 10.

[59] Albert Boiter, "When the Kettle Boils Over," *Problems of Communism*, New York, Vol. XIII, No. 1, January-February, 1964.

[60] Karcz, "The New Soviet Agricultural Program," *op. cit.*, and Bush, *op. cit.*

seems to be yes—for reasons that are, as I see it, only peripherally related to the question of ownership. All the policies considered appropriate by the foremost authorities on the subject have either not been applied in the USSR or else have been frustrated by "the inexorable logic of the command economy."[61] The most fruitful research in agriculture (the Russians have an outstanding tradition in this field) will be of no value if the results are not attractive enough for one reason or another to permit application on the farm. (It is, of course, true that the phenomenon of Lysenkoism is a direct contradiction of scientific research). Little good can come of expensive training of farm specialists if they have to be kept on the farm by administrative fiat alone. Little good can come—as Theodore Schultz convincingly asserts—of supplying new factors of production, such as hybrid corn, if it is not advantageous for the farm to introduce them into actual production.[62] The importance of extension services and the education they provide has been vividly demonstrated elsewhere, but no lasting effect can be achieved in this respect by orders from outside plenipotentiaries or inspector-organizers. Professor Schultz has long stressed the importance of education and new factors of production. He has also insisted that proper handling of these problems may lead to less expensive, more rapid progress than the old-fashioned method of merely chanelling expensive investments into the countryside.

At the beginning of this study, attention was called to the prevailing atmosphere of ferment and potential change in Soviet agriculture on the eve of the Congress of Collective Farmers. Clearly, it would be foolish to expect too much from this and other developments, since the task of rationalizing the command economy is a difficult and protracted one. Soviet leaders would perhaps do well to heed the advice of their former colleague, Bukharin, whose books and ideas are still banished from the Soviet intellectual scene; for their experience with agriculture demonstrates most vividly the applicability of his remark: "We shall conquer because of scientific economic administration or we shall not conquer at all."[63] This has been the case so far, and this is why the record is still incomplete. After a period of forty-nine years it is still correct to stress the potential of Soviet agriculture, its promise, rather than its achievement (in spite of the bumper harvest in 1966). It is also true that the record is a far better reflection of the impact of unbalanced sectoral growth than of socialization as such. The road ahead, however, is now less obscured than at any other period in Soviet history.

---

[61] Schultz, *op. cit.*, *passim*, and Johnston and Mellor, *op. cit.*, pp. 582 ff.
[62] Schultz, *op. cit.*, p. 105.
[63] Bukharin in *Pravda*, January 24, 1929, as quoted by Lewin, *op. cit.*, p. 178.

Appendix I

Derivation of a Deflator for Peasant Incomes in 1928—1940

The Index of Collective Farm Market Prices

It is assumed that prices on rural markets moved in the same fashion as prices on urban markets. Prices on urban markets are estimated here.

According to A. I. Malafeyev, in *Istoriya tsenoobrazovaniya v SSSR, 1917–1963* (The History of Price Formation in the USSR, 1917–1963), Moscow, 1964, p. 131, prices on peasant markets—or on the equivalent of the future collective farm market—changed in the following fashion (percentage of change from the preceding year): 1929, 48 per cent; 1930, 145 per cent; 1931, 83 per cent. From these data, an index of these prices is extrapolated: 1928 = 100, 1929 = 148, 1930 = 363, and 1932 = 664. What is then needed is a price index for 1932 that would allow linking the above index to the index of collective farm market prices for 1932–1937 provided by Malafeyev, *op. cit.*, p. 402, and to the index for 1933–1939 supplied by M. A. Vyltsan, *Istoriya SSSR*, No. 2, 1966, p. 61.

Malafeyev also lists price relatives as an index of prices for five foods (rye flour, potatoes, beef, butter, and eggs) for 1928–1931 and for June 1, 1932 (*op. cit.*, p. 172). These prices relate to the "private market," which is supposed to have disappeared by the end of 1931. The indices are as follows: 1928 = 100.0; 1929 = 146.3; 1930 = 359.7; 1931 = 630.0; and June 1, 1932 = 1,320.0.

The correspondence between these indices and those of prices in the bazaar trade is evident. It is not surprising, even if the data relate to different kinds of trade, because the markets in question represent what were at the time the only free markets. We assume that on June 1, 1932, bazaar prices were also at the level of 1,320.

Malafeyev also obliges by reproducing data from a statistical handbook on bazaar trade published in the early thirties (p. 194). These data show changes in collective farm market prices for the same and other products from June 25, 1932, to September 25, 1932, as well as from September 25 to December 25 of the same year. They are the only price data available for the period. (Archival sources may include monthly data for the 25th day of each month.) It is necessary to assume that there was no price change between June 1 and June 25, 1932. On the strength of this assumption, price changes for four major products are listed as follows (preceding date = 100):

	September 25, 1932	December 25, 1932
Rye Flour	105.9	125.2
Potatoes	74.2	165.2
Beef	116.6	133.1
Butter	127.8	152.2

These relatives are aggregated with the aid of 1932 value weights for grains, potatoes, and meat and milk products as provided by Vyltsan, *op. cit.*, p. 59. The September price comes to 110.2 per cent of the June price on the average; the December price, to 138.4 per cent of the September price. Shifting the base to 1928 = 100, by linking the relatives to that for June 1, 1932, the following indices are obtained: June 1 = 1,320; September 25 = 1,455; and December 25 = 2,013. The index number for 1932 as a whole is estimated at 1,600 or the unweighted average of the three index numbers given above. More refined methods are of little avail, and the underlying assumption is that two-thirds of sales occurred at sharply rising prices in the last seven months of the year. This does not seem unreasonable.

The resulting index is then linked to that provided by Malafeyev, *op. cit.*, p. 402, for the years 1932–1937 (1932 = 100) and Vyltsan, *op. cit.*, p. 61, for 1933–1939 (1933 = 100). The index for 1940 is based on average annual prices for 1932 as given by Vyltsan (p. 61); the estimates of 1940 collective farm market prices are from the appendix to "Quantitative Analysis of the Collective Farm Market" by J. F. Karcz in *American Economic Review*, June, 1964. This calculation includes data on grains, potatoes, vegetables, milk, and meat. Price data for 1932 are from Vyltsan, *op. cit.*, pp. 59, 61; quantity weights refer to 1940 in order to preserve the Soviet practice of calculating price indices with the aid of the Paasche formula. The results are as follows (1928 = 100):

1929......	148	1935......	1,034
1930......	363	1936......	885
1931......	664	1937......	997
1932......	1,600	1938......	856
1933......	2,371	1939......	1,228
1934......	1,453	1940......	2,056

According to this calculation, 1940 prices exceed those of 1939 by a factor of about 1.7. According to Vyltsan, *op. cit.*, p. 61, the corresponding factors for price changes between March 1939 and March 1941 are as follows: rye flour, 5; beef, 1.8; butter, 1.8; potatoes, 1.9; and milk, 1.7.

The reader may wish to consult Malafeyev's discussion (pp. 166–207) on price trends during the entire period. Sharp rises in retail prices occurred in 1932. It was the year of the introduction of compulsory deliveries; in addition, so-called commercial trade was being rapidly developed. In the light of these trends, the increase in 1932 does not seem excessive, especially if it is kept in mind that by the beginning of June of this year prices had doubled in comparison with average prices for 1931. Nor does the price increase between 1939 and 1940 seem excessively large if it is kept in mind that 1939 was a very poor harvest year and that stockpiling and changes in the procurement system during that year must have exerted an unfavourable impact on supply both in the retail network and on the collective farm market. It remains to be said that Soviet sources continue to lack information on the average change in market prices between 1939 and 1940.

The Deflator

It is assumed throughout that one half of peasant purchases occurred at prices that moved as collective farm market prices did during this period and that the remaining half was spent in retail trade. (The assumption is more valid for the late thirties than for 1932, when the market probably absorbed more than 50 per cent of peasant expenditures, but there is nothing to justify an adjustment. Cf. *Planovoe khozyaystvo*, No. 9, 1938, p. 102). The retail price indices are taken from Malafeyev, *op. cit.*, p. 407. The results are shown below.

	State Retail Prices	Collective Farm Market Prices	Deflator
1928..............	100	100	100
1932..............	255	1,600	928
1937..............	536	997	766
1938..............	536	856	696
1939..............	536	1,228	882
1940..............	637	2,056	1,346

The resulting index numbers for 1937–1939 are likely to be somewhat on the low side, since there are some ambiguities about the movement of retail prices in those years (Malafeyev, *op. cit.*, pp. 206, 209–16), but this is not likely to exert a serious influence on calculations designed to illustrate an order of magnitude. More serious errors are likely to result from the difference between the "average" market basket and that purchased by peasants. We are still ignorant of the underlying data, and little purpose would presently be served by guesses based on data from the late twenties. The matter must rest here pending further research.

Appendix II

Notes to Table 2

Indices for Gross Output (Official) are based on data from *Selskoe khozyaystvo SSSR, op. cit.*, pp. 21, 79. Those for Gross Output (Adjusted) are arrived at by raising the indices for 1909–1913 and 1913 by 15 per cent. The sceptic may wish to refer to Arcadius Kahan's article in *Soviet Agricultural and Peasant Affairs, op. cit.*, p. 137. He will find that present estimates of output for 1913 are lower than corresponding estimates made in 1924–1925 and 1926–1927, as follows: for grain, by 19 per cent; for potatoes, by 21 per cent; for flax, by 27 per cent; and for hemp, by 22 per cent. The weight of grain in any index of output for this period exceeds 30 per cent.

Indices of Per Capita Gross Output (Official) are arrived at by dividing Gross Output (Official) by corresponding indices of population based on data in *Narodnoe khozyaystvo SSSR v 1962, op. cit.*, pp. 7–8; those for Per Capita Gross Output (Adjusted), by dividing Gross Output (Adjusted) by the same indices of population.

Indices of Farm Marketings (Per Urban Head) are based on unpublished calculations by this writer. Those for 1909–1913 and 1913 are derived from data in *Selskoe khozyaystvo SSSR, op. cit.*, pp. 86–87. Those for 1928–1929 are estimates based on a variety of sources in order to eliminate differences in data for marketings as printed in *Kontrolnye tsifry narodnogo khozyaystvo SSSR na 1929–1930, op. cit.*, pp. 538–39, and as now reckoned by the Central Statistical Administration. Quantities are weighted by average values of marketings in 1925–1926 and 1927–1928 as calculated in terms of prices given in *Kontrolnye tsifry narodnogo khozyaystvo SSSR na 1929–1930, op. cit.*, pp. 581–82. The calculation includes grains, potatoes, vegetables, sunflowers, sugar beets, raw cotton, tobacco, makhorka, flax fibre, hemp fibre, meat, milk, eggs, and wool. Weighted quantities are then divided by an index of urban population based on data in *Narodnoe khozyaystvo SSSR v 1962, op. cit.*, pp. 7–8, and in *Zernovaya problema v godu sploshnoy kollektivizatsii selskogo khozyaystvo SSSR, op. cit.*, p. 27. Urban population for 1928–1929 is taken as 28,300,000; for 1938–1940, as 54,700,000; and for 1936–1940, as 50,800,000. Data on marketings for 1936–1940 are from *Narodnoe khozyaystvo SSSR v 1958, op. cit.*, p. 351.

Indices of Food Marketings (Per Urban Head) are derived in the same way as those of Farm Marketings (Per Urban Head). In this instance, the calculation includes grains, potatoes, vegetables, sunflowers, meat, milk, and eggs.

Indices of Sown Area are based on data from *Selskoe khozyaystvo SSSR, op. cit.*, p. 127.

Indices of Capital Stock (Total) assume that the value of capital stock, in terms of prices used in the capital census of 1962, was 20,000,000,000 rubles in 1940 and 16,300,000,000 rubles in 1928. These values are arrivied at on the basis of data in *Narodnoe khozyaystvo SSSR v 1964, op. cit.*, p. 52. (According to *Narodnoe khozyaystvo SSSR v 1962, op. cit.*, capital stock in 1940 was 23 per cent larger than in 1928.) The figure for 1940 is reduced by 15 per cent to take territorial differences into account. Investments in 1940 (roughly 700,000,000 rubles, excluding investments in herds) are then deducted from it. No further adjustment is made at this point in the calculation since investment data are in terms of "adjusted 1955 prices" and are, therefore, imprecise for this reason alone. Estimates are also made of the value of 1937–1939 investments in order to approximate an index of capital stock for 1936–1939. Data on investments are from *Kapitalnoe Stroitelstvo v SSSR, op. cit* ., pp. 35, 37, 152–55.

Indices of Capital Stock (Excluding Livestock) are based on the same sources as those of Capital Stock (Total) and are derived in the same manner. No figure for 1936–1939 has been derived, because one is not necessary in further calculations.

Indices of Labour Input (Man-Days) are based on data in Nimitz, *Farm Employment in the Soviet Union, 1928–1963, op. cit.*, Table 1.

The Output Index (Official) is arrived at by recalculating indices of Gross Output (Official) with 1928 as the base year.

The Input Index (Weights I) is calculated on the basis of the indices given in the table for the three inputs: Sown Area, Capital Stock (Total), and Labour Input (Man-Days). The weights employed are land, 13.7; capital, 17.8; and labour, 68.5. These are factor shares for 1958 as calculated by Abraham S. Becker in *Soviet National Income and Product, 1958–1962, op. cit.*, p. 116. For the Input Index (Weights II), the weights employed are land, 25.6; capital, 16.7; and labour 57.7. These weights are, again, from Becker, *op. cit.*

The Joint Productivity Index (Weights I) is arrived at by dividing the Output Index (Official) by the Input Index (Weights I). The Joint Productivity Index (Weights II) is similarly derived using the Input Index (Weights II) as the divisor.

Appendix III

Notes to Table 7 and Table 8

Indices of Gross Output (Official) are based on data from *Selskoe khozyaystvo SSSR*, *op. cit.*, pp. 21, 79; *Narodnoe khozyaystvo SSSR v 1964*, *op. cit.*, p. 246; and *SSSR v tsifrakh v 1965 godu*, p. 70. Those for Gross Output (Adjusted) are arrived at by raising the indices for 1909–1913 and 1913 by 15 per cent.

Indices of Net Output (USDA Index) are taken from the *USSR and Eastern Europe Agricultural Situation*, *op. cit.*, p. 2.

Indices of Per Capita Gross Output (Official) are arrived at by dividing Gross Output (Official) by an index of population based on data in *Narodnoe khozyaystvo SSSR v 1964*, *op. cit.*, p. 7. (All figures are taken as referring to January 1.) Indices of Per Capita Gross Output (Adjusted) are arrived at by dividing Gross Output (Adjusted) by the same index of population.

Indices of Per Capita Net Output (USDA Index) are taken from *The USSR and Eastern Europe Agricultural Situation*, *op. cit.*, p. 2.

Indices of Farm Marketings (Per Urban Head) are based on unpublished calculations by this writer. Those for 1909–1913 and 1913 are derived from data in *Selskoe khozyaystvo SSSR*, *op. cit.*, pp. 86–7. Those for 1928–1929 are estimates based on a variety of sources in order to eliminate differences in data from marketings as printed in *Kontrolnye tsifry narodnogo khozyaystvo SSSR na 1929–1930*, *op. cit.*, pp. 538–39, and as now reckoned by the Central Statistical Administration. (For flax, hemp, tobacco, and makhorka, marketings are assumed to move in the same fashion as state procurements.) Weights used are 1958 values of marketings in terms of average prices realized by the collective farm and the private sector.

Indices of Food Marketings (Per Urban Head) are derived in the same way as those of Farm Marketings (Per Urban Head). The calculation omits wool and technical crops other than sunflowers.

Indices of Sown Area are based on data from *Selskoe khozyaystvo SSSR*, *op. cit.*, p. 127; *Narodnoe khozyaystvo SSSR v 1962*, *op. cit.*, p. 247; *Narodnoe khozyaystvo SSSR v 1964*, *op. cit.*, p. 272; and *SSSR v tsifrakh v 1965*, *op. cit.*, p. 71.

Indices of Capital Stock (Total) are based on data from *Narodnoe khozyaystvo SSSR v 1961*, *op. cit.*, p. 68; *Narodnoe khozyaystvo SSSR v 1962*, *op. cit.*, p. 53; *Narodnoe khozyaystvo SSSR v 1964*, *op. cit.*, p. 68; and *SSSR v tsifrakh v 1965*, *op. cit.*, p. 27. Figures for 1953 and 1956–1957 are estimates based on data from *Selskoe khozyaystvo SSSR*, *op. cit.*, p. 385.

Indices of Capital Stock (Excluding Livestock) are based on the same sources as those of Capital Stock (Total).

Indices of Labour Input (Man-Days) are based on data from Nimitz, *Farm Employment in the Soviet Union*, *op. cit.*, Table 1.

The Output Index (Official) is taken from *Narodnoe khozyaystvo SSSR v 1964*, *op. cit.*, p. 246, and *SSSR v tsifrakh v 1965*, *op. cit.*, p. 69.

The Input Index (Weights I) is calculated on the basis of the indices given in the table for the three inputs: Sown Area, Capital Stock (Total), and Labour Input (Man-Days). The weights employed are land, 13.7; capital, 17.8; and labour, 68.5. These are factor shares for 1958 as calculated by Abraham S. Becker in *Soviet National Income and Product, 1958–1962, op. cit.*, p. 116. For the Input Index (Weights II), the weights employed are land, 25.6; capital, 16.7; and labour, 57.7. These weights are, again, taken from Becker, *op. cit.*

The Joint Productivity Index (Weights I) is arrived at, in the first instance, by dividing the Output Index (Official) by the Input Index (Weights I). In the second instance, Net Output (USDA Index) is divided by an index of input recalculated to the same base as Net Output (USDA Index) and weighted accordingly with Weights I. The Joint Productivity Index (Weights II) is similarly derived in both instances with the difference that Weights II enter into the calculation instead of Weights I.

Fifty Years of Soviet Labour

Norton T. Dodge

The labour policy of the Soviet state has been marked, from the out-set, by obvious conflicts among its goals. The light in which one views these conflicts—whether or not they are regarded as involving fundamental human values and freedoms—will, to a large extent, determine how one evaluates the success or failure of the Soviet regime in fulfilling the prom-ises of the October Revolution in the sphere of labour policy. One such conflict arose early in Soviet history over the issue of basic Party policy towards labour and the trade-union structure. Here, the leadership threw its weight on the side of the doctrine that only the Party, serving in its capacity as "the vanguard of the proletariat," is qualified to determine what policies are in the long-term interests of the working class. This doctrine opened the door for a host of tensions within the ruling elite, ranging, over the decades, from early suppression of syndicalist tendencies among workers to eventual extinction of the independent power position of the trade-union movement. Such policies may have been viewed by the Party leadership as indispensable means for the attainment of Soviet objectives in the realm of international power, but they will not be accepted by dispassionate observers as having been helpful in advancing the inter-ests of workers in the Soviet Union. A second conflict arose in connection with the allocation of economic resources between current welfare on the one hand and investment in rapid economic growth on the other. This conflict was resolved by Stalin in favour of the latter alternative. To be sure, it could be argued that the benefits of economic growth would in due time redound to the advantage of labour and the general population. As a matter of practical experience, however, the real benefit to labour from economic growth has been so severely restricted by the need to continue to maintain a high level of investment that the particular mix of elements of growth and welfare chosen by the makers of basic Party policy can be seen as unmistakably dominated by the political interests of the state.

The several categories of workers in the Soviet Union may be distinguished, as a matter of convenience, as follows: (1) workers and employees of industrial enterprises and other economic establishments of the state, including state farms; (2) employees of the government and of various governmental institutions; (3) employees of the consumer cooperatives, which function largely in rural areas; (4) members of collective farms; (5) individual artisans working at home; and (6) household servants. Of these, only the first three groups, which make up the bulk of the hired labour force in the Soviet Union, will be considered here. It is a well-known fact that collective farmers and artisans work under unique conditions in the Soviet Union and that they are subject to special treatment by the state. Household servants, on the other hand, constitute an extremely small group about which little information is published. For these reasons, this study shall focus on developments over the past fifty years as they have affected the workers (blue-collar) and employees (white-collar) of the Soviet Union who now make up more than three-fifths of the entire civilian labour force of the nation. The passage of fifty years since the establishment of the first workers' state offers sufficient perspective for making a meaningful comparison of the original promises of the Bolshevik revolution with the present status of labour under Soviet socialism. The first and longest part of this study is an attempt to make such a comparison; the final part is an effort to weigh the outlook for Soviet labour during the next few decades. Though discussion in the latter part must be conjectural in nature, it nevertheless seems useful to try to distinguish, where possible, the more permanent features in the condition of Soviet labour from those that are in the process of change or are likely to change in the future.

Promise of the "Workers' State"

One of Lenin's most distinctive ideas as a political theorist grew out of his view of the relationship between the labour movement and the Communist Party. He believed the proletariat by itself was not capable of carrying out the revolutionary overthrow of capitalism, because it was an unwieldy mass composed of diverse elements possessing limited degrees of class consciousness. Some groups of workers, as he saw it, were concerned primarily with their own narrow, immediate material interests and could, at times, act against the interests of other elements of the working class, or even contrary to their own long-term interests. At other times, the entire working class might sacrifice its "true" and "permanent" interests in the pursuit of transitory or contradictory objectives. The Party, however, was quite another matter. As Lenin would have it, the Party he was building was not to be a mass political organization of the working class but rather a select, disciplined vanguard acting *on behalf of* the proletariat.

It is equally clear that this is precisely the way in which Stalin, closely following in Lenin's footsteps, interpreted the relationship between the activist Communist Party and the mass of workers. He wrote:

> The Party cannot be a real Party if it limits itself to registering what the masses of the working class feel and think . . . The Party must stand at the head of the working class; it must see further than the working class; it must lead the proletariat and not follow in the trail of spontaneous movement.[1]

The Party's role, then, was to educate and unify the proletariat, enabling it to pursue its "permanent" interests—the overthrow of capitalism and the establishment of socialism. Thus, at the outset, latent conflict was inherent between the objectives of the Party on the one hand and the aspirations of labour and its representative organizations on the other. For a time prior to the revolution and for some years after, before control of the levers of power was securely in its hands, the Party responded sympathetically to many of labour's "bread and butter" demands; it even appeared to accept trade-union demands for an important role in running the economy. Given the fundamental Bolshevik view of the relationship between the Party and the proletariat, the step from elitism to despotism was a relatively small one. Once entrenched, Stalin did not hesitate to use coercion, along with propaganda, persuasion, and education, to carry out his policies, regardless of trade-union or worker opposition.

Arvid Broderson argues that this elitist conception of the Party's relationship to the proletariat is opposed to the views of Marx himself. "Marx," he states, "consistently expresses a strong aversion to the notion that the workers' party could be anything except a creation of the proletarian class itself. He rejected the idea that it could be an 'elite' outside the proletariat arrogating to itself the power and right to conduct the politics of, or for, the workers themselves."[2] Other students of Marx believe, in contrast, that the genesis of elitist ideas begins with the *Communist Manifesto*, in which Marx and Engels predict that a portion of the bourgeois ideologists will join the proletariat and assert that "The Communists . . . have over the great mass of the proletariat the advantage of clearly understanding the line of march, the conditions, and the ultimate general results of the proletarian movement."[3] Whatever the genesis, the fact remains that from Lenin to Brezhnev, the Party leadership has been convinced that the "vanguard" rather than the "great mass of the proletariat" can know what is in the best interests of the workers.

Dictactorship of the Proletariat. In the light of this long-standing view of the relationship of the Party to the proletariat, it is not difficult to see

---

[1] J. Stalin, *Problems of Leninism*, Moscow, 1940, p. 73.

[2] Arvid Broderson, *The Soviet Worker*, New York, Random House, 1966, p. 16.

[3] Karl Marx and Friedrich Engels, *The Communist Manifesto*, in *Capital, the Communist Manifesto and Other Writings*, edited by Max Eastman, New York, The Modern Library, 1932, pp. 334–35.

why the "dictatorship of the proletariat" meant that the Party as an elite excercised the powers vested in all industrial workers by the October Revolution. The Party felt justified in acting on behalf of the alleged dictator, the proletariat, which was incapable of knowing or acting in its own interest. As Stalin put it, in his usual blunt fashion, ". . . the leadership passed wholly and entirely into the hands of one Party, into the hands of our Party, which does not share and cannot share the guidance of the state with any other Party. This is what we call the dictatorship of the proletariat."[4] It would be difficult to express more unequivocally the real meaning, in practice, of the dictatorship of the proletariat or to reveal more explicitly the Party's arrogation to itself of powers purportedly vested in the workers themselves.

Workers' Control. As Lenin prepared for the seizure of power, he tried to gain the support of the workers by appealing to the vision of a new order in which the workers themselves would manage production in each plant or enterprise. The factory committees that sprang up after the February Revolution were viewed as a first step in this direction, and, after the October Revolution, the Bolsheviks established the principle of workers' control over all industry. Isaac Deutscher points out: "At this stage the Bolsheviks appeared as adherents of the most extreme decentralization of economic power, which gave their Menshevik opponents the opportunity to charge them with abandoning Marxism in favor of anarchism."[5] As the Bolsheviks attempted to exert central control over industry, they inevitably came into conflict with the unruly factory committees and were forced to call upon the trade unions for aid in disciplining them. Late in 1917, the factory committees were incorporated into the trade unions, and the trade unions became the main agency through which the Party assumed control over industry.[6] In this fashion the dream ended of an industrial democracy in which workers themselves would run their factories. Whether or not workers would have an independent voice now became a question of the role of trade unions in the centralized, one-party, Soviet state.

The Fate of Trade Unionism. Control over unions by the Party was not won at once.[7] Trade unions played an active role in economic administration

---

[4] J. Stalin, *op. cit.*, pp. 181–82.

[5] Isaac Deutscher, *Soviet Trade Unions*, London and New York, Royal Institute of International Affairs, 1950, p. 15.

[6] *Ibid.*, pp. 17–18.

[7] For a brief review of the changing position of unions, see Emily Clark Brown, *Soviet Trade Unions and Labour Relations*, Cambridge, Massachusetts, Harvard University Press, 1966, Chapter III. Deutscher, *op. cit.*, provides a more complete treatment.

during the first years after the revolution, and many state functions were trans-ferred to them. As economic crisis deepened during the Civil War, however, changes were needed to counteract the growing economic disorganization. Two extreme solutions confronted the policy-makers. Trotsky urged an authoritarian solution: the militarization of the trade unions and their complete subordination to the state. The Workers' Opposition insisted that the administration of the economy should be turned over to the trade unions themselves. As Isaac Deutscher puts it, the issue was whether the trade unions were to absorb the state or *vice versa*. Lenin took a middle position, which was finally victorious. According to him, the unions could function as a "transmission belt" between the workers and the state and could, while retaining the appearance of autonomy, serve as a "school of communism" and promote labour discipline and productivity.

With the introduction of the New Economic Policy (NEP) in 1921, some of the traditional activities of trade unions were resumed. In private industry, the unions were encouraged by the Party to support the claims of labour, but they were instructed not to assume directly any functions of control over production. Though strikes against state enterprises were not outlawed, the leaders of the trade unions were understandably expected to do their utmost to discourage them or else be prepared to face the disapproval of their superiors in the Party. Trade unions were also elimi-nated from participation in the actual management of state enterprises. Any interference with management was to be regarded as "absolutely harmful and inadmissible."[8] Deutscher also stresses that the Eleventh Party Con-gress made a major step towards eliminating what little trade-union inde-pendence remained by requiring that candidates for "election" as secre-taries and chairmen of the central committees of the unions must be Party members of long standing.[9]

The ambiguous role of the trade unions continued throughout the period of NEP. At the end of 1928, as NEP drew to a close and the First Five-Year Plan was inaugurated, friction between the trade unions and the economic administrators increased. Tomsky and other pro-labour union officials undertook a vigorous fight to retain a measure of independence for the unions. Tomsky contended: "There should be no friendship between the economic administrator and the Trade Unionist, when it comes to carrying out the collective agreement—both sides must fullfil their commitments."[10] Tomsky was removed from office in May of 1929

---

[8] Deutscher, *op. cit.*, p. 62.
[9] *Ibid.*, p. 65.
[10] *Ibid.*, p. 78. Quoted by Deutscher.

and was later purged along with other like-minded trade unionists. From this time forward, the trade unions were wedded to the Party. In official parlance, they became "helpmates of the Party" and were formally committed to serving its interests and those of the government in carrying through the policy of forced industrialization.

After Stalin's death, the new leadership began to recognize that the existing coercive features of labour legislation were outdated, if not counterproductive. Increased labour productivity, it was believed, could be achieved only through less brutal compulsions and by convincing the workers that they were no longer simply tools for implementing decisions in which they had no say. As a result, in 1956, the government carried out what Edmund Nash has called an unprecedented relaxation of labour controls.[11] Authority to transfer workers from plant to plant was terminated; penal liability for unauthorized changes of employment was repealed; and legal prosecution of workers absenting themselves from work without valid reason was discontinued. To give workers a sense of participation and to shift the disciplinary burden from the manager's to the union's shoulders, so-called comrades' courts were set up in enterprises employing more than 100 persons. These kangaroo courts, which have been criticized in the Soviet press as management-controlled, can levy heavy penalties on recalcitrant plant workers whom management prefers to bring before the courts rather than punish by disciplinary sanctions.[12]

Regulations requiring agreement between management and the factory committee on changes in output norms were issued in 1956. The extent to which they increased the power or independence of the unions is debatable, however, since the Central Trade Union Council decreed that in exercising this new responsibility factory committees should make every effort to support management and increase output.[13] Two years later the powers of the factory committees were further expanded on paper. These committees were to participate in the drafting of plans and the determination of wage payments as well as work quotas. They were also to be consulted on managerial appointments. A regulation requiring the factory committee's consent to the discharge of a worker was reintroduced.[14]

---

[11] Edmund Nash, "Recent Trends in Labour Controls in the Soviet Union," *Dimensions of Soviet Economic Power*, Washington, D.C., U.S. Government Printing Office, 1962, p. 393. Many of the controls had been poorly enforced for several years prior to 1956.

[12] Paul Barton, "The Current Status of the Soviet Worker," *Problems of Communism*, Washington, D.C., July–August, 1960, pp. 21–22.

[13] *Ibid.*, p. 23.

[14] *Ibid.*; Nash, *op. cit.*, p. 396.

Nevertheless, the subservience of the committees to management deprived these measures of much of their significance other than the deeper involvement of the trade unions in unpopular decisions. The primary function of the trade unions continues, as before, to be that of encouraging workers to fulfill and overfulfill production plans. Enlarging the prerogatives of local trade unions has in no way provided more effective means for solving the major issues of collective discontent.

Promise of Equal Opportunity

The organization of modern industrial society is such that unfortunately the more desirable jobs at the top of the social structure are scarce and the object of strong competition. The Soviet Union suffers additionally, because, even now, after four decades of rapid industrialization, a large proportion of the labour force—somewhere near 35 per cent—works in agriculture, where employment tends to be less rewarding and physically more exhausting than in other sectors of the economy. Significant questions to answer in evaluating the performance of Soviet society since the revolution are: Who gets the desirable jobs? Do all citizens have an equal chance? Do the children of more favoured families have an advantage? Or, as Inkeles and Bauer ask, will the Soviet regime reverse the usual pattern and give the children of workers and peasants a more favourable chance?[15]

Though persons of bourgeois background or parentage were discriminated against in the years following the revolution, for most Russians the revolution meant the opening up of a multitude of opportunities that had previously been closed to them. Inkeles and Bauer note that Soviet experience in this respect was somewhat more favourable than that of other industrial societies. They report:

> In particular, mobility out of the worker and peasant category into white-collar work, and stability of status among those already in the white-collar milieu, are more evident in the Soviet data ... The rate of Soviet industrial expansion was so rapid that it created rather unprecedented needs for trained technical personnel and associated managerial, professional and clerical employees.[16]

Nevertheless, Inkeles and Bauer find that the Soviet class structure had solidified to a remarkable degree by World War II. They summarize the situation at that time as follows:

---

[15] Alex Inkeles and Raymond Bauer, *The Soviet Citizen*, Cambridge, Massachusetts, Harvard University Press, 1959, p. 80.

[16] *Ibid.*, p. 84.

It is obvious that the ultimate occupational placement of a child, although not absolutely sealed at birth, was heavily determined by his father's position in the occupational structure. Two out of three male children born into a professional or administrator's home could count on attaining to the same level as their father did, whereas only one in twelve of the children of peasants could realistically have the hope of reaching the professional-administrative level. Less than one in five of the sons born into the favored homes was forced to toil with hands, whereas almost eight in ten of the peasants' children earned their living in the "dirty, hot, and hard" jobs. We must repeat that this pattern developed in the face of an early social policy deliberately designed to turn the old social order upside down by selective encouragement of the mobility of the children of workers and peasants.[17]

Among the key factors influencing social mobility are (1) skills and ability, products of intelligence and education; (2) motivation to acquire and apply skills; and (3) opportunity to apply the skills possessed. In Soviet society, as in most others, upper class families are better able to assist and motivate their children in the pursuit of careers and to provide them with more intellectual stimulation, if not, in fact, more inherited intelligence. Perhaps the key difference in the Soviet hierachical bureaucracy is the greater importance of education in securing advancement. As a result, the question of whether or not the Soviet regime provides more nearly equal opportunity for education than do other societies is of central importance.

After the revolution, the rapid expansion of school enrollment and the introduction of a broad system of stipends opened semi-professional and professional careers to many who possessed the ability and motivation to pursue them and who would have been excluded by financial or class disabilities in pre-revolutionary Russia. The formal requirements for admission were largely based upon academic merit. However, political conformity, if not active support of youth and Party activities, was also required, and children of the former elite found admission particularly difficult. Inkeles and Bauer state:

> Far and away the outstanding obstacle to a superior education for those from upper class social backgrounds was not money, but rather the regime's treatment or evaluation of such backgrounds. Three fourths of all those of intelligentsia origins who had a complaint blamed their social origins for holding back their education.[18]

Frequently, persons of "undesirable" origins had to disguise their backgrounds or earn the status of workers by taking manual jobs for a time. More recently, discrimination against Jewish students in the form

---

[17] *Ibid.*, p. 83.
[18] *Ibid.*, p. 146.

of quotas has been alleged.[19] On the other hand, quotas favouring students of certain national minorities exist, and at an earlier time, quotas favouring the admission of women in various technical fields were established.[20] Broad social factors appear to have had more influence in deciding who obtains a secondary specialized or higher education in the Soviet Union than specific governmental policies favouring one group of students or discouraging another. These factors have kept the representation of the peasantry and ordinary workers very low in comparison with the number that might be expected if admissions were by lottery. Inkeles and Bauer found that among respondents in the 21 to 35 year age group, only one out of twenty of those of peasant or ordinary worker social origin obtained a higher education, while among those whose fathers were skilled workers the proportion was one in five. Among those whose fathers were engaged in professional or administrative work, slightly more than two out of five achieved a higher education.[21]

Continuing concern for the small percentage of students in higher education from peasant or worker origin has been shown by the Soviet leadership, although for long periods any public discussion of the matter was suppressed. During the debate on the 1958 school reform, Khrushchev himself charged that children of workers and peasants comprised only 30 to 40 per cent of the students in higher educational institutions in Moscow. The remainder, he said, were descendents of white-collar employees and the intelligentsia.[22] As De Witt points out, this complaint "confirmed what was already suspected by Western observers; namely, that the actual composition of student enrollment in Soviet higher education was far from conforming to the professed communist ideal of equality of access to education."[23] Data from a 1963 survey conducted in Novosibirsk Oblast confirm the perpetuation of this pattern. An analysis of the correlation between the father's occupation and interest in further schooling among secondary school graduates indicates that 82 per cent of the children of the urban intelligentsia entered specialized or higher educational institutions. In contrast, at the other extreme, only 10 per cent of the children of agricultural workers succeeded in entering such institutions. Between these two poles were children of industrial and construction workers (61

[19] Nicholas De Witt, *Education and Professional Employment in the U.S.S.R.*, Washington, D.C., U.S. Government Printing Office, 1961, pp. 358–60.
[20] *Ibid.*, pp. 357–58; Norton T. Dodge, *Women in the Soviet Economy*, Baltimore, The Johns Hopkins Press, 1966, pp. 111–12.
[21] Inkeles and Bauer, *op. cit.*, p. 142, Table 34.
[22] De Witt, *op. cit.*, p. 351.
[23] *Ibid.*

per cent), children of service personnel (58 per cent), and children of transport and communications workers (46 per cent).[24]

The student of peasant origin is handicapped in obtaining an advanced education by the lower quality and reduced availability of rural primary and especially secondary education. Also, while continuing schooling, students of both peasant and worker origin and their families bear a greater burden of income forgone than do others.[25] Perhaps more important, however, are differences in the degree of family support and the strength of individual motivation among students of different social groups. Inkeles and Bauer found that while almost three-fourths of the sons of the intelligentsia reported complete family support in their educational aspirations, only one-third of the sons of workers were able to do so. For daughters, the proportions were two-thirds and one-fourth, respectively. Similarly, the sons and daughters of the intelligentsia were themselves much more strongly motivated than their contemporaries of peasant and worker origin.[26] This circumstance helps to explain why children of the former elite achieved a much higher average level of education in spite of the discrimination practiced against them by the regime.

A hopeful development in recent years is expansion of the specialized secondary and higher educational systems so that an increasing proportion of the young people wanting such education have an opportunity to obtain it. The situation was particularly tight in the latter half of the 1950's when only 20 to 25 per cent of general secondary school graduates could be admitted as regular day students even if all places were made available to current graduates. In recent years, however, ignoring the double class completing secondary school in 1966, between one-quarter and one-third of the graduates could be accommodated as regular day students. Nevertheless, such improvement as has been made may be negated by expected increases in the college-age population in coming years, unless facilities are expanded at an even more rapid rate.[27] In view of continued restrictions on access to specialized secondary and higher education, owing to space limitations, it is not likely that the advantages of a superior social origin will disappear in the foreseeable future. It is evident that the Soviet Union

---

[24] V. N. Shubkin, in N. N. Novikov, et. al., eds., *Sotsialnye issledovaniya*, Moscow, 1965, p. 135.

[25] Tuition, charged students at the high school level or above from 1940 until 1956, increased the financial burden during this period. See De Witt, *op. cit.*, p. 66.

[26] Inkeles and Bauer, *op. cit.*, p. 150. See also Shubkin, *op. cit.*

[27] See James W. Brackett and John W. De Pauw, "Population Policy and Demographic Trends in the Soviet Union," *New Directions in the Soviet Economy*, Washington, D.C., U.S. Government Printing Office, pp. 618–19.

has not been notably successful in giving those from the less favoured classes an equal opportunity to advance within the social system. What is most remarkable in these circumstances is the tenacity with which the advantages of social origin persist despite drastic change in political and economic institutions. Modern industrial society appears to have its own imperatives, which cannot be altered easily by what Marxists might describe as activities at the level of the superstructure. Though equality of opportunity can be provided for in the formal framework of law, it is very difficult indeed, to attain as a matter of fact.

Promise of Equality for Women

Along with other major segments of the population, women were promised greater equality of opportunity following the revolution. For the first time, education in all fields and at all levels was thrown open to women, and many entered specialized secondary and higher educational institutions.[28] The percentage of women in higher educational institutions increased sharply during the Second Five-Year Plan; by 1937, it had reached 43 per cent. During the war, the percentage almost doubled. It returned to the 1937 level six years ago, where it has remained with only a slight variation.[29]

Paradoxically, the participation of women in the labour force as a whole declined slightly following the revolution, largely because of the shift of women from rural to urban areas, where their participation rate has traditionally been lower. However, between 1926 and 1959 the participation rate of urban women increased from 40 to 67 per cent, nearly offsetting the effect of the shift of women to urban areas.[30] Though the participation of women increased in almost every occupation, of particular significance in terms of enlarged opportunity was their increased role in semiprofessional and professional occupations. For example, the proportion of women among specialists with a specialized secondary education increased from 30 to 62 per cent between 1928 and 1965, while among specialists with a higher education, the increase was from 28 to 52 per cent.[31] Some professions in which very few women are found in other economies have a substantial proportion of women in the Soviet Union. Almost one-

---

[28] Surprisingly, women accounted for a quarter of the enrollment in higher educational institutions just prior to World War I. See Dodge, *op. cit.*, p. 103.

[29] *Ibid.*, p. 112; *Narodnoe khozyaystvo SSSR v 1965 godu* (The Economy of the USSR in 1965), Moscow, 1966, p. 700.

[30] Dodge, *op. cit.*, p. 33.

[31] *Ibid.*, p. 185; *Narodnoe khosyaystvo SSSR v 1965 godu*, Moscow, 1966, p. 580.

third of the engineers, two-fifths of the agricultural scientists, and three-quarters of the civilian physicians are women.[32] For these women, work provides real satisfaction and an opportunity to realize their aspirations and potential. It cannot be denied, however, that the proportion of women decreases with each successive increase in rank in the occupational hierarchy, even in fields dominated by women. In medicine, for example, the probability that a woman physician will be the head of a medical establishment or a chief or deputy chief physician is about one in ten, whereas the probability that a male physician would occupy such a position is about three in ten. The probability that a woman will hold a position in the next lower echelon is approximately one in seven, while for a man it is a little better than one in six. Thus, even in the Soviet Union where the situation is more favourable to a woman physician than in any other country in the world, a woman is much less likely to achieve a high position in her profession than a man.[33] The reason fewer women than men reach the top of their chosen professions does not appear to be prejudice against women or less opportunity in a formal sense. Rather, women are more preoccupied with other matters such as caring for a husband and children and are not likely to be as professionally competitive as men. As a result, most women's professional progress is slower than most men's and is likely to have a lower ceiling.

The most striking increase in opportunity for women has occurred in Soviet Central Asia, where the Moslem customs of early marriage and confinement of women to the home have in the past deprived women of both education and the possibility of a career beyond raising and caring for a family. Tremendous strides have been made by the Soviet government in freeing women in these areas from their traditional bondage, but traditional attitudes are tenacious and difficult to eradicate. Though many more young women of local nationalities are now receiving specialized secondary or higher education in the Central Asian Republics, the proportion is substantially less than among the Slavic nationalities in European Russia, particularly for those women of rural origin.[34] Progress in this regard during the 1950's was much slower than in preceding decades, suggesting that it may be many years before equality in educational and employment opportunities is won for the young women of the Central Asian nationalities.

For every Soviet woman for whom the door to a profession has been opened, there are several women workers bending to their tasks in the

---

[32] Dodge, *op. cit.*, p. 194.
[33] *Ibid.*, p. 210.
[34] *Ibid.*, pp. 107 and 118–21.

fields of a collective farm or in the machine shop or on the assembly line of a factory. Also, the fact should not be overlooked that for the bulk of Soviet women work is a necessity. If it were not necessary to work to make ends meet, many Soviet women would prefer to withdraw from the labour force, especially during the period when their children are young. For these women, equality of opportunity has meant simply the necessity to do tiresome, enervating work in addition to bearing the responsibility of raising a family. Equality has, in fact, meant inequality in the sense that women, as a group, bear a heavier burden than men.[35] That the regime has realized this is obvious from its attempts to provide more adequate child-care facilities, to reduce the demands of housework, and to make arrangements for part-time work. Also, protective legislation affecting women, such as provisions for maternity leave, is among the most progressive in the world.[36]

Promise of More Equal Incomes

With the abolition of the capitalist system, some of the inequalities of income that had prevailed under the private ownership system were eliminated in the Soviet Union. To be sure, the principle of "from each according to his ability, to each according to his need" remained a distant goal. Instead, the principle of "to each according to his work" was accepted as operative for the earlier, "socialist" phase of the development. This principle has led to much greater differentials in income than were originally expected. Apart from eliminating the upper extreme of the income distribution curve, the Soviet Union has found itself, in practice, operating with a system of differentials roughly similar to those prevailing under capitalism. In the years immediately following the revolution, egalitarian principles had a considerable influence on wage policy, but under pressure of a real and urgent need to increase production, the reverse became true in 1920 and 1921. The wage pendulum began to swing again in 1927. At the Seventh Trade-Union Congress, Tomsky reported, with some exaggeration, admittedly, that the difference between the pay of skilled and unskilled labour was "of such a colossal magnitude as does not exist in Western Europe" and urged that the gap be reduced.[37] In the next two years, earnings differentials were reduced substantially, but another reversal in policy came in 1931, initiating a period of wide wage differentiation that

---

[35] Time-use studies show that women have less leisure and less time for sleep than men. See *Ibid.*

[36] *Ibid.*, pp. 57–75.

[37] Quoted in Abram Bergson, *The Structure of Soviet Wages*, Cambridge, Massachusetts, Harvard University Press, 1944, p. 187.

continued until after Stalin's death. During this period, wage equality or "levelling," as Stalin called it contemptuously, was identified as a petty bourgeois or utopian policy or worse.

The situation began to change somewhat with the Twentieth Party Congress in 1956. Since then, the main trend in Soviet wage policy has been towards narrowing existing differentials, primarily through raising the minimum wage while holding the highest wages and salaries constant. At the Twenty-first Congress, in 1959, a programme was announced to increase minimum wages from 27–35 rubles per month, the rate that had prevailed since 1957, and to 40–45 rubles in 1962 and 50–60 in 1965. Realization of these goals has been delayed, however, and the present minimum is 40 rubles per month.[38] Since 1956, new wage and salary scales have also been established within individual branches of the economy. At present, the two extremes in wages are in a ratio of 1.8 to 1, as compared with the ratio of 2.8, or more, to 1, which prevailed previously. The actual narrowing of differentials brought about by these new scales is somewhat deceptive, however, owing to the previous practice of upgrading workers into relatively high wage categories, leaving few workers in the two lowest categories. Now, though the extremes of the scales are not so far apart, a substantial number of workers can be found in the lowest categories, bringing the actual extremes in the wage differentials closer to those of the formal categories. A reduction in the percentage of workers paid on a piece-rate basis during the past few years has also contributed to a narrowing of the wage differentials among individual workers in the Soviet Union. The major trends described are shown in Table 1, which gives decile and quartile ratios of money incomes for workers and employees. The decile ratios, in particular, show the increase in inequality from the early 1930's to 1956 and the sharp decline since that date.

Table 1

Differentials in Money Incomes of Workers and Employees in the USSR, 1929–1959

	Decile Ratio	Quartile Ratio
1929	315	182
1934	317	182
1956	338	185
1959	328	184

SOURCE: Murray Yanowitch, "The Soviet Income Revolution," *Slavic Review*, Urbana, Illinois, December, 1963, p. 686. The decile ratio is D9/D1 in per cent and the quartile ratio is Q3/Q1 in per cent.

[38] Janet Chapman, "The Minimum Wage in the USSR," *Problems of Communism*, September–October, 1964, pp. 76–79.

Substantial differences in average pay also exist among the different industries and sectors of the economy. Though these have lessened in recent years, the average earnings of workers and employees in water transport, the highest paid category in 1965, were almost double the earnings in the housing-communal sector, the lowest paid.[39] Perhaps the most striking reduction in differentials is the change in the relationship between earnings of blue-collar workers, on the one hand, and white-collar employees and engineering-technical personnel (ITR), on the other. The dramatic improvement in the position of workers vis à vis these two other groups is shown in Table 2.

Table 2

Comparison of Average Earnings of Workers, Employees, and Engineering-Technical Personnel (ITR) in the USSR, 1932–1965

(In Percentages of Average Earnings of Workers)

	Average Earnings of Employees	Average Earnings of ITR
1932	150	263
1940	109	210
1950	93	175
1955	88	165
1960	—	150
1965	—	145

SOURCES: Murray Yanowitch, "The Soviet Income Revolution," *Slavic Review*, December, 1963, p. 697; *Sotsialisticheskiy Trud*, No. 11, November, 1966, p. 5.

The underlying reasons for the substantial change in Soviet income structure in favour of workers, as shown in Table 2, include: (1) a more rapid increase in the supply of engineering-technical personnel relative to the supply of workers (580 versus 270 per cent); and (2) a greater upward wage drift for workers, many of whom are on piece rates, than for employees on fixed salaries.[40]

Though comprehensive data on income distribution in the Soviet Union are lacking, apparently a remarkable compression of extremes in income has occurred as a result of increases in the minimum wage. The establishment of a minimum wage of 27–35 rubles per month in January 1957 reportedly increased the wages of the lowest paid workers by 33 per cent. Further increases in the minimum wage have more than doubled the incomes of the lowest paid workers and employees in the past decade.[41]

---

[39] *Narodnoe khozyaystvo SSSR v 1965 godu, op. cit.*, pp. 567–68.

[40] *Narodnoe khozyaystvo SSSR v 1960 godu*, Moscow, 1961, p. 216, and *Narodnoe khozyaystvo SSSR v 1965, godu, op. cit.*, p. 140. These figures cover the period 1932–1965.

[41] Janet Chapman, *Real Wages in Soviet Russia Since 1928*, Cambridge, Massachusetts, Harvard University Press, 1963, pp. 180–81.

In addition, increases authorized late in 1964 for persons employed in the service sector have contributed further to the reduction in differentials. During the same decade, the highest salary scales have not been increased. Consequently, the difference between the highest and lowest levels of income has been approximately halved. As an illustration, a member of the Academy of Sciences of the USSR who was at the same time the director of a research institute and a part-time professor would have received a combined income of 1,350 rubles per month a decade ago (500 rubles as Academician, 600 as director, and 250 as a professor teaching half time), a figure seventy times the wage of the lowest-paid service or clerical personnel. Today, the Academician's income would be no higher, but the income of the lowest-paid service or clerical personnel would have more than doubled, reducing the differential from 70 to approximately 33. Admittedly, even after the reduction, the differential remains very large and hardly in keeping with the goals of socialism as expressed by Marx or Lenin. In theory, such differentials are justified on the grounds that at this stage of socialist development they are still necessary.[42] In practice, however, they merely reflect the same relative conditions of supply and demand that place a premium on scarce talent under any economic system. Since income differentials in the Soviet Union remain wide in spite of the narrowing which has occurred in the past decade, it may be concluded that after fifty years, the egalitarian promise of the revolution has only been imperfectly realized.

Promise of a Better Standard of Living

The Soviet revolution promised higher standards of living for workers and peasants through the abolition of exploitation of man by man. Yet the disruption of production caused by the revolution and subsequent civil war caused a drastic drop in real wages and, in some sections of the country where weather conditions were adverse, serious conditions of famine. By the end of NEP in 1928, however, real wages had regained their pre-war level. Then the policies of forced draft industrialization and the collectivization of agriculture precipitated another sharp decline culminating in the famine of 1931–1932. The depth of the decline in real wages is not known, but as the figures in Table 3 indicate, real wages still were more than 40 per cent below the 1928 level in 1935. They came closest to the 1928 level in 1937, but subsequently declined as a result of the disruptive effects of the purges and preparations for war. The destructive

---

[42] See, for example, V. Kelle, "The Perfecting of Social Relations Under Socialism," *Pravda*, April 5, 1967. Translated in the *Current Digest of the Soviet Press*, New York, April 26, 1967, pp. 10–11.

effects of World War II caused yet another major drop in real wages, but, again, the depth of the decline is not known. By 1952, however, real wages had regained their 1928 level.[43] Since then, they have continued to increase at a rate of about 4 per cent per annum, and they now stand some 70 per cent above both the 1928 and pre-revolutionary levels. This represents an increase of approximately one per cent per annum over the past five turbulent decades. If one includes in the period since 1928 only what Bergson calls "the effective years" of Soviet economic growth by eliminating the abnormal years 1941 through 1947, the proportion is increased to almost two per cent per annum, a respectable but not unusual rate of growth.

Table 3

Composite Index of Real Wages of Nonagricultural Wage Earners and Employees in the USSR (1928–1965)

(1928=100)

1935	58	1952	100
1937	85	1954	123
1940	79	1958	138
1944	73	1960	142
1948	60	1965	170

SOURCES: Based on Janet G. Chapman, *Real Wages in Soviet Russia Since 1928*, Cambridge, Massachusetts, Harvard University Press, 1963, p. 144; Alec Nove, "Wages in the Soviet Union, A Comment on Recently Published Statistics," *British Journal of Industrial Relations*, London, June, 1966, p. 220; and *Narodnoe Khozyaystvo SSSR v 1965. godu*, Moscow, 1966, pp. 567 and 652. Chapman's section of the index is her "Real wages, gross formula (7), given year prices" which produces rather more favourable results than her index using 1937 prices. This alternative index shows real wages at only 75 per cent of the 1928 level in 1952 and reaching the 1928 level only in 1958. When Nove's and more recent Soviet data are tied to this index rather than the former, they show only a 25 per cent increase in real wages over the 1928 level rather than 70 per cent.

Changes in real wages per worker do not, however, tell the full story; for although real wages in 1937 were substantially lower than in 1928, per capita consumption levels for the nation as a whole were higher. This paradox is explained by a number of factors. First, the process of urbanization improved the living standards of many former peasants in spite of the overall decline in real wages. Second, unemployment disappeared. Third, the number of dependents per wage earner decreased sharply from 2.5 to 1.5.[44] With more members of the typical family working, it was possible for per capita consumption to increase despite lower average real wages.

---

[43] Chapman, *Real Wages, op. cit.*, p. 144, provides several indices computed with different weights. As indicated in the note to Table 3, the different weights give rather different results, but it is not possible to state that one index is superior to the other.

[44] *Ibid.*, p. 167. The 1938 figure is an interpolation between 1935 and 1940.

These changes also reshaped family life in several important respects. Families became smaller, and many urban women with children had to enter the labour force to make ends meet. More young children were placed in child-care facilities, and the state took over some of the functions of raising children.

The rate of increase in per capita consumption between 1928 and 1937 was 3.8 per cent per annum; for "the effective years" between 1928 and 1958, the rate was 4.3 per cent per annum.[45] These are very impressive rates by any standard. In the United States, for example, per capita consumption increased at an average rate of 3 per cent per annum from 1869 to 1899 and at a rate of 2 per cent per annum from 1899 to 1958.[46] Since 1958, however, the rate of growth in per capita consumption in the Soviet Union has decreased dramatically to only 2.3 per cent per annum in conjunction with the overall decline in economic growth.[47] The burden of this decline fell most heavily on consumption because of the stagnation in agricultural production, affecting the availability of foodstuffs and fibres, and the reduction in housing construction, resulting from the larger demands of an increasingly complex and expensive defence effort.

The situation in housing warrants special attention in any discussion of the standard of living. A few facts and figures will tell the story in general terms. Before the revolution, the average urban family in Russia had only 7 square metres of living space available per person. By 1928, this figure had shrunk to 5.8 square metres. A growing population and increasing urbanization during the 1930's resulted in even more extreme crowding, and the average living space per person was reduced to only 4.5 square metres in 1940.[48] Major efforts were made to improve housing conditions after the war, but average urban dwelling space per person was still only 5.4 square metres in 1958, well below the 1928 level. By 1965, it had increased to 6.4 square metres but still remained below the pre-revolu-

---

[45] Abram Bergson, *The Real National Income of Soviet Russia Since 1928*, Cambridge, Massachusetts, Harvard University Press, 1961, pp. 225, 237, and 252, using the composite, 1937 base; Janet G. Chapman, "Consumption," in *Economic Trends in the Soviet Union*, Abram Bergson and Simon Kuznets, eds., Cambridge, Massachusetts, Harvard University Press, 1963, pp. 238–39.

[46] Chapman, "Consumption," *op. cit.*, pp. 246–47.

[47] David W. Bronson and Barbara S. Severin, "Recent Trends in Consumption and Disposable Money Income in the U.S.S.R.," *New Directions in the Soviet Economy*, Washington, D.C., U.S. Government Printing Office, 1966, p. 521; Stanley H. Cohn, "Soviet Growth Retardation: Trends in Resource Availability and Efficiency," *New Directions in the Soviet Economy*, Washington, D.C., U.S. Government Printing Office, 1966, pp. 99–132.

[48] Broderson, *op. cit.*, p. 113–14.

tionary level. In terms of occupancy, this meant an average of 2.3 persons per room. In Western Europe and the United States, anything over 1.5 persons per room is considered excessive crowding.[49] Housing remains, therefore, an area of major disappointment and dissatisfaction among Soviet workers.[50]

Promise of Job Security

The guarantee of the right to work in Article 118 of the 1936 Constitution has been hailed by the Soviets as a unique and major innovation. On the surface it appears to guarantee the Soviet citizen freedom from fear of unemployment. It states: "The citizens of the USSR possess the right to work, that is, the right to guaranteed employment, their work being remunerated according to quantity and quality." As Broderson points out, however: "It says nothing about the kind or place or condition of employment . . . The paragraph still leaves it to the discretion of the government, not the worker's own choice, how or where he has the right to be employed."[51]

Official Soviet sources state that the USSR knows no unemployment and defines unemployment as "a phenomenon peculiar to the capitalist system." It is admitted, however, that unemployment and rural overpopulation were a problem during the 1920's.[52] In 1928, for example, 1.5 million, or 11 per cent of a labour force of 13.1 million, were unemployed.[53] By 1930, unemployment had reportedly disappeared. Nevertheless, unemployment and underemployment remain very real problems for the Soviet Union today. The present sources of unemployment include the following: (1) minors refused employment, (2) new graduates not assigned to jobs and unable to find work, (3) workers in the normal process of changing jobs, (4) workers displaced by technological change, and (5) persons resident in areas lacking suitable employment opportunities.[54] Each of these sources of unemployment will be examined in turn.

---

[49] Timothy Sosnovy, "Housing Conditions and Urban Development in the U.S.S.R.," *New Directions in the Soviet Economy*, Washington, D.C., U.S. Government Printing office, 1966, pp. 544—45.

[50] It is sometimes argued that the poor quality of housing is compensated for by its low cost, but undoubtedly most workers are eager to move into new housing and willing, if able, to pay a higher price to acquire additional privacy and space desperately wanted and needed.

[51] Broderson, *op. cit.*, p. 48.

[52] *Entsiklopedicheskiy slovar*, Moscow, 1953, Vol. I, p. 158; and *Bolshaya Sovetskaya entsiklopediya*, Moscow, 1949—58, Vol. 4, p. 388.

[53] Chapman, Real Wages, *op. cit.*, p. 167.

[54] Seasonal unemployment, although a problem, is not considered here.

(1) Minors refused employment. A decree of the Presidium of the Supreme Soviet in 1956 required that young workers between the age of 16 and 18 years work only six hours a day but receive pay for eight hours of work. Since no additional funds were provided factory managers to cover the added costs of young workers, some factory managers responded by refusing to admit minors to work. Though the number of young workers denied jobs cannot be large, the problem has attracted considerable attention in the press.[55]

The problem of "voluntary unemployment" among young people has been, it would appear, a more serious one than their being denied employment. This problem was particularly acute during the latter half of the 1950's, when higher educational institutions had space for only a small percentage of the graduates of ten-year schools. Many of the graduates who failed to gain admission to the school of their choice preferred to wait another year to try again at the same or another school rather than to work at a job unattractive to them. The problem was exacerbated by the policy permitting a graduate to apply to only one institution at a time. Khrushchev summed up the situation in a speech in April 1958:

> Moreover, some boys and girls having graduated from the ten-year school are loath to go to work in factories, plants, collective farms and state farms, considering this an insulting proposition. Such a genteel, patronizing, incorrect attitude toward physical labour is found in families here and there. When a child learns badly at school, many a parent will tell him: If you learn badly, you will not get into a higher school and must instead go to a factory as a simple worker. In this fashion many people are making a bugaboo out of physical labor. I do not have to emphasize here, that this kind of attitude is an insult against (sic) the workers of a socialist society.[56]

One of the aims of the 1958 school reform introduced by Khrushchev was to correct this prejudice against physical work. The attitude is a deep-seated one, clearly, and the school reform had little effect on it. Even if the government should provide sufficient higher educational facilities to accommodate all the qualified applicants, the fact remains that as in any economic system there are fewer attractive than unattractive jobs available. Ultimately, the less talented Soviet youths must come to terms with this fact.

(2) New graduates not assigned to jobs. In theory, all graduates of training programmes in the labour reserves, specialized secondary schools, and higher educational institutions are assigned for a period of two to four years following graduation to specific jobs by a special commission. For

---

[55] See, for example, *Sovetskaya Latviya*, September 16, 1958.
[56] *Pravda*, April, 1958, quoted in Broderson, *op. cit.*, pp. 152–53.

a variety of reasons, however, some graduates are given their diplomas without specific assignments. For example, a young woman married to a man working in a city where there is no request for a graduate with her special training may be left to her own devices to find employment. Sometimes these unassigned graduates have difficulty finding employment in which they can use their special training.

A. N. Shelepin has commented as follows on the problem of placing labour reserve graduates:

> The educational institutions of the labour reserves graduate annually a significant section of young workers whose skills are not in demand. Some of the graduates remain unassigned for a long time or are forced to retrain.[57]

The following quotation indicates that similar problems exist for graduates of higher educational institutions:

> ... there are specialties for which there is not a great demand in general or at a particular time. ... Increased admissions, which a VUZ [higher educational institution] may obtain, justified or not, sometimes lead to unemployment for some university graduates.[58]

The long lead time necessary to estimate the demand for specialists trained at higher educational institutions with a four- or five-year programme makes it unusually difficult to graduate the precise number of students needed in all specialties. As indicated above, this may result in unemployment or, at best, the improper utilization of the young specialists in excess supply.

(3) Workers in the normal process of changing jobs. High rates of labour turnover have plagued the Soviet economy since the First Five-Year Plan. In the early 1930's, the rates averaged more than 100 per cent per annum. In recent years, the rate has been averaging approximately 20 per cent. Rates one-third higher are found in the northern and eastern regions, where living conditions are more difficult. Rates are also higher for married women, who sometimes withdraw from the labour force during the summer months, when their children are out of school and need looking after. Turnover rates also differ among various sectors and branches of the economy at any given time and over a period of years. No distinct pattern in these differences may be found, however.

The extent of the loss to the economy from frictional unemployment depends, of course, not only upon the rate of turnover but also upon the average length of time between jobs. Murray Feshbach has estimated, on

---

[57] *Komsomolskaya Pravda*, April 16, 1958.
[58] *Ibid.*, June 26, 1958.

the basis of scattered Soviet sources, that the average length of time lost between jobs in the Soviet Union is approximately 20 days. On the basis of this figure, it may be estimated that the total loss to the economy owing to turnover is 1.5 per cent of the man-days worked per year.[59] Other estimates have placed the figure as high as 2.6 per cent of the labour force.[60] In a country suffering from a labour shortage, such high figures reflect the absence of an organized labour market and represent a considerable loss to the economy.

What begins as an economic problem evolves into a social problem in the Soviet context because the social insurance system does not provide unemployment benefits. In ostrich-like fashion, all unemployment—even frictional—is declared as nonexistent, to the satisfaction of doctrinaire officialdom but at the expense of the workers who fail to find satisfactory employment within a few weeks. Most Soviet workers have very small cash reserves or other assets, so that unemployment for only a short period can be a severe economic blow. The failure of the government to provide payments to job-seeking workers represents a rather callous willingness to sacrifice generally accepted human values in order to maintain the fiction of full employment.

(4) Workers displaced by technological change. In addition to normal labour turnover, there are workers who lose their jobs and are forced to find other work, not through their own volition but as a result of technological change. As technological change occurs, jobs are eliminated and readjustments in the utilization of the labour force are required. The advent of automation, which usually results in a sharp drop in the labour-output ratio, has intensified the problems of job displacement and readjustment. The Soviet economy has been no more immune from these problems than any other modern industrial economy, although the slower pace at which automation is being introduced has postponed the problem in some sections of the economy. V. V. Grishin, Chairman of the All-Union Central Trade Union Council, recognized the seriousness of the problem in a report in 1960:

> It is known that as a result of the introduction of new technology, mechanization, and automation into production, labour requirements are diminished. Already today many enterprises have labour surpluses. In our view this problem requires an organizational solution. It is imperative that the *sovnarkhozy*, the planning organs in the union republics, and the Gosplan of

[59] Murray Feshbach, "Manpower in the U.S.S.R.: A Survey of Recent Trends and Prospects," *New Directions in the Soviet Economy*, Washington, D.C., U.S. Government Printing Office, 1966, pp. 733–34.

[60] Jay B. Sorenson, "Soviet Workers: The Current Scene, Problems and Prospects," *Problems of Communism*, May–June, 1965, p. 29.

the U.S.S.R. elaborate measures for the better utilization of labour reserves. The consideration of questions of labour utilization and organized placement of freed workers should be included in the compilation of annual production plans.[61]

At the more human level, the problem of technological unemployment was dramatized in a novel by Fedor Panforov entitled *In the Name of Youth*. He writes of a large automobile plant that was partially converted to automation, leading to the displacement of 900 workers. At once, fulfillment of the production programme lagged behind. The workers tacitly decided: "By automation you deprive us of work. Well, then, take that: we will not fulfill the program." Later, one of the characters asks: "Imagine that you came from a village or a city high school to the oil fields and learned a trade of which you could be justly proud, and then all at once you are classified as 'unemployed.' How would you feel?"[62] The response of many displaced Soviet workers clearly would be to question the meaning of the constitutional guarantee of employment.

Though the Soviet economy has long offered itself as a model for an economic order based on comprehensive central planning, it has failed thus far to develop the institutional framework necessary to cope with the problems of man-power supply and distribution. This lack lies at the root of the problem of redistributing workers displaced by technological change. Paradoxically, labour exchanges have existed in the past. They were set up in the 1920's to aid in the placement of workers but were summarily abolished in 1933 along with the People's Commissariat of Labour. The reestablishment of labour exchanges has been recommended by leading Soviet labour economists such as M. Sonin. The call for an "organizational solution" to the problem, issued by Grishin in the quotation above, further underscores the need for institutional reform. Yet these pleas have fallen on deaf ears. To date, the government has introduced few concrete measures designed to aid in the relocation or retraining of displaced workers. Most hopeful, perhaps, was the decision at the end of 1966 to establish State Committees on the Utilization of Labour Resources in the republics. This could presage the reestablishment of a comprehensive labour exchange system.[63]

---

[61] Quoted in Soloman M. Schwarz, "Unemployment in the Soviet Union," *Current History*, Philadelphia, November, 1960, p. 281.

[62] Quoted in *ibid.*, pp. 280–81.

[63] *Byuletin Ministerstva Vysshego i Srednogo Spetsialnogo Obrazovaniya SSSR* (Bulletin of the Ministry of Higher and Specialized Secondary Education in the USSR), Moscow, No. 5, 1967, p. 11.

Such limited action is especially difficult to explain in the face of increasing pressures from above to lay off redundant workers and decrease costs. Prior to the current economic reforms, there were many reasons for plant managers to hoard labour and few deterrents. The emphasis of the new reforms upon the criterion of profitability can only be expected to lead to the discharge of more redundant workers. The government has already found it necessary to warn plant managers that the reduction in their work force should not exceed that brought about by normal departures and retirements, but the problem can be expected to grow more acute during the next two years, as the remainder of industry is converted to the new system.

(5) Persons resident in areas lacking suitable employment opportunities. This problem concerns women more than men. In medium-sized and small cities job opportunities for women are more limited than in larger centres, and a relatively high proportion of the women spend full time in housework or the cultivation of private garden plots rather than working in the socialized sector. A similar situation exists in certain areas of the country where heavy industry and mining predominate such as in the Donbas and Kuzbas. Here the employment opportunities for women, for work in the socialized sector, are severely limited, particularly since the enforcement in the late 1950's of the prohibition against most kinds of underground work for them.[64] Until a better balance is achieved in areas such as the Donbas and Kuzbas between light industry, with jobs suitable for women, and heavy industry and mining, with jobs more suitable for men, many women will continue to suffer from "structural" unemployment. The high percentage of Soviet women who are compelled to work by economic circumstance makes this particular problem more acute in the Soviet Union than in other industrial countries. Elsewhere, a higher proportion of women in places where there are unbalanced labour opportunities would be content to remain at home.

Information about the magnitude of the various forms of unemployment discussed above is insufficient to estimate accurately their full scope. Official concern suggests that their total impact is considerable, but official embarassment has apparently deterred an attack sufficiently vigorous to reduce or eliminate all forms of unemployment. The only form of unemployment from which the Soviets have not suffered since the early 1930's is that resulting from inadequate aggregate demand. During the 1930's, their superiority over the capitalist countries in this respect was quite

---

[64] Dodge, *op. cit.*, pp. 70–71; Feshbach, *op. cit.*, pp. 720–21.

obvious. In more recent years, however, the leading capitalist economies, especially those in Europe, have shown considerable skill and effectiveness in reducing all forms of unemployment, including that attributable to inadequate aggregate demand.

Promise of Improved Working Conditions

One of the revolution's promises for improving working conditions was a reduction in the hours of work. Introduction of the eight-hour work day in 1917 was one of the first acts of the Bolshevik government, and the Labour Codes of 1918 and 1922 reinforced and elaborated this measure. Such legislation was advanced for the times. Overtime work was also forbidden, but exceptions were soon introduced and overtime became an accepted practice. In 1927, further progressive legislation was passed, providing for a seven-hour work day and a 42-hour work week.[65] During the First Five-Year Plan, experiments were made in many plants with the continuous, day-in, day-out operation of the plant with individuals working on staggered schedules of four out of every five days. It was soon found, however, that because part of the workers were off each day, workers failed to feel responsible for the proper care of their machines. To fight such "depersonalization," continuous operation of plants was largely eliminated, and a five-day work week with the sixth day off was introduced at the end of 1931.

The 1936 Constitution guaranteed a seven-hour work day, but in 1940, by a simple edict of the Presidium of the Supreme Soviet, the work load was increased to eight hours a day, six days a week with the seventh day off. Although motivated by a justifiable fear of war, this action displayed the rather cavalier attitude of Soviet officialdom toward constitutional procedures. During World War II, many workers worked as many as eleven hours a day, six days a week, but in the post-war period, the eight-hour day, six-day week became standard again, until 1956, when the length of the working day on Saturday or before a holiday was cut to six hours.[66] In May, 1960, the seven-hour day was made law, and the 41-hour work week became common practice.[67] As a result of these reductions, the

---

[65] Alexander Baykov, *The Development of the Soviet Economic System*, Cambridge and New York, Cambridge University Press, 1946, p. 214; W. W. Kulski, *The Soviet Regime*, Syracuse, Syracuse University Press, 1954, p. 339.

[66] Nash, *op. cit.*, p. 394.

[67] *Ibid.*, p. 397.

average number of man-hours worked annually in Soviet industry is less than in any other leading industrial nation.[68]

During the late 1950's, at the time of the drafting of the Seven-Year Plan, the Soviet government indicated its intent to introduce a 35-hour work week, beginning in 1964. Thus far, however, the regime has not found conditions sufficiently favourable to warrant a change to such a reduced work week throughout the economy. At present, the work week, which is still 41 hours long, is being adjusted to provide two free days a week. This shift was scheduled for completion by the fiftieth anniversary of the revolution—none too soon in the minds of many Soviet workers.[69]

Though initially Soviet policies regarding hours of work were quite advanced and have become so again, during Stalin's ascendency workers bore a heavy burden in long work hours. In addition, they suffered from a "speed-up" rivalling any of the fabled speed-ups of the "harsh and grasping" capitalists. Central to the Soviet speed-up was the extensive use of straight and progressive piece rates among production workers. These put great pressure on the workers to produce as rapidly as possible, and the rates were periodically adjusted upward to maintain the pressure. In addition, many devices—posters, articles, and medals—were employed in the plants to praise and reward the most productive workers and to shame the laggards. The regime also organized a series of special campaigns to increase the effort and output of labour—the Subbotnik, Udarnik, Stakhanovite, and more recent movements. As a result of such efforts and campaigns, the Soviet worker's environment was much more production-oriented than that of the European or American worker, and neither individually nor collectively could he do much to make it more congenial, not to say less exacting.

There are many other aspects of working conditions which merit comment—safety measures, conveniences, penalties for infractions of regulations, relationships with superiors, and so forth—but here we can only stress that in the absence of effective and independent trade-union organizations representing the workers' interests, management usually has done no more for the workers than was considered necessary to achieve satisfactory production. In the case of disputes with management, only "individual grievances" are handled by arbitration or the courts. Collective action, such as a strike, is prohibited. Indeed, to strike is a criminal offence

[68] Stanley H. Cohn, *op. cit.*, p. 115.
[69] Bureau of Labour Statistics, United States Department of Labour, *Labour Developments Abroad*, June, 1967, p. 16.

in the Soviet Union rather than a civic right.[70] Under such circumstances, it is not surprising that in regard to conditions of work the Soviet Union still lags behind Europe and the United States.

Promise of Freedom from Oppression

Revolution freed the Russian worker from the "oppression of capitalist bosses," but a modern industrial economy requires that the worker be directed by bosses however they may be labelled. Having no independent trade union to defend him, the Soviet worker may often wonder whether or not he has fared better under the new generation of plant managers. The regime soon found that it was extremely difficult to direct an economy by relying solely upon economic incentives. It was found easier, if not essential, to reinforce incentives with more direct pressures and controls. As early as 1920, Trotsky demanded that an individual's freedom to choose his own place of work be abandoned. The 1922 Labour Code for the RSFSR states that in exceptional instances, such as fighting the elements or in case of a shortage of labour for carrying out important state work, all citizens of the RSFSR, with certain exceptions based on age and sex, could be called up for work in the form of compulsory labour service.[71] Further extensive restrictive legislation was passed in the late 1930's in an effort to stem the high rates of labour turnover and to strengthen the control of the government over labour in the face of increasing international tensions. An internal passport compulsory for urban dwellers over 16 years of age had already been introduced in 1932. It controlled the movement both of those who had passports and those who did not (mainly the rural population), because a passport was necessary to move into an urban community. In 1938, every worker was obliged by law to carry a work-book showing his record of employment and release from his previous job. Severe penalties were also introduced for absenteeism or tardiness. In 1940, as war clouds began to threaten, workers and state employees were forbidden to leave any enterprise or institution arbitrarily. In the autumn of that year, the State Labour Reserves were established to mobilize and train large numbers of youths, and soon after ministries were empowered to shift certain categories of skilled workers and technicians from enterprise to

---

[70] Broderson, *op. cit.*, p. 128. Despite the illegality of strikes, they are still held. Several recent violent ones are mentioned by Albert Boiter, "When the Kettle Boils Over . . . ," *Problems of Communism*, January–February, 1964, p. 35.

[71] Bureau of Labour Statistics, *Principal Current Soviet Labour Legislation, A Compilation of Documents*, Washington, D.C., U.S. Government Printing Office, 1962, p. 3.

enterprise regardless of personal desire or geographic location. Thus, even before the war began, the labour force of the Soviet Union had been placed on a mobilized, quasi-military footing.

Though most of these incursions on the freedom of workers can be explained by the war, for a decade after the war many continued on the books. For example the draft of youths (boys 14 to 17 years of age and girls 15 to 17) into vocational schools was formally abolished only in 1955 and compulsory transfers only a year later.[72] The system of organized recruitment of labour (*orgnabor*) still continues. As Murray Feshbach has pointed out, in the past dozen years this system has recruited less among the rural and more among the urban population. Since 1961, it has been authorized to recruit professionals with specialized secondary or higher education as well as skilled workers.[73] Though coercion apparently is not normally employed, a plant can be directed to release some of its workers for reassignment. Men recruited in this way usually must sign a contract for two or three years and may be transferred to distant places of work. Many are now being sent to remote eastern and northern regions, where labour turnover is high and forced labour camps until recently were major suppliers of man power.[74]

Today, freedom to change jobs seems to be a fact for most ordinary workers, provided the worker can find other employment and new housing, if required. For established professionals and workers with special skills, there is less real freedom even though they possess the same legal rights to change jobs. Pressure and persuasion from administrators and the Party result in many higher level personnel being assigned to their jobs with little or no real choice.

The other major category that today lacks freedom of choice in employment is graduates from technical-vocational schools and full-time students graduating from specialized secondary or higher educational institutions. These young people are assigned to jobs for a period of two to four years. Though their wishes may be consulted in the assignment process, usually many students are not satisfied with their jobs; and as a result, there has been a major problem in enforcing compliance with the work assignments.[75]

Of course, the most serious denial of freedom in the Soviet Union has been the imprisonment of many thousands in the forced labour camps

---

[72] Nash, *op. cit.*, p. 393; Barton, *op. cit.*, p. 23.
[73] Feshbach, *op. cit.*, pp. 739–40.
[74] Barton, *op. cit.*, p. 20.
[75] Feshbach, *op. cit.*, p. 737.

that originated at the time of the Civil War and have continued until the present day. During the period of NEP (1921–1928), forced labour did not assume any great significance. However, following the inauguration of the First Five-Year Plan, forced labour became an important element in the planned economic growth of the country, especially in construction, mining, and lumbering in Siberia and in other inhospitable areas. Estimates of the number of persons working in the camps have varied widely. At one extreme is Dallin's and Nicolaevsky's estimate of 10–12 million in 1940,[76] while Jasny estimates "as high as 3,500,000" at approximately the same time.[77] Two of the more comprehensive estimates, made by Peter Wiles and Abdurakhman Avtorkhanov, are given in Table 4.

Table 4

Estimated Number of Prisoners in the USSR, 1927–1941

	Wiles	Avtorkhanov
1927	—	140,000
1928	30,000	—
1930	660,000—730,000[1]	1,500,000
1931	2,000,000	—
1932	—	2,500,000
1936	—	6,500,000
1937[2]	2,000,000	—
1937[3]	3,000,000	—
1938	—	11,000,000
1939	8,000,000	—
1940	6,500,000	—
1941	9,000,000	13,500,000[4]

[1] For 1929–1930.
[2] For January.
[3] For December.
[4] For June.

SOURCE: S. Swianiewicz, *Forced Labour and Economic Development*, London, Oxford University Press, 1965, pp. 33 and 37.

As might be expected, the two estimates differ considerably because there are no adequate underlying data. Wiles perhaps underestimates the effects of collectivization upon camp population in the early and mid-1930's, while Avtorkhanov may overestimate the numbers for the late 1930's and 1941. With these qualifications, the estimates suggest that although forced

[76] David J. Dallin and Boris I. Nicolaevsky, *Forced Labour in Soviet Russia*, New Haven, Yale University Press, 1947, pp. 86–87.

[77] Naum Jasny, "Labor and Output in Soviet Concentration Camps," *Journal of Political Economy*, October, 1951, p. 416.

labour was not the foundation of Soviet economic development, the role of forced labour was significant and large, particularly in certain industries and areas.

During and immediately following the war, large numbers of civilians from occupied areas swelled the ranks of the camps along with military prisoners, members of certain Soviet nationality groups, and displaced Soviet citizens.[78] This influx may have totalled as many as 15 million people, but, as a result of high mortality in the camps, the number could not have been nearly so high at any given time.[79] By the end of the 1940's, sources of new forced labour had largely dried up, and the role of the camps began to decline. A massive but abortive uprising in Vorkuta in 1948 was echoed again, after Stalin's death, in a wave of strikes throughout the camps. Conditions improved as a result of the strikes and the number of prisoners began to be rapidly reduced. By 1957, P. J. Kudryavtsev, Deputy Procurator General, reported that the total number of prisoners was only 30 percent of those in the camps when Stalin died.[80] There is no indication, however, that the forced labour system is being liquidated. Though no longer a mass phenomenon, it is a stain on the record of the first fifty years of the Soviet regime.

Future Prospects for Soviet Labour

It is difficult to look ahead and divine what the next fifty years hold for Soviet labour. Labour's future is so closely intertwined with broader economic and political developments that prediction is hazardous. Our efforts here will be modest. We shall simply attempt to point out some of the likely constants in labour's future as well as changes already in progress or very likely to occur in the next few decades.

Unchanging Features. That the Party's top leadership will continue to determine major economic policies and priorities is evident. Though the Party is now less able to ignore public opinion than during the Stalin regime, the leaders themselves still make the final decisions regarding such key questions as the size of military spending, the allocation to investment, and the share of consumption. While current and foreseeable economic reforms are likely to improve the efficiency of management and the functioning of consumer choice, they certainly will not establish consumer sovereignty. We can expect, therefore, much the same investment-oriented

---

[78] These are Soviet displaced persons repatriated from Germany and Italy, and elsewhere in Europe, and sentenced to camps as suspect.

[79] Swianiewicz, *op. cit.*, pp. 44–45.

[80] *Ibid.*, p. 50.

economic policy that has in the past placed the aim of national economic growth ahead of increases in consumption. Only if the overall rate of economic growth is restored to high previous levels can any significant reallocation of resources in favour of the consumer be expected.

Party domination of labour and trade-union policy also seems certain to continue. Neither an individual worker nor any group of workers is more likely in the future than in the past to influence the policies regulating their work. Nor is it likely that factory committees will acquire real autonomy or independent voices in operating their plants. Up to the present, the Soviets have shown no indication of following the Yugoslav example of granting real powers and responsibilities to the workers. Nevertheless, it seems probable that the recent Soviet actions giving more formal responsibility to factory committees will be expanded. Indeed, the present economic reforms giving greater independence to the enterprise would seem to call for more union independence. But there is little doubt that, as in the past, the Party and management will effectively dominate the factory committees.

Wage differentials roughly based on productivity do not seem likely to disappear in the foreseeable future. Transition to full communism would, of course, drastically alter the present incentive system, but before such a transition can be conceived, a multifold increase in per capita income is required, and, even more necessary, a drastic change in individual attitudes, motivations, and personal values. The existing incentive system in the Soviet Union attests that even after fifty years of socialism most citizens are still motivated by much the same material considerations as persons living and working under capitalism. It seems doubtful, therefore, that the next fifty years will bring more basic changes in human nature than there have been in the past.

Though the labour sector of the Soviet economy is much less planned than other sectors, the assignment of many new graduates to jobs for a term of several years seems a feature of labour planning that is likely to continue. Undoubtedly, persuasion and various forms of compulsion will continue to supplement economic incentives in directing workers to jobs the state considers essential. However, as in recent years, most workers will be relatively free to choose their places of work. The role of forced labour, which has already declined in significance, seems unlikely to regain its importance. There is no indication, however, that forced labour will cease to be a part of the system.

Probable Changes. Though no basic changes in the fundamental features of the Soviet system as it relates to labour seem likely in the next few decades, other less fundamental changes are already in progress or can be expected in the near future. First, the standard of living of workers and employees will continue to improve. Nevertheless, in view of the many competing claimants for resources and the recent retardation of economic growth, it seems unlikely that the rate of improvement in the near future will be more rapid than in the recent past. Assuming that the present rate holds steady, living standards will rise approximately 50 per cent in the next two decades. On the other hand, the rate of increase achieved before the recent slowdown in economic growth would permit a doubling of living standards over the same period. Even if this impressive rate of growth should be achieved, Soviet living standards would still lag far behind those of most Western European countries and the United States.

Second, greater equality of opportunity can be expected in the future. From our previous discussion, it seems unlikely that the social structure will be drastically altered in the foreseeable future, but the concern of social scientists with the problem of social mobility suggests that the government may take some action to further equality. Discrimination against Jews and other minorities will certainly decrease, and more equality for Moslem women is inevitable with the passage of time. Whether or not women will play a larger role in the economy in the future is difficult to predict. More part-time work, smaller families, enlarged child-care facilities, and increased employment opportunities in light industry and the service sector should tend to increase female participation in the labour force. On the other hand, the growing proportion of males in the working age population, and rising incomes, which make it less necessary for women to work to make ends meet, could lead to a decline in female participation. Of equal interest is whether, in the future, professional women will have opportunities for career advancement more nearly equal to those of men. Since the burden on women as housewives and mothers seems a major reason for their lower social productivity and reduced competitiveness, expected reductions in the burden should make the career patterns of women more nearly approach those of men.

Third, despite the regime's ostrich-like approach to the unemployment problem, it seems likely, from steps already taken, that a comprehensive system of labour exchanges will be established to reduce several of the more serious forms of unemployment from which the Soviet Union suffers. However, disguised unemployment in some sectors of the economy may become actual unemployment as the current economic reforms progress and as managers, seeking to reduce costs and increase profits, discharge redundant or less productive workers. Similar reforms rationalizing agriculture, where disguised unemployment has been endemic, could greatly intensify the unemployment problem.

Fourth, many of the undesirable features of present working conditions should improve in the next decades. Ultimately, the 35-hour, five-day work week will be introduced, safety measures will be improved, better facilities will be provided for workers, regulations will become less harsh, and so forth. It is doubtful, however, that worker relations with management can be fundamentally improved. Management can be expected to continue to use its prerogatives to get the maximum production from workers at the smallest expense. In a production-oriented environment this is inevitable. Indeed, there is small chance that the Soviet Union will set an example for the rest of the world in the area of creating more congenial working conditions.

Conclusion

In the economic sphere, the promises raised by the October Revolution turned out to be far too sweeping to be fulfilled, at least within the first fifty years of the new regime. The revolution promised an economic order that would be the most productive ever devised by man, based on the most progressive social system in history, a system in which ownership of all productive assets would pass out of private hands into the possession of society as a whole. Given this new social milieu, it was believed that the Soviet economic system held the promise of developing "at a rate utterly beyond the reach of the capitalist system, because its development [would be] free of the anarchical features of capitalism and [would] not contain within itself the antagonisms peculiar to capitalism."[81]

Today, it is quite plain that the original, politically inspired optimism— not to speak of the rhetoric generated by it—was less than fully justified. The output of the Soviet economy after fifty years of development is still considerably behind that of Western Europe and the United States. At the same time, the labour force employed in the production process is nearly 50 per cent larger than the American. This bespeaks neither a rate of growth nor a labour productivity "beyond the reach of the capitalist system." However, the general record of Soviet economic development does compare favourably with that of the pre-Soviet, capitalist system of

---

[81] *Social Economic Planning in the Union of Soviet Socialist Republics*, The Hague, The International Industrial Association, 1931, p. 126, the report of a delegation from the USSR to the World Social Economic Congress, Amsterdam, August, 1931.

production in Russia. The Soviet method of economic development has, after all, succeeded in lifting Russia to the position of the second largest economy in the world in contrast with its standing of fifth largest on the eve of World War I.

When the leaders of the revolution promised to create an economic order motivated first and foremost by a concern for social justice, they did not foresee that in order to achieve an adequate level of productivity, let alone to surpass the West in the economic sphere, they would be required to develop the same kind of technical capabilities and human skills as were possessed by the capitalist nations, but in the long run the means have devoured the end. The indispensable system of occupational differentiation involved in building a modern industrial society has left its indelible mark. The normal pressures of economic development have produced a new class of bureaucrats and technicians who have been given a larger role in the management of production as well as greater economic power and more social privileges than the proletariat. Broadly speaking, society has divided into a minority composed of those who draw up plans and give orders and a majority who perform the labour required to carry them out. When faced by two conflicting options, the heirs of the Bolshevik Revolution passed up the possibility of impressing the world with a uniquely high level of worker welfare. They chose, rather, to leave their imprint upon world history by enhancing their capacity to maintain a high level of investment and by promoting maximum production in the politically vital spheres of heavy industry and military strength.

Marxist Economic Theory in the USSR
Jack Miller

> The bankruptcy of ideology should not entail either a decline
> of national energy or destruction of faith.
>
> *Professor V. I. Grinevetsky*, June 1918

Marxist theory has been subjected to a severe test in being employed
for half a century in the service of the Russian state. This employment has
taken two forms: as a factor in policy-making, and as a systematic ideology.
The economic part of the theory is, at least conceivably, of special importance for Marxism both in respect of policy formation and as ideology
capable of stimulating confidence and energy.

Broad Periodization

The fifty years of Marxist economics in the USSR fall into three main
periods of very different kinds in terms of general intellectual quality and
belief in the ideology. The specialist economic discussions of the 1920's
offer a sharp intellectual contrast to the poverty of published thought in
the period from 1930 to 1952, when the economic situation did not need
theory for the practical activities of the state, or when in any case use
could not be made of it. The revival of serious economic discussion since
the late 1950's has shown a cleavage between the theorists of Marxist
economics and those who are outside Marxism but who unavoidably pay
some lip service to it. These non-Marxist economists appear to be much
more like the Marxists of the 1920's in their intellectual competence and
genuine concern for the economy of their country than are the Marxist
economists who are their contemporaries. However, the serious economists of today, in contrast to those of the 1920's, show little interest in
adapting Marxist economics to the needs of the time, as distinct from
expressing their thoughts with just enough Marxist terminology to meet
the conventional requirements of publication. This circumstance, of course,
is more likely to hasten the demise of Marxist economic theory than to
give it new life. Moreover, it is difficult to imagine that real life, in the
sense of effective adaptation to the actual needs of the economy, is being
put into Marxist theory by the present-day traditionalists: in their books
and articles on the Marxist economics of socialism and communism they

appear to be trying, without conviction, to tidy up ideologically in the wake of unavoidable economic reforms. The Marxist economists of the 1920's leave a powerful impression on the mind; those of the 1930's struggled in bad conditions to· make a political economy of socialism; those of today leave a peculiarly empty impression.

If the function of the economic part of Marxism is considered as an ideological factor outside the ranks of the economists, the three periods look rather different. This function was of little importance in the 1920's: Marxism had not effectively spread beyond the ranks of the Bolshevik and Menshevik intellectuals. In the 1930's, however, and especially in the second half of that decade, when a generation of young *apparatchiki* was emerging from the uneducated masses and beginning to exercise real power under Stalin, the ideology was of fundamental importance. Without it, these people would not have had the absolute and simple faith that enabled them to carry out their tasks. It was not necessary to know the theory fully, but it was necessary to know that Stalin knew it fully. The fact that there was not yet a political economy of socialism did not bother them. They had no doubt that all such intellectual problems would be resolved in due course, just like the practical problem of catching up and overtaking America. Meanwhile, they read prescribed sections of *Das Kapital* with the same kind of satisfaction as others in their time have read the Bible. The truth was there, even if it was not quite comprehensible; its interpretation for application to current tasks was safely in Stalin's head; and all his analyses and instructions glowed with its special, illuminative light. The 1960's contrast sharply in this respect. Against a much more generally sophisticated intellectual background, few of the several million students required to enroll in Political Economy or Scientific Socialism as part of their compulsory education in Marxism get any of this kind of satisfaction and little of this kind of certainty out of it. This is probably true even of those students who aspire to becoming Party functionaries.

Value Theory

A brief account of Marx's economic model is unavoidable. In an economy where independent owners of goods exhcange them freely among themselves, the exchanges will take place according to the value of the goods, which in these conditions are called commodities. In Marx's time, economists were ceasing to assume or to search for a metaphysical "value" underlying price. Modern non-Marxist economics simply takes value as price. For Marx, the value of a commodity is the socially necessary labour it contains, i.e., the amount of work normally needed to produce it at the period and in the economy concerned. Marx took the medieval idea of labour embodied in goods and developed it into a logical concept of "abstract labour," a homogeneous term denoting the total quality of all the kinds of actual work that are performed in the economy concerned and that cannot themselves be directly measured against each other.

In this scheme, there are, at any moment, two kinds of labour: living and embodied. Living labour is actual workers working. Embodied (or dead) labour is the value put into products by past work. This stored work is in turn transferred to new products as the materials or machinery in which it inheres is used up in production. Embodied labour is called constant capital, because it does not increase, i.e., it does not create more value but is simply carried over. Living labour, however, being a quality of people and not of things, has the capacity to create more value than that embodied in it, by encompassing, for example, the value of a worker's food, housing, and clothing, and presumably of his education and much else. Living labour is therefore called variable capital. It is the source of all new value in the economy, because the value embodied in it makes, not its labour, but its capacity to work: the term "labouring power" is Marx's rendering of this concept in English. The working class sells its only commodity, labouring power, for wages. These are in principle equivalent to its value. What the employer gets, however, is not labouring power but labour, which is usually greater in value. The difference between the two is surplus value, a factor put to use by the capitalist class partly for its own consumption and partly to increase constant capital.

Now, constant capital increases faster than variable capital, i.e., the proportion of embodied labour to living labour increases. Since profit, which comes from surplus value, is obtainable only from living labour, the rate of profit as a percentage of capital (constant plus variable capital) declines. Moreover, since profit is the motive of capitalist production, this slow but inevitable decline undermines capitalism in the long run, notwithstanding various capitalist expedients. (The main expedients are to force down the value of labouring power by reducing wages, at the same time maintaining or increasing the hours and intensity of work performed, and to secure foreign low-wage areas by imperialism, but both domestic and colonial workers resist these measures. Since there are several imperialisms, war becomes a necessary part of the mature system, too.) For purposes of secular analysis, products are divided into producer goods (department I) and consumer goods (department II), and the interrelations of I and II are studied under conditions of a static economy (simple reproduction) and growth (expanded reproduction). Marx's model is material: only material goods, and services most obviously necessary to them, like transport, embody value. People engaged in other activities, however necessary or desirable, are living on the surplus value created by productive workers. The model is also industrial. There are no peasants in it, but the peasantry is shown as having historically been a source of primitive accumulation by early capitalists in the creation of industry and capitalism. After capitalism, money wages and other features of the market and class economy would disappear, but a surplus product would still be needed to support necessary unproductive occupations and expanded reproduction.

The follwing points should be noted: (1) The theory concerns commodities, i.e., goods whose ownership is transferred, whether by primitive exchange or in a capitalist market. It does not apply to goods which are produced and consumed by a single owner. (2) the value of a commodity is due exclusively to the labour embodied in it, and is not affected by its use-value or the demand for it. (Of course, a commodity will not pass to another owner unless he wants it, so some use-value or demand is implied, but the degree of use-value or demand is irrelevant). (3) Marx's concept of value, whether logically valid or not as the key concept of his scheme, is doubtless highly abstract. Prices at any particular time and place are facts. Marx, like everybody else, treats actual prices as due to actual supply and demand at the time and place concerned. He does not demonstrate any connection between actual prices, or their long-term movements, and his value concept, nor has anybody else done so. The theory, however, assumes that the prices of commodities are somehow governed by their relative values.

The 1920's

The Bolsheviks shared this economic theory with most of the other Russian revolutionaries, but for them it had a special significance. They were the heirs of that strand of the Russian revolutionary tradition that placed the most emphasis upon organization, whether of self, party, or society. The cardinal enemy was *stikhiynost*—the enslavement of man to blind forces that he did not comprehend. Marx's economic theory was the key both to *stikhiynost* in its mature capitalist form and to its replacement by the conscious organization of society. Without this theory, or one of equivalent scope and intellectual strength, explaining the same thing and providing the same solution, the Bolsheviks could not have had the confidence to seize power and keep it. The law of value was the critical element in the theory, both in a positive and a negative sense. It was the mechanism of *stikhiynost* that they fought to overcome, and it would have no place in the market-less, commodity-less, planned society they would construct. It is impossible to visualize Bolshevism without Marx's value theory as the intellectual rationalization for its source of quasi-religious strength.

On the practical side, the Bolsheviks found support for the possibility of economic planning in the versions of the German war economy that reached them from abroad and, nearer home, in a book published in Kharkov in 1919 entitled *Post-war Perspectives of Russian Industry*. (Its author, the monarchist engineer V. Grinevetsky, was disgusted with the unpractical idealism of the liberal intelligentsia and in particular with the lack of interest in economic fundamentals displayed by the Provisional Government.) Lenin's intention to socialize the economy by stages gave way to the political and military necessities of the Civil War, with its economic outcome in the period of so-called war communism, during which the state controlled and allocated everything it could reach. Even the more practical of the Bolsheviks came to see in war communism the advent of the real thing, which would need only to be made more productive and sophisticated when the fighting was over. Realism supervened in policy after the Civil War, when the system became too dangerously intolerable to the country, and the limited market of the New Economic Policy (NEP) was allowed in order to avoid a collapse.

The mood of war communism, however, powerfully influenced economic theory throughout the 1920's. In particular, Nikolay Bukharin's work, *Economics of the Transition Period*, published in 1920, sought to generalize the experience of war communism. In it, Bukharin repeats the traditional view that Marxist value theory is applicable only to commodities, that is, to goods exchanged between independent owners through the anarchy of the market. He adds that in a planned economy, where man is sovereign over his material circumstances, political economics is replaced by a normative science. Writing before the introduction of NEP, he proclaimed the end of political economy.

As the importance of the market sector engaged in private enterprise increased in the NEP economy, and as even the state trusts evolved a quasi-market relationship among themselves, the view that political economics was a thing of the past in the USSR could not be sustained. Analysis of market forces could not be avoided for the purposes of either short-term or long-term policy. For moral, ideological, and political reasons, it was, however, difficult to admit that value theory retained anything like the importance it had in capitalist political economy. The question of whether value existed in a socialist system was to become the critical issue delaying the construction of "a political economy of socialism" until the 1950's, when the problem was not so much resolved as glossed over in a debased intellectual climate. Meanwhile, in the 1920's, two main approaches to this problem emerged. The logical view—that value remained insofar as the market did, since the concept of abstract labour is relevant only to the extent that actual kinds of work are generalized through a market mechanism—was expounded by the Menshevik economist Rubin and tended to be accepted by the Bolshevik theorists. The opposing view was essentially an attempt to construct a new theory of value: abstract labour was proposed as an abstraction from the universal physiological components of work, such as muscular and nervous energy. The *Rubin-shchina* (the Rubin school, in a pejorative sense) was denounced, and its author subsequently sentenced, following the issuance of a Central Committee statement on the controversy in 1930. The statement provided no solution, though it leaned towards the physiological or mechanist school, whose approach must have looked more promising for a Marxist theory of planning in physical quantities. Nothing seems to have come of it, but this is not surprising, since Marxism is a social, not a physiological, system. Nevertheless, mechanist ideas eased the way to the present view that the law of value does operate in socialism.

The best-known element of the economic debates of the 1920's is the issue of the practical means of industrialization. On this subject, E. Pre-obrazhensky's famous study, *New Economics*, published in 1926, considers the interrelation between the market sector and the planned sector of the actual Soviet economy. The first is seen as subject to the law of value, but the second is seen as analogous to the formative period of capitalism in that it must obtain the resources for investment, on which to establish itself, from the outside, which in Soviet circumstances meant the peasantry. Thus, the law governing the socialist sector, and also its relations with the market sector, is "the law of primitive socialist accumulation," and the course of development of the Soviet economy as a whole is governed by the outcome of the contradiction between these two laws. It should be remembered that Preobrazhensky's book is the first part of a much larger work he intended to write, and cannot be judged as offering a complete theory. Other attempts to elaborate a theoretical definition of the mixed economy of NEP generally leaned towards the law of value as the law governing the whole economy, on the view that the socialist sector had to come to terms in some way—i.e., have a market relationship—with the peasantry. Here differences in theory most directly reflect the policy differences of the period.

Another centre of attention in the industrialization debate is of interest primarily outside Marxist theory. This is the use to which Marx's structural analysis of the capitalist industrial economy was put in order to trace the movement of products (and, for Marxists, the values they embody) between department I (producer goods) and department II (consumer goods). These discussions, which were connected with the practical problem of balances within Gosplan (the State Planning Committee), constitute the earliest substantial body of systematic work on the internal relationships of an industrial economy, and thus provide a foundation—partly in fact but mainly in retrospect, as this work was scarcely known until recently—for a basic field of development within modern economics. The element of Marxist theory in this aspect of the economic discussions of the 1920's is accidental, in the same sense that the relevant parts of *Das Kapital* are not directly connected with the theory and could, in substance, have been written without it.

One more aspect of the debates of the 1920's should be noted here, if only because it acquired special labels—that is, the argument between the "genetic" and the "teleological" schools. The geneticists were mainly Mensheviks working in Gosplan who emphasized the "genetic" or inherent structure of the Russian economy in such matters as proportions of industrial to agricultural production and difficulties in the way of establishing radically new proportions. The teleologists took the position that a new structure would afford the desired key to the situation. The genetecists were condemned, with Rubin, in the trial of Menshevik economists in 1931.

The Stalin Period

Political economy, like any other science, intellectual discipline, or theory, implies the determination of necessities or laws defining limits for freedom of human action. The official outlook of the 1930's, and the personal outlook of the new men of the time, did not take kindly to this idea. Their mood is expressed in the statement attributed to Stalin at the outset of the period: "There are no fortresses that Bolsheviks cannot capture." There is, however, one practical need for political economy, and it became evident in this period. It is impossible to teach a subject without systematizing it to some extent, if only for the purpose of exposition, and large numbers of people had to receive formal training in order to work in administering the rapidly growing Soviet economy. In addition, the importance of Marxist economic theory within the whole ideology made it impossible to avoid efforts to construct a political economy of socialism.

Stalin's promulgation of socialism in December 1936, and his announcement a year later of "a full correspondence" between the forces and the relations of production, meaning that the Soviet system perfectly fitted the needs of contemporary technology, provided a special stimulus to efforts on the theoretical front. However, nothing tangible came of these efforts. The Soviet economy was taught descriptively, and this was done very poorly, for lack of a theoretical framework. Ideology had to be content with the teachings of Marx on capitalism. In all fairness, it could scarcely be expected that a viable theory for a new kind of economy could be constructed without a delay of many years, but the intellectual standard of the work that was visible to a Western resident, and the conditions in which this work was being done, showed little prospect of achievement.

Of course, the practical needs of the economy itself provided some stimulus. One of these was the problem, faced below the level of the central plan, of deciding how to implement its directives. For example, how was the specified construction of a certain amount of generating capacity for electric power in a particular area to be accomplished? Several different technological variants could be employed, but no particular variant was ever laid down in the plan. The literature on this question in the 1930's is to be found in the journals of particular industries rather than in the central economic publications. The problem was met by taking a national rate of interest—under another name—on which to compare different capital costs with operating costs at the state-fixed prices and wages. Thus, the discussion remained on the level of people's commissariats, and of localities, and did not emerge into the central press as a stimulus to study of the economy as a whole.

The other practical problem was inside Gosplan, where balances had to be drawn up to ensure the production and movement of all the goods needed in the plan, and the utilization of all the goods produced in the plan, at the right time and in the right place, in the correct amount and by the correct commissariat or committee. I received the impression in the later 1930's that this work was getting out of hand, leading to the elaboration of more and more charts on which the flows of goods and services were displayed. In order to help the planners find some way of coping with the number and size of their charts, at least two groups of economists were working on a theory of balances, one at the Gosplan Institute of Economic Reserach and another at the Soviet Academy of Sciences. Their work appears to have been bogged down by the difficulty of providing a Marxist framework, in terms of the labour theory of value, without having clear leads from above as to how value theory was to be employed in the socialist economy, so that the balance charts could show the proportions of embodied labour, living labour, and surplus value (or, a politically more admissible term, surplus product) in all the goods or aggregates of goods, and demonstrate the movement of the interrelation of these theoretical categories in any particular plan.

The urgent needs of the Gosplan staff, who had to plan the actual flows of goods, were of a more practical nature, and there seems to have been little relation between the staff and the theoretical workers, even though a group of the latter worked in Gosplan's own economic research institute. At least some of the theorists would have liked to simplify their problem by taking, as a first approximation of Marxism, the peasantry as living labour, and state income from them as surplus value. The whole of industry could then be seen as living on the surplus value, and theorists could get down to analyzing the internal relationships of industry without having to bother about value theory. This, of course, was politically impossible. Another political stumbling block was the need to divide goods in terms of their origin and consumption into socialist, co-operative, or private production. How was the production of the household plot of the collective farmer, a most important producer, to be classified? In general, published writings by these theorists leave the same hollow impression as those on the teaching of a political economy of socialism. However, three articles by Strumilin, head of the group working on balances theory in the Academy of Sciences, seem to have broken new ground in one respect at least. The articles were all published about the same time, in 1936, though in three different periodicals. They differ only in their classification of the household plots: in one version, these are included with the collective farms; in another, they are regarded as belonging to the remaining individual peasants; in the third, they are treated as a category of their own. This surely must have been a brave protest on the part of Strumilin. In any case, it led to threats against him. Nonetheless, it did not break the deadlock.

With the exception of such semi-market areas as those represented by collective farm bazaars, illegal transactions among state enterprises, and some purely local economic activities, all prices in all market sectors were set by the state. At first glance, the task of pricing seems to have been one that might have stimulated work on theory. There is no evidence, however, that this was the case. In practice, though Marxist economists worked in the pricing departments, their function was, necessarily, to make purely *ad hoc* adjustments arising out of economic policy decisions made by the government. The absence of any connection between Soviet pricing and value theory is explained by two circumstances. First, it is not at all clear that any such connection exists in the nature of the theory. Second, until 1943, it was more or less assumed that value theory had ceased to apply to the Soviet economy, since the market had been superseded by planning.

In the middle of the war, a work on a political economy of socialism suddenly emerged in the famous unsigned article of July-August 1943 entitled *Pod znamenem marksizma.*[1] By then, Soviet victory appeared certain, and the article, which is on the teaching of political economy, has the purpose of integrating the subject into both the curriculum and the ideology after the war. Contemporary experience is acknowledged in the part of the article dealing with the teaching on capitalism and imperialism. A new differentation is made between the political economy of fascism and that of the capitalist democracies, but this differentation limits itself to politics and completely evades the questions facing Marxist political economy in this connection. So far as the treatment of socialism is concerned, the practical problem is the old one of validating the use within socialism of such elements of the capitalist economy as money, price, and profit, and providing some theoretical framework for their future. Similarly, the question of criteria for planning and the relation of the plan to the market elements of the Soviet economy could scarcely avoid being treated in this first authoritative statement on the political economy of socialism. A Marxist treatment of these questions must turn on value theory, and what we get about value in this document can be reduced to the following summary.

Objective law does exist in socialism, but it operates through the full awareness and will of the state. (A more or less absolute contrast is made here with the traditional Marxist view of blind or *stikhiynyy* economic law in capitalism.) Collectivization and industrialization are economic necessities in the transition to socialism, and are therefore laws of the transition; there are various such necessities within socialism, such as planning and distribution according to work done, which are likewise laws. "The mistakes of previous teaching, in which operation of the law of value in socialist society was denied, created insuperable obstacles to an explanation of such categories as money, banks, credit, and so forth in socialism." The law of value operates in socialism, owing to the fact that labour is of different kinds, mental and manual, skilled and unskilled, rural and urban, etc. The products of these different kinds of labour are commodities. Commodities explicitly include "all the output of enterprises of a fully socialist type." The state obeys the law of value in that state prices are based on the socially necessary costs of production, except for deliberate divergencies to implement policy.

There is a surprising inconsistency within the article at this point. The final paragraph of this section contradicts the view that all products of the state sector are commodities by saying that in socialist society the equipment

---

[1] "Teaching of Economics in the Soviet Union," translated in *American Economic Review*, Evanston, Illinois, Vol. XXXIV, No. 2, June, 1944, pp. 500–530.

of factories, plants, MTS, state farms, and so forth are no longer commodities, because they are not freely bought and sold as in capitalism. Thus, the article does not in fact give a decision on the question of the law of value in the state sector, or rather it gives two more or less opposite decisions. The second is presumably a sort of minority report, but the inconsistency is not made explicit, and seems in fact to be deliberately slurred over. It is also possible that the two views are stated simply in order to have the best of both worlds: state sector goods are commodities, hence the categories of money, profit, etc., in this sector; and state sector goods are not commodities, hence no crises in Soviet industry.

The ambiguous framework of this article lasted until 1952. Its "laws" of the socialist economy, in slightly varying lists, such as balanced or proportionate development, the overtaking of capitalism, distribution according to work, incessant improvement in productivity, incessant improvement in material and cultural level, and incessant increase in output of all industries, were published in numerous editions by so many authors that they can be said to have been poured for years over the heads of the population. Virtually no other treatment of the Soviet economy appeared. There was an apparent break in 1948, with the appearance of Notkin's *Essays in the Theory of Socialist Reproduction* and Voznesensky's famous account of the war economy.[2] Notkin was disappointing: for all that this once original economist could do in this atmosphere, he might as well have remained silent. As for Voznesensky, while his references to theory are entirely in line with the 1943 pronouncement, the general flavour of his book is such as to play down objective necessity and to stress the power of the state to do what it wants. Whether or not this tendency played any part in Voznesensky's destruction, it is expressed in many other sources in this period, for example, in a *Pravda* editorial of August 8, 1949, in which there are such comments as the following: "...the role of the so-called 'objective' factors is reduced to the minimum.... Our people has become able to influence every aspect of life to a desired end."

The study of language is a less ideological subject than political economy. The discussion in the same period of the linguistic theories of N. Y. Marr, which came to a head in 1950, involved a more serious attempt to handle the question of objective social law, in this case the very difficult question of law operating in a human activity which is immediately willed, but willed in ignorance of the laws governing this activity. The problem would

---

[2] N. Voznesensky, *Voennaya ekonomika SSSR v period otechestvennoy voiny*, Moscow, 1947.

appear to be simpler in economics than in language, but the standard of analysis was lower in economics.

Stalin's collection of comments on the unpublished draft of the textbook on political economy, issued in October 1952 under the title *Economic Problems of Socialism in the USSR*, comes down heavily on the side of objective necessity, or law, as a constraint upon the freedom of action of the socialist state. (In a study of Stalin's function as conductor of the ideological orchestra, this emphasis in 1952 would be as relevant as the opposite observation attributed to him twenty years earlier about no fortresses that Bolsheviks could not capture.) The emphasis on necessity is sound economics, and in general the 1952 document sets a sober tone. The series of "laws," such as balanced or proportionate production, is put in its place as a feature of a socialist model, not necessarily attained in practice. Laws cannot be abolished or "transformed," but systems to which they are proper can be changed. Commodities do and will exist as long as there are market relations between the state and the collective farms, and the state and the private consumer. To this extent, the law of value does operate, in the sense that if state prices are unfair to the collective farms, they will react accordingly. Stalin firmly equates market relations, commodities, and the operation of the law of value as three aspects of the same sphere of the Soviet economy that is said to be foreordained gradually to diminish over a long period until it disappears in full communism. Meanwhile, since the state sector is in extensive contact with the law of value, through its market relations with the collective farms and with private consumers, including its labour force, such manifestations of value as prices, costing, and profits are also used within the state sector, though they do not originate there. (The idea of "shadow" profits in the state sector had also been put forward in the 1920's.) These devices, though they are market categories, are no threat to the socialist economy, because the market is not the primary feature of the Soviet economy. They can therefore be safely used and developed, and are indeed of great benefit for socialist efficiency if wisely used.

Stalin is unrealistic at many points where he touches on conditions of the actual world, including aspects of contemporary capitalism, and where he puts forth the idea that the collective farms of his day enjoyed market relations with the state. (He does give a realistic example of agricultural pricing policy.) His Marxism, however, is sound enough, and his treatment is logical: he does not mutilate the theory as the "majority report" section of the 1943 document does. Nor does he revise the theory, though he points out the urgent need for its revision, for "replacing the old concepts with new ones that correspond to the new situation."[3] In his tidying-up operation, however, Stalin does not face up to what is involved in his solution of the relation between state sector and market. His point that the entire state sector is permeated by a market relation with its own labour force is a useful one for validating the use of derivative value categories in relations between state enterprises, but, unless a suitable, special conceptual species of "commodity" is invented for state products acquired by the private consumer, this market realtion involves labouring power, which the workers exchange for consumer goods, as a commodity in the socialist economy, a circumstance that Stalin explicitly repudiates elsewhere in his 1952 materials. This repudiation has been widespread in Soviet ideology, on the emotional grounds that Soviet labour cannot be a commodity like capitalist labour.[4]

In 1946, the pre-war discussion on criteria of alternative investments emerged from the pages of the branch publications into the central economic press, where it tried, without much success, to break out of the bounds imposed on it by the 1943 article. This discussion could not contribute directly to a theory of the Soviet economy, because the problem was restricted to alternative ways of implementing the national plan; the criteria by which the national plan itself was set up, so far as any existed, could not be questioned. Nevertheless, original thinking on social costs and time-discounting was manifested in this discussion, which reappeared throughout the 1950's and has now merged with the general discussion of pricing, interest charges, etc., on which investment decisions depend. It should be

---

[3] "Mutilation" is used here to denote alteration of part of a theory or model without concern for the effect on internal logical consistency. For alteration made with due concern for consequential change in other parts of the theory to preserve its logical coherence, "revision" seems an appropriate term. A third term is needed for the degree of correspondence between a theory and reality—perhaps "realism." In these terms, Stalin was asking for realist revision, and the general history of Soviet-Marxist political economy is one of pseudo-realist mutilation.

[4] See, for example, an indignant letter in *Voprosy ekonomiki*, No. 3, 1967, pp. 133–134, on the suggestion in *Ekonomika Sovetskoy Ukraini*, in an article by Kornienko and Pakhomov, in No. 9, 1966, that the labouring power of Soviet workers could be considered as a commodity. The article is significant as a plea for serious work to construct a political economy of socialism. The letter of protest is supported by a brief statement by the editors of *Voprosy ekonomiki*, but not in the violent terms that would have been used a year or two earlier.

Kornienko and Pakhomov could have made their proposal less offensive to ideological susceptibilities by saying that the employer to whom the Soviet workers sell their labouring power is the state, representing the whole community, which includes themselves, and that the surplus value, or surplus product, likewise belongs to the whole community.

noted that this problem, because of its practical urgency in the increasingly complex economy, forced the ideological authorities into legitimizing, in 1954 and more fully in 1958, the actual practice of using a national rate of interest on capital. This practice was not squared with the ideology, which could not accept a charge on capital, because embodied labour does not create value, but it was nevertheless simply accepted and even encouraged. Concern here is not with Soviet analysis of the capitalist economies. It is worth noting, however, that the condemnation of serious attempts in this direction published in the late 1940's, notably Varga's assessment of the American economy, must in due course have helped the political leaders to become aware of an element of danger in relying on ideological writers incapable of analysis.

Since Stalin

By 1955, there was at least open admission of the situation, and in a form that implicitly questions whether Marxism can be relevant. For example, at this time, a writer in *Voprosy ekonomiki* is to be found complaining:

> ...for years there has not been a single worthwhile general theoretical work... Not a single work has been published which examines in what ways the objective character of economic laws finds expression, how the requirements of any of these laws are put into effect, and how breaches of these laws can be identified.

In the middle fifties, the element of Soviet political economy most directly related to policy appeared in public after a silence of over twenty-five years. This was the question of the proportions between departments I and II, in the form of rates of growth of producer goods and consumer goods output. The discussion was one-sided, since the existence of proponents of change had to be inferred from the attacks upon them. One of these attacks, by the then Khrushchev supporter Shepilov, was couched in hysterical language. In this atmosphere, reason could play little part. The Stalinist assumption that department I must grow at a faster rate than department II for the economy as a whole to continue to grow, though never demonstrated, was reasserted. Other aspects of this question were given no hearing, in particular the importance of the composition of department I, the proportion of producer goods for making producer goods and of producer goods for making consumer goods. (Khrushchev himself publicly raised this obvious question not long before his fall.)

The textbook on political economy, which at last appeared in 1954, after so many years in preparation, makes no theoretical contribution whatever, nor do its subsequent editions, which simply reflect, as is natural for an official textbook, the prevailing modifications of ideological exposition.[5] One of these is an extension of the concept "commodity," from Stalin's goods entering into market relations, to all goods, including those transferred between state enterprises, on the grounds that such transfers are effected as sales and purchases.[6] It is remarkable that the Marxists who can commit this solecism on Marxist political economy without bothering to make the adjustment in the theory necessary to accommodate it, find (or found, until the 1965 reforms) such difficulty in legitimizing interest and rent, which would involve less severe adjustment.

The view of transfers within the state sector as commodities could be legitimized either by redefining the market within the theory, or by pronouncing Soviet state enterprises to be legally independent owners, but such radical changes in Marxist theory or Soviet law would raise more problems than they solved. Still, if adequate revisions are not made, such mutilations of the theory as the admission of intra-state commodities will kill it. From the point of view of elementary internal logical consistency, ideological tidying up after the practical reforms now commencing had better not be done at all. On the other hand, to do nothing would kill the ideology in another way, by totally severing it from its tenuous connection with reality.

The concern of this study, of course, is with Marixst economic theory in the USSR, not with the revival of economics as such since the late 1950's, nor with the use of Marxist concepts or terms for the purpose of facilitating publication of contributions that are in themselves independent of Marxism. A possibly significant development in Marxist economics is the reexamination of the thought of the 1920's, for guidance on the legitimation of value theory in the state sector. The most direct expression of this new tendency at the time of writing is to be found in a recent, if back, issue of the journal *Ekonomicheskiye nauki*,[7] which, apparently for the first time in the USSR,

---

[5] A directive of the Russian government on textbooks in 1818 is still relevant. Only those were to be used that were thought to be best in helping to achieve "an enduring and blessed harmony between faith, knowledge and authority" (L. Greenberg, *The Jews in Russia*, p. 32).

[6] At a conference on the law of value in 1957, the more or less official validation of intra-state commodity relations was made on the different, but equally surprising, ground that wages paid by state enterprises represent a relation of equivalent return between the enterprise and its workers, and thus state production is permeated by the principle of equivalent return. See Ostrovityanov's speech in *Voprosy ekonomiki*, No. 8, 1957.

[7] D. Manevich, "Diskussiya o predmete politicheskoy ekonomii" (pp. 86–92), and N. Petrakova, "Problema plana i rynka v sovetskoy ekonomicheskoy literatury 20 godov," (pp. 92–99), *Ekonomicheskie nauki*, No. 5, 1966.

gives informative and even respectful accounts of the great debates of those years, in certain selected aspects. These articles, which appear to be first of a series on the history of Soviet economic thought, deal mainly with efforts in the 1920's to handle the problem of the relation between the state sector and the market sector, with the explicit purpose of helping to meet the felt need for the ascertainment and use of market-type criteria in the present state economy. Thus, the articles evince a tendency to go further than mere ideological validation. In other current Soviet publications, there is an implied tendency to draw some kind of analogy between NEP, as a return to the pre-civil war policy of market relations between town and country, and the reforms now beginning, as a return after the Stalin period to something in the spirit of NEP. Thus, war communism and the Stalin period are shown as the two deviations from the proper line. An example of this approach is the pamphlet *Plan and Market* by G. S. Lisichkin.[8]

There is something unpleasant in tracing the degeneration of what was once a powerful system of ideas, both in the intellectual and moral sense, to the position now occupied by political economy in the USSR. Marx, concerned with the future of his own country to a greater extent than is often realized, built a remarkable tool for broad historical analysis, out of the intellectual materials and social conditions accessible to him, to forewarn and stimulate his country, and in addition any other country, that might find his forecast relevant. It is not surprising that the Russian state has not been able to use this tool either in running or describing its economy, but it seems unable to admit this fact.

---

[8] G. S. Lisichkin, *Plan i rynok*, Moscow, 1966.

Satisfaction of Consumer Needs

Heinrich Vogel

The competitive struggle directed at satisfying consumer needs in a market economy is, of course, conspicuously missing from the command economy of the Soviet Union. In its place, central planning takes on the function of allocating the factors of production. Looking over the past fifty years of the Soviet economy in terms of satisfaction of consumer needs, one might try to derive historical comparisons of results achieved with promises made, but one might also choose to concentrate on an analysis of the present situation of the Soviet consumer, viewing it as the cumulative outcome of the half century of experimentation vesting the power of control over the nation's economy in its rulers rather than its consumers.

The approach of this study will reflect economic decisions, leaving historical analysis aside. It is, after all, well known that there were no specific promises made to Soviet consumers at the time of forced industrialization. As early as 1917, in fact, Lenin put the whole problem quite bluntly: "Either perish or overtake and outstrip the advanced countries economically ... Perish or drive full steam ahead. That is the alternative with which history has confronted us."[1] Stalin referred explicitly to this quotation in his speech "Industrialization of the Country and the Right Deviation" at the Soviet Party Plenum of November 19, 1928, which marked the actual beginning of the Soviet experiment in central planning. Obviously, rapid growth in a totally planned economy depends on the large savings gained by holding down consumption. The historical background of forced industrialization, considered here as an external factor, has been frequently documented, and need not be described in detail. The framework of domestic and foreign affairs ought to be mentioned only to call attention to the enormous time pressure under which the Bolsheviks operated their economic policy.

Considerable research has been done on the lot of the Soviet consumer by such well-known scholars as Janet Chapman, M. Miller, M. E. Ruban, and Alec Nove, but their studies follow a predominantly descriptive, largely statistical line. This study will raise a few methodological questions

---

[1] English translation in Nicolas Spulber, ed., *Foundations of Soviet Strategy for Economic Growth,* Bloomington, Indiana, Indiana University Press, 1964, p. 266.

in an effort to prepare the ground for some theoretical reflections on the changing position and role of the consumer in Soviet society. Presuming that the reader is informed about the degree of social and economic backwardness in Russia at the beginning of the Soviet economic experiment, a few general conclusions about the actual development of living standards in the Soviet Union will finally be drawn.

Up to now, scholarly discussion of the economic idea of "consumer needs" has not provided much of a basis for theoretical conjecture about the relative value of living standards.[2] The term "consumer needs" ought perhaps to be replaced by the term "consumer wants" if a more precise understanding of what goes on in the structure of the Soviet economy is to be got at. A common term in economic theory, "consumer wants" describes the attitude of the consumer towards categories of goods or services, such as food, housing, safety, and employment, that represent individual and social welfare functions. The principal concern here will be with the mechanisms that are at work between the levels of individual and social welfare functions and that serve to coordinate wants on both levels in terms at least of economic plans. The enumeration of discrepancies between individual and social welfare functions ought not to be taken as implying the impossibility of interrelations or correspondences between public requirement and private necessity. (Even so, K. Arrow has contended that an individual social welfare function is a contradiction in itself and that each empirical social welfare function would include an element of dictatorship.)[3] Finally, it should be mentioned that though this study has reference to developments over the entire period of Soviet rule, the statistical review offered gives only a bare minimum of data, limiting itself to the period after 1950, because the significance of discrepancies between individual and social welfare functions has mainly increased since then.

The Changing Position of the Consumer

A look at the planning process in the Soviet Union will show the crucial points of divergence between the preferences of planners and of consumers in respect of welfare functions. The first phase of the planning procedure is seen as fixing the rate of investment and its regional and sectoral allocation. Investment, of course, means non-consumption. According to growth theory, the rate of investment and its regional and

---

[2] "A feeling of deficiency, combined with the endeavour to put an end to it." See Georg von Stakelberg, *Grundlagen der theoretischen Volkswirtschaftslehre*, Tübingen, 1951, p. 3.

[3] See *Social Choice and Individual Values*, New York and London, John Wiley & Sons. 1955. p. 76.

sectoral allocation determines the time-lag between the act of investment and its effect on consumption. The second phase of planning is seen as fixing the share of collective consumption in total consumption. Collective consumption, of course, is financed by diverting the necessary funds from the monetary income of the population. It is only in the third phase of planning that the actual production and distribution of goods for individual consumption are dealt with. In this scheme, types and dimensions of production that have been limited by the decisions of the first and second phases of planning are established as residual categories. They are influenced by the degree of knowledge about actual demand structures, which in turn depends on the competence of the institutions engaged in planning, and particularly on their information about correct price relations.

The Rate of Investment. The strategy of Soviet industrialization is considered by some to be generally applicable to developing economies. This suggests that some effort must be made to place *ex-post-facto* reflections on the changing position of the Soviet consumer in the context of this model. In most theoretical growth models, a maximum rate of saving is postulated as a constant constraint having the objective of maximum growth. The fact that a socialist state can more easily fit the rate of saving to the objectives of growth strategy led to the erroneous assumption that the amount of saving could be left entirely to the discretion of the planners. Indeed, the famous growth model of G. A. Feldman, dating from 1928, is based on the assumption that saving can be adjusted to investment without difficulties.[4] The rate of growth is then determined only by the production of investment goods directed to sector A. This constitutes the theoretical core of the famous "Law of priority growth of sector A." Feldman examines three possible cases: (1) where total consumption is constant; (2) where total consumption increases at a constant geometric rate; and (3) where total consumption increases at a rising rate. He stresses that the rate of saving that can be enforced by the state depends upon the attained degree of industrialization. The importance of Feldman's model is, of course, that it demonstrates how thoroughly the effects of plans for industrialization on consumption were discussed by the Soviet institutions concerned.[5] Clearly, the objective of long-term planning has been to raise the standard of living.

The planners, it should be noted, were by no means free when they fixed the pace of industrialization. In 1943, O. Lange wrote: "Soviet

[4] *Planovoe khozyaystvo*, Nos. 11 and 12, 1928.
[5] See also Michael Kaser, "Welfare Criteria in Soviet Planning," in *Soviet Planning, Essays in Honor of Naum Jasny*, J. Degras and A. Nove, eds., Oxford, Basil Blackwell, 1964; New York, Frederick A. Praeger, 1965, pp. 153–161.

economic planning did not serve the objectives of a harmonious social welfare economy but served political and military objectives to which all other aspects of economic planning were sacrificed."[6] This statement can be accepted as valid for the period up to 1950. Elsewhere, Lange refers to the Soviet economy as a war economy, a term that is justified by the relevant methods of organization and enforcement in effect at the time. The people in charge knew how to mobilize patriotic emotions for their goals. Obviously, the realized rate of saving under the early Five-Year Plans, and especially during World War II, to a large extent comprised voluntary reduction of consumption. The slow expansion of consumption may be explained further in terms of over-investment practices caused by inadequate methods of planning and inefficient organization. "Over-investment cuts consumption at both ends: the total product is smaller than it otherwise would be, and in this smaller product the share of investment is greater than necessary."[7] Investment directed to such non-European areas as Siberia, Central Asia, and the Far East resulted in additional cuts in total consumption. Naturally, it is beyond the scope and intent of this study to judge whether the decision to develop these areas was based on political or economic considerations, but it seems important not simply to disregard the possibility that the reasons were purely economic ones.

Malenkov's speech to the Supreme Soviet of the USSR on August 9, 1953, marked a major turning point in economic policy in the Soviet Union in favour of the consumer. The motives of the Soviet political leadership in this endeavour are perhaps best summed up by Nove: "Soviet leaders . . . may wish to give their people the most that can be spared, or the least that will persuade them to work—such fine distinctions can be left to philosophers."[8] Beyond political and philosophical considerations, however, there seem to have been strong economic reasons for strengthening the position of the consumer, whose interests are directed towards consumption here and now, and not towards consumption in generations to come. First, the attained state of economic development provides the conditions for further differentiation of production. Likewise, further economic development requires differentiation, from which favourable effects on production of consumer goods may result. Second, there is the necessity of mastering Soviet-type inflation caused by excessive credit and excessive money in circulation. Under conditions of centralized planning

---

6 "The Working Principles of the Soviet Economy," in *USSR Economy and the War*, New York, Russian Economic Institute, 1943, p. 43.

7 B. Horvath, *Towards a Theory of Planned Economy*, Belgrade, 1964, p. 186.

8 "The Pace of Soviet Economic Development," *Lloyds Bank Review*, London, April, 1956, p. 17.

of production, the acceptance of consumer's free choice, combined with material incentives, such as wage differentials, poses the permanent danger of disequilibria on markets of consumer goods. Such disequilibria become evident in queues at state shops and in stocks of unsaleable goods. There is, in the long run, only one way out of this dilemma: production must be adjusted to the demand structure of the population. Third, persuasion to work, as practiced in the Soviet Union, is only efficient under certain circumstances and for a limited period of time. Highly specialized and qualified workers in modern industrialized economies continually demand improvement of their nutrition, living and working conditions, and social welfare in general. The influence of this factor on labour productivity, in comparison with the influence of the factor of technical progress, has been neglected for a long time by Soviet planners. The term *materialnoe stimulirovaniye* characterizes the new trend towards making allowances for the growing importance of individual and collective consumption and its influence on labour productivity. Nevertheless, the increasing importance of consumption in relation to investment cannot be expressed properly in this relation only. The share of gross fixed investment going to industries of sector B must also be taken into account (see Tables 1 and 2). This share reached about 12 per cent as an average for the period 1959-1963. The Soviet economy thus approaches the standard of inter-industry distribution of investment in industrialized countries in the West—that is, an estimated 15 per cent.[9]

Collective versus Private Consumption. In long-term economic policy, determination of the relationship between private and collective consumption is a crucial problem. Soviet ideological concepts of this relationship should by no means distract attention from the fact that in the Soviet Union, too, collective consumption constitutes "policies of the welfare state, based on necessities and possibilities of developed industrialism."[10] In this respect, there seem to be no basic differences between the Soviet economy and the the mixed economies of the West; minor differences emerge from the preponderance of the state sector in the socialist economic system. Discussions of the specific communist character of social funds, which have proved to be fruitless, should, therefore, be replaced by the approach used in public finance in the West.

---

[9] See Rolf Krengel, "Die quantitativen Veränderungen der sowjetischen Wirtschaft," in *Bilanz der Ära Chruschtschow*, Erik Boettcher, ed., Stuttgart, p. 77.

[10] Hans Raupach, "Das kommunistische Verteilungsprinzip: Jedem nach seinen Bedürfnissen in der Praxis," in *Methoden und Probleme der Wirtschaftspolitik*, Hans Ohm, ed., Berlin, 1964, p. 224.

Table 1

Relative Shares of Investment and Private Consumption in Gross National Product at Factor Cost

(Percentages)

	1928	1937	1940	1950	1955	1964
Private Consumption ..	64.7	52.5	51.0	51.0	50.6	46.5
Gross Investment	25.0	25.9	19.2	23.0	25.3	30.5

SOURCES: A. Bergson, *The National Income of Soviet Russia Since 1928*, Cambridge, Harvard University Press, 1961, p. 237; Stanley H. Cohn, "Soviet Growth Retardation: Trends in Resource Availability and Efficiency," Joint Economic Committe, U.S. Congress, *New Directions in the Soviet Economy*, Washington, D.C., Part II-A, 1966, p. 129.

Table 2

Distribution of Investment to Sectors A and B

(Rubles and Percentages)

	Total Investment	Investment in Sector A	Investment in Sector B	Share of Investment in Sector A
1928	260,000,000	210,000,000	50,000,000	81
1940	2,000,000,000	1,700,000,000	300,000,000	85
1953	6,500,000,000	5,900,000,000	600,000,000	91
1961	14,900,000,000	13,200,000,000	1,800,000,000	89
1964	16,900,000,000	14,800,000,000	2,100,000,000	87

SOURCES: Rolf Krengel, "Die quantitativen Veränderungen der sowjetischen Wirtschaft," in *Bilanz der Ära Chruschtschow*, Erik Boettcher, ed., Stuttgart, p. 77; *Naradnoe khozyaystvo SSSR 1964* (The Economy of the USSR in 1964), Moscow, 1965, p. 513.

In this field, the general scope of public activity is defined as relating primarily to "social wants proper."[11] These social wants must be satisfied by public goods, that is, goods that everybody is free to consume, such as public security and public roads.[12] Imperfections in market distribution also serve to justify the idea of collective consumption. This, of course, implies a value judgment in respect of patterns of income distribution. All kinds of social economies or diseconomies for which collective consumption will act as a corrective are to be included in this sphere. Never-

---

[11] R. A. Musgrave, *The Theory of Public Finance*, New York, McGraw-Hill, 1959; E. Sohmen, "Grundlegung, Grenzen und Entwicklungsmöglichkeiten der Welfare Economics," in *Probleme der normativen Ökonomik und der wirtschaftspolitischen Beratung*, Schriften des Vereins der Sozialpolitik, Berlin, Vol. 29, 1963; O. H. Brownlee and E. D. Allen, *Economics of Public Finance*, 2nd ed., Englewood Cliffs, N.J., Prentice-Hall, 1954; and B. A. Weisbrod, "Collective Consumption Services of Individual Consumption Goods," in *Quarterly Journal of Economics*, Cambridge, Massachusetts, Vol. 78, 1964.

[12] Critical statements were made by B. Sucharevsky, "Zarabotnaya plata i obshchestvennyye fondy potrebleniya," in No. 8, 1961, and N. Buzlyakov, "O razvitii obshchestvennykh fondov potrebleniya," in No. 4, 1962, *Voprosy ekonomiki*.

theless, at this point it still appears extremely difficult to set up a catalogue of wants covered optimally by measures of collective consumption. The reason for this is that the categories presented lack a clear definition of their limits. Moreover, identification of imperfections in market distribution, as well as of social economies and diseconomies, require value judgments. Obviously, a term like social economies or diseconomies must be looked upon as unsatisfactory for practical purposes of economic policy. In some cases, however, the economic advantage of substituting distribution through the budget for distribution through the market is calculable. This is true, for example, when "the costs of measuring the product and collecting from buyers on the basis of the amount purchased by each may be high compared to other costs involved in producing the service."[13]

Decisions of any government, socialist or capitalist, that interfere with consumer choice "may occur simply because a ruling group considers its particular mores superior and wishes to impose them on others." However, even Musgrave, whose approach is based on the individualistic concept, admits: "A position of extreme individualism could demand that all merit wants be disallowed, but this is not a sensible view."[14] Of course, conformity or non-conformity of objective governmental functions with those of the consumer can be determined, if at all, only by indirect observation and measurement of consumer reactions. From all this, the conclusion might be drawn that the relation of collective to private consumption is arbitrary and dependent on the discretion of the ruling group. Yet, some historical studies that have been made in the United States and West Germany lead to the assumption that a correlation exists between industrialization and the amount of budget expenses taken as an expression of economic activity of the state.[15] Technical progress, urbanization, and the growth of per capita income increase the importance of private consumption, and as a consequence, also of collective consumption.[16] However, a

---

[13] Brownlee and Allen, *op. cit.*, p. 161.
[14] R. A. Musgrave, *op. cit.*, pp. 13 and 14.
[15] S. Fabricant, *The Trend of Government Activity in the United States since 1900*, Princeton, 1952; M. S. Kendrick, *A Century and a Half of Federal Expenditures*, New York, 1955; L. Edelberg, "Public Expenditures and Economics Structure in the United States," in *Social Research*, New York, Vol. III, No. 1, 1936; K. Littmann, "Strukturen und Entwicklungen der staatlichen Aktivität in der BRD 1950–1970," in *Strukturwandlungen einer wachsenden Wirtschaft*, Schriften des Vereins für Sozialpolitik, Berlin, Vol. II, No. 30, 1964; and T. Pütz, "Wirtschaftliche Entwicklung und zunehmende Staatstätigkeit," in *Zeitschrift für Nationalökonomie*, Vol. II, Vienna, 1960.
[16] This increases present production of consumer goods and also creates new production sectors.

considerable time-lag is caused by the political process in Western democracies, where a consensus on public intervention by means of the budget is required, as Kenneth Galbraith points out in *The Affluent Society*.[17]

In the Soviet Union, the system of social funds (*obshchestvennyye fondy potrebleniya*) means contributions to collective consumption at public expense, and comprises, with a few exceptions, transfer payments, subsidies, and non-monetary benefits.[18] This is little different from those systems in Western welfare states. The Party Programme of 1961 announced that the scope of collective consumption would be broadened. It says: "After twenty years, social funds of consumption as a whole will increase to half of the population's total real income."[19] Services like housing, public transportation, and other public utilities will be financed through the budget. "Personal needs shall be satisfied more and more by social funds, which will grow faster than individual payments fixed according to achievements."[20] In this sentence, attention should be paid to a significant formulation that seems almost like a failure in the Freudian sense: individual wages and salaries, i.e., monetary income, are equated with satisfaction of wants, i.e., private consumption by expenditures.

Basic data are too inadequate to form an opinion cf Soviet reality insofar as the correspondence of the decisions of planners with the wishes of consumers is concerned. Sporadic references in Soviet publications indicate that a correspondence has not yet been achieved. The following example might serve to make this evident. Apparently, free medical care is considered unsatisfactory as far as consumers are concerned. According to a report, more than fifteen hundred patients visit a clinic on Kirov Street in Moscow every day, paying a fee for their treatment.[21] This indicates a growing need for more individual treatment in clinics and a strong distrust of the efficiency of free medical care. The discrepancy between planner preferences and consumer wishes is evident in this case. The consumer has the opportunity to choose private consumption, because the clinic is officially tolerated.

It would seem that in the course of time the function of the consumer has become more important than that of the planner. The bargaining power of consumers is based on the amount of purchasing power available from current income, savings, hoards, and credits, which, together, form

---

[17] *Gesellschaft im Überfluss* (German translation), Munich-Zurich, 1963.
[18] These derive from governmental and communal budgets, from social insurance, social organization, enterprises, and collective farms.
[19] *Program der KPdSU* (German translation), Moscow, 1961, p. 116.
[20] *Programm der KPdSU, op. cit.*
[21] *Literaturnaya gazeta*, October 12, 1965.

so-called discretionary income. If fundamental needs are covered by collective consumption goods, discretionary income will increase and enable the consumer to counteract discriminatory price policy. As Tables 3 and 4 suggest, the share of social fund payments in total money income of workers and employees has remained at about 33 per cent since 1946.[22]

Table 3

Disposable Money Income and Transfers from Social Funds Since 1950

(Rubles)

	Disposable Money Income	Transfers from Social Funds
1950......	39,100,000,000	8,900,000,000
1958......	70,450,000,000	14,700,000,000
1960......	78,940,000,000	17,100,000,000
1961......	87,590,000,000	18,200,000,000
1962......	94,760,000,000	20,000,000,000
1963......	98,600,000,000	21,900,000,000
1964......	104,170,000,000	23,600,000,000

NOTE: According to the official definition, which is used here, social funds comprise transfer payments, except those for paid leave.

SOURCES: D. W. Bronson and B. S. Severin, "Recent Trends in Consumption and Disposable Money Income in the USSR," *New Directions in the Soviet Economy*, Joint Economic Committee, U.S. Congress, Part II-B, Washington, D.C., 1966, p. 526; *Narodnoe khozyaystvo SSSR v 1962* (The Economy of the USSR in 1962), Moscow, 1963, p. 487; *Narodnoe khozyaystvo SSSR v 1963*, Moscow, 1964, p. 505; and *Narodnoe khozyaystvo SSSR v 1964*, Moscow, 1965, p. 590.

Table 4

Relative Share of Real Income from Social Funds in Total Monthly Real Income of Workers and Employees

(Rubles and Percentages)

	Average Monthly Income from Work	Average Monthly Income from Social Funds	Total Real Monthly Income	Share of Income from Social Funds in Total Real Income
1946..........	47.5	14.9	62.4	31.4
1950..........	63.9	18.5	82.4	28.9
1955..........	71.5	20.3	91.8	28.4
1958..........	77.8	26.6	101.4	34.1
1959..........	79.0	27.7	106.7	35.0
1960..........	80.1	27.6	107.7	34.4
1961..........	83.4	27.3	111.7	32.7
1962..........	86.2	29.5	115.7	34.2
1963..........	87.6	30.4	118.0	34.7
1964..........	90.1	30.9	121.0	34.3

SOURCES: *Narodnoe khozyaystvo SSSR v 1964* (The Economy of the USSR in 1964), Moscow, 1965, p. 555.

[22] *Narodnoe khozyayastvo SSSR v 1964 godu* (The Economy of the USSR in 1967), Moscow, 1965, p. 555.

These data represent merely a rough average of transfers made from social funds. It is admitted, of course, that there are considerable regional differences.[23] Official statements of today concerning the development of the population's welfare fail to give information on the exact share of income from social funds in total income. (This practice was usual only in the first years after 1961.) The reason for this is doubtless the necessity of practicing *materialnoe stimulirovaniye*. Additional income must be met with additional consumer goods. As an unforeseen consequence, patterns of private consumption expand at the expense of collective consumption.

Mainly for ideological reasons, the announcements in the 1961 Party Programme have often been interpreted as a "forward flight." However, there is an economic argument that might make the above-mentioned changes plausible.[24] The direction of consumer wants may lead to calculable economies. The well-known alternative of public or private transportation may serve as an example. If the primacy of public transportation were enforced, considerable amounts of capital could be set free for other purposes, because public investment in gasoline stations, repair shops, and traffic lights could then be postponed. On the other hand, the recent decision to produce 800,000 automobiles per year after 1970—to be sold, for the most part, to private buyers—contradicts the Party Programme of 1961. It is not necessary to emphasize that this decision meets the wishes of the Soviet consumer.[25] A greater supply of this "luxury good" will serve as an instrument to skim off surplus purchasing power in the Soviet Union. Of course, it will require more investment in road construction and related automotive industries.

On the whole, then, it may be concluded from these and other recent developments in the Soviet Union that the Soviet leadership has failed to convince the consumer that a reasonable relation maintains between the dimensions of collective and private consumption. This circumstance is also based on the influence of Western standards that have been imported into the USSR. Moreover, the Soviet leadership has proved unable to organize efficient market distribution of consumer goods, a shortcoming that further affects control of consumer cash. In this context, price inflexibility is, of course, the most important factor. In its basic features, the Soviet system of social funds pursues optimal satisfaction of the population's wants for social security. It also aims at attaining social justice

---

[23] See *Planirovaniye narodnogo potrebleniya v SSSR*, V. F. Mayer and P. N. Krylov, eds., Moscow, 1964, p. 48.

[24] First formulated by Hans Raupach in his article "Das kommunistische Verteilungsprinzip . . .," *op. cit.*

[25] There are numerous letters to the editor in the Soviet press to attest to this.

through the redistribution of income by taxation and assistance from social funds. Soviet officials admit, though, that until now this has been realized only to an unsatisfactory extent.[26] The degree of correspondence between the objectives of planners and the wants of consumers in the whole sphere of social funds, particularly in collective consumption, is a socio-economic problem, and therefore, it cannot be examined merely by economic methods. For a comprehensive analysis, sociological data are an indispensable requirement.

Planning for Private Consumption. The interrelation between the second and third phases of planning consumption is probably already apparent. In the third phase, the consumer's decision to buy or not to buy proves a most efficient check on plans for the amount and composition of consumer goods. After 1950, monetary income increased significantly as a result of wage reforms, more comprehensive aid from social insurance, price reforms for collective farm products, and reduced taxes on low income groups. Redistribution of income in favour of the collective farm population has resulted from the concession to free collective farm markets. D. W. Bronson and B. S. Severin state that there was an increase in disposable per capita real income of 264.9 per cent from 1950 to 1964.[27] Attention should be drawn to the fact that this comparison includes collective farmers and their families, who, until recently, were neglected factors in Soviet income policy (see Table 5).

As a matter of fact, the figures, as seen in retrospect, do not indicate if this development corresponds with the calculations of the planners. No

Table 5

Per Capita Annual Disposable Money and Real Income

(Rubles)

	1950	1958	1950	1961	1962	1963	1964
Money Income	217.1	340.7	368.5	402.0	428.0	438.8	457.3
Price Index	100	77.4	76.3	76.4	77.9	78.7	79.5
Real Income	217.1	440.2	483.0	526.2	549.4	556.9	575.2
Price Index	100	202.8	222.5	242.4	253.1	256.5	264.9

SOURCE: D. W. Bronson and B. S. Severin, "Recent Trends in Consumption and Disposable Money Income in the USSR," *New Directions in the Soviet Economy*, Joint Economic Committee, U.S. Congress, Part II-B, Washington, D.C., p. 526.

---

[26] *Planirovaniye narodnogo potrebleniya v SSSR, op. cit.*, p. 47.

[27] D. W. Bronson and B. Severin, "Recent Trends in Consumption and Disposable Income in the USSR," in *New Directions in the Soviet Economy*, Joint Economic Committee, U.S. Congress, Part II-B, Section 4, Washington, D.C., 1966, p. 526.

doubt, payments exceeding the planned wage funds are of great importance. Because central planning requires, above all, plan fulfillment in real terms, short-term lending from the bank system became one of the loopholes through which enterprises could escape the extreme pressure of the plan. As a rule, short-term credits from the state bank were not paid back under pre-reform conditions, and were eventually cleared from the enterprise's books by the ministry. Credit, however, is identical with additional wage payments for overtime work and bonuses, though frequently with a time-lag. A number of other legal or illegal causes of "wage-creep" also exists.

As mentioned above, central planners generally start from the erroneous assumption that disposable income amounts to income spent, or in any case to savings frozen to eternity in bank accounts. The planners aim at achieving an equilibrium of monetary demand and supply of consumer goods that will skim off the amount of money in circulation, so that voluntary savings are reduced to a negligible quantity. As a consequence of inadequate supply of consumer goods, both in terms of quantity and quality, this equilibrium has not been achieved up to now. The publication *Narodnoe khozyaystvo SSSR* points to the amount of savings as proof of the population's increasing welfare (*blagosostoyaniye*), but this seems to be making a virtue of necessity.[28] We cannot interpret savings under conditions of the Soviet state welfare system as being induced by the traditional motive of security. They are pent-up demands, which, together with the considerable hoards of collective farmers, are available practically every day for storming better supplied markets (see Table 6). The decision to in-

Table 6
Growth of Savings in Savings Banks
(Rubles)

	Total Volume	Increase Over Previous Year	Average Size of Savings Account
1950	1,900,000,000	—	124
1958	8,700,000,000	6,800,000,000	185
1960	10,900,000,000	2,200,000,000	209
1961	11,600,000,000	700,000,000	222
1962	12,700,000,000	900,000,000	238
1963	13,900,000,000	1,200,000,000	260
1964	15,700,000,000	1,800,000,000	285
1965	18,700,000,000	3,000,000,000	326

SOURCES: *Narodnoe khozyaystvo SSSR v 1962* (The Economy of the USSR in 1962), Moscow, 1963, p. 492; *Narodnoe Khozyaystvo SSSR v 1964*, Moscow, 1965, p. 595; *SSSR v Tsifrakh v 1965* (The USSR in Figures in 1965), Moscow, 1965, p. 144.

---

[28] This was done for the first time in *Narodnoe khozyaystvo SSSR v 1962 godu*, Moscow, 1963, p. 482.

crease production of automobiles, and the extensive discussion on augmenting the share of privately owned flats in total housing, are remedies for this threat to the monetary equilibrium.[29] Until now, planners have not been willing to consider the adaptation of assortment to actual demand, nor have they had an adequate knowledge of demand structures. The lack of working methods for the calculation of prices according to actual scarcities proves to be crucial in this connection.

The distribution of disposable income reveals a continual shift in favour of the rural population, caused by the regionally differing revenues from sales on collective farm markets. As a consequence of the higher planned prices for collective farm products, owing to the 1965 reform, farmers derived an additional income of two billion rubles from over-plan sales. Western scholars see an inflationary process in the disproportionate development of monetary income and the production of consumer goods.[30] The lack of data makes it difficult to estimate the degree of this inflation. A comparison of consumer expenditures on state and collective farm markets is available, but it shows only the development in a continually diminishing sector of consumer demands, disregarding the fact that on these two markets the assortments of goods on sale differ. Still, the statistical data available do suggest inflationary pressure.

Retail sales rose during the period 1961-1965 at an average annual rate of 5.7 per cent; personal savings accounts, at an average annual rate of 10.4 per cent (see Table 7).[31] The production of goods corresponding to the increasingly differentiated and changing tastes of consumers has proved to be completely inadequate. This becomes evident in a comparison of sales of stocks of durables and soft goods (see Table 8). The

Table 7

Retail Sales and Personal Savings Accounts
(Per Cent Increase over Previous Year)

	1961	1962	1963	1964	1965
Retail Sales	3.4	7.3	4.7	5.1	7.9
Personal Savings Accounts	7.0	8.5	10.2	12.1	19.1

SOURCES: D. W. Bronson and B. S. Severin, "Recent Trends in Consumption and Disposable Money Income in the USSR," *New Directions in the Soviet Economy*, Joint Economic Committee, U.S. Congress, Part II-B, Washington, D.C., 1966, p. 515.

[29] See A. Birman, "Khozyaystvennaya reforma i puskovoy impuls," *Pravda*, March 6, 1966, p. 3.
[30] F. D. Holzman, "Soviet Inflationary Pressure, 1928-1957: Causes and Cures," in *Quarterly Journal of Economics*, May, 1960, p. 515.
[31] D. W. Bronson and B. S. Severin, "Recent Trends in Consumption and Disposable Money Income in the USSR," *op. cit.*, p. 515.

Table 8

Index of Retail Trade Sales and Stocks, Selected Goods

(1958 =: 100)

	1960	1963	1964
Sales of Textiles	117	135	122
Sales of Consumer Durables	125	153	177
Stocks of Textiles	142	207	223
Stocks of Consumer Durables...	343	522	546

SOURCES: *Narodnoe khozyaystvo SSSR v 1964* (The Economy of the USSR in 1964), Moscow, 1965, pp. 629, 630, 637.

Table 9

Disposable Income and Retail Trade Sales

(Rubles)

	Disposable Income	Retail Sales[1]	Residual	Residual Minus Annual Increase of Savings Accounts
1960 ...	78,940,000,000	82,250,000,000	—	—
1961 ...	87,590,000,000	85,000,000,000	2,590,000,000	1,890,000,000
1962 ...	94,760,000,000	91,160,000,000	3,600,000,000	2,700,000,000
1963 ...	98,600,000,000	95,320,000,000	3,280,000,000	2,080,000,000
1964 ...	104,170,000,000	100,360,000,000	3,810,000,000	2,000,000,000

[1] These figures represent retail sales of state, cooperative, and collective farm markets. Sales on collective farm markets for 1964 have been estimated.

NOTE: If the figure for disposable income in 1960 is compared with the figure for retail sales, it may be concluded that the calculations for disposable income made by Bronson and Severin and used here are too low. It seems improbable that the excessive amount of retail sales in 1960 was due to dishoarding in this amount.

SOURCES: D. W. Bronson and B. S. Severin, "Recent Trends in Consumption and Disposable Money Income in the USSR," *New Directions in the Soviet Economy*, Joint Economic Committee, U.S. Congress, Part II-B, Washington, D.C., 1966, p. 526; *Narodnoe khozyaystvo SSSR v 1964* (The Economy of the USSR in 1964), Moscow, 1965, p. 625; and *Sovetskaya torgovlya* (Soviet Trade), Moscow, 1964, p. 39.

increase of sales on credit should also be taken into consideration. Sales on credit went from 633 million rubles in 1960 to 2,572 million rubles in 1964. This represents a 434 per cent increase.[32] Obviously, the consumer has had the opportunity to countervail discriminatory pricing, because monetary demand has increased during the planned period through credit. Table 9 shows an estimate of the surplus of monetary demand less the increase of savings in accounts. The calculated amount reveals the inefficient planning in the retail trade sector; planning in this sector clearly fails to anticipate the demand structure.

[32] *Narodnoe khozyaystvo SSSR v 1964 godu*, Moscow, 1965, p. 628.

The industrial reform of 1965 aims at improving the situation in several respects through a new system of direct coordination on the enterprise level, with fines for delayed supply, and the like. General prospects seem to be good for the consumer, since better organization and the trend towards material incentives are apt to have a positive influence on the quantity and quality of goods, but these remarkable changes relate only to the sector of consumer goods production. Detailed central planning for input supply apparently causes difficulties for the factories concerned, as the Bolshevichka-Mayak experiment has shown.[33] Price formation is another crucial problem in this respect, having not yet been solved. The reform is not likely to lead to a decrease in inflationary pressure. On the contrary, the weak aspects of the new system alluded to above, as well as recent reports on its progress, complete the picture of the difficulties to be expected in the elaboration of private consumption.[34]

Summary

The position of the consumer and his wants in the Soviet economy reflects a permanent conflict on different levels. Inevitably, in all societies there are conflicts growing out of the divergent objectives and functions of the leadership and the consumer. In the Soviet system, the political and economic mechanisms for communication that ordinarily serve to coordinate the differences were cut off in the late twenties. Notwithstanding official exorcism, some of these mechanisms, such as monetary disequilibria, have remained in force; others, such as statistical analysis of demand structures, have been rehabilitated as useful methods.[35]

The development of the Soviet economic experiment over the past fifty years, with its turning points in 1928, 1953, 1961, and 1965, has been a continual struggle against enormous difficulties and obstacles originating primarily in external factors. Since a fair evaluation must take into account the start under extremely poor conditions in 1917, it must be admitted that the position of the Soviet consumer has improved greatly. During recent years, moreover, the consumer has gained a large measure of sover-

---

[33] See H. Vogel, H. Kontetzki, and P. Schütterle, "Betrieb und zentrale Plannung in der UdSSR nach den Wirtschaftsreformen vom Herbst 1965," *Gegenwartsfragen der Ost-Wirtschaft*, Schriftenreihe des Seminars für Wirtschaft und Gesellschaft Osteuropas, University of Munich, 1966.

[34] A. Kursky and E. Slastenko, "Nekotoryye itogi perevoda gruppy predpriyatiy na novuyu sistemu planirovaniya i ekonomichiskogo stimulirovaniya," *Voprosy ekonomiki*, No. 10, 1966, p. 8.

[35] See P. Maslov, "Primenimost koeffitsientov elastichnosti v statistike i planirovanii tovarooborota," *Vestnik statistiki*, No. 8, 1966.

eignty, though this does not mean that satisfaction of all his wants has been achieved. Exact findings on the degree of his satisfaction depend on measurements that raise methodological problems and that are complicated by the interdependence of private and collective consumption.

Soviet planners are pragmatists and politicians. They justify their constant practical efforts to achieve social equilibrium with prolix ideological sermons. These could act as signposts for scholars to concentrate on categories and definitions that would distract them from the essential task in this field as we see it: determining whether or not the methods of production and distribution are efficient.

The Promise of Economic Self-Sufficiency under Soviet Socialism

Leon M. Herman

The October Revolution in 1917 was a political undertaking motivated by many ambitions. The Bolshevik leaders of the revolution represented the overthrow of the weak and ill-defended Provisional Government not as an end in itself, not as a mere fulfillment of their own power ambitions, but as an historic act made inevitable by the patent need to break the chain of continuity with Russia's despised past. Without this abrupt break, Russia, though newly liberated from centuries of despotism, would, in their opinion, find it impossible to build its own new world. By the same token, the October Revolution was designed to help Russia execute a forward leap of historic proportions into the next stage of human development, into the age of socialism. In this sense, the revolution was perceived by its leaders as a ringing declaration of independence from the rest of the world, especially from "the exploiter nations," that is, the economically more advanced capitalist countries of the West. The implied warning was that the torch of economic leadership would thereafter be carried by the nation that had been propelled by this revolution ahead of the rest of the world into a new historical era.

Most immediately, according to the leaders of the revolution, the people of Russia would be liberated from their inherited condition of hopelessness, instilled over the centuries by class division, oppression, and exploitation. They would emerge into a new era of human history, characterized by social cooperation, communal prosperity, and free development of all members of society. "The social revolution of the proletariat," proclaimed the Programme of the Communist Party of Russia in 1919, "marks an end to the division of society into classes, and thereby liberates the whole of oppressed mankind, thus abolishing all forms of exploitation of one section of society by another."[1]

Design for a New Economic Order

The early pronouncements of the Soviet regime were not, however, limited to hazy projections of the shape of things to come. They also contained a number of specific commitments to action. One such commit-

---

[1] "Programme of the Communist Party of Russia," 1919, *The A.B.C. of Communism*, London, 1922, pp. 389-402 (Appendix).

ment was to the immediate pursuit of an historically new economic policy designed "to secure a universal increase in the productive forces of the country." This goal would be achieved, the Party Programme of 1919 promised, by following a new "governmental design" described briefly as including "the maximum centralization of production" in the sense of "consolidation of individual branches and groups of branches." On the plane of governmental action, this design began to take shape during the first months in which the Soviet state existed. The new rulers of Russia wasted no time in setting out to create the society of the future, seeing their way in violent divorce from Russia's past and defiant estrangement from the political and economic norms of the capitalist world. Only by breaking with the exploiter nations, ran the official argument of the period, was it possible to build an independent and efficient economic order, self-contained and self-renewing, and proof against the anarchy of the market ruling the economic affairs of the outside world.

In the realm of international cooperation, just one kind of effort was provided for in the early plans of the Soviet government. This was the provision, in the words of the Party Programme of 1919, "to establish a unified economic plan in conjunction with those among [the nations] that have already established a Soviet system." An early act of symbolic commitment on the part of the Soviet leaders to economic isolation as a policy came in January 1918, in the letter and spirit of their decree on the cancellation of all foreign debts. It must have been quite clear to Lenin and his associates at this time that the countries most immediately affected by this kind of "nationalization" policy were precisely those that were Russia's most important actual and potential trade partners. These were, quite obviously, the countries to which the Soviet regime would have to turn if and when it ever felt the need to reinstitute any kind of normal exchange of commodities based on mutual economic confidence. It can only be assumed, therefore, that the new world that the Bolshevik leaders were planning to build in Russia was conceived of as a world without normal external economic relations, a world in which such legal and moral refinements as the inviolability of the economic rights of foreign owners would no longer have to be respected.

After the first flush of victory over Russian capitalism—"the weakest link in the chain of world capitalism"—the Soviet leaders were not inclined to be excessively impressed with the higher stage of economic development already achieved by the West. They were disposed, rather, to see in this highly advanced technical system a promise of growing internal social tension: over-production followed by under-consumption and unemployment at home and accompanied by frequent and fierce struggles for markets abroad. They foresaw a series of economic crises, and very little else, as "the inevitable outcome of the development of productive strength in bourgeois society," to use the language of the programme. These were the symptoms and "the necessary conditions of the imminent social revolution." It followed, in their opinion, that the victorious proletariat of Russia could not conceivably be expected to build its future on a policy of extensive and continued economic cooperation, individual or collective, with the nations still clinging to the doomed economic and social order of the West.

Another significant commitment to economic isolationism came in April 1918, with the establishment of a state monopoly over foreign trade by the Soviet government. The intent behind this move, plainly enough, was to erect around the economic structure of Soviet Russia something like an insuperable administrative barrier against economic influences from the outside world. It was to be, more specifically, the kind of a barrier through which the government of the USSR alone could make, as a mater of exception, the necessary provisions required for a controlled exchange of goods with the economies of the outside world, in accordance with the changing economic conditions and interests of the Soviet state.

Lenin's Design for Limited Economic Collaboration

As long as internal economic conditions were in disarray, the Bolshevik leadership could not, understandably enough, proceed to foreswear active economic exchanges with the outside world. In the early period, following the seizure of power by Lenin and his monolithic Bolshevik Party, there were certain minimum requirements that had to be imported from abroad to help in the revival of economic life in Russia. There were, for example, such critcal items as locomotives, generators, compressors, pumps, and trucks, which could, at that time, be procured only from outside the national economy. These critical shortages were rather generally characterized by Soviet officialdom of the period as strictly temporary in character, induced by a variety of passing emergency conditions. Faced by the persistence of these temporary shortages, however, Lenin declared himself ready to enter into any kind of contractual arrangements with private individuals and firms in the West, but only, in his own words, "in order to learn from the enemy" as quickly as possible. In spite of this, the principle of eventual economic disengagement from the capitalist world, from a "world plagued by endemic economic disorders," remained unchanged as a basic condition for building the new and unique socialist economy of the future.

Still, even in the balmy climate of the early years of the New Economic Policy (NEP) in Russia, Lenin argued vehemently against any attempt made by his associates to find a more efficient substitute for the cumbersome state monopoly instituted in 1918 to preempt all activity in the field of foreign trade. He rejected Nikolay Bukharin's well-reasoned proposal, which was, in effect, to replace the trade monopoly, along with the general condition of economic isolation fostered by it, with a system of high protective tariffs. He was especially stung by Bukharin's favourite epithet for the inflexible, largely negative state trading system: namely, *sistema glavzapora*, or literally, the system of the bolted gate. On this issue, Lenin took the position that "even a partial opening of the frontiers carries with it a most serious danger." He was prepared to agree with Bukharin, he said, that Russia had a lot to learn from its more advanced neighbours, and that some of these skills could be learned through the medium of foreign trade, but he was clearly not willing to open the door to a normal, legally regulated exchange of goods, and, at the same time, to the development of a process of economic interdependence between Soviet Russia and the outside world. Instead, Lenin continued to search for some form of *ad hoc* economic collaboration that would specifically benefit the industrial sector of the economy, and that would remain at all times under the effective control of the Soviet government.

In the early years of NEP, the internal pressures for a more active form of economic intercourse with the industrial nations of Europe nevertheless continued to rise. In order to meet these pressures, Lenin came up with a proposal for the formation of a number of international "mixed companies," each dealing with a specific area of commodity trade. In these joint companies, he explained, "the foreign and the Russian merchants would work side by side," thereby helping to overcome the "bad work" of the state trading monopoly and to teach the inexperienced officials of the People's Commissariat of Foreign Trade the skills required for the conduct of international trade. Lenin concluded this proposal with the following blunt comment: "If we shall not be able even under these conditions to learn, and ultimately to master [the skills of foreign trade], then our nation is a completely hopeless nation of fools."[2] Lenin's main concern during these formative years was to try to avoid, by any and all means, the kind of relationships with the economies of the outside world that might turn out to be open-ended. Almost any temporary system of co-operation, however radical, seemed to him to be preferable, under the circumstances, "in order to help us learn seriously and lastingly." He preferred such make-shift systems precisely because they could be terminated at any time by a unilateral decision of the Soviet government.

---

[2] Lenin, *Sochineniye*, Vol. 33, pp. 417-420.

Foreign Trade of the USSR

(In Rubles, at the 1950 Official Exchange Rate of One Ruble = $ 0.25)

	Exports	Imports	Turnover
1913	5,298,000,000	4,792,000,000	10,090,000,000
1918	28,000,000	367,000,000	395,000,000
1919	300,000,000	11,000,000,000	11,000,000,000
1920	5,000,000	100,000,000	105,000,000
1921	70,000,000	734,000,000	804,000,000
1922	286,000,000	941,000,000	1,227,000,000
1923	760,000,000	498,000,000	1,258,000,000
1924	1,174,000,000	906,000,000	2,080,000,000
1925	2,119,000,000	2,882,000,000	5,001,000,000
1926	2,527,000,000	2,401,000,000	4,928,000,000
1927	2,600,000,000	2,642,000,000	5,242,000,000
1928	2,799,000,000	3,321,000,000	6,120,000,000
1929	3,219,000,000	3,069,000,000	6,288,000,000
1930	3,612,000,000	3,690,000,000	7,302,000,000
1931	2,827,000,000	3,851,000,000	6,678,000,000
1932	2,004,000,000	2,454,000,000	4,458,000,000
1933	1,727,000,000	1,214,000,000	2,941,000,000
1934	1,458,000,000	810,000,000	2,268,000,000
1935	1,281,000,000	841,000,000	2,122,000,000
1936	1,082,000,000	1,077,000,000	2,159,000,000
1937	1,312,000,000	1,016,000,000	2,328,000,000
1938	1,021,000,000	1,090,000,000	2,111,000,000
1939	462,000,000	745,000,000	1,207,000,000
1940	1,066,000,000	1,091,000,000	2,157,000,000

SOURCE: *Vneshnyaya torgovlya SSSR za 1918—1940* (Foreign Trade of the USSR for 1918—1940), Moscow, 1960, p. 14.

Recent Trends in Imports and National Income in the USSR

(In Rubles, at Current Prices)

	Imports	National Income	Import Coefficient
1950..........	1,310,000,000	74,000,000,000	1.8
1955..........	2,755,000,000	97,600,000,000	2.8
1956..........	3,251,000,000	105,600,000,000	3.1
1957..........	3,544,000,000	111,100,000,000	3.2
1958..........	3,915,000,000	126,700,000,000	3.1
1959..........	4,566,000,000	132,900,000,000	3.4
1960..........	5,066,000,000	142,800,000,000	3.5
1961..........	5,245,000,000	151,000,000,000	3.5
1962..........	5,810,000,000	162,500,000,000	3.6
1963..........	6,353,000,000	166,400,000,000	3.9
1964..........	6,963,000,000	179,700,000,000	3.9
1965..........	7,248,000,000	192,600,000,000[1]	3.8

[1] This figure is from *Narodnoe khozyaystvo SSSR v 1965 g.* (The Economy of the USSR in 1965), Moscow, 1966, p. 589.

SOURCE: Official Soviet Foreign Trade Returns; A. L. Vainshtein, *Ekonomika i Matematicheskie metody*, Moscow, No. 1, 1967, p. 28.

The need for international trade as a permanent condition of economic activity was considered by Lenin to be a uniquely capitalist phenomenon, arising directly out of the capitalist form of economic organization and, specifically, out of its "need of an over-expanding market" and its pre-occupation with relative costs, fluctuating prices, and rates of profit. Such a need for ready access to foreign markets, Lenin assumed, was the motive force behind the public policy of all the major countries of Western Europe. It was this assumption, in fact, that served to keep alive his hopes for a rather easy and early political reconciliation with the rest of Europe, regardless of the character of Soviet internal economic and political institutions. He was convinced that the compulsive urge on the part of the trade-minded capitalists of Western Europe to enjoy the benefits of the "huge" Russian market would, in due time, compel the governments of these countries to accept the legitimacy of the Soviet regime, in spite of their strong antipathy for the political system of communism.

At the same time, however, Lenin did not perceive any comparable permanent pressures for external trade that were likely to develop in the kind of planned and inward-looking economy that he hoped to build in Russia. He regarded the observable need for foreign trade on the part of his government to be prompted by dislocations and imbalances in domestic supply brought about by years of living under abnormal economic conditions. Purchases made abroad at this time were considered to be justified on the grounds that they were unique and transitory, a function of the emergency conditions following the prolonged civil war. These purchases were limited, it was generally explained, to the kinds of implements and materials that would, eventually, in Lenin's words, "enable our factories to produce on their own all that is necessary."

Not all the principal leaders of the country during the mid-twenties, it should be noted, were convinced that economic isolation was indeed the most practical goal to be pursued by a country as backward in industrial development as Soviet Russia was at that time. This was particularly true of some Bolshevik leaders who had a close knowledge of the facts of inter-national economic life. Such a man was Leonid Krasin, the first People's Commissar of Foreign Trade. Krasin was well aware that the progressive industrialization of a country tends to increase rather than diminish its need for and participation in world trade. In a speech delivered in November 1924, Krasin characterized as "completely mistaken" the popular notion that the division of labour among nations in the world market is mainly oriented towards exchange of goods between nations engaged exclusively in industrial production on the one hand and nations engaged primarily in agricultural and mineral production on the other. The most intensive growth of trade in the modern world, he pointed out, was actually taking place among the very highly industrialized nations of Europe, such as Germany, England, and France. His own knowledge of the world economy, he said, and his practical experience as a former businessman, brought him to the conclusion that "the industrial development of a country like the Soviet Union will hardly result in a decline of demand in the USSR for the products of foreign industry."[3] Unlike many of his associates, Krasin was personally inclined, on the evidence at hand, towards a dynamic view of the process of industrialization. He argued that by the very nature of things, Soviet foriegn trade agencies would always have to count on the appearance in the world market of "more complex machines, new chemical products, various patented products...which our own industry would not be in position to manufacture." There is no evidence, however, that he succeeded in winning Stalin over to his own pragmatic view of the value of keeping open the channels of external trade in the interest of sustaining a condition of balanced industrial growth in the Soviet Union.

Foreign Concessions versus Technical Aid Contracts

In keeping with Lenin's preference for terminal forms of economic collaboration with the West, the Soviet government proceeded, even before the coming of NEP, to establish a system of "foreign concessions" under which duly qualified and licensed companies from abroad were permitted to operate a number of mining, industrial, and commercial enterprises in Soviet Russia. This arrangement was worked out by Lenin, who considered the concessions to be most suitable as a means of resolving the very real conflict between the immediate need for outside technical help and the long-term commitment to economic self-sufficiency. Under a decree, published on November 23, 1920, the Soviet government declared itself ready to conclude concession agreements with "reliable foreign firms" and to provide the necessary guarantees that property invested in such enterprises would not be nationalized, confiscated, or requisitioned. The decree further guaranteed that no arbitrary orders of any kind would be issued which might in any way adversely affect the concession agreements.

It seems unnecessary, in this context, to explore the reasons why Lenin's carefully devised programme of foreign concessions failed to develop any real momentum or, eventually, to produce any significant economic results during the ten years of its existence. The fact is that by the end of 1929 there were only 59 foreign concessions in operation in the

---

[3] L. B. Krasin, *Voprosy vneshney torgovli* (Questions of Foreign Trade), Moscow, 1928, p. 318.

country, most of them small in size. The value of their aggregate output
was only 44 million dollars, or no more than a fraction of one per cent
of the total annual product of state industry in the Soviet Union.[4] It is even
more to the point to recall that by this stage in Soviet history—that is, the
late twenties—Stalin was already firmly in the saddle and that, as one
might expect, he had his own ideas of the best way to proceed to transplant
foreign technology onto the Soviet economic landscape under political
conditions acceptable to him. Stalin's preferred method of economic
cooperation with industrial firms from the West, as it turned out, was the
"technical assistance contract." Under his leadership, therefore, the foreign
concessions were gradually squeezed out of existence, largely by means
of a variety of "labour disputes," long before the expiration of their legal
duration, which usually ranged from 10 to 20 years.

Soviet Foreign Trade, Total Turnover, Exports Plus Imports
(In Rubles)

1909–1913 (Average)	11,508,000,000
1913....................	12,618,900,000
1929....................	7,902,800,000
1930....................	9,176,800,000
1931....................	8,393,000,000
1932....................	5,601,700,000
1933....................	3,692,600,000
1934....................	2,850,400,000
1935....................	2,666,500,000
1936....................	2,711,600,000
1937....................	3,069,900,000
1938....................	2,754,800,000

NOTE: The ruble used in the above table had an official valuation of 18.8 U.S. cents—that is,
one dollar equals 5.3 rubles.

SOURCE: Alexander Baykov, *The Development of the Soviet Economic System*, Cambridge
University Press, London, 1946, p. 274.

Stalin had evidently changed his mind quite abruptly. He came out
strongly in favour of a contract arrangement for technical assistance that
was not only basically different in character from the concession agreement
but also much shorter in duration. The technical aid contract appealed to
him for a number of reasons. To begin with, it offered a direct choice to the
Soviet government of the individual Western firm to be invited to assume
a given set of obligations. These amounted typically to an undertaking to
build and equip a complete new plant for a major branch of industrial

---

[4] N. Lyubimov, "The Soviets and Foreign Concessions," *Foreign Affairs*,
New York, October, 1930, p. 95.

production. Under such a contract, each Western firm was required, as part of the pattern, to place at the disposal of the Soviet government, among other things, "its technical processes and trade secrets." In addition, it was required to undertake "to send engineers and skilled workmen to the USSR to act as instructors, as well as to admit Soviet engineers to its own workshops."[5] Contracts of this type, covering periods of two to five years, were arranged for most of the basic industries in the USSR. At the height of this phase of economic collaboration with the West, between 1928 and 1933, up to 2,000 technical experts from the United States alone— including designers, engineers, and mechanics—were employed in the USSR.[6] No contract in this series, incidentally, is known to have been cancelled by the Soviet government prior to its legal date of expiration.

There is no reason to believe that Stalin ever regretted his choice of this method of accelerated technological transfer from abroad. He seems to have remained confirmed in his judgement that the technical assistance contract, which could be tailored to suit the current operational needs of every essential industry in the country, was by far the more appropriate instrument for the pursuit of the goal of eventual economic self-sufficiency in the USSR. At the same time, this method enjoyed the added advantage of involving the Soviet government in legal arrangements with outside firms that provided for short periods of duration and called for the fulfill-ment of a number of specified technical tasks. Meanwhile, the foreign trade monopoly continued to be managed by the leadership of the USSR in such a way as to "permit the Soviet state to utilize most fully the economic interest of the capitalist nations in [its] market."[7] The obverse of this condition—namely, the interest of the Soviet state in the capitalist market— continued as before to be treated as a strictly short-term affair. It was regarded as motivated primarily by the need to strengthen Soviet industry until it could reach the stage of self-sustained growth.

Stalin's Drive towards Economic Disengagement

The objective of economic disengagement from the outside world remained high on the Soviet political agenda. Thus, for eaxmple, writing on the occasion of the tenth anniversary of the Bolshevik revolution, an authoritative commentator on foreign trade considered it appropriate to restate the standard formula for a successful national economic policy as

---

[5] *Ibid.*, p. 104.
[6] W. H. Chamberlin, *The Soviet Planned Economic Order*, Boston, 1931, p. 82.
[7] *Sotsialisticheskoe narodnoe khozyaystvo SSSR, 1933–40 g.g.* (The Socialist Economy of the USSR, 1933–40), Moscow, 1963, p. 615.

follows: "Everything that can be procured or produced within the country must gradually disappear from the import plan."[8] There was no hint in this formula that the Soviet government was giving any thought to the possible value of foreign trade as a means of arriving at a more effective utilization of the economic resources of the country. Nor is there any evidence in general that the economic planners of the country showed any interest during this period of relative international calm in discovering the areas of production in which the USSR enjoys a comparative advantage or in developing the channels necessary for the exchange of these competitive domestic goods through the world market for the products of the most efficient producers abroad. Foreign trade was perceived wholly as an operation oriented towards import substitution. The same writer, in fact, ended his survey of the economic situation in the comparatively quiescent year of 1927 with a call for "the strengthening of Soviet industry in order to diminish more and more our dependence on foreign countries."

The task of strengthening Soviet industry for technological self-sufficiency, through the medium of technical assistance contracts and foreign trade, was envisioned by Stalin as a readily attainable, short-term objective. He seems to have defined "modern technological capability" in strictly static terms. As he saw it, once Russia imported all the known important technical processes and innovations of the period, the goal of national technical and economic independence would be fully attained. In order to speed up the movement towards this objective, Stalin settled on a carefully screened list of "essential" industries that were in need of "strengthening" according to a clearly determined order of priorities. In due time, the branches of industry important enough to be included in this list began to enjoy the benefits of preferred treatment, from the standpoint of capital investment and modern technology. They were provided with the best productive equipment available abroad and introduced to the latest known foreign technological processes. They received, in addition, the benefit of the services of foreign engineers and technicians imported from the leading industrial countries cf the West. These foreign technicians, working under the terms of technical assistance contracts drafted by Soviet specialists, were obliged, in the case of each individual selected industry, to elaborate an up-to-date construction design for an integrated industrial plant or complex of plants, to install the necessary equipment, and to supervise consequent production during a trial period of operations.

As a result, the period from 1926 to 1933 witnessed something of a high-water mark in economic cooperation between the USSR and the

---

[8] Ya. Ganetsky, *Desyat let Sovetskogo stroitelstva* (Ten Years of Soviet Construction), Moscow, 1927, p. 111.

world industrial community at large. While it lasted, moreover, it was a cooperative undertaking of broad scope, designed to keep wide open the channels of technical communication with the outside world. As it turned out, the duration of this undertaking was limited, lasting only as long as it was considered officially necessary to fulfill the country's quota of import requirements as perceived at that moment in history. Owing to this drive to import technology, and partly because of the world-wide economic depression, the USSR emerged as the leading importer of machinery and equipment in the world at this time. In 1931, about one-third of the machinery moving in international trade—excluding automobiles—went to the Soviet Union. These imports were utilized, in keeping with official objectives, not for meeting the current capital needs of existing plants but "almost exclusively for the equipment of newly built enterprises in the heavy industrial sector."[9] The will of history, in Stalin's view, seemed quite clear at this juncture: it called for a change in the direction of the systematic curtailment of foreign trade. Accordingly, a resolution adopted at the Seventeenth Party Congress held in 1934 stipulated that "during the Second Five-Year Plan the USSR must be converted into a country that is independent in a technical and economic sense, into the leading techno- logical state in Europe."[10]

After the passing of this water-mark, the People's Commissar of Foreign Trade, A. P. Rosengolts, was ready to explain how the government of the USSR viewed the future of its external economic relations now that the intensive industrialization programme of the First Five-Year Plan had been brought to a satisfactory conclusion. He stressed two points: (1) "our interest in imports has declined considerably" and (2) "we can now . . . display greater endurance than ever before by utilizing our considerable manoeuvring possibilities." To this he deemed it appropriate to append the familiar official proposition that "Soviet interest in external trade is now less than the interest displayed in our orders by the capitalist countries." [11] Against this background, the official press began, around 1935, to pronounce the campaign for the industrialization of the country, partly with the aid of foreign imports, as an accomplished fact. Soviet spokesmen started assuring the public that the growth of industry had reached a stage where the nation could "sharply curtail imports without

---

[9] *Sotsialisticheskoe narodnoe khozyaystvo v 1933–40 gg.*, *op. cit.*, p. 616.

[10] *KPSS v Rezolyutsiyakh* (The CPSU in Resolutions), Part III, Seventh Edition, Moscow, 1954, p. 221.

[11] A. P. Rosengolts, *Fifteen Years of the Foreign Trade Monopoly of the USSR*, Moscow, Leningrad, 1933, p. 16.

Index of Physical Volume of Soviet Foreign Trade, 1929–1937
(Compared to World Export Trends)

	Soviet Exports	Soviet Imports	World Exports
1929.........	100.0	100.0	100.0
1930.........	135.7	141.3	93.0
1931.........	146.1	161.5	85.0
1932.........	127.8	115.8	74.5
1933.........	118.5	62.5	75.5
1934.........	102.9	47.1	78.5
1935.........	90.5	51.9	81.8
1936.........	68.2	60.0	85.9
1937.........	68.4	53.2	97.6

SOURCE: *Vneshnyanya torgovlya SSSR*, edited by D. D. Mishustin, Moscow, 1941, pp. 91–92.

any loss whatsoever for the domestic economy."[12] Henceforth, the official view ran, Soviet trading organizations would be authorized to engage in trade transactions only in cases where they were certain to receive especially attractive conditions, either on the export or import side of the trade. After the mid-thirties, in fact, Soviet foreign trade experts began to react somewhat defensively in regard to any observed increase in the level of trade, especially in the case of imports. When they reported "a certain increase" in the value of imports between 1935 and 1936, for example, they explained to their readers that "in a relative sense," that is, in relation to the rising level of industrial consumption in the country, such an increase was no real cause for alarm: it did not have to be considered as a serious deviation from the basic position of the Soviet government that the need for foreign trade had substantively diminished.

In keeping with this basic attitude, and with the new policy behind it, the organizational structure of the foreign trade in the country was ordered to be changed. Official spokesmen contended at the time:

> ...we must destroy the long-established practice under which our trading organizations sent people abroad in order to look there for buyers of our export goods and for sellers of import goods to us.... The Party has placed before us the task of so organizing our work as to make sure that foreign firms come to us and conclude transactions for export or import here, in Moscow, directly with our export and import organizations.[13]

This shift towards Moscow as the main centre for the conclusion of foreign commercial transactions, ordered in June 1935, was greeted

---

[12] D. D. Mishustin, *Vneshnyaya torgovlya i industrializatsiya SSSR* (Foreign Trade and the Industrialization of the USSR), Moscow, 1938, p. 79.

[13] D. D. Mishustin, *op. cit.*, p. 86. The discussion on the next few pages is based largely on the authoritative views expressed in this volume.

by the official press as the "organizational expression" of the end of Soviet dependence on imports from the economies of other nations. The specialists pointed with particular pride to the fact that the level of machinery imports into the USSR declined by nearly 90 per cent between 1931 and 1937.[14] In Stalin's opinion, made public in an address to graduates of the Red Army Academy in May 1935, this vigorously enforced control over imports, with emphasis on self-sufficiency, had advanced the situation to a point where "we have in the main outlived the period of famine in technical resources." One official commentator on the above Stalin text developed this idea still further, concluding with a flourish to the effect that "this was an import that has led to curtailment of imports, thanks to the colossally expanded, powerful, technically advanced Soviet heavy industry."[15]

Once the Second-Five-Year Plan had been completed, by the end of 1937, Soviet officials began to celebrate a dual achievement in the economic development of the USSR. They glorified both the completion of ten years of "scientific economic planning" in the country and the liquidation of its temporary "technical economic backwardness." Both achievements, it was asserted, were made possible as a direct result of the "innate advantages of the socialist order." Typically, the completion of the Second Five-Year Plan was hailed in the following language:

> The USSR has fulfilled the grandiose plans of the Second Five-Year Plan, with the aid of an insignificant volume of imports, and in the future we can fulfill our plans, without the need for imports. Nearly everything that is at all needed for a powerful country—everything—is being produced in the USSR.[16]

In order to present evidence in support of this sweeping conclusion, Soviet experts in the field, academic as well as official, cited some comparative statistics on the importance of foreign trade to the major economies of the world. In these comparisons, Japan and the leading countries of Europe were shown to be exporting some 20–25 per cent of their aggregate domestic product; even the United States was shown to have exported as much as 10 per cent of its total national product before 1929. In contrast, they pointed out, "the dependence of the Soviet Union [on foreign economies] was less than that of any other country." The USSR, these figures showed, exported only 1.3 per cent of its total national product in 1935; on the import side, Soviet involvement in the world market was even more

---

[14] From 2,076 million to 278 million rubles. See *Vneshnyaya torgovlya SSSR za 1918–1940* (Foreign Trade of the USSR for 1918–1940), Moscow, 1960, pp. 301, 368.

[15] D. D. Mishustin, *op. cit.*, p. 35.

[16] *Ibid.*, p. 139.

insignificant, accounting for only one per cent of the entire domestic product of the nation in the same year.[17] Such a development was no mere accident, according to the official experts: "This is a characteristic feature of the socialist economy, which bases itself entirely on the internal market." To be on the safe side, this Soviet writer proceeded to quote a dictum pronounced by Stalin in 1926. To no one's surprise, he used much the same words as the leader: "Our industry bases itself on the internal market." He did not, for his own good reasons, include the final qualifying phrase of Stalin's remark—"primarily the peasant market."[18]

When the German author Marx-Reinhard suggested in a book published in 1930 that the Soviet Union, despite the rapid build-up of its own industrial plant, was likely to continue to import machinery from the West, citing as his reason the fact that it usually takes many decades to achieve self-sufficiency in the entire range of existing industrial equipment, he was ridiculed in the official Soviet literature on foreign trade. Specifically, he was accused of not understanding the socialist character of the economy of the USSR. According to one Soviet author, this was a case in which "the low-brow ideologues of capitalism" were not really to blame. Being culture-bound bourgeois intellectuals, they could "hardly have expected that the Soviet nation would be able to utilize the importation of machinery so effectively, with such exceptional goal-directedness, with such a profoundly conceived plan."[19]

At the highest level of authority within the Party, it became fashionable towards the end of the thirties to associate a high level of foreign trade with a state of "backwardness and poverty," especially insofar as the Soviet Union was concerned. The Soviet success in liberating itself from backwardness, and at the same time from external commerce, was summed up as follows by A. Mikoyan, then the highest authority on foreign trade in the USSR:

---

[17] During this period, official opinion in the USSR tended to heap scorn on the claim of the Nazi government in Germany that it was leading a worldwide movement towards autarky. The Soviet view was that the German leadership was throwing "good money after bad" into a useless effort to stimulate production of synthetic raw materials. In the light of Marxist theory, it would seem, fascist economic policy was inherently incapable of producing real autarky, as long as it continued to base its economic activity on capitalist practices. "These fascist attempts to attain independence of imports in regard to the supply of raw materials have not, and could not, attain any major results, in view of the capitalist contradictions."

[18] Stalin, "On the Economic Situation of the Soviet Union and Party Policy," Address of April 13, 1926, *Works*, VIII, p. 131.

[19] D. D. Mishustin, *op. cit.*, p. 210.

In the period when we were still backward and poor, when we did not have our own developed machine-building industry and we had to build industry at any cost, we were forced to export abroad a great deal of raw materials and foodstuffs, which we needed ourselves, and we exported these in order to obtain foreign exchange, and to use these earnings to buy machine tools for industry, equipment for tractor and automobile plants.[20]

In the absence of any serious interest in the relative scales and costs of production, in the late thirties trade came to be regarded as something in the nature of a burden on the economy, a physical drain of commodities out of the country that ought normally to be consumed within the domestic economy. As one official text expressed it, with reference to this period, "the urgent need for large-scale imports disappeared," and it was no longer necessary "to expend vast resources that could be effectively applied toward socialist construction."[21]

The Grand Illusion of the Parallel World Market

The traumatic experience of the Second World War, and along with it the massive economic support received by the USSR from the Western capitalist nations, brought little change in the fundamental bias of Soviet leaders in favour of autarky. For all their continued concern with reading the signs of history correctly, in the final analysis the rulers of the Soviet Union chose not to allow their post-war policy to be influenced in any way by the whole-hearted and massive support obtained from the West during the struggle for survival as a nation. If anything, their deep-seated urge towards isolation from the world economy was visibly reinforced by the consequences of the Second World War, if in a somewhat altered form.

In the wake of the westward advance of the Red Army, the Soviet Union moved rapidly to establish a broad belt of communist-ruled states as a means of achieving greater military security. At the same time, however, this enlarged domain served to bolster Soviet hopes for increased political and economic self-sufficiency. More particularly, the emergence of a group of communist nations in Eastern Europe appeared to Stalin to make his ceaseless quest for autarky more attainable at last. It helped to provide new impetus for the pursuit of the goal of economic self-sufficiency, this time on a broader territorial basis, i.e., no longer on the scale of a single nation but on the basis of a "new, socialist, world system of states."

---

[20] Address of A. I. Mikoyan before the Twenty-eighth Party Congress, Stenographic Report (in Russian), 1939, pp. 218–19.

[21] *Sotsialisticheskoe narodnoe khozyaystvo SSSR, 1933–40, op. cit.*, p. 618.

It is clear from the authoritative remarks of the chief economic planner of the period, Nikolay A. Voznesensky, that the Soviet government had no intention of abandoning its apprehensive approach towards the world economy as a result of its shattering war experience. Nor did it see any reason for discarding autarky as an ideal. When called upon to spell out the economic policy of the Party for the first post-war five-year plan, Voznesensky followed closely both the reasoning and the language used by Soviet policy-makers and theorists before the war. He gave his official opinion in these words:

> The USSR will continue in the future to maintain economic ties with foreign countries in accordance with the tested line of the Soviet government, which is directed towards the attainment of the technical and economic independence of the Soviet Union.[22]

During the early years of the post-war period, it became evident to outside observers that Stalin had grown very infatuated with his own unique political creation, "the new and parallel world market," which extended over the territory of the USSR and the communist states that came into existence after World War II. He considered the creation of this rival market to be the most important political consequence of the war and a tangible result of his own activist policies in the post-war period. In the official language of the period, the international economy will never be quite the same again, for, it was said, "a world democratic market had arisen alongside the world capitalist market."[23] The old, single capitalist world market, as Stalin saw it, had begun to disintegrate. Accordingly, the main thrust of Soviet foreign trade policy was to be directed towards "strengthening economic cooperation among the socialist countries." Henceforth, Soviet foreign trade would be assigned a new function: service as an instrumentality for the "planned link-up" of the economic development of these countries, "on the basis of the international socialist division of labour and fraternal cooperation and mutual assistance."

The advantages of the "world democratic market" were, in the Soviet view, economic factors of far-reaching political significance. It was at one and the same time a greatly enlarged political domain and a brave new economic world independent of the resources under the control of capitalism and sufficient unto itself. "The world democratic market has at its disposal," in the words of the official textbook, "sufficient resources to provide every country with everything necessary for its economic development."

----

[22] *Planovoe khozyaystvo*, Moscow, No. 2, 1946.
[23] *Politicheskaya ekonomiya* (Political Economy), Moscow, 1954, p. 610.

If the men in power within the USSR were troubled by any shadow of doubt on this score, they made sure not to reveal it to the outside world. They all reported in unison that they were continuing to find their original assumptions about the innate superiority of the socialist world market validated by "the steady growth and consolidation" of this market. In other words, they were delighted to accept the results of their own arbitrary administrative orders for expanding intra-bloc trade as the judgement of history, as amounting to "irrefutable proof of the historic progressiveness" of the new, parallel world market. One of the major consequences of the establishment of the world socialist market, this theory stated, came in the form of an unprecedented body of benefits growing out of the economic cooperation between the Soviet Union and its new allies, the countries of Eastern Europe. "The experience of this cooperation," Stalin wrote in 1952, "shows that not a single capitalist country could have rendered such effective and technically competent assistance to the People's Democracies as the Soviet Union is rendering them."[24]

By contrast, because of the lack of a similar climate for cooperation, the outlook for the major trading nations of the West was adjudged by Stalin to be rather hopeless. In the future the capitalist economies could expect to be confronted by increasingly severe competition, including an unexpected form of economic pressure from the countries making up the new, parallel world market. Indeed, as far as the immediate future was concerned, "it may be confidently said," Stalin predicted, "that with this pace of industrial development [among the communist countries], it will soon come to pass that these countries will not only no longer be in need of imports from the capitalist countries, but will themselves feel the necessity of finding an outside market for their surplus products."[25]

Nonetheless, even under these circumstances—so dramatically new and so clearly favourable for the pursuit of ever closer economic cooperation within the socialist camp—official Soviet opinion, it should be noted, did not advocate a complete severance of commercial ties with the West. A measure of contact was still thought to be necessary for the socialist countries in the interest of "furthering the improvement of their economies." It was quite plain on the evidence, moreover, that continued commercial contact of this kind was favoured primarily because of assumed strong interest on the part of the West in selling its "pressing surpluses"

---

[24] J. V. Stalin, *The Economic Problems of Socialism in the USSR*, Moscow, 1952, p. 36.

[25] *Ibid.*

to the socialist market. It was reasoned that such an interest could, under proper conditions, be usefully engaged in any process of negotiation on economic or political matters. In the standard language of Soviet editorial comment of the period: "There need be no obstacle to the development of mutually beneficial trade with the nations of the capitalist camp." Such trade, however, was not a matter of particular significance on the Soviet side of the world-wide political barrier. "The development of trade relations among the nations of the two camps is of considerably greater significance for the capitalist countries, especially in connection with the continuous contraction of the world capitalist market."[26]

The reorientation of Soviet foreign trade toward the socialist market, as shown by the record, had gone a long way by the end of the Stalin era. Some 60 per cent of the entire foreign trade of the USSR was devoted to its European communist trade partners in 1953. By comparison, the same group of countries accounted for only 1.5 per cent of Soviet foreign trade in 1938. Similarly, in 1953 trade with China had grown to a point where it represented 18 per cent of total Soviet trade, as compared with only 4 per cent in 1938. Taken together, all the communist-ruled countries accounted for 83 per cent of the foreign trade of the Soviet Union in the last year of the long Stalin era.[27] The degree of self-isolation within the confines of a regional market was most conspicuous; the large and diverse economies of the world industrial community had been successfully relegated to a peripheral role in the economic life of the USSR.

Nikita Khrushchev's Opening to the West

After the death of Stalin, the external economic behaviour of the Soviet Union began to suggest quite strongly that a serious revaluation of official policy on the part of the new leadership was under way. The severe degree of studied isolation from the international economy, which had been the hallmark of Soviet policy during the preceding eight years, diminished somewhat during the last months of 1953. By their action, if not by their words, the new leaders left no room for doubt that they had found some of the arguments used by Stalin in support of his policy of economic isolation rather unconvincing. He had argued, it will be recalled, that the West had entered its long-awaited phase of economic decline after the fatal blow that was delivered to its stability by "the great historic victories of communism" in Europe and Asia. As far as practical policy

[26] *Politicheskaya ekonomiya*, Moscow, 1954, p. 611.
[27] *Spravochnik po vneshney torgovle SSSR* (Reference Book on Foreign Trade in the USSR), Moscow, 1958, pp. 116–118.

was concerned, it followed from this argument that the capitalist countries could be effectively helped along the road to oblivion if the Soviet government could continue to keep their access to the communist world market as limited as possible. The observable facts of international economic life, however, pointed clearly in the opposite direction, namely to a state of general economic good health among the nations making up the industrial West. By the early fifties, both foreign trade and industrial production in the major Western nations were showing a strong upward trend. Industrial production of Western Europe was 36 per cent higher in 1952 than it was in 1948. Industrial employment increased by 8 per cent.[28] During the same four-year period, the export trade of all non-communist countries increased by one-third, from 60 billion to 80 billion dollars.

Three years later, at the Twentieth Party Congress, Mikoyan felt free to articulate the views of the new leaders on the basic issues related to the international economy. He reported that they had found Stalin's analysis of the economy of contemporary capitalism "hardly helpful or hardly correct."[29] Stalin, he recalled, had forecast that "the volume of production in these countries [would] shrink." It was now quite clear to his successors that it was impossible to square Stalin's properly optimistic forecast with the hard facts as they had evolved around "the complex and contradictory manifestations of contemporary capitalism," especially "the fact of the growth of capitalist production in many countries after the war." To refute Stalin's highly doctrinaire analysis, Mikoyan noted, all you had to do was to look at the real world beyond the frontiers of the USSR. You would find, he contended, that throughout the post-war period, the developed capitalist countries were both expanding their economies and increasing their trade, among themselves as well as around the world. Evidently, this was a case in which history itself was plainly not tending to its business. In these circumstances, it was argued, why should the Soviet Union deny itself the obvious benefits of a modest increase in trade with the highly productive and technologically sensitive economies of the industrial West?

The Imperatives of Technical Modernization. After he succeeded in eliminating his own peers and rivals from their positions of power, Party chieftain Khrushchev was left free to apply his prodigious energies towards the task of improving the operation of the domestic economy, as he perceived this task. One after another, he unveiled new initiatives designed to

---

[28] *Economic Survey of Europe in 1953*, United Nations, Geneva, 1954, pp. 219–220.

[29] *Twentieth Congress of the Communist Party of the Soviet Union*, Moscow, 1956, Vol. I, p. 323.

raise the operational efficiency of the domestic production plant, in the hope of thereby increasing the ability of the Soviet system to pay dividends, economic as well as political. In his new capacity as supreme leader, after June 1957, Khrushchev also tried hard, and not without a certain amount of success, to breathe a measure of new vitality into the old political slogans, to inject some variety into the flow of simulated optimism from the official media of opinion.

In the course of coming into closer daily contact with the operation of the domestic economic order, Khrushchev stumbled upon a number of unpleasant circumstances. Being a man of gregarious disposition, he often shared these findings with his captive audiences, and, in the process, helped to enliven his all too long and frequent official speeches. On one such occasion, in May 1958, he reported having learned that the entire procession of new techniques and products generated by the welter of discoveries made within the modern chemical industry had literally by-passed the Soviet economy, while its leaders were preoccupied with the pursuit of the will-of-the-wisp of "technical and economic independence," i.e., with the protection of the domestic economy against possible negative influences from the outside world.

Information of this nature helped to steer Khrushchev in the direction of broadening his contacts with the business world of the West. In March 1959, for instance, Khrushchev took the initiative in delegating himself as "a representative of Soviet business circles," and travelled in that capacity to the Leipzig Fair in East Germany. Using the massive Soviet pavilion as his backdrop, he addressed a large group of businessmen for the West who were assembled there for his benefit. He dwelled in some detail on the advantages that awaited them if and when they decided to expand their commodity trade with the Soviet Union. He explained, in accordance with the standard Soviet formula on this subject, that he was thinking primarily of the economic interest of the capitalist countries. It is you, he informed them, who need the trade in order "to use your industries to capacity, to reduce unemployment, and to obtain normal income and profits."[30]

About the time of this historic visit, Soviet economic relations with the industrialized countries outside the bloc became perceptibly more active as well as more purposive. The Soviet government revived an old technique, not actively used since the late 1930's, for the promotion of its own

---

[30] *Pravda*, March 7, 1959. See also U.S. Congress, Joint Economic Committee, *A New Look at Trade Policy Towards the Communist Bloc*, Washington, D.C., 1960, p. 13.

economic development. It resumed the practice of importing complete industrial plants from the West, along with the patents and the engineering services required for launching these units into production. After several decades of self-imposed isolation, this technique, plainly enough, still recommended itself to the Soviet leadership as the most effective means by which newly developed ideas embodied in these sets of equipment, technical processes, and finished products could be physically transplanted onto the industrial landscape of the USSR.

As a man with a practical bent of mind and a competitive interest in building up an efficient production system at home, Khrushchev rated the acquisition of new, market-tested technology from the world market very high, considering it a direct stimulus to the economic development of the USSR. A campaign for systematic procurement of this type, he had previously explained, with specific reference to the chemical industry,

Foreign Trade Turnover

(In Rubles, at Prices of Respective Years, with Foreign Currency Recalculated into Rubles of the Exchange Rate Introduced in January 1961)

	Exports	Imports	Turnover
1913*	1,192,000,000	1,078,000,000	2,270,000,000
1917	382,000,000	1,901,000,000	2,283,000,000
1928	630,000,000	747,000,000	1,377,000,000
1932	451,000,000	552,000,000	1,003,000,000
1937	295,000,000	229,000,000	524,000,000
1938	230,000,000	245,000,000	475,000,000
1940	240,000,000	245,000,000	485,000,000
1946	588,000,000	692,000,000	1,280,000,000
1950	1,615,000,000	1,310,000,000	2,925,000,000
1955	3,084,000,000	2,754,000,000	5,838,000,000
1958	3,868,000,000	3,915,000,000	7,783,000,000
1959	4,897,000,000	4,566,000,000	9,463,000,000
1960	5,005,000,000	5,066,000,000	10,071,000,000
1961	5,398,000,000	5,245,000,000	10,643,000,000
1962	6,327,000,000	5,810,000,000	12,137,000,000
1963	6,545,000,000	6,353,000,000	12,898,000,000
1964	6,915,000,000	6,963,000,000	13,878,000,000
1965	7,350,000,000	7,248,000,000	14,598,000,000

* For the territory covered by the former Russian Empire.

NOTE: Based on the respective gold content of the ruble and the dollar, the value of the ruble, over the years, as officially determined by the Soviet government, has been as follows: In 1913 (also 1917, 1928, 1932), one dollar equalled 1.94 rubles; in 1937 (also 1938, 1940, 1946), one dollar equalled 5.3 rubles; in 1950—1960, one dollar equalled 4 rubles; and since January 1, 1961, one dollar has equalled 0.90 rubles.

SOURCE: *Narodnoe khozyaystvo SSSR v 1963 g.* (The Economy of the USSR in 1963), Moscow, 1964, p. 548.

in his address to the May 1958 Plenum, would contribute directly "to the more rapid fulfillment of our programme for the construction of new . . . enterprises without wasting time on the creation of designs and mastering the process of production of new types of equipment."[31]

When it came to spending hard currency, Khrushchev was not a man given to impulsive behaviour. He was willing enough to spend scarce foreign exchange, but only if he knew of no more promising alternative. He had gradually become convinced that continued Soviet economic isolation from the world industrial community, under conditions of rapid technological change, would ultimately prove to be a costly exercise in political self-indulgence. He was too competitive a politician to permit the Soviet Union, under his leadership, to lose ground in the international economic race. Accordingly, after he had acquired the necessary practical experience in this sphere, Khrushchev began to suggest, in his numerous formal and casual remarks, that he was not impressed by the methods which the economic bureaucracy of the USSR was using to keep up with technical progress in the West. These methods consisted, in the main, of employing one, or both, of the following two approaches: (1) screening thoroughly the published technical literature of the West for the purpose of incorporating its findings into the current flow of Soviet industrial research; and (2) importing prototypes of more advanced models of foreign machinery for the purpose of imitating and eventually assimilating them into the production process at home. Both these approaches, Khrushchev discovered, left a great deal to be desired. Soviet industry lost a vast amount of valuable time and remained, for the most part, outside of the mainstream of technical modernization. Production equipment supplied to factories, and finished products, were, as a result, conspicuous by their display of a visible layer of technological dust.

Khrushchev was acutely aware of the direct bearing of continued technical modernization on the current efficiency of production. In keeping with this awareness, he never hesitated to compare Soviet equipment with that of the West, usually to the disadvantage of the former. On one occasion, for example, he reported that the Soviet aviation industry was producing engines that operated for only 500 hours, while British aircraft engines of the same class worked 2,500 hours.[32] On all such occasions, he made it known that he had become too impatient to wait for the established, routine approach to technical innovation in the USSR to continue its familiar bureaucratic course. He declared himself willing, if necessary,

---

[31] *Pravda*, May 7, 1958.
[32] *Pravda*, December 15, 1963.

to pay in cash for any foreign patents involved in order to acquire directly, and for immediate use, the most efficient industrial technology available. One practical outcome of this change in approach, begun under Khrushchev, was formal Soviet adherence, effective July 1, 1965, to the Paris Convention for the Protection of Industrial Property.

Thus, by the time of Khrushchev's displacement from power, the long-standing commitment to autarky as a practical goal for economic development had weakened perceptibly among the Soviet political elite. Khrushchev was a willful man, who pressed hard on this issue, and finally succeeded in convincing his associates of the importance of his own practical discovery that the modern tempo of technical progress had created an immense, world-wide reservoir of new production ideas fed from international sources and emptying continuously across national frontiers as part of the process of international trade. Given this situation, no single nation could afford either to reproduce this vast and ever-expanding reservoir on its own, or, still less, to isolate itself from it. Stalin, in his own, more "heroic" time, may have succeeded in imposing a state of economic self-isolation upon the USSR, while building his elaborate myth about the unique economic potential of his "parallel world market," but working in a better informed, more skeptical environment, Khrushchev could not realistically undertake to turn his back upon the practical realities of contemporary international economic life.

The Changing Realities of the Socialist Market. During most of his years in high office, however, Khrushchev had no difficulty in accepting the second premise of Stalin's parochial foreign economic policy. This was the proposition that the Soviet state, given its "special role in history," should continue to pursue external economic relations primarily along political lines. Most immediately, of course, this meant the closest economic cooperation with the other communist-ruled countries of the world, those countries that had already "forever broken with the capitalist system." Khrushchev was quite naturally persuaded that a policy of utmost concentration of foreign trade activity within its own political orbit would enable the Soviet Union to achieve the dual purpose of "unifying and strengthening the socialist system of states," and, at the same time, deny the major trading nations free access to the markets, as well as the commodity resources, of the communist group of countries. The latter objective is generally expressed in official doctrine as "narrowing the sphere in which the principal capitalist countries have access to world resources."[33]

---

[33] *Politicheskaya ekonomiya*, Moscow, 1954, p. 612.

The various putative advantages of growing trade within the bloc, as officially recited, are too numerous to be examined here. As might be expected, they cover the whole gamut of economic benefits considered to be attainable through the pursuit of the theory and practice of Soviet economic development. In the context of this study, it is important to indicate that the advantages of maximum intra-bloc trade include, among others, benefits of a protective character. What this means, in effect, is that by maximizing intra-bloc trade turnover, the Soviet economy is assumed to be gaining added protection for itself against the unqualified evils of competition, anarchy of production, and economic exploitation holding uncontrolled sway over the capitalist market. Large-scale trade among communist partners, according to official doctrine, is certain to yield benefits bearing directly on the collective growth of the economic power of the communist camp. By their "collective, planned utilization of available resources, [they will be certain] to help develop the productive

Volume of Foreign Trade of the USSR Distributed by Groups of Countries
(In Rubles)

TOTAL

	Turnover	Export	Import
1946	1,280,300,000	588,300,000	692,000,000
1950	2,925,500,000	1,615,200,000	1,310,300,000
1955	5,838,500,000	3,084,000,000	2,754,500,000
1958	7,782,400,000	3,867,800,000	3,914,600,000
1960	10,071,100,000	5,005,500,000	5,065,600,000
1965	14,598,900,000	7,349,500,000	7,248,400,000

COMMUNIST COUNTRIES

	Turnover	Export	Import
1946	697,600,000	340,500,000	357,100,000
1950	2,372,800,000	1,350,200,000	1,022,600,000
1955	4,662,400,000	2,453,700,000	2,208,700,000
1958	5,754,300,000	2,822,600,000	2,931,700,000
1960	7,370,800,000	3,790,300,000	3,580,500,000
1965	10,048,300,000	4,999,400,000	5,048,900,000

COUNTRIES OF THE COUNCIL FOR ECONOMIC MUTUAL ASSISTANCE (COMECON)

	Turnover	Export	Import
1946	583,000,000	309,100,000	273,900,000
1950	1,752,800,000	938,400,000	814,400,000
1955	3,267,300,000	1,722,400,000	1,544,900,000
1958	4,174,000,000	2,146,400,000	2,027,600,000
1960	5,468,600,000	2,880,600,000	2,588,000,000
1965	8,471,300,000	4,210,200,000	4,261,100,000

NON-COMMUNIST COUNTRIES

	Turnover	Export	Import
1946	582,700,000	247,800,000	334,900,000
1950	552,700,000	265,000,000	287,700,000
1955	1,176,100,000	630,300,000	545,800,000
1958	2,028,100,000	1,045,200,000	982,900,000
1960	2,700,300,000	1,215,200,000	1,485,100,000
1965	4,459,600,000	2,350,100,000	2,199,500,000

INDUSTRIALLY DEVELOPED COUNTRIES

	Turnover	Export	Import
1946	491,000,000	209,100,000	281,900,000
1950	440,200,000	235,900,000	204,300,000
1955	904,300,000	502,500,000	401,800,000
1958	1,223,500,000	632,200,000	591,300,000
1960	1,917,300,000	913,300,000	1,004,000,000
1965	2,806,000,000	1,340,600,000	1,465,400,000

NEWLY DEVELOPING COUNTRIES

	Turnover	Export	Import
1946	91,700,000	38,700,000	53,000,000
1950	112,500,000	29,100,000	83,400,000
1955	271,800,000	127,800,000	144,000,000
1960	783,000,000	301,900,000	481,100,000
1965	1,743,600,000	1,009,500,000	734,100,000

NOTE: The ruble is officially valued by the USSR at $1.11.

SOURCE: Supplement to *Vneshnyaya torgovlya*, Moscow, No. 11, 1965; No. 8, 1966.

forces of the individual member countries and thereby increase the economic power of the socialist camp as a whole."[34]

During the early sixties, however, it became quite apparent that Khrushchev's devotion to the cause of the socialist market had begun to wane. His attempt to steer the regional economic organization of Eastern Europe (Comecon) in the direction of joint economic planning in June 1962 ended in failure.[35] He discovered that some of the member countries of Comecon were more interested in the feeling of pride and power they derived from their diversified industrial expansion programmes than in the higher economic returns they were likely to secure from a more rational division of labour within the socialist market. He could not help being discouraged to find, for example, that the leaders of many of these countries were too bent upon the endless diversification of their undersized industrial plant to be seriously concerned, as he was, over the persistence of small-scale, inefficient production in most of the national industries of the

---

[34] *Ibid.*

[35] *A Background Study on East-West Trade*, United States Senate, Committee on Foreign Relations, April, 1965, pp. 26–38.

smaller countries in the region. Nor were these leaders as eager, as he was, to make a better showing in the economic competition with the Common Market or with the West in general. Instead, most of the smaller countries of Eastern Europe seemed rather to incline to give the Soviet Union a free hand in its efforts to solve the problem of competition between the two world political systems if their big neighbour would only give them in exchange the freedom to dispose of their economic resources in accordance with their own national interests, as they perceived them.

In the course of his search for ways to improve the climate for intra-bloc cooperation, Khrushchev found the forces of economic nationalism and administrative inertia all too well entrenched in Eastern Europe. The leaders of the smaller countries of the region had been clearly over-educated in the fundamental Soviet approach to economic success. Like their earlier Soviet counterparts, they came to regard a rapid rate of indus-trial growth as the hallmark of successful economic development. Working with ambitious quantitative plans, in the manner of the Soviet Union, they had also become worshippers of "the cult of the ton." At the same time, the economic policies pursued by the smaller countries of Eastern Europe left little elbow room, and little real incentive, for the full play of the forces of innovation. As evident from Khrushchev's occasional public complaints, the managers of production in the command economy tended to be rather passive on this score: they had no incentive to exert any pressure upon their own research institutes either for machines or products of a better design. There were, plainly enough, no real rewards in the system for the time to be spent and the risk to be incurred in introduc-ing a more efficient manufacturing process or a better quality product.

Khrushchev was perceptibly puzzled by the lack of incentive to manu-facture products of a high standard of quality in the countries of the socialist camp. At times, in fact, he gave expression to his puzzlement in public, though he always sought to explain away this critical weakness of the quantity-oriented economies of Eastern Europe in the usual terms of "the temporary shortcomings of our dynamic economic system." For example, in the course of a tour he made through several factories in Hungary in 1964, Khrushchev digressed from the main topic of his speech to muse over a question that had apparently been long weighing on his mind. He reflected:

> As a rule, the plants and factories in the capitalist countries turn out fine products. But these goods are made not by the capitalists but by men and women workers, by engineers. If the workers, engineers and employees manufacture excellent goods while working for the capitalists, why then must we, the workers, engineers and technologists in the socialist countries, work

less well, producing goods of lower quality. After all, we are doing it all for ourselves, for our own people, for the building of socialism, for the building of communism.[36]

In general, the momentum of intra-bloc commodity exchange has remained strong throughout the recent period. Trade between the USSR and Eastern Europe has continued to expand in volume. In 1965, for instance, the value of Soviet imports from Eastern Europe reached 4.7 billion dollars, a figure nearly three times the value of imports from the industrial West. It is most doubtful, however, whether Khrushchev, during his latter years in office, saw in this routine escalation of intra-Comecon commercial exchanges the making of a really self-sufficient regional economy in Eastern Europe, equal to and independent of the actively trading, cost-conscious industrial community of the outside world.

The Withering Away of the Self-Sufficient State

Only three years have passed since the fateful power play, known formally as "the decision of the October 1964 plenum," that toppled Khrushchev from his position of supreme control. In most areas of policy-making, the style of leadership in the Soviet Union has changed conspicuously during this period. The official climate has come to be dominated by a mood of caution and a policy of general avoidance of new initiatives. As seen from the outside, the new men at the top of the Soviet power structure have succeeded in maintaining their collective leadership over a significant period of time, but they have done so largely by way of keeping open most of their options. This general mode of behaviour cannot, however, be described as applying to the sphere of foreign economic policy. In regard to the issue of autarky, in particular, the post-Khrushchev leadership has not hesitated to show its hand, which indicates rather clearly that it favours a much more active engagement in economic intercourse with the world industrial community. Ever since Kosygin's speech to the September 1965 Plenum, the new leaders have spoken and acted consistently in support of a more economically informed approach to foreign trade, both within and beyond the socialist market.

Through a More Expedient Approach to Socialist Trade. As part of the present reexamination of established policy, the whole subject of the utility of the socialist market has, for the first time, come to be viewed in a more sober light. While the rhetoric that suffuses all references to the realm of external trade has undergone little change, some of the practical issues involved in intra-bloc trade have begun to be aired in public discussion with a relative degree of candour. Foreign trade experts now feel

---

[36] *Pravda*, April 2, 1964.

free to discuss "the unresolved problems" that have arisen in commodity trade between the USSR and its socialist partners. These problems, it turns out, are quite fundamental, touching upon the stubborn facts of production costs and market prices. In its recent discussion of these issues, the Soviet economic press has begun to present evidence to the effect that the commodity structure of its trade with other Comecon members was ill-conceived, and has often been unprofitable for the USSR in a number of ways.

Soviet trade analysts now contend openly that the enormous volume of fuels, minerals, and other raw materials that the USSR exports annually to its socialist partners represents a growing burden on the capital resources of the country. Such exports require continued heavy outlay of new investment. Yet, the cost of this capital outlay, say the Russians, is not being recaptured by the prices currently in effect in the socialist market. While on this subject, the trade experts of the Soviet Union also make clear that they are quite dissatisfied with the other side of the bargain—i.e., with the fact that the merchandise that the Soviet Union imports from the other bloc members is all too heavily weighted on the side of machinery and consumer goods. Goods of this type, according to their calculations, require much smaller capital input for sustained expansion of their production.[37]

One Soviet economist has recently calculated that in order to obtain one "foreign exchange ruble" from the sales of some of its typical raw material exports to the Comecon countries, the USSR has to invest between five and eight times as much as is normally required to earn such income from its own machinery export items.[38] Nor is this all. What also emerges from these recent, more candid discussions is that the machinery the Soviet Union imports from its socialist trade partners is overpriced in relation to its quality. The same Soviet writer volunteers the opinion, with the kind of restraint that is generally indicated in all public discussions of intra-bloc problems, that "some socialist machines could be resold on the world market only at sharply reduced prices."

The new tone that has crept into these discussions in the mid-sixties suggests that Soviet officialdom has found it difficult to continue to ignore the salient fact that an exchange of goods that rests on a sound ideological base is not necessarily always a good economic bargain. In the present, less dogmatic political climate, the trade officials of the USSR have exhibited a strong tendency to pursue trade primarily for the opportunity it affords

---

[37] The share of machinery in total Soviet imports from Comecon countries was 45.5 per cent in 1964. It had risen to this level from 43.6 per cent in 1960. See *Vneshnyaya torgovlya*, No. 12, 1966, p. 12.

[38] O. Bogomolov, *Mirovaya ekonomika i mezhdunarodnye otnosheniya*, No. 5, 1966.

to obtain real and measurable economic benefits. It takes no rare political insight to recognize that the trade pattern now followed by countries of Eastern Europe among themselves is essentially a product of the cold war. As a matter of record, this trade assumed its particular commodity structure under the pressure of the political tensions that developed between East and West during the late 1940's. This, of course, was a period in which the Soviet Union was pressing relentlessly to expand westward by way of imposing minority governments on its weak neighbours immediately to the West. This display of expansionism, in turn, evoked a strong response on the part of the Western nations. One response, it will be recalled, took the form of barring the shipment of advanced types of machinery to Russia and its new captive alliance. The situation obviously called for a quick response in order to find a substitute source of imports, especially of machinery, needed to help rebuild the seriously demolished industrial plant of the USSR.

Faced by an urgent need for imported equipment, the Soviet leaders filled it, in large part, by directing the more industrially developed countries of Eastern Europe towards adaptation of their economies to meet the conditions of the cold war. In the early years after the war, it was a relatively easy matter for the Soviet leadership to impose a drastic change of domestic production patterns on some of its newly acquired weak allies, in particular Czechoslovakia and East Germany, two countries that were to initiate the production of a wide variety of heavy industrial equipment for export to the USSR. The USSR, for its part, was thereby enabled to keep its own basic production and trade pattern unchanged: it continued to provide, in its commodity exchange within Eastern Europe, roughly the same range of raw materials it had exported in the past to its highly industrialized trade partners in the West. Today, the economic rationality of this commodity exchange between the USSR and its small allies is clearly far less compelling. An exchange in which Russia imports from Poland, for example, 277 million dollars worth of machinery, while the flow of equipment in the other direction amounts to only 108 million dollars, can be explained only on the grounds of economic inertia. In time, however, a great deal of this kind of exchange pattern has come to be so patently indefensible that most of the trade partners within Comecon would like to find an escape. High Polish officials, such as Deputy Premier Jaroszewicz, have, on occasion, complained openly that the schedule of machines and vehicles assigned to the smaller trade partners for production, under the aegis of Comecon commissions, is altogether too long, with the result that these countries find it impossible to establish economically rational—that is, profitable—scales of production for most of the equipment on the list.

As a result, the prices they receive from their socialist trade partners—these are generally world market prices based on the cost structure of large-scale producers in the West—do not pay back the full cost of their inputs of materials, labour, and capital, under their conditions of small-scale production.[39]

Share of Machinery in the Mutual Export Trade of the Comecon Countries
(Percentages of Total National Exports)

	1955	1960	1964	1965
Bulgaria	2.8	15.2	29.0	29.9
Hungary	37.6	46.2	44.6	42.8
East Germany	—	56.3	55.8	58.6
Poland	17.4	37.4	46.6	48.7
Rumania	6.1	16.1	23.0	24.5
Czechoslovakia	51.1	47.3	54.3	56.3
USSR	17.3	14.1	18.3	18.0

SOURCE: *Vneshnyaya torgovlya*, Moscow, No. 12, 1966, p. 10.

The evidence at hand suggests that the present pattern of specialization and exchange among the Comecon group of nations is badly out of joint, and in need of a searching review and modification. Soviet specialists in the field no longer hesitate to make this point explicit. They are now contending that in the past the approach to specialization has been all too broad, too superficial: for example, finished goods versus raw materials. In the future, it is said, the approach needs to be more selective, more oriented towards specific products. Ways should be found, it is recommended, to work out areas of national specialization within, rather than between, the individual branches of rapidly expanding processing industries: for example, those producing types of steel plate, generators, etc. At the same time, Soviet writers make the point that they would like to see a greater effort made towards specialization within the various branches of the more capital intensive industries, mining operations in particular, in the belief that "[this] would make it possible to increase the reciprocal exchange of raw materials among Comecon members."[40] Such a drastic modification of the present commodity exchange pattern would obviously require a long and difficult process of negotiation and gradual readjustment.

Through a More Active Contact with the World Reservoir of Technology. Following the 1964 change in the personnel and style of leadership in

---

[39] See, for example, *Trybuna Ludu*, December 5 and 31, 1965; and February 13, 1966. See also Ye. Orlova, in *Planovoe khozyaystvo*, August, 1961.

[40] *Vneshnyaya torgovlya*, No. 12, 1966, p. 12.

the Soviet Union, Premier Kosygin emerged as the principal spokesman on issues involving the industrial and commercial policies of the Soviet government. In this capacity, he soon revealed himself as a man who is more concerned with the state of the industrial arts in the USSR than with the political image of Soviet socialism. Generally, his diagnosis of the state of affairs in domestic manufaturing has been, from the beginning of his accession to power, quite frank, within the limits of public discussion permitted in the USSR. In his now historic address of September 27, 1965, treating at some length all facets of the current economic reform, Kosygin summed up his own findings on the subject quite succinctly, if uninspiringly: "The pattern of production of machinery and equipment by many branches [of Soviet industry] does not conform to modern standards."[41] His recommended remedy was equally straightforward: "In vigorously developing our machine-building industry," he advised, "we must make wider use of the achievements of engineering abroad." In the years that have passed since that address, Kosygin has continued to remind his associates in the Soviet leadership that they live in an efficiency-conscious world, distinguished by an incredibly fast tempo of technical change, and that it is neither in their interest nor in their power to turn their collective backs upon the existing world economic order. Rather, they must become more alert, availing themselves of all existing opportunities "to improve . . . production techniques" and "to satisfy . . . the needs of our export trade."

The most dependable way to keep in touch with the rapid pace of industrial change in the world, as seen by Kosygin, is to expand more widely than before the exchange of goods through the channels of international trade. This new faith in the healing power of external trade was made fairly explicit in the text of the Directives designed to govern the new, eighth Five-Year Plan, adopted at the Twenty-third Party Congress in April 1966. As might be expected, the formal statement on trade policy that issued from this Congress was replete with the familiar verbal formulas bestowing fulsome praise upon the official tenets of post-war Soviet foreign trade policy. At the same time, however, a number of new nuances of a significant character did come to the surface. Thus, the Congress, for example, placed itself on record as being wholeheartedly in favour of "an increase in the turnover of goods between the USSR and the other socialist countries," but this familiar objective was at once carefully qualified by a rather novel call for a more economic approach to this proliferating but rather slapdash commodity exchange. What was needed, the statement

---

[41] *Pravda*, September 28, 1965.

said, was "an improvement in the structure of exports and imports and the raising, on that basis, of the economic effectiveness of [this] foreign trade."[42]

In the same statement, second place of honour, as usual, was again assigned to the newly developing countries. The latter were promised "more Soviet machinery and other types of industrial products needed for the creation of their national economy." To this was added the standard pledge that the Soviet Union would continue to render technical assistance to them, as well as train personnel and provide research facilities to assist in the creation of a domestic industry and in the improvement of agriculture, transport, communication, and geological prospecting.

The really novel and interesting element of official trade policy, in respect of the Directives of 1966, is to be found in the passages dealing with the need for a new approach to the third and last group of trade partners, i.e., "the industrially developed capitalist countries." Here, in new and strong language, one encounters a call for "a profound study of foreign markets" as the only way to develop a truly reciprocal relationship, based on the unique capabilities of the USSR in production, with the world economy at large. Here, one also finds an unusually clear affirmation of "the advantages of the international division of labour" and an expression of serious intent to make more complete use of them in the future. As a token of their seriousness in this respect, it should be noted, the Soviet leaders have gone so far in this statement as to direct the authorities at the level of the Ministry of Foreign Trade to introduce the kind of "improvements" (read: changes) in the commodity structure of Soviet trade, both on the import and the export side of the exchange, that would in fact make it possible for the USSR to take part in a rational division of labour on an international scale.

Most interesting of all, in the present context, is the clearly expressed judgement that previous Soviet practice in this regard has left a good deal to be desired. Past practice in planning domestic production, it is now recognized, has all too often resulted in the dissipation of economic resources, thanks largely to the enforcement of the principle of "universal production," to which official economic doctrine has long been dedicated. In the future, the new leaders indicate in their recent pronouncements, they will be guided, in ordering the structure of their domestic production, by the principle of comparative costs with reference to the world market. Specifically, they have committed themselves, in the words of the Directives

[42] *Pravda*, April 10, 1966.

of 1966, not to produce any longer but rather from now on to import "articles whose production inside the country entails greater costs and capital investment."

This new recognition of the value of close and continued cooperation with the international economy, through the exchange of products and technical processes, was expressed even more vigorously in the economic report delivered by Kosygin to the same Twenty-third Party Congress. In his own report, the Soviet premier related the growing official interest in trade with the West, more directly than it has ever been done in the past, to the principal imperative of the present inter-dependent world, that is, "the scientific and technical revolution unfolding in the contemporary world."[43] This revolution, he asserted, "calls for more freedom of international economic intercourse, creates a basis for a broad economic exchange between socialist countries and the nations of the capitalist system." His judgement was based, he said, not on a mere theoretical perception of what trade with the West may bring in the future. This trade, he explained, had already expanded by some 50 per cent during the preceding five years, under conditions of mutual economic advantage.[44] What was more important, in his view, was the fact that the recent commodity exchange between Russia and the West had already helped "to solve a number of national economic problems." He could have added further weight to his argument by showing, on the authority of official Soviet data, that during the most recent period on record, from 1959–1965, trade with the industrial West grew more rapidly than did trade with the countries of the communist world system.

Recent Growth Trends in Soviet Foreign Trade

(In Millions of Rubles)

	1958	1965	Index (1958 = 100)
Total Trade Turnover*	7,782	14,598	187.6
With Communist Countries	5,754	10,048	174.6
With Comecon Countries	4,174	8,471	203.1
With Industrially Developed Countries ..	1,223	2,806	229.4
With Newly Developing Countries......	805	1,774	216.6

* Exports plus Imports.

SOURCE: Annual Foreign Trade Returns of the USSR.

---

[43] *Pravda*, April 6, 1966.

[44] According to official Soviet statistics, total turnover of trade with the industrial countries of the West increased from 1.9 to 2.8 billion rubles between 1960 and 1965.

For all that, Premier Kosygin reported with disapproval, Soviet response to existing opportunities in world trade had been somewhat lethargic. There was still a serious educational job to be done, in his opinion. A great deal of bureaucratic inertia still remained to be overcome. He pointed in particular to the conservative disposition of the industrial managers who go about their accustomed rounds, absorbed in their day-to-day production schedules, indifferent to the varied and valuable contribution that a modest increase in external trade could make towards the modernization of their productive equipment as well as towards lowering the cost and raising the quality of their finished product. "We must change this essentially incorrect view, and strengthen our business contacts between industry and foreign trade." There is, in the view of Kosygin and his entourage, a very particular role that foreign trade can play in connection with the present campaign of economic reform. Trade, if properly utilized, can become a prime channel through which the higher layers of authority in the country can maintain systematic pressure upon the industrial managers, the kind of pressure that would serve to infuse ideas of cost-consciousness into the production process and thereby enforce a greater sense of discipline in the allocation of resources throughout the domestic economy.

In his own eminently pragmatic view of the future, Premier Kosygin seems to feel assured that many benefits would inevitably accrue to the Soviet industrial establishment as a result of an imaginative and sustained contact with the more industrially developed countries of the West. He is aware that Soviet industry in the years immediately ahead will need to be exposed, on a continuing basis, to a wide variety of new influences that could be helpful in the current drive to instill a sense of economic discipline among its managerial class, chiefly in the form of a compulsion to reduce costs to a minimum at every step of the production process. Above all, however, he knows his own environment well enough to realize that a national economy that is impelled, as Russia's has been over the past five decades, by a mission to catch up with the more advanced industrial nations in terms of physical output, enlarging its productive capacity at a forced pace, cannot at the same time be as sensitive as it should be to new processes of production, new manufacturing equipment, or new finished products. In this respect, the leaders of the country do not really have an acceptable choice at their disposal. They are faced by the alternative of either pursuing their economic growth on a narrow, purely national base of industrial research, or opting in favour of a much more systematic involvement in economic and technical exchanges with the growing community of technologically restless, industrially advancing nations of the world.

Retrospect

Among the many expectations raised by the Bolshevik Revolution and the founding of the first Soviet socialist state, the promise of economic self-sufficiency has long exercised a special fascination upon the minds of the ruling elite of the country, partly for reasons of national prestige and partly for reasons of security. Today, however, this promise is gradually but perceptibly evaporating into thin air. True, the foreign trade monopoly has never been allowed to lower its guard; it still mans the administrative barriers that protect the economic security of the USSR. The trade monopoly remains to this day deeply embedded in the institutional framework of the Soviet state structure, but the tantalizing prospect of economic independence from the rest of the industrial community of the world, which the monopoly trading institution was designed to achieve, continues to elude the USSR today as much as ever before. Even the enormous territorial expansion of the socialist camp, climaxed by the inclusion of Mainland China in 1949, accomplished precious little by way of creating an alternative, self-sustained reservoir of technological innovation.

Most discernible signs seem to point to the conclusion that the present generation of Soviet leaders has grown skeptical about the whole notion of a studied, politically justifiable isolation from the world industrial community. Their own experience of a lifetime has helped to make them aware that the scientific and technical revolution now under way in the world of production is concentrated among the actively cooperating economies of the industrially more developed nations outside the communist bloc. Having recognized this fact, the Soviet leaders are genuinely concerned over the danger of being cut off from this vital centre of technological change and economic progress. Accordingly, they no longer find it difficult to accept the proposition that in our time economic progress is in fact indivisible.

To this extent, then, it may reasonably be concluded that the Soviet political system has demonstrated its capacity to shed unworkable ideas, if given enough time and a clear record of negative results. The whole record of Soviet experience with the concept of autarky, national as well as regional, has indeed been demonstrably negative. A close reading of the current literature on this theme would suggest, in fact, that Soviet economic writers would like to forget about the whole thing. If possible, they would prefer to characterize the notion of autarky as some alien idea, invented by someone with an interest in keeping the Soviet Union in a state of economic retardation. "From an economic point of view," we read in a recent issue of the journal of the Ministry of Foreign Trade, "autarky is disadvantageous, because it tends to slow down the development of the productive forces, to brake the growth of labour productivity."[45] The author of the article then goes on to explain, in the manner of a man who has just stumbled on a rare discovery, that any society which attempts to produce everything at home, without paying the closest possible attention to the comparative cost of production of the same article abroad, is inviting the waste of social labour. In light of this reasoning, he concludes, the Soviet Union and the other socialist countries now "do not believe in secluding themselves within the bounds of their national markets, or of the world socialist market, but are striving to utilize the advantages of the international division of labour on a world-wide scale."

The withering away of old ideas is obviously proceeding apace in Russia today. The present leaders of the Soviet government seem to be ready to accept the premise, now generally adopted among the economically more experienced nations, that the critical ingredient of an effective production system in our times is technology, and that the market for technological ideas must be as inclusive as the entire industrial community of the world. It is now quite clear to them that a national or regional market for technical innovation is, by definition, a needlessly impoverished storehouse of ideas. They are manifestly no longer willing to be confined to an economically retarding environment of this variety.

It is almost as if the rulers of Russia were now ready to agree with John Stuart Mill that it is the business of the state not to try to innovate but rather "to make itself an active circulator and diffuser [of experience] . . . to enable each experimentalist to benefit by the experiments of others, instead of tolerating no experiment but its own." The process of disllusionment with regard to the promise of autarky has been going on for a number of years in the Soviet Union. This goal, which once seemed within easy reach and full of glittering promise, is no longer held to be either attainable or desirable. The original urge to maintain the Soviet economy as an island, enjoying a state of splendid isolation from the main theatre of economic activity and experimentation, is now clearly recognized as a fond illusion, as a condition which, if only partially attained, would deprive the Soviet Union, or any other nation in its place, of the right of free access to the growing abundance of the economic harvest made possible in our age by the studied application of human ingenuity and social cooperation.

---

[45] *Vneshnyaya torgovlya*, No. 2, 1965, p. 5.

The Kosygin Reforms: New Wine in Old Bottles?

James H. Blackman

This year, the fiftieth anniversary of the Bolshevik Revolution, finds the Soviet economy in a state of flux. The old institutional forms continue to dominate the economic landscape, but in altered and still altering ways. Change and its accompaniment, uncertainty, have, in fact, been on the increase throughout much of the Khrushchev and post-Khrushchev era. The Soviets themselves frequently characterize the present as a period of transition, leaving the terminus, as well as many of the interim stations, vague. This study investigates, in the brief perspective of Soviet history, the nature of the so-called ongoing transition. It asks the questions: From what? Towards what?

Some observers, both Soviet and Western, have taken the position that the reforms currently in progress constitute, or at least presage, a radical break with the command economy fashioned by Stalin. The well-known Soviet economist, A. Birman, in what may have been an excess of wishful thinking, has stated that "the present change in our country's economic life is the most important one in the last thirty-five years."[1] As a matter of fact, he regards it as the third great reform in Soviet history, ranking alongside Lenin's New Economic Policy (NEP) of the twenties and the forced draft industrialization and collectivization of Stalin's First Five-Year Plan.[2]

Similarly, in the West, certain early evaluations of the Kosygin reforms have described them as "remarkable by past Russian standards,"[3] involving a "titanic reorganization."[4] In the opinion of Dr. John Hardt, the Soviet Union is in the early stages of its second economic revolution, one in which indirect fiscal and monetary controls probably will supplant direct political controls.[5]

Other assessments, apparently in the majority on each side of the Iron Curtain, have viewed the import of the reforms in a more conservative

[1] A. Birman, *Izvestia*, February 11, 1966, p. 3.
[2] A. Birman, *Novy mir*, December, 1965, p. 194.
[3] *Business Week*, New York, April 29, 1967, p. 93.
[4] Gilbert Buck, "The Toughest Management Job in the World," *Fortune*, New York, July, 1966, p. 73.
[5] *Ibid.* p. 74.

light. They do not deny that substantial changes have occurred, or that more may be expected, but the foundations of the system, it is argued, are left essentially intact. For example, though he agrees that a number of novel changes are being made, the reforms, according to Professor Abram Bergson, "are by no means radical."[6] It is in this latter camp that the present writer finds himself, for reasons that constitute the burden of the discussion to follow. In the metaphor of the title, it is evident that new wine—I think, on balance, an improved wine—is in prospect, but its basic disposition is constrained by the same old economic bottles.

This study will focus attention primarily on the reforms ushered in by Kosygin in his famous speech to the Central Committee of the Soviet Communist Party on September 27, 1965.[7] Hence, the use of his name in the title. This is not, however, to imply that the changes are uniquely his proposal or that other leaders—Brezhnev, for instance—dissociate themselves from "the new system of management and incentives." What I have called "the Kosygin reforms" represents the programme of the collective leadership that supplanted Khrushchev, and might more accurately be labelled as such. My reference to Kosygin is intended simply to recognize the division of labour in the higher reaches of the Party and does not reflect, as far as known, a division of ideas. Kosygin's basic concern, which this study shares, is with industry. Agriculture, thus far, has been less caught up in institutional tinkering, but the evidence mounts that it is about to follow suit.[8] Notwithstanding increasing resemblances in the patterns of agrarian and industrial reforms, I shall concentrate on the latter, occasionally noting significant interaction with the agricultural sphere.

Though I have been speaking of the recent Soviet reforms in the plural, their actual multiplicity and variety are poorly conveyed by a single word, which would fail, likewise, to indicate the degree, large or small, of their internal harmony. It is important, therefore, to stress at the outset the self-contradictory nature of the changes being wrought. The Party's economic

---

[6] A Round-Table Discussion, "Soviet Economic Performance and Reform: Some Problems of Analysis and Prognosis," *Slavic Review*, Urbana, Illinois, June, 1966, p. 223.

[7] *Pravda*, September 28, 1965.

[8] The main formula relied on to strengthen agriculture has been the channelling of more resources to it. Recently, however, the pressure has mounted to adapt and extend the new reform system to it. Witness, for example, the announcement of the "transfer of 390 state farms and state agricultural enterprises to full economic accountability in 1967 by way of experiment." Cf., *Pravda*, April 15, 1967, p. 1.

programme is replete with inconsistencies, more pronounced in implementation than in formulation, but considerable in each case. The total thrust of the reforms, characterized above as moderate, if not conservative, reflects the operation of these cross-directional and partially offsetting pulls.

A persistent theme may nonetheless be detected in the reforms—namely, to accord value categories more prominence at all levels of management and planning. It is this aspect, perhaps more than any other, that has prompted certain analysts to conclude that the reforms establish, or promise, a significant decentralization of economic decision-making. Even so, however, the increasing monetization of the economy cannot be so simply equated with the devolution of power from the centre to the field. The precise nature of the enhanced role of money and the purposes it is to serve are altogether crucial for determining any net decentralizing or centralizing tendency. It is necessary to ask whether the monetary indicators, as refurbished and elaborated by the reforms, are designed primarily to heighten central control, or if they are intended chiefly to widen the area of balanced, decentralized choice. In other words, in the context of historical continuity and change, is the present Soviet leadership using monetary levers (profits, cost accounting, and so on) in appreciably different ways and for different ends than the classic Stalinist model, or is the rationale basically the same? If different from the Stalinist model, can the new, or incipient, monetary functions nevertheless be interpreted as the descendants of remoter Soviet economic models, notably, the New Economic Policy of Lenin? Should this prove to be the case, the Kosygin reforms would indeed deserve the label "radical," though sustaining a diminished claim to originality. At the risk of gross oversimplification, let me turn now to a brief sketch of these main historical antecedents, which are of interest and relevance for the present inquiry.

NEP, Lenin's compromise with capitalism, was a move taken to stem peasant unrest and to gain time for the building of a Marxist society. It was officially enacted by the Tenth Congress of the Communist Party in March 1921, when the Red Army was preoccupied with the Kronstadt mutiny and the regime again hovered on the brink of counter-revolution.[9] Through the process of trial and error, a novel and in some ways highly successful mixed economy evolved. Institutionally speaking, NEP was neither capitalist nor socialist, though its long-term socialist objective was always fully explicit. Under the new arrangements, market forces were permitted to organize and actuate the agricultural sector, as well as much

---

[9] See, for example, the account given in Anatole G. Mazour, *Soviet Economic Development: Operation Outstrip: 1921–1965*, Princeton, New Jersey, D. Van Nostrand Company, Inc., 1967, p. 22.

of domestic trade, while the state reserved for itself the so-called commanding heights of heavy industry, banking, transportation and foreign commerce. Though the span of control afforded by these heights eventually proved inadequate for Stalin's needs, it did facilitate the initial abridgements of consumer sovereignty and the favouring of industry in its terms of trade with agriculture.

When NEP began its restoration of the market, it faced the task of re-creating a stable pecuniary system, money having been effectively repudiated by the printing presses of war communism. Though a sound monetary circulation was not achieved at once, it was understood to be indispensable for the commercial operations and principles that the regime now espoused. By 1924, a stable ruble—the chervonets—was attained, thanks to the government's conservative methods of finance. Significantly, the reestablished institution of money was to persist, even if with varying importance, after most of NEP's expedient compromises had succumbed to Stalin's administered economy.

A number of scholars have characterized NEP as "primarily a new agricultural policy."[10] The essential aim of this policy was to enlarge the agricultural surplus by inducing the peasants, who comprised some twenty-four million households, to pursue their own financial gain on free, competitive markets. Buttressing this profits "come-on" was an important, related measure abolishing the requisitions of surplus grain. Instead of the irregular, often confiscatory, levy of the period of war communism, under NEP, peasants were obliged to pay a regular tax in kind (after 1923, in money) on their agricultural products and were free to expand and market the surplus as they chose. "Every peasant must realize," so an early decree read, "that the more land he cultivates the greater will be his surplus of grain which remains his personal property."[11]

NEP's industrial innovations, though of somewhat lesser importance historically than its agricultural policies, hold greater interest for this particular study. Among the most significant changes introduced in the industrial sphere, was decentralization of the operation of state-owned industry through the formation of trusts, along side of which some small private businesses were permitted to exist. The transactions of the trusts and their subordinate enterprises were carried out on markets providing exchange links both within industry and to private households. Altogether, about 300 trusts were required to control the enterprises of the state sector.

---

[10] V. N. Bandera, "The New Economic Policy (NEP) As An Economic System," *The Journal of Political Economy*, Chicago, June, 1963, p. 268.

[11] Mazour, *op. cit.*, p. 24.

In turn, some dozen syndicates coordinated the distribution and other activities of the trusts in line with the general policies of the central government bureaus (the Supreme Economic Council, the State Planning Commission, etc.).

It should be emphasized, however, that the market itself was a critical element in directing and controlling the economic units. At first, the rule of *khozraschet* (economic accounting) was applied only to the trusts; later, financial responsibility was decentralized to the level of the enterprises. The essence of *khozraschet* was the separation of the economic agency (trust or enterprise) from the state budget. The behaviour of the new, quasi-independent units was made subject to two general rules, supplying "an incentive and a check."[12] The first of these was an injunction to maximize profits; the second charged managers with conducting "their" businesses economically, so that, at a minimum, they would "pay for themselves." This entailed, among other things, tightening labour discipline and gearing wages more closely to productivity. With most prices formed on the market, NEP's profit-maximizing criterion, as Peter Wiles has observed, was tantamount to an order to adapt outputs to the market.[13] Thus, according to Wiles, *khozraschet* began as an indirect injunction to the producer to satisfy the consumer.[14]

The specific functions of the profits rule under NEP were several. Realized profits enabled the executives of the system—from enterprise managers to Supreme Economic Council officials—to gauge roughly the efficiency of their operations and to respond to the patterns of demand. The quest for efficiency was served by both intertemporal and cross-sectional comparisons. Additionally, profits performed the familiar incentive function of capitalist economics. A good profits record was not only a valuable career stepping stone (and conversely), but it also exerted direct and increasingly important income leverage. The introduction of the "Director's Fund" provided for the retention by the trust of 20 per cent of the profits. Half of this accumulation was earmarked as capital reserve, and the other half enabled the payment of bonuses and wage supplements as well as the enhancement of the communal economy: housing, educational facilities, and the like. In the interest of meeting costs and in order to

---

[12] Bandera, *op. cit.*, p. 271.

[13] Peter Wiles, *The Political Economy of Communism*, Cambridge, Massachusetts, Harvard University Press, 1965, p. 34.

[14] It should be added, of course, that allowances were made for monopolistic pricing and various direct interventions of the state.

facilitate the mobilization of capital, enterprises were enjoined to include in their prices minimum profits.[15]

In sum, the NEP economy contained a mixture of private and state enterprise, both of which produced for profit. Markets of varying degress of imperfection and regulation transmitted the signals by which the profit-seeking activities of businesses, whether state or private, were channelled. The private units, however, were restricted in their market conduct by innumerable orders, many of them discriminatory, as well as by the monopoly powers of state enterprise. The latter, in turn, were considerably constrained themselves by the production quota and price-fixing proclivities of the central bureacracy.

The regulated markets of NEP socialism, not to mention the private elements of the economy, were never ideologically sanctioned in the long-run sense.[16] Basically, they were tolerated only as long as the achievements and prospects for growth were high. In any case, during the NEP period, the greatest stress was never on the market or on rational prices, but rather on the devolvement of decision-making to the periphery in order to counter the inefficiency and waste of the central bureacracy. In Wiles's telling phrase, "market socialism came almost in a fit of absence of mind," the Bolshevik leaders perceiving dimly, if at all, the organic connection between the market and decentralization.[17]

As will be seen, NEP's profit-maximizing calculus both resembles and significantly diverges from the new incentive system emerging from the current Kosygin reforms, but before exploring or interpreting these intersystemic comparisons, attention must be turned to the radically altered arrangements of Stalin's command economy. Since the general outlines of the Stalinist model are reasonably familiar, it should suffice here to note its primary stress on physical targeting and its consequent attentuation of market activities and value calculations. Reduced in scope and transformed in function, money did not, however, become insignificant under the Stalin Five-Year Plans.[18] Likewise, the pratice of cost accounting

---

[15] Bandera, *op. cit.*, p. 271.

[16] Actually, Lenin referred to his mixed NEP system as "State Capitalism." On this, see Maurice Dobb, *Soviet Economic Development Since 1917*, London, Routledge and Kegan Paul, 1948, p. 145.

[17] Wiles, *op. cit.*, p. 32.

[18] Economic accounting was contradictory in that it exhibited both functional and dysfunctional features from the standpoint of the dominant command model. For example, the use of money made possible a certain amount of unplanned, decentralized initiative, of which the central authorities might (or might not) approve. See the interesting development of this theme in David Granick, "An Organizational Model of Soviet Industrial Planning," *The Journal of Political Economy*, April, 1959, pp. 109–130.

or *khozraschet* continued in an essential, if modified and semi-contradictory, role. What remained was a limited sphere of enterprise autonomy and financial manoeuvre, partly illicit, but in part also winked at by the authorities on pragmatic grounds.

In the command economy the plan is law, and with the restoration of detailed central planning, money shifted from a preponderantly "active" (allocative) use to a largely "passive" (control) use, to borrow Wiles's concept and terminology. Apart from several genuine markets, to be acknowledged presently, money, in essence, afforded Stalin and his administrators the means of a continuous audit, the famous "control by ruble." Though enterprises were no longer free to dispose of resources in the light of monetary relationships (as, in the main, they had been during NEP), the results of their activities were, nonetheless, recorded in financial terms. Thus, their accounts at the state banks were kept under constant scrutiny, and in theory only plan-approved transactions could be consummated. Because it followed the course of the bank balances, the administrative hierarchy could mete out appropriate corrective orders and rewards.

In this milieu of direct allocation of supply and central targeting of outputs, the practice of *khozraschet* lost most of its original consumer or customer orientation. NEP-style profit-maximizing was soon reduced in Stalin's interpretation of *khozraschet* to the injunction: "Be watchful of costs." For the enterprise, this stricture, somewhat expanded, meant: "Produce, as economically as possible, the assortment and quantities of goods laid down in the plan; do so, moreover, in the prescribed way, with the given production function and designated suppliers, all transactions to be accomplished at the centrally fixed prices."[19] If an enterprise managed to fulfill its planned production programme at lower unit costs than budgeted in the plan, then it could secure an above-plan profit.[20] Alternatively, if it worked at lower efficiency than projected by the plan, it might sustain an actual loss, or would in any case fall short of the planned profits goal. Finally, the rewards or penalties that it received rested in part on its financial performance.

The disposition of enterprise profits was regulated in detail by the central government, but the portion assigned to the "Director's Fund" could be used for certain welfare purposes and income supplements at the

---

[19] Often, even these fairly restricted cost considerations were casualties of the mania to achieve above-plan gross outputs.

[20] Here, for simplicity, I abstract from planned subsidies that were prominent in the Stalin era, especially in heavy industry.

discretion of the enterprise.[21] As a function of the level of rewards involved, the incentive effect of this pecuniary element in the Stalin system tended in practice to be rather weak. The key service of *khozraschet* for Stalin lay rather in its contribution to the generalized system of economic control. As a source of economic stimulation, its value was much less, and as an allocative criterion, virtually nil. If not in the customary operations of state enterprises, where then was money "active" under the Stalinist system? Where did it serve as something more than a unit of account or medium of exchange—namely, as a significant motivator and guide to choice?[22] The answer is to be found in three main areas and at least two subsidiary ones.

Stalin's retention of NEP's genuine market for consumer goods, as well as, to a modest degree, the market for labour, made of his command economy something less than a pure model. Typically, Soviet consumers were free under Stalin to spend their money incomes (mostly earned from work) on any objects of their choice. Interspersed periods of rationing, some quite long, were crisis-born and were officially regarded as abnormal. Nevertheless, if freedom of consumption obtained in normal times, the Soviet consumer was still not "sovereign," since his demand patterns could not determine production. Presumably, Stalin reckoned the welfare gains and the attendant incentive effects of the free disposal of income on retail markets as more than outweighing the financial problems thus created. The latter, it might be mentioned, were problems of both a micro- and a macro-economic nature—problems, that is, of individual and of aggregative market balance.

Though he emasculated the trade unions, Stalin still rejected the extreme command formula of Trotsky for a labour army. Instead, he opted for a labour market, which—at times, at least—was relatively free. With the exception of the forced labour camps and the collective farm sector in general, Stalin relied on wage differentials and premiums, both to channel workers to the priority sectors where he wanted them and to coax productivity gains from workers in given occupations. On the worker side of the wage bargain, Stalinist money unquestionably was "active."

Another area where the market mechanism played a decisive role within Stalin's command economy was in the production and distribution of certain farm products. These were grown mainly, though not exclusively, on the private plots of collective farms and sold on free peasant markets.

---

[21] Dobb, *op. cit.*, p. 354.

[22] Accuracy demands the qualification that Stalin's use of money as a unit of account and as a medium of exchange left much to be desired, and even these traditional functions of money were from time to time obliterated.

The share of these "free marketings" in the gross value of agricultural output was substantial, sometimes exceeding thirty per cent, and as such provided the major source of peasant money income.

Finally, Stalin permitted or utilized various markets for "interstitial activities," as Grossman has called them, outside of agriculture.[23] Included in this miscellaneous category were diverse services such as legal and medical assistance and certain handicrafts and strictly local undertakings. Individually, as well as in total economic weight, the dimensions were minor. Black markets, likewise free, and underground commerce in the cities, constituted illicit offshoots of recognized private trade.

The fifth market or monetary element that merits reference derives from the impossibility of planning an economy in complete detail from the centre. Data and time considerations simply make it necessary for many "small" decisions to be taken at the local level in order to speed the economic process and exploit knowledge either partly or wholly inaccessible at the centre. Under Stalin, the operation of *khozraschet* offered the most important means for harnessing local managerial initiative and for tapping the peculiarly local stores of information. Basically, the market criteria, and more generally the monetary criteria, were used by managers to disaggregate the broad production assignments contained in their more general plans. The true priorities of the state were not necessarily served by the exercise of this decentralized initiative, but apparently no better alternative for lightening the impossible burden of the central planners was found.

In an insightful article, David Granick has argued that *khozraschet* stands "in flat contradiction" to the "fundamental, i.e., command model."[24] It is his thesis that command and market orders coexist in the Stalin economy, expressing a certain relationship of dominance and subordination. By interaction and joint accommodation, the mixed systems may prove durable, but their essential opposition, he contends, cannot be erased. This is a plausible view, though it insufficiently recognizes the highly circumscribed nature of *khozraschet* during the Five-Year Plans. For Stalin, the basic purpose of money and accounting was to effectuate commands; it was not primarily to express market forces—not certainly in the manner of NEP. Because of this, the contradiction that Granick sees may be more implicit, more a tendency, than a fact. True, "passive" money always contains the seeds of "active" money, but neither a quick nor a certain evolution can be assumed. By the same token, the power of Soviet

---

[23] Gregory Grossman, "Gold and the Sword: Money in the Soviet Command Economy," in Henry Rosovsky, ed., *Industrialization in Two Systems*, New York, John Wiley and Sons, 1966, pp. 204–236.

[24] Granick, *op. cit.*, p. 123.

enterprises to exercise initiative may be seen as a direct function of their liquidity; offsetting forces, including some monetary instruments, may still secure and perpetuate the dominance of the command system.

In view of the onrush of administrative change since Stalin's death, it is perhaps well to ask if the basic model was already altered beyond recognition by the time of the Kosygin reforms. Clearly, a new spirit is rising and virtually a whole new team of players is on the stage, but these circumstances in no way signify a drastic change in the rules. On the contrary, the evidence of the post-Stalin era still testifies to the primacy of the plan; even the specific output priorities of the dead dictator have shown remarkable persistence. The most significant reform that Professor Grossman could point to on the tenth anniversary of Stalin's death was the replacement of the economic ministries by the regional councils of the national economy (sovnarkhozes). Though this particular step was heralded by the Soviets(and others, too) as an important move in the direction of decentralization of power, the consensus of expert opinion in the West reached just the opposite conclusion—namely, that power at the centre was actually augmented and on the enterprise level somewhat lessened. This regionalization, as Alexander Erlich put it, "shortened the distance between planning agencies and enterprises, but it didn't essentially modify the nature of the relationship."[25] Furthermore, the enhancement of regional economic authority that did occur proved rather fleeting, for consolidation of the sovnarkhozes and recentralization of their duties commenced almost at once in Khrushchev's losing battle with localism.

More important than any concrete institutional change in the post-Stalin years was the intellectual ferment that Khrushchev sparked with his de-Stalinization speech and thereafter intermittently encouraged. The prolonged debates on price principles, investment criteria, and planning methodolgy that marked the 1950's and 1960's amounted to nothing less than the discovery, or rediscovery, of economics. Rationalization of the economy did not occur simultaneously with the new ideas (indeed, it may never occur), but an atmosphere conducive to such a change plainly was taking shape; meanwhile, some promising economic experiments, especially in the consumer goods area, were being launched.

The first of these experiments in decentralized control of enterprise administration was begun on July 1, 1964, at the Bolshevichka and Mayak clothing combines. These reforms, which Khrushchev inaugurated, or blessed, aimed essentially at greater satisfaction of and faster adjustment to consumer wants. The principal means by which it was hoped to achieve

<hr>

[25] *Slavic Review*, June, 1966, op. cit., p. 225.

these ends were use of profitability as the primary success indicator for evaluating and rewarding managerial performance,[26] and use of direct contracts between producers and retailers to plan and schedule production. Still left under central jurisdiction were the decisive matters of investment, prices, and general targets for sales and profitability.

The experiment with the clothing firms was not an unmitigated success, but the boost it gave to profits and sales was sufficiently promising to prompt the new leadership, which had ousted Khrushchev, greatly to expand its scope. Thus, during 1965, some 400 enterprises in light industry were shifted to the Bolshevichka-Mayak basis of operations, or modified variants of it. Most of the changes introduced were of a mildly restrictive sort, in which managerial freedoms to fix or raise prices and to let contracts were somewhat curbed. The rationale of increased flexibility to enable efficient response to changes in consumer demand and the drive to upgrade quality, however, remained the same. This enlarged experiment with decentralism was, of course, at a very early and inconclusive stage when the far-reaching Kosygin proposals affecting all of industry were promulgated in late 1965. The relationship of the two reform tracks was left somewhat vague, but the slowness of the initial pace of the Kosygin reforms indicated some longevity for the earlier experimental system.

The rapid build-up of reforms in the consumer goods field was climaxed at the close of 1965 by Kosygin's wide-ranging recommendations for "a new system of planning and incentives." The unveiling of the Kosygin programme in particular served to underscore the leadership's belief that the traditional forms of Soviet economic organization were in need of substantial overhaul. The broad debate and experimentation of recent years were not to be shut off, but certain issues called for immediate resolution, and the subsequent discussion could not fail to be shaped by the dominant Kosygin themes. Thus, the managerial economics of the Liberman school received a strong endorsement, while the models of "perfect computation" were tabled. Profit, not cybernetics, became the leitmotif of the Party.[27]

---

[26] It should be noted that the profitability indicator for the Bolshevichka-Mayak test was defined as the ratio of profit to the cost of production, that is, the traditional Soviet usage in this regard. On the other hand, profitability as applied to the Kosygin reforms was defined as profits divided by total investment, inclusive of fixed and working capital. The difference has an important bearing on the incentive to economize capital. Cf. Imogene Erro, "Economic Reform in the Soviet Consumer Industry," in Joint Economic Committee, U.S. Congress, *New Directions In the Soviet Economy*, Part II-B, Washington, D.C., 1966, p. 558.

[27] This basic policy decision did not reflect a rebirth of the old mathematics stigma of the Stalin period but rather represented a consensus that the so-called push-button economy was not practicable, a view shared, it may be noted, by most of the nation's leading mathematical economists.

Remarkable though it was for its fresh initiatives, Kosygin's prescriptions for reform nevertheless suffered a number of perplexing ambiguities, with essential elements in apparent conflict. On the one hand, the centre was to be strengthened by the recreation of the economic ministries; on the other, the enterprises were accorded—on paper, at least—considerably widened authority. Here, as well as in other areas, much remained to be spelled out. The revision of prices was billed as a critical item on the agenda of reform, but the specific principle of price formation was left open, or at any rate was not then disclosed.

For these reasons, in the aftermath of Kosygin's speech, it was difficult to gauge precisely its major thrust. Nor is the interpretative problem much easier today, increased knowledge of the specifics of the programme notwithstanding. It is evident that the Soviet leaders themselves do not yet see clearly the systemic implications of the reforms they have launched. Hence, they contrive to keep a number of options open as they pragmatically explore the terrain. The result is a continuing ambiguity as to the dominant vector of change. The pressures for change are, however, not so difficult to spot. Reforms usually have their origins in trouble, and the present organizational flux in the Soviet Union is no exception. Though the problems eliciting reform are numerous and varied, they tend to have common expression in the lagging growth rate of the economy. At the recent Party Congress, N. Baybakov, the Head of Gosplan (State Planning Commission), reported that the average annual growth rate of the national product had declined to a level of 6 per cent during most of the period 1961–1965, as compared with 8.2 per cent in the preceding five years.[28] This was so despite the maintenance of high and stable rates of investment. The most conspicuously lagging sector was agriculture, which, though it received considerable attention, remained virtually stagnant throughout the Seven-Year Plan (1959–1965).

The decelerating growth curve is not traceable to a single cause, but several basic retarding influences can be distinguished, each of which has a significant bearing on the Kosygin reforms. First, the traditional Soviet allocational pattern has been disrupted, partly by international factors, so that growth-producing activities are no longer given exclusive attention. Though in most years the investment rate has remained high, the competing demands of consumption and defence have prevented an increase in the rate of capital formation as an offset to its greatly diminshed yield.[29]

---

[28] Quoted in Joint Economic Committee, U.S. Congress, *New Directions in the Soviet Economy*, Part I, Washington, D.C., 1966, p. ix.

[29] The marginal efficiency of capital has been approximately halved in the past decade.

Second, the old techniques of planning and supply are no longer effective owing to the vast increase in the size and complexity of the economy. The product assortment has become more variegated and of higher quality, and demand—at least in the expanding consumer goods sector—has become less predictable. Machine technology today is more pervasive than in earlier years, as well as more complex in terms of design, construction, and upkeep. Likewise, the interdependence of production activities in general has greatly increased, with consequent added burdens for planning. The extensive feedback and chain reactions derived from these technological linkages render an already bottleneck-prone system still more vulnerable. Moreover, the knowledge and communications needs of the economy have outstripped its present data-generating capacities and transmission speeds. Paradoxically, the system appears to have a super-abundance of information, but too often it is not of the right kind, or else it is not placed in the hands of the right users at the right time. Thus, the economy often lacks crucial signals amid the general deluge of reports.

Third, by the testimony of Soviet economists themselves, the failure of incentives, together with associated bureaucratic inertia, constitutes a serious brake to economic progress. Such sluggishness is perhaps most alarming because of the diminished innovational propensity that accompanies it. The level of incentives has not only proved increasingly inadequate, but their directional pull has all too frequently been perverse. This is the celebrated problem of the malfunctioning "success indicators." The general, though belated, conclusion reached by Soviet leaders is that the interests of the state and the individual must be unified. "What is good for the state must also be good for the enterprise and its personnel." This slogan has become the contemporary Soviet equivalent for the late Charlie Wilson's assertion: "What's good for General Motors is good for the country." The breakdown of incentives has not only adversely affected management. Soviet reports also indicate that the inadequate system of rewards for workers has likewise slowed advances in productivity. In brief, under the pre-reform system, the connection between wage payments to workers and overall production achievements had become harmfully wide.

Fourth, there is some justification for singling out Khrushchev for special blame. True, he made a number of positive economic contributions, notably in the early years, but his subsequent bureaucratic improvisations created a jungle of overlapped and conflicting jurisdictions. At the end, sheer administrative mess stood in the way of his overriding goal of rapid growth. Thus, his most visible legacy to his successors was a substantial job of cleaning up. The question of reform, however, involves much more than simply tidying up. In essence, it reduces to the discovery of a greatly improved, if not optimum, mix of centralized and decentralized decision-making. The Soviets themselves see the problem in these terms. What is sought is a more effective harnessing of local knowledge and initiative to the basic tasks prescribed by the centre. These, in turn, must be more consistently and, in other senses, better formulated than before.

It may be noted that the search for the optimum degree of centralism is not peculiar to the present leadership. Stalin was continuously absorbed in this effort, though the pendulum in his day was never permitted to swing very far in the direction of dispersed authority. Notwithstanding wider amplitude, the swings of the pendulum increased in frequency under Khrushchev. First, he tried to escape the stultifying evils of central management by various decentralizing measures—for example, the creation of the sovnarkhozes—only to encounter another evil, which was worse from his standpoint, namely, lack of coordination and violation of state interests. These twin results of his non-market method of extending some decision-making responsibility to the periphery inevitably prompted recentralization.

The new element in the present situation derives from the altered role of economics and the corresponding vision of this role. Brezhnev and Kosygin plainly appreciate the need to render the Soviet economic process more efficient, a circumstance that accounts for their genuine reformist zeal, but they also appreciate, though perhaps only dimly as yet, the decentralist logic of economic efficiency. The threat that this poses to the continued exercise of their vast and arbitrary power evidently makes them hesitate and induces the familiar zigzag approach. Their apparent dilemma is that the political conditions for the optimum degree of centralism depart significantly, and, I think, increasingly, from the optimum defined by economics. On the other hand, this is not to imply that only polar models can be effective. Whether the Soviets can come up with a viable distribution of central and peripheral power, within an overall authoritarian framework, however, remains to be seen. Nevertheless, it would be premature to exclude this possibility before the Kosygin reforms have run their course. The Soviet leaders and many economists, too, insist that they have the solution in sight. Meanwhile a unity of "plan" and "market"—incipient, if not yet actual—is proclaimed on all sides.

Kosygin's voluminous reform proposals[30] comprise what he calls "an entity," though they may perhaps best be understood in terms of a twofold division, which he, incidentally, also observes. The first category consists

---

[30] The text in one translation runs to 25 large pages. Cf., *Problems of Communism*, Washington, D.C., October, 1965, No. 6, pp. 3–28.

of his recommendations for improving planning and increasing local initiative; the second relates to questions regarding proper administrative structure at all levels. The key idea put forward for rationalizing national economic planning emphasizes the content of the plans rather than the technique of their formulation. According to Kosygin, central planning should concentrate on macro-economic goals and policies, divesting itself of the crippling burden of detailed physical targeting. From now on, the planners should direct their attention to the achievement of high growth rates and the maintenance of correct basic proportions. Thus, the investment plan is moved to the forefront and the long-term planning function enhanced. Similarly highlighted is the planning of technical advance.

In this context, it is interesting to note several criticisms specifically aimed at Khrushchev, and some implicitly at Stalin as well. Kosygin contends that long-range national targets have borne little relation to the prospective plans of enterprises. Moreover, the target figures for the Seven-Year Plan were not even broken down into annual goals, a circumstance that tended further to reduce their impact. Though Khrushchev allegedly neglected long-term planning, he nonetheless stretched out the planning horizon. In place of the traditional five-year plans, he went to the seven-year period, and just before his removal, he was looking towards a ten-year planning interval. Plainly, Kosygin did not like this. Instead, he proposed to establish or resestablish the five-year plan as the basic form, with the important proviso that annual assignments be made so as to dovetail with and facilitate long-term contracting at the enterprise level.

Khrushchev's sin of voluntarism in planning also served to generate numerous disproportions, geographic as well as sectoral. Though he can scarcely be charged with neglect of agriculture, his bungling assertedly contributed to a dangerous lag in this important sphere. For this and other reasons, too great a disparity obtained in the growth rates of producer and consumer goods. By calling for a relative as well as an absolute rise in the volume of consumption, Kosygin appeared, in his speech, to reverse the time-honored priority of heavy industry, a point to which I shall return. Kosygin's emphasis on the relief of planners from minute programming of production and supply had the obverse effect of freeing enterprises from the deleterious influence of petty tutelage. One gains the impression that the partial escape of enterprise management from the detailed web of central commands is expected to confer the greatest benefits of all the interrelated reforms. In any case, it is precisely here that reconciliation of the simultaneous centralizing and decentralizing moves is supposed to occur. On the one hand, the central planning function is to emerge stronger by reason of its new uncluttered focus and closer accord with reality. No longer, for example, will the centre issue detailed orders on where to plant a particular grade of corn, or how and where to cast small bolts. Rather, the broad issues of the economic structure—such matters as level and distribution of income and securing the best developmental pace—are to be central preoccupations. Of course, direct commands are not to be dispensed with, but there is to be increasing reliance on a variety of new and rejuvenated financial levers. Among these are to be such potent instruments as central fixing of prices, setting of norms for payments on fixed capital and for deductions from profits, not to mention wage policy guidelines and the determination of wage structure. In addition, the crucial programming of capital investment (or the lion's share of it) and the planning of new production units are to continue as the special province of the centre.

At the same time, on their side, enterprises are meant to enjoy greater independence in the selection of both inputs and outputs. Managers, properly guided by prices and sufficiently encouraged to economize by profit-sharing incentives, will be induced to act more effectively in implementing the centre's basic aims. Or so, at least, the theory goes. As one Soviet economist puts it: "A plan that is not based on a market is as powerless against disproportions as is a market that is not organized by a plan."[31]

Mention has been made of the somewhat surprising omission from the reform agenda of proposals on planning techniques. Only a few years ago these topics were at the centre of attention. At that time, input-output and related programming methods were hopefully looked to, to rescue a clogged and creaking hand-operated plan, but a variety of technical and other problems slowed the harnessing of the electronic computer to the tasks of planning. This application was not ruled out by Kosygin, but for the time being the emphasis of the reforms was placed elsewhere. The whole subject of planning methodology was accorded only a paragraph in his speech, in which he called for "a more profound and thorough elaboration of national economic balances."[32] Doubtless, Kosygin will need these, as well as a huge expansion of computers to process them, the switch to macro-planning notwithstanding.

Perhaps the key element of the reforms, as I have said, was the creation of a new environment for enterprise activity. Basic to this approach was the reduction of centrally set indicators from about thirty or more to the following nine items: (1) volume of goods to be sold; (2) main assortment of goods; (3) size of the wage fund; (4) level of profits and profitability;

---

[31] *Izvestia*, February 27, 1966, p. 2.
[32] *Pravda*, September 28, 1965.

(5) payments, from profits, into the state budget; (6) allocations from the budget; (7) volume of centralized capital investment and commissioning of production capacities and fixed assets; (8) main targets for introducing new technology; and (9) indices for supplying materials and equipment. All other economic indices and related decisions were to be left to the enterprises. Among the norms that they could now fix for themselves were labour productivity, cost reduction, and gross and commodity output. Accounting standards for all indicators, however, were to continue to be set by the state. The merit of the changes lay not simply in the lessening of harmful interference, but equally in the nature and role of the retained indicators. In particular, the discarding of the old gross output measure of success and its replacement by sales or profits tests promised greatly to improve enterprise efficiency and the quality of goods turned out. Thus, if expectations were realized, the Humpty-Dumpty world of positively-sloped demand curves in the state enterprise sector would disappear.

Another reform instrument for promoting enterprise economy was the placing of an interest charge on fixed and working capital. The rate, while varying, was, apparently, to average about six per cent, or approximately one quarter of the expected profits. The serious decline in the productivity of capital was to be countered, additionally, through the mechanism of incentive payments. Under the new system, profitability no longer was to be calculated with respect to operating costs, but rather in accordance with Western practice, as Liberman had advocated—that is, as the ratio of profits to fixed and working capital. In terms of the rationale of the reform, enterprises, in striving for incentive pay, would be led to improve both the numerator and the denominator of the profitability ratio. To the extent that capital could be husbanded and employed in an optimum way, the profitability ratio and incentive funds would be enhanced.

The specific incentive arrangement provided for by the reforms was somewhat complicated, but the essential points can be put fairly succinctly. The first claims on the incomes of enterprises after meeting production costs were to be profits deductions for the budget, or the so-called payments for funds, and interest payments, if any, on bank loans. Residual income was to be channelled, then, into three funds—namely, the production development fund, the material incentive fund, and a fund for social and cultural undertakings and housing construction. Though the nomenclature of the several funds is reasonably self-explanatory, a word or two may help to clarify their purposes. The first fund, that for production development, was to enable a certain amount of decentralized investment, the sources of which were to include not only a share of profits, as indicated above, but also a portion of the accumulated depreciation allowance and any proceeds from the sale of excess equipment. The explicit aim was to spur local innovation in modernization projects, where the costs, at any rate, were not too high.

The material incentive fund, as the name implies, was set up to reward deserving employees in a successful enterprise. The fund was designed to be fed by profits in such a way that the share for overfulfillment of the profits or sales plan would be less than the rate paid for the fulfillment of the indices specified in the plan. By this device, it was hoped that enterprises would be dissuaded from their usual practice of concealing reserves at the time of plan formulation in the interests of soft targets. Rather, the reduced rates for profit-sharing on above-plan performance were counted on to induce firms to seek high, though realistic, plan targets at the outset. This particular element in the reform derives from the original Liberman scheme, which sought to unify state and enterprise interests in high production goals, always, on the premise, of marketability.

The stake of the enterprise in the design of realistic plans was further augmented by the operation of the social and housing incentive fund. This fund was intended to supplement centrally allocated resources for housing and the communal economy—the building of rest homes, for example—and for other socio-cultural needs. The potential pull of such a fund, given adequate levels, can be readily appreciated in view of the proverbial scarcity of Soviet housing space. This question of the intensity of the pull, which is determined by the total volume as well as the enterprise share of profits, is, of course, crucial to the effectiveness of each of the newly established incentive funds. Further, it is this prerequisite of adequate profitability that makes the upward revision of prices, primarily for producer goods, an integral part of the reform programme. Probably more than any other consideration, the immensities of the task of price-changing dictated the gradualness of the transition to the new system.

Last on our list, but near the top in importance, was the new power granted to enterprises in respect of labour. Within the limits of the wage fund, still centrally prescribed, management was to be given the opportunity to determine the size of its labour complement, its composition, and also, to a degree, rates of remuneration.[33] With profits fixed as a prime objective, it was assumed that stimulation of labour efforts and reduction of surplus labour would follow. The government acknowledged that

---

[33] Before the reform, many economists had argued that the size of the wage fund and the disposition of it should be left to the discretion of the enterprises. Kosygin, while endorsing the principle, nevertheless, deferred this grant of power to the indefinite future.

specific unemployment might result from this tightening process (in fact, in a sense, that was the short-run aim), but the discharged, locally redundant workers, it was believed, could be quickly reabsorbed.

In order to get workers to produce more, under the new system management was accorded considerable leeway in the determination and distribution of bonuses. Rewards to workers were to depend not only on their individual production performance at piecework or timework but also on their participation in a successful collective, brigade, shop, or other production unit. Moreover, even though an enterprise might fail to achieve its planned goals, workers in components of the enterprise fulfilling assigned tasks could also expect bonuses from the incentive fund. Thus, the state had to guarantee a certain portion of the planned incentive fund.[34]

As noted previously, improvement of the organizational apparatus of the economy comprised the second major division of the Kosygin reform package. The change in this connection that has been most publicized, and probably deservedly so, is the replacement of Khrushchev's territorial principle of administration by the old branch principle. The regional councils, with their localist propensities, did not, it was contended, sufficiently concentrate and centralize the forces for industrial management. Despite the related perils of departmentalism, ministerial organization, suitably rehabilitated, was to be preferred. The explicit centralist language of the reform, in bald contradiction to the tenets of enterprise autonomy, reads: "The ministries will plan and control production." It is further explained that they will deal with the issues of technical policy, material and technical supply, financing, labour and wages.[35] In addition, branch research institutions will be subordinated to them. The centralist theme also predominated in the proposed new structure of the ministries. Some nine all-union ministries were to be set up as well as eleven of the union-republic variety. Additional ministries were to be left to the republics to form, provided their activities were purely local in nature.

Earmarked for discard, along with the regional councils, were two other Khrushchev brainchildren, the USSR Supreme Economic Council and the USSR Economic Council, but central administrators were hardly to lack for jobs under the new regime. Retained on a reorganized basis were three powerful USSR State Committees: (1) the Committee on Science and Technology; (2) the Committee on Construction; and (3) the Committee

---

[34] Cf. E. Nash, "Labor Aspects of the Economic Reform in the Soviet Union," *Monthly Labor Review*, Washington, D.C., June, 1966, pp. 601–602.

[35] *Pravda*, September 28, 1965.

on Material and Equipment Supply. The fuzziness of the reforms in fixing the boundaries of power was nowhere more pronounced than in the new or revised central administrative agencies. Thus, for example, the State Committee on Material and Equipment Supply was charged with the realization of supply plans and interbranch cooperation. At the same time, enterprises were admonished to step up direct contracts with their customers as well as with the appropriate agencies of wholesale trade, bypassing, it would seem, the instructions of central supply. The direct contract, or direct link, approach was regarded as a successful feature of the trial run in 1965 of the 400 consumer goods enterprises. Improvements in quality and assortment and an associated reduction of inventories were among the most impressive benefits of closer customer relations.

Another organizational device, reputedly pre-tested with good results in recent years, was the establishment of the so-called associations. These were combinations of enterprises linked together financially to improve their cost accounting, their coordinative planning, and their basic division of labour. The spread of amalgamations was called for by Kosygin, although, in a sense, they served to dilute the emphasis of the reforms on the enterprise as the basic economic cell. During the first quarter of 1965, the number of these producer associations (or *firmy*, in Soviet parlance) passed 500, with an estimated payroll of one million workers.[36] If the new associations do not simply become transmission belts for central and ministerial directives, as is alleged to have happened in Poland, if, that is, they behave as commercial entities, their proliferation may prove to be a genuinely decentralizing step. The step, it should be clear, would be towards the decentralism of an oligopolistic structure, not a perfectly competitive one.

It will perhaps be helpful to provide a brief survey of the calendar of reform before undertaking to explore its implementation in somewhat greater detail. For this purpose, two questions will be asked: (1) How much of the economy has been transferred to the new system thus far (i.e., through the first quarter of 1967)? (2) What does the schedule look like from here on out? The revised administrative structure blueprinted by Kosygin in his Plenum speech took shape swiftly during the last months of 1965. By the new year the ministries were formed, and, ostensibly, were ready to discharge their considerable planning and supervisory tasks with

---

[36] In the opinion of Leon Smolinski, this horizontal merger movement represents "the first major organizational innovation on the enterprise level in thirty years." The innumerable dwarf shops and tiny enterprises constitute a major efficiency drag on the Soviet economy, which the larger-scale associations promise at least partially to alleviate. Cf. L. Smolinski, "The Soviet Economy in Search of A Pattern," *Survey*, London, April, 1966, pp. 88–101.

respect to both the old- and new-style enterprises.[37] As might be expected, however, a number of organizational and staffing gaps remained, not to mention overlaps with the old command agencies that lingered on the scene. Furthermore, no general statute governing ministry conduct and analogous to the new statute on enterprises was forthcoming, nor, apparently, was one "in the mill." In legal terms, it was simply presumed that any powers not explicitly granted enterprises by their statute belonged to the ministries.

Meanwhile, the preparation of specific plans for shifting industry to the new system was left to an *ad hoc* commission of representatives of seven high-level central agencies.[38] The first fruit of its labours came in the form of an announcement on January 1, 1966, that forty-three enterprises from seventeen different ministries were beginning operations under the reform arrangements for planning and material incentives. Of the pioneer group of enterprises, it is interesting to note, over three-quarters were from heavy industry, including twenty-two machine-building plants. Light industry and food processing contributed only ten. All told, about 300,000 workers were directly affected by the shift.[39] Each of the chosen enterprises had passed a stringent qualifying test based partly on its record of above-average profits and superior overall economic performance. Each enjoyed a steady market for its products and had skilled economic cadres at its disposal. Some also could claim further salutary experience with the direct links approach experimented with the year before. Among those selected, were twenty plants in Moscow and Moscow Province, plus some in Leningrad, Kharkhov, Gorky, and a few other cities.[40]

The nature of the selection evidenced the regime's strong desire for an auspicious introduction of the new measures. For this purpose, it was prepared to move slowly and to work with only sure-fire winners. Though this

---

[37] The reasons for junking the regional economic councils before the year was out are not apparent since the revisions in the year-end reports must have been greatly complicated thereby. Similarly, the immediate need to recouch the budget and plan data for the subsequent period must have entailed analogous difficulties and an altogether excessive amount of administrative confusion.

[38] Included were the State Planning Commission, the Ministry of Finance, the State Planning and Wages Committee, the State Bank, the State Construction Bank, the State Price Committee, and the Central Statistical Administration. Cf. *Current Digest of the Soviet Press*, New York, Vol. XVIII, No. 9, March 29, 1966, p. 24.

[39] *Pravda*, January 5, 1966, p. 2.

[40] A good review of the reform sequence is given in Keith Bush, *The Progress of the Industrial Reforms*, Radio Liberty Research Paper, No. 7, 1966. See, also, his "The Reforms: A Balance Sheet," *Problems of Communism*, July-August, 1967, pp. 30–41.

approach plainly had its propaganda uses and could serve to indicate the upper performance bounds of the programme, the general feasibility of the reforms and their macro-economic impact could scarcely be illumined by the initial biased sample. Undoubtedly, Khrushchev, had he determined on such a programme, would have taken a much larger first stride, but the contrasting mark of his successors, who were at least equally receptive to change, was still on the side of cautious and deliberate speed.

The second quarter of 1966 witnessed the transfer of another 200 enterprises, most of which had demonstrated impressive profit-making capabilties, and some of which were very large.[41] Thus, paradoxically, the rescue operation for the economy continued to focus on the very strongest elements. With these additions, the number of workers and employees in the new system approximated one million. Momentum picked up still more at the half-year point, when 430 enterprises were converted. Included in this new group were entire sub-branches of the food industry, such as tea and tobacco concerns, whose wholesale prices were judged to be suitable to support the programme without change. The cumulative total of workers now stood at two million. By the end of the year, one third of industry was scheduled to be operating on the new basis; however, in August, presumably as a result of growing pains, an interdepartmental commission under Gosplan recommended that no further individual enterprises be transferred in 1966. For the most part, the commission's recommendation was followed, with only a small number of enterprises— thirty-one, to be exact—being converted during the remaining months. This brought the total number of enterprises working under the new arrangements to 704 by the end of 1966. In economic weight they accounted for about 10 per cent of the industrial work force and something over 12 per cent of gross industrial production.[42]

During the early part of 1967, the first complete ministry was brought under the new system, and by the end of the first quarter of the year some 2500 enterprises were covered, accounting for as much as one-fifth of the nation's industrial output. Plans for the rest of the year remained somewhat tentative, but the original expectation of completing the entire changeover by January 1, 1968, seemed unlikely to be realized. From this time on, an enterprise's profit potential rather than a prior record of regular profits was to suffice to qualify it for inclusion in the new system. Thus,

---

[41] *Izvestia*, March 30, 1966, p. 2.

[42] Bush, *Problems of Communism, op. cit.*, p. 31. Besides the industrial enterprises, the government reported the conversion of 259 trucking firms, four sea and river fleets, six communications enterprises, and four civil aviation units in 1966.

the pace and sequence of the remaining transfers was to be closely geared to unfolding price revisions.

In turning now to the reform experience, the administration view is paraphrased first, and the reader is warned that it suffers from the usual defects of official optimism. However, the fact that the controlled press has been made to play an especially bouyant campaign tune has significance in itself, evidencing as it does the determination of the Soviet leaders to carry through the whole programme. The first measure of success to which enthusiastic officials point falls in the area of plan formulation. According to N. Drogichinsky, head of Gosplan's department for intro-ducing the new system, each of the converted firms sought to have its sales and profits targets raised above pre-reform levels. This contrasted sharply with the customary lobbying efforts of enterprises to secure soft goals to facilitate plan fulfillment and overfulfillment. The high rates of profit retention for the several incentive funds (between 60 and 90 per cent of "the additional profits"[43]) apparently proved to be effective lures for coaxing out the harder plans.

Performance reports for the first year, with only minor exceptions, evoked extravagant official praise. Much is made of the fact that for the group as a whole gross industrial production grew by 8.6 per cent as compared with the planned 6.7 per cent. According to Gosplan's Chairman, N. Baybakov, the reformed enterprises fulfilled their sales volume plan, an index subject to approval, by 103.3 per cent. In comparison with the preceding year, total sales of the affected group rose by more than 10 per cent, profits by a reported 25 per cent, and labour productivity by 8 per cent. For industry as a whole, the corresponding gain for profit over 1965 was 10 per cent, and for labour productivity 5 per cent. Returning to the reform group, the average wage (inclusive of bonuses from the material incentives fund) rose 4.8 per cent, as compared with an all-industry figure of 3.1 per cent. No figures are given for the number of people employed, an index that does not require central approval, but it is reported either to have decreased as compared with the plan or to have remained the same as for 1965.[44]

---

[43] The new system recognizes three categories of profits. The chief one is "planned profit," jointly formulated by the central government and the enterprise. The second category is "additional profits," in which the enterprises, having uncovered additional reserves, themselves assume higher plan goals. As indicated, a very high rate of profit retention is authorized for this category. Finally, there are "above-plan" profits, a high proportion of which flow to the state budget, the rationale for this being to encourage enterprises to assume higher commit-ments in advance. Bush, *op. cit.*, p. 35.

[44] See Bush, *op. cit.*, p. 35; N. Baybakov, *Pravda*, November 4, 1966, pp. 2–3; *Pravda*, January 29, 1967.

Though somewhat bewildering at first glance, this profusion of statistical claims is also very impressive. Nonetheless, there appear to be many pitfalls, enough to prompt a variety of interpretative reservations, some of which, I might add, have been entered by individual Soviet commentators themselves. Government officials doubtless are aware that some of these released indicators of success are inconclusive, if not downright misleading, but propaganda considerations normally prevail. An example of this is the reference to the overfulfillment of the output plan (and, similarly, the sales plan). Though this is not necessarily a "minus" result, it would have been preferable from the regime's standpoint and also that of the enterprises to have formulated more accurate targets. Furthermore, the net effect quite possibly may be negative, as the increasing emphasis on the overall smothness of production seems to suggest. That is, overfulfillments inevitably occasion departures from scheduled allocations, and the upsets in the weak supply system may ramify.

Secondly, it should be noted that the profit comparisons are a bit ambiguous and, in any case, too fragmentary for the drawing of firm conclusions. Under the new arrangements, the profits account includes items previously treated as costs, among them the interest on bank loans and the so-called "white-collar" bonuses to managers and technical and office personnel. Whether Soviet statisticians have made the necessary adjustments for comparability is not revealed, but it seems unlikely.

The Soviet Academician, N. Federenko, has been especially critical of the paucity of statistics released on profits, as well as on other key indicators. With respect to the 25 per cent gain in profits over 1965, he argues: "...we ought to know how their profit rose in 1965 as compared with the preceding year, and in 1965 as against 1963—i.e., the dynamics of the main plan indicators over a number of years, taking into account the changes in assortment, prices and so on. Such an analysis could show the efficacy of the measures that have been carried out." But, Federenko concludes: "It cannot be made because the necessary data are lacking."[45]

Official comparisons of the performance of the reform enterprises with that of the total economy also tend to inflate the index of success. For example, announced labour productivity, though interesting, is not very relevant as a test of success. It is enough to recall that the reform enterprises were chosen for their special economic merits, which is to say that they exceeded national productivity (and profits) averages both before the reforms and after. Sound interpretation requires, among other things, the more extended time series study that Fedorenko is seeking.

---

[45] N. Fedorenko, "The Reform in Industry: Initial Results and Problems of Increasing Its Efficacy," *Planovoe Khozyaystvo*, April, 1967, pp. 5–17.

Evaluations are frustrated in some degree by still another problem of comparability. Reference here is to the cited superiority of the reform group over the total economy in the growth of average wages. Not only do the general strictures of the foregoing paragraphs hold true for this type of comparison, but in this instance even the specific numbers may have been ill-chosen. If the reported 3.1 per cent increase in average wages for industry as a whole does not include incentive supplements, as may be the case, then the corresponding figure for the reform group becomes 2.8 per cent rather than 4.8 per cent, which counts the bonus increment, too.

The techniques of comparison, discussed thus far, have supported, if not engendered, the rosy official view of the reform's immediate success. It should be noted, however, that there are some factors working in the other direction. Most of these difficulties derive from the appeal to the plan as a standard of evaluation, a problem endemic to the Soviet system. To be concrete, if it is granted that the reform enterprises acquire relatively hard goals whereas the old firms cagily manage soft ones, then comparisons of their degrees of overfulfillment are muddied. In general, more mileage can be got from other frames of reference than the fuzzy criterion of the plan. "It was demonstrated long ago," Federenko asserts, "that the main thing is not plan overfulfillment, but the actual contribution an enterprise makes to the national economy."[46] One might add, however, that this fact has been lost on Soviet statisticians.

It might be supposed from the concentration of this study on the reform group, the elite few, that no organizational progress has been made by the so-called old enterprises. This would be wrong, of course, for many experiments and improvements have been wrought outside the reform sector proper. For example, changes in success indicators, away from gross production, institution of new credit practices, new payment procedures designed to speed the completion of construction projects, new mergers—these and many other salutary developments were being pursued pending transfer to the full Kosygin reform structure. Indeed, for the experimental consumer goods firms, on the direct-links approach, a straight conversion to the Kosygin formula could be construed as a backward step.

The non-statistical indicators of the reform's success, which abound in Soviet sources, are often more impressive testimonials, though not any easier to handle, than the bare statistics. Each reform enterprise has its success story to tell, fragments of which are recorded in the Soviet press. In any frequency distribution, the following claimed improvements would probably rank near the top: (1) quality is now a major concern of

---

[46] *Ibid.*

management and workers alike; (2) for related reasons of incentive, acceleration of shipments and sales is emphasized; (3) rhythmical production is increasingly replacing the Soviet "storming" habit; (4) cost consciousness is now the rule at all levels; and (5) hidden reserves, high goals, and additional profits are objects of constant search. Such are the qualitative generalizations of success. The roll call of concrete examples is endless.

Whatever the initial degree of success, the road of progress for the reforms, the Soviet literature makes amply plain, has been a rocky one. Though the problems confronting the reforms are refracted by the official lens to yield a brighter picture, they nonetheless have received considerable official attention. There is also a large, officially sanctioned, but not endorsed, grass-roots literature of complaints. These domestic criticisms, stemming from the academic community as well as from the economic participants themselves, are quite revealing, and it may be assumed that the government is an attentive, if not necessarily happy, listener.

Conceptually, it is useful to divide the reform problems into those that might be seen as transitional and those that might be identified as fundamental. The particular areas of transitional difficulties, on which attention is focussed first, are treated under five headings: personnel, statistics and accounting, norm determination, unemployment, and mixed system problems. This fivefold grouping, as with any other classification, reflects a certain internal overlap that will become apparent as we proceed. It should also be noted at the outset that some of these designations reappear, though in a different guise, in the category of so-called fundamental problems.

Personnel. The short-run personnel difficulties that have slowed and otherwise disturbed the progress of the reforms have typically involved an insufficiency of skilled cadres, or certain psychological impediments, or both. In brief, the reservoir of economically-minded managers and bureaucrats, who are amenable to, if not experienced, in the ways of the market, has been too thin to permit extensive, fully effective application of new techniques. The reform's emphasis on the use of economic, as opposed to administrative, levers has also placed the professional economist in acutely short supply. It can be argued that the small size of the pool of qualified executives will become a more severely limiting factor as the reform programme widens in scope, that, in fact, the problem will worsen rather than improve with time. And this, in a sense, is true. When, as is unavoidable, the second and third teams of managers undergo conversion (at first only the cream of the crop was involved), the problems of implementing and taking advantage of the potentials of the reform must surely mount. On the other hand, this need not imply a long-run situation of indefinite duration. Whether the main personnel difficulties can be resolved within a short-run span of, say, five years, will depend on a pervasive recasting of mental attitudes. For the provision of market experience and formal economic skills simply will not be self-sustaining without the proper psychological climate. Both the higher and the lower reaches of the command economy must be reoriented psychologically for the reforms to take root and survive.

What makes this task so formidable is the "chicken-and-the-egg" quality of the twin pre-requisites of success. Broad marked experience is needed to generate decision-making and innovatory skills; at the same time, the appropriate managerial psychology is needed at the outset in order to assure that the market experience is not malformed from birth. Something of this sort was accomplished in the creation of reliable executive cadres during the First Five-Year Plan, which likewise faced multi-faceted problems demanding simultaneous solution.

Today, the readying or retooling of the needed executive cadres, and the labour force at large can be construed as essentially a transitional task, but establishing the necessary moral climate is a much tougher proposition. Quite possibly, a longer thaw is needed or a swifter-running political upheaval. Not only must Soviet managers learn new and more venturesome ways, casting aside their ingrained pursuit of *"val,"* but bureaucrats and party activists must shed their lifelong habits of meddling. In this connection, it may be observed that the Party elections in 1966 offered scant grounds for optimism in the reform camp. According to Hough, the startling fact is "that they failed to give recognition to the men directly associated with the economic reforms or those who might be expected to gain importance as a consequence of those reforms."[47]

Statistics and Accounting. The Chief of the Statistical Administration, V. Starovsky, is on record to the effect that "the entire system of statistical indices must be brought into complete conformity with the new conditions occasioned by the profound reform."[48] It is widely recognized that statistical data must be rendered both more serviceable and less voluminous, but one of the paradoxes of the early reform period is that the statistical and reporting burdens of the new enterprises have actually increased. One new system director has estimated that the volume of economic processing (i.e., paper work) has doubled. "To collate what has been achieved and

---

[47] "None of the major advocates of the reform," Hough continues, "were included in the all-union bodies, and only one of the lesser advocates was named to a republican Party committee."

[48] *Pravda*, December 18, 1965, p. 2.

what is being planned with the results of previous operations," he says, "the old indices, have to be recalculated to bring them into line with the new ones."[49] Moreover, the problems are made more difficult by the shortage of qualified bookkeepers, not to mention economists, and the increasing complexity of their work.

However appalling these perverse-seeming results of the reform may be, the reasons are not hard to find, nor should the cures be especially difficult. The managerial comment quoted above simply testifies to the fact that the transitional economy is currently operating on two distinct bases. Thus, accounts still must be rendered according to both the old and the new categories for the calculation of macro-balances as well as for the diverse needs of comparability and other purposes. Obviously, most of this duplicative statistical load should abate, save for the less urgent purposes of historical studies, once the whole economy is converted to the new basis of operation.

Much the same thing applies to the tendency of the central administration to saddle the new enterprises with exceptionally large reports because of its day-to-day interest in the progress of the reforms during the first phase of operation. This extraordinary volume may be expected to subside once the reform system has shaken down and, as it were, proved itself, but it still must be admitted that there is a counter-tendency, perhaps common to bureaucracies everywhere, to proliferate reports or cling to superfluous routines. Presently, according to Starovsky, there is a lag in deleting report categories that are unnecessary for the working of either the old or the new systems.[50]

These mixed considerations are not susceptible of a precise balance, but one is left with the impression that the statistical picture should brighten somewhat in the near future. Discussion has already commenced on the possibility of replacing a large part of the detailed operational reports with periodic reports on substantial deviations from plans or on other special circumstances. Where, for example, an enterprise is unable to eliminate the consequences of some breakdown without the help of a superior agency, a report would be submitted. On their part, the central departments of the government might rely on spot inspections in place of the present costly continuous audit, at least as far as certain indicators are concerned.

---

[49] *Sovetskaya Rossiya*, August 3, 1966, as extracted in *Radio Liberty Dispatches*, dated August 29, 1966.

[50] *Pravda*, December 18, 1965, p. 2.

Were these anticipated economies in the collection of statistics to be realized, it is plain that Soviet information requirements would still greatly exceed the statistical minima of a true market economy. The Soviet government continues to emphasize to the reform enterprises that indices of gross output, labour productivity, number of workers, average wages, production costs, and certain other factors, though no longer planned from above, are nevertheless necessary for economic evaluation and must be maintained. As long as the plan is dominant and the bureacracy intact, the level of the sea of paper may not diminish appreciably.

Considerations of space preclude all but a bare mention here of "the information revolution" that the apostles of "Computopia"[51] are still pushing despite the Party's rejection of a computerized economy. On a more modest level of aspiration, the computer people do have government support. This extends to the long-range reassessment and revision of data flows keyed to regional and central computer centres. At a minimum, the standardized bits of information are meant to serve efficiently the needs of various input-output matrices that foreseeably will be in use whether or not the old command processes of physical targeting are actually abandoned. Heavy discussion of the computer centre network concept has not yet produced agreement on a single practicable model. Once this decision is made, it is apparent that a long while, perhaps ten years or more, will be required to progress from the drawing boards to a fully operational system.

Norm Determination. At the time of his speech, Kosygin left most of the details of the reform up in the air, or, more properly, delegated the concretizing tasks to various bodies, of which the ministries were probably the most important. The many norms that the centre had retained in its province had to be given a conceptual base on which the detailed calculations could then proceed. Fundamental questions regarding the level, uniformity, and flexibility of the norms had to be answered and the range of managerial discretion determined, if only later to be corrected by experience. Each ministry was charged with confirming its own norms under the new system, after first clearing each one with a labyrinth of agencies: the State Planning Commission, the State Labour and Wages Committee, the Ministry of Finance, the USSR State Bank, and the Central Council of Trade Unions.[52] It is hard to resist the inference that so many cooks may have spoiled the soup, or at least impossibly complicated its preparation.

---

[51] This apt term was coined, if I am not mistaken, by Professor Egon Neuberger. See his "Libermanism, Computopia and Visible Hand: The Question of Imformational Efficiency," *American Economic Review*, Evanston, Illinois, May, 1966, pp. 131–144.

[52] *Izvestia*, January 30, 1966, p. 2.

Two complaints that run through the early literature of reform are especially worth noting. The first asserts that the actual incentive payments have been too modest to exert much influence. Implicit is a criticism of the level of profits, or the norms of retention, perhaps both. Professor Birman has argued that bonuses should be greatly increased, not by any inflationary budget grants but rather through the proverbial search for new reserves. These, he insists, are exceptionally large and only need efficient management to tap them.[53]

The second objection usually made concerns the distribution of bonuses under the new system. A prime difficulty here has been the disparity of the incentive pull for managers and that for workers. In the case of managers, and other white-collar personnel, the income supplements, which derive from enterprise profits, have averaged one-third of the official base pay, a not inconsiderable amount. With workers, on the other hand, bonuses to date have formed a very small portion of their take-home pay, ranging from 4 to 7 per cent of annual wages. Obviously, the lure is scarcely sweet enough to call forth the zealous effort the press describes. Moreover, since only about half of the worker bonuses come out of profits and the rest from the wages fund, the collective stake in the profitability of the enterprise is further diluted. Another complaint concerning the distribution of premiums among workers is that the approximately egalitarian shares in a number of instances have dulled the incentive effect. The principle of bonus payments, it is argued, should be one of differential rewards according to contributions made.

It would be a mistake to suppose that these and similar problems are exclusively transitional, that bureaucratic trial and error will suffice to establish correct, or at least good, norms in a fairly short time. Doubtless, this will prove to be so in many instances, but it is also true that the fate of some norms is inextricably bound up with basic issues that may defy immediate resolution. Suppose, for example, that the level of incentives is thought to be too weak. Presumably, it is real income, not money wages, that counts here, and so the norming answer hinges on the politically acceptable aggregate rate of real consumption. Given the rate of growth of the national product, will defence, and investment, and perhaps other priorities permit the desired upgrading of consumer income? It is interesting to note that though Kosygin called for an expanded relative volume of consumption, the directives of the Five-Year Plan provide only for an absolute rise of consumer goods production. Of course, the projected absolute increment may be "eneough" for incentive purposes, but the

---

[53] *Pravda*, March 9, 1966, p. 3.

long delay in the issuance of the final Five-Year Plan gives rise to the speculation that some important new controversies actually have arisen over the distribution of GNP (gross national product). In view of recent record harvests, however, I would be surprised, if the economy's real income targets were not scaled upwards to implement a deeper and wider incentive system.

Before turning to the next topic, mention may be made of another norm that has great conceptual significance but that to date has had little practical import. I refer to the interest rates that the new system has imposed on fixed and working capital as a spur to economizing this scarce resource. Rates have apparently varied in the range of 3 to 8 per cent, with a modal rate of about 6 per cent. All appear to be well below the level of equilibrium implicit in Soviet conditions, exerting only a mild influence on cost calculations. Expressed as a fraction of enterprise payments to the central budget, interest at times amounts to as low as three per cent of the of the total and seldom exceeds 25 per cent. In the words of the Soviet economist, Nikitin: "The payment on capital is essentially pushed into the background."[54]

Unemployment. It has been argued that the most far-reaching feature of the Kosygin reforms is the new power accorded managers to hire and fire employees, within the overall limits of the centrally determined wage fund. At the same time, executives at various levels of industrial administration have recognized from the inception of the reforms that the induced economizing of labour would create problems. It was concluded that better organizations would have to be provided to facilitate transfers of workers between enterprises and also between geographic regions. The general tenor of thought, however, continued to deny the possibility of a national unemployment problem.

Reports of drastic layoffs by individual reform enterprises have been common, but thus far no aggregative statistics have been released on the volume of dismissals during the first eighteen months of the programme. Official figures indicating a more rapid rise in gross output than in labour productivity during the first year, however, have been released. Hence, for that period, it would seem to follow that the new system of enterprises added more personnel than they layed off. This unexpected result may reflect still another case of offsetting pulls in the reform arrangements. On the one hand, the self-interest of the enterprise in greater profits suggests a general concern with cost economies, and more particularly, with labour

---

[54] T. Frankel, "Soviet Reforms: A Tentative Appraisal," *Problems of Communism*, May-June, 1967, p. 40.

economies. On the other hand, the linking of the material incentives fund and the socio-cultural and housing fund with the total number of workers—namely, via wage disbursements—serves to pull management in the opposite direction, towards the augmentation of payrolls.

Mixed System Problems. Only a few of the multiplicity of problems engendered by the "mixedness" of the present system shall be mentioned. Perhaps the most conspicuous transitional difficulty derives from the linkage, through sales, of old and new enterprises. Complaints are numerous, not only about the delays in deliveries that the double system so often involves, but also about the late settlement of accounts that results and the discrimination against the new enterprises that obtains in penalties for contract violations. For example, if a plant operating on the new system fails to fulfill its programme through the fault of the supplier operating under the old system, it suffers by far the greater material damage of the two. Moreover, redress has not been forthcoming through the traditional channels for arbitration. This has led some managers under the new system to call for the establishment of centres from the city to the republican level to study and communicate the practical experience gained in implementing the economic reform.[55]

Many of the new enterprises have been thwarted in their attempts to develop direct links, as encouraged by the reforms, because suppliers have still had their own output assortments rigidly fixed from above, or as is quite common, because the old trade organizations pre-empted the sales decisions to maximize their own outputs and bonuses. Two Soviet authors recently objected that the wholesale and supernumerary depots of the Ministry of Trade were "the main obstacle to the further improvement and development of direct contacts."[56] Wholesale depots, allegedly, do not like direct contacts, because these tend to reduce their own trade turnover, with the result that their personnel and profits diminish.

The trouble, of course, may go deeper. Kosygin, while giving lip service to the idea of establishing contractual relations between enterprises directly rather than through the ministries, nevertheless saw fit to create several very powerful central agencies whose weight is thrown in just the opposite direction. They are the State Committee for Technical and Material Supplies, headed by the influential V. Dymshits, and the Chief Directorates of Supply and Marketing. By their very existence, these central bodies have discouraged enterprises from freely participating in and shaping wholesale trade.

---

[55] *Radio Liberty Dispatches*, August 29, 1966, p. 2.
[56] *Ekonomicheskaya gazeta*, No. 32, August, 1966, p. 28.

Interference by the industrial ministries has had substantially the same effects in frustrating enterprise initiative as the aforementioned supply and trade conflicts. In reestablishing the ministries, the Kosygin reforms accorded them great powers, or at least allowed them to be assumed, even though duplicative of the new enterprise authority. Meanwhile, the ministries have been having a field day, it appears, "doing what comes naturally," namely, appropriating supervisory responsibilities and indulging in the practice of "petty tutelage," which had been so roundly condemned.[57] The upshot has been a heightening tension between the new enterprises and the bureaucrats in the ministries.

Greatly perterbed by these developments, Liberman called earnestly in the spring of 1966 for a "Brain Trust" to protect enterprises against the old ways of central agencies. "Such a body," he wrote, "should be empowered to repeal decisions that prevent the enterprise from effecting reorganization."[58] Since an enterprise cannot argue effectively with its superiors, even when it is right, it must receive economic and legal guarantees of its independence. An inter-agency arbiter was created some months after Liberman's recommendation, but its early performance has evoked mixed reactions. In part, it seems simply to have slowed up decisions without affording the necessary shield for enterprise that Liberman envisioned.

In a similar vein, Birman has called for a Statute on Ministries setting forth their rights and duties consistent with the October 1965 Statute on Enterprises.[59] The latter leaves much to be desired from the standpoint of effective enterprise autonomy, but at least some safeguards for the enterprise powers already granted would be welcome. Birman's emphasis on legal forms may seem a bit surprising when one remembers the cynical disregard for the Model Collective Farm Charter and the sham democracy of the Great Stalin Constitution, but times have fortunately changed somewhat. Thus, while charters are as yet no firm guarantee against arbitrary usurpation and exercise of power, they may be genuinely helpful mobilizing instruments.

Nevertheless, Birman is not content to stop here in his effort to win and preserve enterprise independence. It is his idea that the higher ad-

---

[57] The Soviet press bulges with complaints about the power-happy ministries. One reform enterprise, for example, had its plan changed sixteen times in nine months by the "parent" ministry. A number of ministries have continued to specify reductions in administrative outlays and personnel, contrary to the statute on enterprise rights, etc. Cf. *Literaturnaya gazeta*, February 1, 1967, p. 10.

[58] *Komsomolskaya pravda*, April 24, 1966.

[59] *Pravda*, March 9, 1966, pp. 3, 4.

ministrative and planning agencies should be made financially responsible for the losses that their own mistakes impose on the enterprises under them. He does not reckon sufficiently, however, with the possible inhibition of valid central action that his punitive apparatus might cause. He simply states: "Whenever an assignment is not backed up materially, whenever an index set for an enterprise is not based on solid economic calculations . . ., the assignment or index should be cancelled on principle, and then those responsible should be punished."[60] Perhaps a better method would be to extend the controls of *khozraschet* much further up the administrative ladder.

It should not be inferred from Birman's defence of enterprise that he wishes to coddle it. Quite the contrary. His views are symmetrical and consistent, though as yet largely unheeded. Where, on the one hand, he would make higher bodies responsible for losses imposed on the lower, on the other, he would confront enterprise with only two paths: "Work well or close down." To bail out poor performers indefinitely, as both the old and new systems actually do, is the farthest thing from his purpose. Superior agency responsibility is one thing, subsidies another. The former must be installed, Birman contends, and the latter must go. Otherwise, the profits rationale and drive for efficiency will be thwarted.[61]

It turns out, thus, that Liberman and Birman are after considerably more than the protection of the present legal rights of enterprise, though this in a sense becomes the first step. Each sees the ultimate success of the Kosygin reforms as depending on the progressive expansion of enterprise independence and rights. They attach perhaps the greatest significance to the strengthening of direct contractual links and the complete restructuring of supply through a reorganized wholesale trade system. The notorious central rationing basis for supplying materials and equipment, now still very much intact, in their view, must go. Here they are at one with the late Academician Nemchinov, who in his last years hammered on the theme that planned orders must give way to orders for goods placed with the enterprises, else the independence of the latter becomes illusory. Except for some high-level nods in this direction, centralized supply shows little signs of departure.

In other respects, too, the amount of central interference in the work of enterprises is much too great for the effective discharge of cardinal tasks at either level. Restriction on the enterprise of its use of wage funds constitutes an example. Liberman, among others, has urged that this control

---

[60] *Ibid.*
[61] *Literaturnaya gazeta*, No. 2, January 1, 1967, p. 10.

be moderated and soon abandoned. So, also, with the number of executive posts filled by the Party, the so-called nomenclature positions. Frequently, to cite one further case of unwarranted interference, enterprises today receive their normative working capital, as called for under the new system, but they also have specified for them the detailed distribution of such funds, which runs distinctly counter to reform precepts. Moreover, as Birman laments, financial agencies consider deviations from any normative allocation a violation, and lacking a reliable arbitration service, the enterprise is once more caught in the middle.

Even if the rules of enterprise conduct were to be considerably relaxed beyond the present provisions on paper, and further still beyond the actuality, and even if the managers were really permitted to play the profits game unimpeded, it would remain true that the ruble indicators to which enterprises respond and in terms of which their success is measured are still economically distorting. This was unquestionably so in the case of the pre-reform price structure, and now that we have had a glimpse of the revisions, it appears that most of the basic difficulties persist. The pricing formula, recently approved at long last, provides for selective price increases to bring prices more in line with the costs of production and to put all enterprises, or nearly all, on a profitable basis. The main aim of the Kosygin reforms, the government apparently believes, is satisfied by these revisions, that is, by having made the broad run of enterprises, particularly in the producer goods area, accessible to the operation of the profits system.

It is impossible to square this sanguine view of the adequacy of the reform prices with the failure to adopt equilibrium pricing. Though not without their advocates, equilibrium prices are not even remotely in prospect. Even the potential benefits from the new capital charge may be largely missed by reason of their low level, as well as owing to the government's decision to follow the old ways of sectoral differentiation. In underscoring the primacy of the central government—for it, not the market, will determine all but a handful of prices—the basic decision on prices points up the boundaries presently set for decentralization. "We cannot," says the Chairman of the State Price Committee, V. Sitnin, "go in for free price formation."[62] This far and no farther, he is saying; but the trouble with poor prices, not to say centrally fixed prices, is that they induce, where money is active, broad recentralizing forces because of the havoc they wreak. Thus, the area of decentralized choice is not frozen as of the establishment of the revised prices but may be expected to shrink in size.

---

[62] *Economist*, London, October 8, 1966, p. 148.

For all its deficiencies, the new price administration need not spell the end of the new economic stimulation. As a matter of fact, it may strengthen profits and profit-tied incentives, as its architects contend. The real casualty is scarcity pricing. In the absence of a valid signalling system, the prospects for improved resource use are greatly dimmed. In short, it will not help managers much to push Party controllers aside when it comes to economic questions, as the reforms bid them do, if they themselves will as a result be deprived of accurate economic moorings. The reform fillip to intensified effort is fine, but it is simply not enough to solve the problem of economic efficiency, as the Soviets by now should have learned. Meanwhile, it may be asked, whatever became of the reform's aim to relieve the centre from its self-inflicted snare of detailed management and to loosen the enterprise straight-jacket? Is it not deeply contradictory to declare the reformed centre's chief concerns to be macro and then to make it responsible for fixing and continuously updating virtually every price in the land?

The meaning of the Kosygin reforms, which have had so short a life, cannot be understood save with reference to their anticipated future course. Hopefully, the meagre windows that this study has opened on the past will facilitate this speculation, but the conclusions should nevertheless be skeptically regarded. If evaluations prove irreststible, as in the present case, the least that can be done is to emphasize their tentativeness. Attention will be directed first to the short-run period of 1965–1970, and second, if briefly, to the short-term influences.

One of the pitfalls in this admittedly premature assessment is that the reform enterprises have had so little experience—at most, only eighteen months—in operating under the new conditions. This, as Federenko notes, is a very short period "if account is taken of the length of time required for the cycle of technological improvement, for deepening the specialization, concentration, and integration of production, and for training personnel to work in the new way."[63] The effect of the measures being carried out, he concludes, will only be fully felt after four or five years. This much time, and more, he believes will be required for eliminating bottlenecks in the economy, in particular, for eliminating shortcomings in material and technical supply. In terms of these factors, one might expect, therefore, that the reforms will begin to harvest some of their most significant dividends around 1970, at the close of the present Five-Year Plan.

The benefits of the learning process—for instance, in the improvement of key norms—should likewise provide a cumulative boost, at least for

---

[63] Fedorenko, *op. cit.*, pp. 5–6.

several years. In addition, once the conversion has been completed, the cross-pulling and the confusion between the old and the new ways should be substantially lessened. It is also true, however, that some of the early sources of gain will have spent themselves in a few years time. This suggests that the oppositely directioned influences may approximately net a fairly smooth performance rating. According to Fedorenko:

> The initial period of reform is a period of mobilization of the most apparent and most easily discovered potentialities: a reduction of the stocks of raw materials and supplies to the necessary levels; sale of stocks of above-norm finished goods; sale of superfluous assets; and proper organization of production. These measures yield a big return and improve the results of an enterprise's activity, but such potentialities are limited.[64]

If these significant, "one-shot" gains are not fully or sufficiently replaced by dependable, long-term yields, then the fate of the reforms would appear to be retrogression, or alternatively, another injection of change. It may be asked: "How long is the transition?" As previously noted, the administration's plans call for the whole of industry to be working according to the new system by 1968. This goal, it appears, will not be met, but with the accelerated pace of price revisions the changeover schedule should not seriously lag. It should also be noted that the reform has widened to include parts of agriculture and other areas of the economy not in the original blueprint, which, so to speak, puts the regime ahead of the game.

In the elementary sense of being on, or nearly on, schedule, the reforms may be said to be going well, but the wisdom of the schedule itself is in question, as are a number of the consequences of the reforms, which may have a bearing on their longevity. Many observers have applauded Kosygin for his gradualist approach, which contrasts strikingly with Khrushchev's impulsive, often contradictory, sweeps. On the other hand, there is some evidence that the transition-mix combines the worst, not the best, elements of the two systems. Furthermore, a dynamic consideration, to which Rush Greenslade has called attention, may exert appreciable importance.[65] His point is that the very slowness of the pace of reform enables its numerous natural enemies to regroup and to make of their private battles for self-preservation a common cause. Its economic promise notwithstanding, the programme could be derailed before it becomes widespread and firmly fixed. That danger certainly can be read in the above accounts of the

---

[64] *Ibid.*

[65] Rush Greenslade, "The Soviet Economic System in Transition," in Joint Economic Committee, U.S. Congress, *New Directions in the Soviet Economy*, Part I, pp. 1–18.

performance of the ministries, whose stripes have changed but little, it would seem, since Stalin's day.

In my view, the pervasive and possibly cumulative pulls of counter-reform should have a slowing, not a crippling, effect, during the next few years. It is reasonable to expect a continued pragmatic testing of the programme, with adjustments and refinements in the light of experience, for the remainder of the quinquennium. In general, too, the relatively modest goals of the new Five-Year Plan appear likely to be met, which should impart some solidity to the emerging institutions of the Kosygin reforms. I would suppose that in 1970 Soviet leaders will pronounce the reforms a success, just as they are doing in mid-stream. And they would not be blatantly incorrect, for considerable good has already been done piecemeal, and more is impending. On the other hand, I would not expect the liberal advocates of the reforms to be so pleased, for its liberal (i.e., market) promise was curbed and neutralized almost from the start. The practice of *khozraschet* has gained ground, but it is still unquestionably subordinate, and still, in any case, primarily a Stalinist instrument of control. The seed of market socialism (NEP, or some other form) is there, but fertilization has yet to occur.

Today, and I would guess the same would hold true for 1970, planners prefer to plan in much the old-fashioned way, which means that pecuniary considerations still must take a back-seat. Likewise, the bureaucrats and Party controllers at all levels do not appear willing to let their diverse empires be dissolved in the interest of enterprise autonomy and rational, market-guided decision-making. The hope of the reform, or at any rate of some of the reformers, that elevation of the profit criterion would enable the economy to be less rule-ridden and slothful has simply not materialized. The bureacracy has just ground out, and is continuing to emit, new sets of rules, as complicated as the old and probably as contradic-tory. In Stalin's day, as Granick has astutely observed, the Party played a positive role in enabling enterprise managers to resolve their multiple, conflicting commands. In the Kosygin economy, despite the hope of some, the Party is unlikely to suffer technological unemployment, for in a system of manifold and inconsistent orders, Party members have a mission, analogous in size and substance to their role under Stalin.

Thus, though the new incentives may energize and channel the nation's effort somewhat more effectively than the former methods, the large economies needed to boost the sagging growth rate will simply not be forthcoming. At some point—in 1970, or shortly after perhaps—the major impetus of the Kosygin reforms may be fairly spent, and it is a safe guess that the Soviet economy will find itself beset by nagging pressures, familiar for thirty odd years. This state of affairs will be traceable in part to the gathering of counter-forces to restrict incipient managerial powers and nip limited consumer sovereignty in the bud. More significantly, however, the loss of steam will be due, I think, to the fact that the reforms failed to go far enough in the first place towards achieving a durable and dynamic institutional base, which I equate with the advent of true scarcity prices and a greatly enlarged sphere of decentralized authority.

What may be the responses of the regime in the long haul, when the present reforms lose their momentum-giving power? How will the alternatives appear to the leaders five years or so from now, when they turn once more to a crash effort to reinvigorate their unwieldy and overcommitted economy? Let me in concluding offer some speculations on four possible "ways out," from which the Party may take its basic long-term line. First, the leadership may in effect opt for a future much in the image of the recent past, the various disappointments of this time notwithstanding. Which is to say, the Party may continue to tinker and patch, with relaxations here and tightenings there, but most probably with some net decentralist motion. Coupled with this, there very likely may come a scaling down of objectives to relieve the economy of intolerable strain from the demand side. This, of course, is what has been happening recently. Kosygin's cautious outline of the new Five-Year Plan, as it were, ratifies the slowdown. The sights are respectable—from our vantage point, we would say high—but they are, nonetheless, reduced in almost every instance from the optimistic Khrushchevian perspectives. Clearly, much depends on the ability of the regime in following this pragmatic model to depressurize its chronic seller's market. This it may choose to do through the softer targets referred to above or by new practices with respect to excess capacity and reserve stocks. Tentative beginnings in this direction have scarcely made a dent in the overtaut, bottleneck economy to which the Soviets are accustomed.

Second, it is possible that the Party will listen to those who perceive the need, or think they do, for more drastic medicine. This view regards the present mix of plan and market as incompatible, and sees a move in either direction as offering greater effectiveness. Under present conditions, the plan is still dominant, but in hamstringing the market it essentially deprives itself of the information and motive power it needs to achieve its own goals. Accordingly, the radical change that this particular alternative poses, as the Kosygin reforms did not, is to reverse the dominance relation. Let the market organize economic activity through socialist institutions,[66] confining the centre strictly to macro-planning, possibly on the Yugoslav model. Parenthetically, it may be observed, that for both the micro- and macro-endeavours, the Soviet economy at the moment is extremely ill-prepared, but at least "scarcity" is in the vocabulary now, and desperation could prompt successful learning in action.

As a third possibility, the conservatives may realize their wish to turn the clock back to Stalin, not to his pervasive terror necessarily, but to his heavy industrial priorities, and, with only minor adjustments, to his planning techniques. This nostalgic view of the full-blooded command economy, is, it seems to me, a wholly misleading one, for its practitioners as well as for others, but it might conceivably prevail. If such a reversal of the trend since Stalin's death should be carried out, it might well bring in its train a period of strife and counter-revolution, because Stalinism at this time appears less stable than even the transitional model of Kosygin.

The fourth possibility that I wish to raise for the long-run salvation of the Party's authoritarian role in life is simply to restore the command economy to undiluted eminence. This would be done not through Stalin's administrative fiat, but rationally and effectively through the currently shelved route of "computopia." The latter may be rehabilitated by hardware breakthroughs, as well as by sheer electronic accumulation in the form of a vastly swollen computer park, or there may occur from unknown quarters a new surge in the cybernetics revolution. Even so, I doubt whether economists will ever possess sufficient knowledge of their environment to be able to instruct the machines how to take over. This ignorance is not a matter of statistical lacks, which are to some degree reparable, but more fundamentally of causal relations, of economic dynamics. The latter are sufficiently enduring, I presume, to inhibit, or render ineffective, fully automated planning.

The alternatives sketched do not exhaust the possibilities, and the several paths, which differ greatly in their likelihood, might be bent this way or that. In terms of probability, I would strongly favour the first, or pragmatic, model, though it is more akin to British muddling-through techniques than communist dialectical leaps. On the other hand, the repairs and improvisations of this alternative will become decreasingly effective, while forces of disequilibrium cumulate towards new crises. Of the two radical solutions or alternatives provoked by the new impasses, I would expect the decision to go to the market way of economic rationalization.

---

[66] Given the weight of history, it seems that state enterprise or cooperatives would much more likely be the institutional accompaniments of any new Soviet market socialism than the mixed, private-public ownership model of NEP.

However, if the more advanced experiments with the market socialist model, as found today in Yugoslavia, Hungary, and Czechoslovakia, should badly falter, Soviet leaders might hesitate at the brink and recoil to the more or less known, though unsatisfactory, terrain of centralism. Besides habit, the most powerful instincts of self-preservation pull in that direction.

Some Reflections on the Growth of the Soviet Economy

G. Warren Nutter

The promise of any revolution is, one must suppose, to right the wrongs of the system being overthrown, fulfilling the hopes of the masses who overthrow it, and carrying forward the historical forces that undermined and weakened existing institutions to the point where new ones could displace them.[1] The promise is implicit in the powerful social movement leading to revolution, and becomes explicit in the slogans of those who seek to capture mass support and thereby channel and control the inevitably amorphous and chaotic revolutionary upheaval. The Russian revolution did not, of course, take place in October 1917. As the culminating acts in the overthrow of an established social order, it unfolded over a dozen years beginning in 1905, the symbolic climax occurring in February 1917 when tsardom came to an end. The events of October marked the capture of leadership by an organized minority, the Bolshevik faction of the Social-Democratic Workers' Party.

The rhetoric of revolution seldom deserves careful analysis in retrospect, but it would be wrong to ignore the slogans put forth by the Bolsheviks as they engaged in the struggle for leadership. If Lenin did not take them seriously, the masses doubtless did, for they heard in them an echo of popular demands. Paraphrased, the slogans promised land to the peasants, bread to the workers, and freedom, peace, and brotherhood to all. In these terms, the achievements measure up poorly to say the least. Far from giving land to the peasants, the communist government took it away. The people may finally, a half century later, have more to eat and wear, but this is primarily because more of them work harder and longer and live in the cities rather than the countryside. There is little reason to believe that either the rural or urban population enjoys a significantly higher

---

[1] This paper is not intended to be a thorough exposition of the economic performance of the Soviet Union. It began as a set of comments on the papers by Dr. John Hardt and Professor Stanley Cohn, and was designed for oral presentation at the Munich conference on the theme "The October Revolution: Promise and Realization." It has been expanded into a somewhat more coherent and self-contained essay at the request of the sponsors of the conference. Dr. Hardt's and Professor Cohn's papers appear on pp. 1 and 24 of this volume respectively.

standard of living on balance—that is, when all components of consumption are taken into account—than before the revolution, but the living standard is higher in the city than in the country now just as it was then, and a larger fraction of the population lives in the city. One hardly needs to comment on how little freedom, peace, or brotherhood the Soviet people have enjoyed or enjoy today, though this question is perhaps beyond the scope of my topic.

In appraising achievements, it is obviously not enough to look at conditions now, fifty years after the revolution. Let us agree that there has been impressive economic growth. Let us agree that the people as a whole are now materially better off than before the revolution. There still remains the question of what happened over the course of this half century, of how the people fared over the years. On that score we see a system stumbling from one crisis to another while the masses paid the price. It was not until the 1950's that growth of agricultural production began to outpace population growth, and in the intervening years it went as often down as up. Not even during the last decade has there been a reasonably steady upward trend. In the field of industrial consumer goods, the record is scarcely better.

Was this suffering "necessary"? Has there been some "higher" purpose or accomplishment to justify continual neglect of what one would suppose, from the ideals of the revolution, is the fundamental task: improvement of the welfare of the masses? As a matter of fact, the promise of the revolution has not been fulfilled, because the Soviet government has not had freedom and prosperity as its aim, but rather enhancement of Soviet power—more accurately, the power of the ruling elite. Such growth as has been achieved has come through forced saving and forced industrialization, through attending to easy tasks and neglecting difficult ones, through domination of the economy from the centre.

So much for the matter of fact. But, as John Hardt asks in his paper: "Was Stalin necessary?" He suggests that he was, given the aims of the Soviet economy. To me, this is simply to say that Stalin was necessary for Stalin. There is no other imperative of history that required this kind of leadership or direction. Nor was there need for this kind of system in order "to overcome backwardness" or to meet the problems of development in an underdeveloped economy, as has been amply demonstrated throughout the rest of the world. Nor to create a powerful nation, if that is supposed to be a legitimate end in itself. The question to ask is not whether Stalin was necessary, but whether the things for which he was necessary were necessary themselves. If one goes back to the hopes and expectations of the Russian revolution, the answer is clear: No, Stalin was not necessary—not then, not now, not ever. Even that statement is too weak. Stalin and the Soviet system were more than unnecessary; they were completely antithetical to the avowed aims of the revolution.

One could go on, as Dr. Hardt does, and ask whether the rigidities and inflexibilities of the Soviet economic system must persist beyond Stalin. He thinks so for two reasons: first, because an authoritarian system is implicitly inflexible; and, second, because the imbalances inherited from the Stalinist period make it virtually impossible to introduce more flexibility into the economy. I agree fully with the first reason but not the second. Greater flexibility and decentralization—more accurately, polycentricity— are essential if the imbalances are to be remedied. Yet they are slow to come. Why? Because the overriding objective of the political leadership is to preserve the autocracy. We see, in modern dress, "the dilemma of the tsars." For more than a century, the last tsars were quite aware that the social and economic system over which they presided was rotten and bound to collapse some day. While recognizing the urgent need for reforms, they were reluctant to introduce them, because they knew that curing the patient would kill the doctor. The social order demanded by reason had no place for an autocratic ruler, and the tsars were more interested in keeping their jobs than in benefiting the masses. And so they let things drift, responding only to overwhelming pressures as they built up.

The same dilemma faces the Soviet rulers of today. To improve the efficiency of the economy, they must relinquish some of their control. Multiple centres for making economic decisions must be created and dispersed throughout the economy. Impersonal markets and forces of competition must displace administrative planning. Where does the process stop? How can one avoid the specter, dreadful to contemplate, of independent foci of power, each competing with the other? What justification remains for a monopoly of power in the hands of a single party dominated by a self-perpetuating elite? How can the appetite for political freedom, once whetted, be suppressed? These are the questions running through the minds of Soviet leaders in their more candid moments.

But let us turn away from such speculations and ask how well the objectives actually pursued and the methods used have worked in generating economic development. How has the Soviet system compared in performance over a half century with other kinds of economic systems? Any discussion of this sort must be introduced with the usual words of warning about the extraordinary difficulties encountered in trying to measure Soviet economic performance. For a variety of well-known reasons, Soviet statistics leave much to be desired. It is therefore natural that scholars will differ in their evaluation of growth trends in the Soviet economy. I shall give here my own evaluation, indicating where it seems appropriate how my figures diverge from those of others.

If we look first at the economy as a whole, it seems reasonable to say that the average annual growth rate in the Soviet gross national product over the last half century has been around 3 per cent, after proper adjustment is made to remove the effects of territorial expansion. On this matter, the calculations of Professor Abram Bergson in his comprehensive study of Soviet national income agree with mine.[2] While there is considerable room for dispute here, I doubt that the growth rate over the last four or five years has been significantly higher than the long-run average. A long-run rate of 3 per cent a year is quite respectable but by no means exciting, particularly when one considers the relatively unadvanced stage of development from which the Soviet economy started and the extraordinary expansion in investment and employment undertaken under the policy of forced industrialization, so well summarized by Professor Cohn in his paper. One might well wonder whether the results have justified the cost, and whether some other economic system would not have done better.

Let us take a brief look at industry, the favoured sector. The long-run growth rate for industrial production has been about 4.6 per cent a year, again with the effects of territorial expansion removed. More disagreement is to be expected from other scholars on the accuracy of this figure, though the index of Kaplan and Moorsteen for 1928–1958 implies a similar result.[3] For the last five years or so, I would put the average annual growth rate at around 5 per cent, while others would put it at around 7 per cent.[4] If my figures are substantially correct, the performance of Soviet industry over the last half century, while impressive, is neither unusual nor unprecedented. Despite the all-out effort to industrialize, overall growth has been less rapid than it was in Russia or the United States in the period 1870–1913.[5]

---

[2] See G. W. Nutter, "The Effects of Economic Growth on Sino-Soviet Strategy," in D. M. Abshire and R. V. Allen, eds., *National Security: Political, Military, and Economic Strategies in the Decade Ahead*, New York, Frederick A. Praeger, 1963, p. 166.

[3] *Ibid.*, p. 167; and G. W. Nutter, *Growth of Industrial Production in the Soviet Union*, Princeton, Princeton University Press, for National Bureau of Economic Research, 1962, pp. 337–340.

[4] See *Current Economic Indicators for the U.S.S.R.*, Joint Economic Committee, U.S. Congress, Washington, D.C., 1965, p. 45; and J. H. Noren, "Soviet Industry, Trends in Output, Input, and Productivity," in *New Directions in the Soviet Economy*, Joint Economic Committee, U.S. Congress, Washington, D.C., 1966, Part II-A, p. 281.

[5] Nutter, *Growth of Industrial Production, op. cit.*, p. 229.

Most of the Soviet growth is attributable to expansion in inputs of capital and labour rather than to improved productivity of resources, by contrast with the situation in the United States, for example, over the last half century.[6] Indeed, the evidence indicates that the stock of industrial capital has actually grown considerably faster than production, so that growth in productivity of capital has been negative.[7]

One should also note that the growth rate for industry reflects the fact that the economy has, because of the inherent nature of administrative planning, followed the path of least resistance. Heavy emphasis has been placed on those tasks that are most easily accomplished, a process of natural selection operating in favour of those production targets most readily fulfilled. Any economy can generate a higher measured rate of growth if it concentrates on growth for growth's sake rather than on satisfaction of other values. There is much to be said for the characterization of the Soviet economy, attributed to Professor Wassily Leontief, as an "input-input system." This is the basic reason why the Soviet economy faces critical re-allocative problems at the moment. The emphasis on growth and power has led to the various distortions so familiar in the Soviet economy: sophisticated weaponry and primitive plumbing; abundance of steel and shortage of grain; spacious subways and pitifully overcrowded housing; jet aircraft and dirt roads; complex machinery and shoddy consumer goods; and so on. As concern for consumer welfare mounts on the part of leaders as well as the masses, these distortions present formidable obstacles in the way of rapid orientation of the economy towards better fulfillment of consumer wants.

In commenting on Soviet economic performance, one must not leave out of account the almost unbroken string of catastrophes that has marked the course of Soviet history and hindered progress. Some were endemic in the system. Thus, the toll of radical and violent revolution levied during the period of so-called war communism, in addition to immediate suffering, generated a population deficit of almost twenty million persons, along with a distorted age and sex distribution, both leaving their indelible mark on the course of events over the following decades. Scarcely had the economy recovered from its initial shock, thanks to the period of New Economic Policy, when a second blow was struck in the form of forced collectivization of agriculture, causing another large population deficit and destroying about half the capital in agriculture. Next came the Great Purge of the late 1930's, placing its own heavy burden on the economy.

[6] *Ibid.*, p. 232.
[7] *Ibid.*, p. 236.

The effects of World War II, even more disastrous, lie in another category in that this event cannot be blamed on the Soviet system itself. Soviet foreign policy no doubt played a role in helping to build up the tensions leading to World War II, and the Hitler-Stalin pact must bear a major responsibility as the proximate cause of the outbreak of hostilities in 1939, but it would be a gross distortion of history to suggest that this great conflict was essentially the product of the communist revolution. Hence, due allowance must be made in Soviet economic performance for the catastrophic impact of World War II; however, it must be remembered that the Soviet Union was not the only country to suffer from the war and that Stalin was willing to resort to more drastic policies of post-war recovery than were available to other countries. For example, the Soviet Union collected at least twice as much in reparations as all of Europe received in the form of Marshall Plan aid from the United States.[8] As the years recede, World War II must be reckoned as less and less of a factor in explaining long-run Soviet economic performance.

As an incidental matter, I should like to record my disagreement with the general view, echoed by Professor Cohn in his paper, that preparation for war was the major reason for Soviet economic stagnation during the period 1937–1940. While the Soviet military programme was very large by standards of the time, it had been under way since at least 1934, with few signs of acceleration in the later years except for expansion in the size of the armed forces. Intensive industrial mobilization was not undertaken until after the German invasion. Sluggishness of the economy during the Third Five-Year Plan is to be attributed primarily to the Great Purge and to the relaxation of effort that followed the signing of the Hitler-Stalin pact.[9]

If, then, we are to appraise how well the promise of the October Revolution has been realized, we must measure performance over the entire Soviet period and not merely over the most favourable years, while making due allowance for the adverse effects of events thrust upon the economy from the outside. At the back of our minds, of course, there always lurks the question of how much differently things would have been under another kind of economic system facing the same basic circumstances, but we can never give a definitive answer to that question since we lack the power to reconstruct history. I am, nevertheless, prepared to advance the speculative opinion that the economy would have grown at least as rapidly as it has while providing far more welfare for the masses if the revolution of 1917 had resulted in the establishment of a constitutional government

---

[8] *Ibid.*, p. 215.
[9] *Ibid.*, pp. 210–213.

and a private enterprise economy along Western lines. I view the communist revolution, now marking its fiftieth anniversary, as one of the great reactionary events of all time. As I read the history of tsarist Russia, it is the story of a slow and tortuous movement over the centuries away from oriental despotism and towards a liberal order in the Western tradition. Reform of the system accelerated in the last half of the nineteenth century and the first decade of the twentieth, reaching a climax with the constitutional revolution of February 1917, but the Bolshevik coup of October and its ultimate aftermath threw the country back to conditions of despotism, terror, and serfdom unsurpassed under the worst of the tsars—all in the name of "construction of socialism." The slow and tortuous movement towards liberalism continues to assert itself beneath all the turmoil, and we may perhaps expect reaction to be overcome eventually. As it is, the promise of the revolution may gradually be realized.

Contributors

JAMES H. BLACKMAN, Professor of Economics at the University of North Carolina, received his M.A. and Ph.D. degrees from Columbia University. He has served as a consultant for the RAND Corporation and the United Nations, and has written widely on Soviet economics. At present, he is on leave from the University of North Carolina, serving as Program Director for Economics with the National Science Foundation.

STANLEY H. COHN, a graduate of Reed College in Oregon, received a Ph.D. degree from the University of Chicago in 1952. He has served as a specialist in Soviet economic affairs and as a general economist for the Research Analysis Corporation, and has contributed to several publications of the Joint Economic Committee of the United States Congress. Presently, he is a member of the economics faculty of the State University of New York at Binghamton.

NORTON T. DODGE is an economist specializing on the Soviet Union. A graduate of Cornell University in 1948, he completed Harvard University's Russian Regional Studies Program and was a graduate student fellow at the Russian Research Center before receiving his Ph.D. from Harvard. He is now Associate Professor of Economics at the University of Maryland. He recently completed *Women in the Soviet Economy: Their Role in Economic, Scientific, and Technical Development.*

ROBERT FARRELL is a graduate of Dartmouth College in Hanover, New Hampshire. In 1962, he was a staff member of the United Nations in the Bureau of Economic and Social Research. In 1963, he travelled in Poland, the Soviet Union, and Czechoslovakia under the auspices of the Experiment in International Living. Since 1964, he has been an editor at the Institute for the Study of the USSR in Munich. Assistant Director of the University of Oklahoma Munich Center for Russian Language and Soviet Area Studies, he is editor, with Robert A. Rupen, of *Vietnam and the Sino-Soviet Dispute.*

JOHN P. HARDT received a Ph.D. degree in economics and a Russian Institute Certificate from Columbia University. He is editor of *Mathematics and Computers in Soviet Planning* and author of *The Cold War Economic Gap.* He is currently Head of the Strategic Studies Department of the Research Analysis Corporation and a staff member of the Institute of Sino-Soviet Studies at George Washington University.

LEON M. HERMAN, Senior Specialist on the Soviet Economy with the Library of Congress, also holds the position of Adjunct Professor of the School of International Service at American University in Washington, D.C. As consultant for the Joint Economic Committee of the U.S. Congress, he has edited several of the comprehensive studies on the Soviet economy undertaken by the Committee. The most recent work in this series, published in July 1966, is titled *New Directions in the Soviet Economy.* He is author of a number of articles dealing with foreign trade policy and other aspects of the current Soviet economic scene.

Jerzy F. Karcz is Associate Professor of Economics at the University of California in Santa Barbara. A graduate of Alliance College in Pennsylvania, he received a Ph.D. degree from Columbia University in 1958. A former consultant to the RAND Corporation, he has taken part in academic exchanges with the Soviet Union, Bulgaria, and Czechoslovakia, He is author of *Soviet Agricultural Marketings and Prices* and editor of *Soviet and East European Agriculture*.

Roy D. Laird is Associate Professor of Political Science at the University of Kansas. He has written numerous articles on various aspects of the politics of Soviet agriculture, and is editor, with Edward L. Crowley, of *Soviet Agriculture: The Permanent Crisis*.

Jack Miller graduated from the University of Sheffield in England in 1935. He is on the staff of the Institute of Soviet and East European Studies at the University of Glasgow, and has been an editor of the quarterly *Soviet Studies* since 1949.

G. Warren Nutter is Professor of Economics at the University of Virginia. A graduate of the University of Chicago, he received his Ph.D. degree in 1949. He has been a member of the research staff of the National Bureau of Economic Research since 1955, and is author of *Growth of Industrial Production in the Soviet Union*.

Vladimir G. Treml received his Master's degree in economics at Columbia University in 1956 and his Ph.D. degree from the University of North Carolina. He has served in various research and consultatory positions with the Center of Industrial Development at the United Nations, the Research Analysis Corporation, and other private and governmental organizations. Dr. Treml is author of *The 1959 Soviet Intersectoral Table* (two volumes, Washington, D.C., 1964) and of numerous papers on Soviet economic planning and development. Presently, he is Associate Professor of Economics at Duke University in Durham, North Carolina.

Heinrich Vogel is a research associate of the Ost-Europa Institut of the University of Munich. He holds diplomas in political science and in East European questions (from the Economics Faculty of the University of Munich).

Eugène Zaleski, a graduate of Jean Casimir University in Lwow, Poland, and Docteur en Droit of the University of Paris, has served as Research Associate of the Russian Center at Harvard University and Senior Research Fellow in the Thomas Jefferson Center of the University of Virginia. At present, he is Maître de Recherche of the Centre National de la Recherche Scientifique in Paris. He is author of *Les Courants commerciaux de l'Europe danubienne* (Paris, 1952), *Mouvements ouvriers et socialistes — La Russie* (Paris, 1956), *Planification de la Croissance et Fluctuations économiques en URSS, 1918 –1932* (Paris, 1962), and *Planning Reforms in the Soviet Union* (Chapel Hill, 1967).

Carl R. Zoerb is an agricultural economist on the staff of Radio Free Europe in Munich. A graduate of the University of Wisconsin, he holds an M.A. degree in economics from Harvard University. From 1930 –1934, he served as an agricultural advisor to the USSR Commissariat of State Farms, working directly at the state farm level and witnessing first-hand the aftermath of collectivization in the Ukraine and the Northern Caucasus.